THE WORKS OF JOHN MILTON

THE WORKS OF
JOHN MILTON

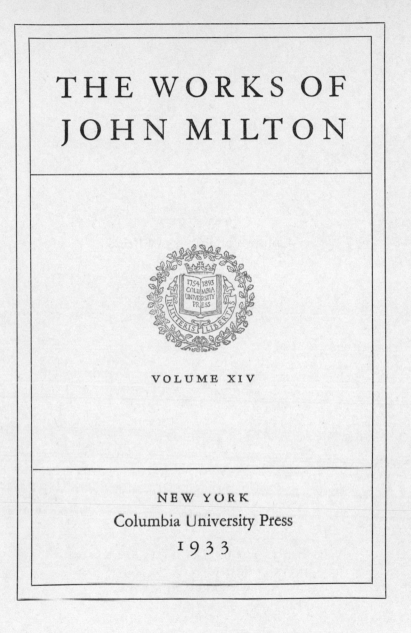

VOLUME XIV

NEW YORK
Columbia University Press
1933

PRINTED IN THE UNITED STATES OF AMERICA
BY THE PRINTING HOUSE OF WILLIAM EDWIN RUDGE, INC.
MOUNT VERNON, NEW YORK

EDITORIAL BOARD

CONTENTS
De Doctrina Christiana
EDITED, WITH THE TRANSLATION OF
CHARLES R. SUMNER, D.D., BY JAMES HOLLY HANFORD
AND WALDO HILARY DUNN

[Præfatio] 2

Liber I. Caput I 16
    Quid sit Doctrina Christiana, quotque
    eius partes

Liber I. Caput II 24
    De Deo

Liber I. Caput III 62
    De divino decreto

Liber I. Caput IV 90
    De prædestinatione

Liber I. Caput V 176
    Præfatio . . . de Filio Dei

Liber I. Caput VI 356
    De Spiritu Sancto

DE DOCTRINA CHRISTIANA

IOANNES MILTONVS

ANGLVS

Universis Christi Ecclesiis, nec non omnibus Fidem Christianam ubicunque Gentium profitentibus, pacem et Veritatis agnitionem, salutemque in Deo Patre, ac Domino nostro Iesu Christo Sempiternam.

———————————

CUM ab ineunte superiore sæculo, ex quo Religio contaminata perpetuis plus mille tercentum annorum corruptelis, ad puritatem suæ originis aliqua ex parte revocari cœpta est, tot institutiones prodierint purioris
5 Theologiæ, quibus Doctrinæ Christianæ capita fere singula nunc breviter nunc satis copiose satisque distincto ordine contineri videantur, cur Ego, si quid in hoc genere, quantum fieri potest, elaboratum iam exiit, in eo opere non acquieverim, aut si id omnes parum feliciter aggressi sunt, ipse ab eodem in-
10 cœpto non sim deterritus, æequum est ut in primis exponam.

Equidem si dicerem propterea quod nihil æque ac religio Christiana duas teterrimas pestes, servitutem ac metum, ex vita ac mente hominum eiiciat atque expellat, me idcirco studiosum huius potissimum doctrinæ esse factum, non religione
15 sed maximis vitæ commoditatibus adductus fuisse arguerer.

JOHN MILTON

ENGLISHMAN

To all the churches of Christ, and to all who profess
the Christian Faith throughout the world, Peace, and
the Recognition of the Truth, and Eternal Salvation
in God the Father, and in our Lord Jesus Christ.

SINCE the commencement of the last century, when religion began to be restored from the corruptions of more
than thirteen hundred years to something of its original
purity, many treatises of theology have been published, con-
5 ducted according to sounder principles, wherein the chief
heads of Christian doctrine are set forth sometimes briefly,
sometimes in a more enlarged and methodical order. I think
myself obliged, therefore, to declare in the first instance why,
if any works have already appeared as perfect as the nature of
10 the subject will admit, I have not remained contented with
them; or, if all my predecessors have treated it unsuccessfully,
why their failure has not deterred me from attempting an
undertaking of a similar kind.

If I were to say that I had devoted myself to the study of
15 the Christian religion because nothing else can so effectually
rescue the lives and minds of men from those two detestable
curses, slavery and superstition, I should seem to have acted
rather from a regard to my highest earthly comforts, than
from a religious motive.

Verum cum æternæ salutis Viam non nisi propriæ cuiusque fidei Deus aperuerit, postuletque hoc a nobis, ut qui salvus esse vult, pro se quisque credat, statui divinis in rebus, non aliorum niti vel fide vel iudicio, sed quid credendum in reli-
5 gione est, id fide non aliunde quam divinitus accepta, et quod mearum erat partium non omisso, ex ipsa Dei scriptura quam diligentissime perlecta atque perpensa, unumquodque habere mihimet ipsi, meaque ipsius opera exploratum atque cognitum.

10 Cœpi igitur Adolescens (dicam enim quibus rebus profecerim, si quem forte posthac proficiendi spes eadem ad eandem viam ingrediendam invitaverit) cum ad libros utriusque Testamenti lingua sua perlegendos assiduus incumbere, tum Theologorum Systemata aliquot breviora sedulo percurrere:
15 ad eorum deinde exemplum, locos communes digerere, ad quos omnia quæ ex scripturis haurienda occurrissent, expromenda cum opus esset, referrem. Ad uberiora deinde Theologorum volumina et disputatas in utramque partem de capitibus quibusdam fidei quæstiones, fidentius demum me con-
20 tuli: liceat candide non minus quam libere dicam, multa ibi adversariorum argumenta misere elusa, aut elenchorum ostentatis putide formulis aut interiectis ubique Grammaticorum inanibus vocabulis, in speciem potius quam solide refu-

But since it is only to the individual faith of each that the Deity has opened the way of eternal salvation, and as he requires that he who would be saved should have a personal belief of his own, I resolved not to repose on the faith or judg-
5 ment of others in matters relating to God; but on the one hand, having taken the grounds of my faith from divine revelation alone, and on the other, having neglected nothing which depended on my own industry, I thought fit to scrutinize and ascertain for myself the several points of my religious belief,
10 by the most careful perusal and meditation of the Holy Scriptures themselves.

If therefore I mention what has proved beneficial in my own practice, it is in the hope that others, who have a similar wish of improving themselves, may be thereby invited to
15 pursue the same method. I entered upon an assiduous course of study in my youth, beginning with the books of the Old and New Testament in their original languages, and going diligently through a few of the shorter systems of divines, in imitation of whom I was in the habit of classing under certain
20 heads whatever passages of Scripture occurred for extraction, to be made use of hereafter as occasion might require. At length I resorted with increased confidence to some of the more copious theological treatises, and to the examination of the arguments advanced by the conflicting parties respecting
25 certain disputed points of faith. But, to speak the truth with freedom as well as candor, I was concerned to discover in many instances adverse reasonings either evaded by wretched shifts, or attempted to be refuted, rather speciously than with

tata, sane dolens, reperi: quam autem ipsi partem pro vera mordicus tenerent, vel scripturæ locis male intellectis, vel consequentiis inde fallacibus arreptis, contentiosius esse sæpe quam validius defensam; hinc veritatem pro errore atque
5 hæresi nonnunquam acerrime oppugnatam: errorem atque hæresin pro veritate habitam; consuetudine ac studio partium quam scripturarum auctoritate commendatiorem.

Cum itaque his ducibus neque summam fidei, neque spem salutis posse me recte committere arbitrarer, et tamen aliquam
10 doctrinæ Christianæ methodicam institutionem, aut saltem disquisitionem, quæ subvenire vel fidei, vel memoriæ, vel utrique possit, apprime esse necessariam, nihil mihi tutius neque consultius visum est, quam ut ipse aliquid huiusmodi quod ad manum mihi esset, labore ac lucubratione propria ex
15 ipso adeoque solo Dei verbo, et fidelissime quidem, nisi mihimet forte infidus esse volebam, de integro componerem. Quod cum per aliquot annos agere attentissime perseverassem, reformatæ religionis arcem animadverti, qua parte Pontificios quidem spectat, satis munitam: cæteris in locis compluribus
20 neglectam, neque operibus neque propugnatoribus firmatam satis aut defensam: perpetuæ diligentiæ verique reperiendi indefesso studio, non credulitati supinæ proposita esse a Deo

solidity, by an affected display of formal sophisms, or by a constant recourse to the quibbles of the grammarians; while what was most pertinaciously espoused as the true doctrine, seemed often defended, with more vehemence than strength
5 of argument, by misconstructions of Scripture, or by the hasty deduction of erroneous inferences. Owing to these causes, the truth was sometimes as strenuously opposed as if it had been an error or a heresy, while errors and heresies were substituted for the truth, and valued rather from deference to custom and
10 the spirit of party than from the authority of Scripture.

According to my judgment, therefore, neither my creed nor my hope of salvation could be safely trusted to such guides; and yet it appeared highly requisite to possess some methodical tractate of Christian doctrine, or at least to attempt
15 such a disquisition as might be useful in establishing my faith or assisting my memory. I deemed it therefore safest and most advisable to compile for myself, by my own labor and study, some original treatise which should be always at hand, derived solely from the word of God itself, and executed with all
20 possible fidelity, seeing that I could have no wish to practice any imposition on myself in such a matter.

After a diligent perseverance in this plan for several years, I perceived that the strongholds of the reformed religion were sufficiently fortified, as far as it was in danger from the
25 Papists, but neglected in many other quarters; neither competently strengthened with works of defence, nor adequately provided with champions. It was also evident to me, that, in religion as in other things, the offers of God were all directed,

etiam in religione omnia, tum facile perspexi; restare adhuc plura quam putabam ad scripturarum normam sanctius exigenda, accuratiusque reformanda. Mihi certe hanc rationem ineundo ita satisfactum est, ut quid credendum in sacris, quid 5 duntaxat opinandum sit, percepisse nunc non diffiderem: summoque solatio fuit, magnum me, Deo bene iuvante, subsidium fidei mihimet comparasse, vel thesaurum potius reposuisse: neque imparatum dehinc fore, neque semper animi dubium quoties reddenda fidei ratio fuisset.

10   Hæc si omnibus palam facio, si fraterno quod Deum testor atque amico erga omnes mortales animo, hæc, quibus melius aut pretiosius nihil habeo, quam possum latissime libentissimeque impertio, tametsi multa in lucem protulisse videbor quæ ab receptis quibusdam opinionibus discrepare statim re-15 perientur, spero tamen omnes hinc mihi potius benevolos, quam iniquum ullum aut inimicum futurum. Illud oro atque obtestor omnes quibus veritas odio non est, ne libertate hac disserendi ac disquirendi quæ scholis conceditur, nullis certe credentibus non concedenda, turbari ecclesiam clamitent, 20 cum explorare omnia iubeamur, et veritatis luce indies aucta, illustretur atque ædificetur longe magis Ecclesia quam turbetur. Equidem non video qui magis investiganda veritate

not to an indolent credulity, but to constant diligence, and to an unwearied search after truth; and that more than I was aware of still remained, which required to be more rigidly examined by the rule of Scripture, and reformed after a more 5 accurate model. I so far satisfied myself in the prosecution of this plan as at length to trust that I had discovered, with regard to religion, what was matter of belief, and what only matter of opinion. It was also a great solace to me to have compiled, by God's assistance, a precious aid for my faith; or 10 rather to have laid up for myself a treasure which would be a provision for my future life, and would remove from my mind all grounds for hesitation, as often as it behoved me to render an account of the principles of my belief.

If I communicate the result of my inquiries to the world at 15 large; if, as God is my witness, it be with a friendly and be-nignant feeling towards mankind, that I readily give as wide a circulation as possible to what I esteem my best and richest possession, I hope to meet with a candid reception from all parties, and that none at least will take unjust offence, even 20 though many things should be brought to light which will at once be seen to differ from certain received opinions. I ear-nestly beseech all lovers of truth, not to cry out that the Church is thrown into confusion by that freedom of discussion and inquiry which is granted to the schools, and ought certainly 25 to be refused to no believer, since we are ordered "to prove all things," and since the daily progress of the light of truth is productive far less of disturbance to the Church, than of illumination and edification. Nor do I see how the Church

turbari Ecclesia possit aut debeat, quam turbari gentes annun-
tiando primitus Evangelio: quandoquidem auctoritate mea
nihil suadeo, nihil impono; imo vero hortor omnes, atque imprimis auctor sum, ut quibus in sententiis non plene satis-
5 factum esse putaverint, assensum eo usque sustineant quoad
scripturarum evidentia vicerit, assensumque et fidem rationi
persuaserit. Latibula non quæro, doctioribus quibusque hæc,
aut si doctissimi quique non semper optimi harum rerum
disceptatores ac iudices sunt, adultis ac fortibus et doctrinam
10 Evangelii penitus intelligentibus, longe maiore cum fiducia
quam rudioribus propono. Cumque eorum pars maxima qui
his de rebus quam plurima scripserunt, suis sensibus expli-
candis totas fere paginas occupare consueverint, scripturarum
loca, quibus id omne quod docent maximopere confirmatur,
15 numeris duntaxat capitum versiculorumque strictim adnotatis
in marginem extrudere, satius duxi mearum quidem pagi-
narum spatia confertis undique auctoritatibus divinis etiam
eadem ingerentibus redundare, meis verbis, ex ipso licet con-
textu scripturarum natis, loci quam minimum relinqui.
20   Id denique ago, ut ex iis quæ sive vetera sive nova attulisse
censebor, pro eorum pondere ac momento, imo pro scripturarum potius auctoritate quarum nituntur creberrimis testimoniis, intelligere omnes possint, quanti intersit religionis

can be more disturbed by the investigation of truth, than
were the Gentiles by the first promulgation of the gospel;
since so far from recommending or imposing anything on
my own authority, it is my particular advice that every one
5 should suspend his opinion on whatever points he may not
feel himself fully satisfied, till the evidence of Scripture prevail, and persuade his reason into assent and faith. Conceal-
ment is not my object; it is to the learned that I address myself,
or if it be thought that the learned are not the best umpires
10 and judges of such things, I should at least wish to submit
my opinions to men of a mature and manly understanding,
possessing a thorough knowledge of the doctrines of the gospel; on whose judgments I should rely with far more confidence, than on those of novices in these matters. And whereas
15 the greater part of those who have written most largely on
these subjects have been wont to fill whole pages with explanations of their own opinions, thrusting into the margin the
texts in support of their doctrine with a summary reference to
the chapter and verse, I have chosen, on the contrary, to fill
20 my pages even to redundance with quotations from Scripture,
that so as little space as possible might be left for my own
words, even when they arise from the context of revelation
itself.

It has also been my object to make it appear from the
25 opinions I shall be found to have advanced, whether new or
old, of how much consequence to the Christian religion is the
liberty not only of winnowing and sifting every doctrine, but
also of thinking and even writing respecting it, according to

Christianæ, concedi libertatem non excutiendæ solum cuius-
cunque doctrinæ, palamque ventilandæ, sed etiam de ea,
prout cuique fide persuasum est, sentiendi atque etiam scri-
bendi. sine qua libertate, religio nulla, Evangelium nullum
5 est; sola vis viget; qua stare Christianam religionem, turpe et
probrosum est: servitus adhuc durat; non legi, ut olim, divinæ, sed, quod miserrimum est, humanæ; vel, verius ut
dicam, inhumanæ tyrannidi servienda. Illud tamen ab hominibus ingenuis et cordatis, utpote indignum plane, non
10 expecto, ut pro more iniquorum quorundam hominum et
rationis expertium, quicquid abhorrere a doctrina vulgo
tradita iudicaverint, id non scripturæ testimoniis collatis, sed
invidioso quolibet nomine vel hæretici vel hæreseos impacto,
per calumniam damnent. Horum instituto satis est infamem
15 hanc notam temere cuivis inussisse, uno verbo, nullo negotio
confutasse; solo nomine hæretici incusso quasi uno ictu con-
fecisse se hominem putant. Quibus Ego, id solum fuisse
hæresin, quoties hoc nomen in vitio ponitur, ætate Apostolorum, quicquid eorum doctrinæ, viva voce traditæ, cum libri
20 Evangelici nondum extarent, repugnabat; eosque solos fuisse
hæreticos, qui, iuxta illud Rom. xvi. 17, 18. *dissidia et scan-*
dala præter doctrinam Apostolicam faciebant; non Domino
nostro Iesu Christo servientes, sed suo ventri: conscriptis

our individual faith and persuasion; an inference which will
be stronger in proportion to the weight and importance of
those opinions, or rather in proportion to the authority of
Scripture, on the abundant testimony of which they rest.
5 Without this liberty there is neither religion nor gospel—
force alone prevails—by which it is disgraceful for the Christian religion to be supported. Without this liberty we are still
enslaved, not indeed, as formerly, under the divine law, but,
what is worst of all, under the law of man, or to speak more
10 truly, under a barbarous tyranny. But I do not expect from
candid and judicious readers a conduct so unworthy of them,
that like certain unjust and foolish men, they should stamp
with the invidious name of heretic or heresy whatever appears
to them to differ from the received opinions, without trying
15 the doctrine by a comparison with Scripture testimonies. According to their notions, to have branded any one at random
with this opprobrious mark, is to have refuted him without
any trouble, by a single word. By the simple imputation of
the name of heretic, they think that they have despatched
20 their man at one blow. To men of this kind I answer, that in
the time of the apostles, ere the New Testament was written,
whenever the charge of heresy was applied as a term of re-
proach, that alone was considered as heresy which was at
variance with their doctrine orally delivered, and that those
25 only were looked upon as heretics, who according to Rom.
xvi. 17, 18. "caused divisions and offences contrary to the
doctrine" of the apostles, "serving not our Lord Jesus Christ,
but their own belly." By parity of reasoning therefore, since

demum libris evangelicis, pari ratione nihil nisi quod iis
repugnat, posse iure nominari hæresin respondeo. De me,
libris tantummodo sacris adhæresco; hæresin aliam, sectam
aliam sequor nullam; hæreticorum, quos vocant, libros perle-
5 geram nullos, cum ex eorum numero, qui orthodoxi audiunt,
re male gesta scripturisque incautius tractatis, sentire cum
adversariis quoties illi sentiebant cum scripturis primo didici.
Hoc si hæresis est, fateor equidem cum Paulo, Act. xxiv. 14.
me secundum viam illam quam hæresin dicunt, ita servire
10 *patrio Deo, ut qui credam omnibus quæ in lege et in prophetis,*
addo, quæ in libris evangelicis etiam *scripta sunt:* alios fidei
Christianæ iudices aut summos interpretes fidemque omnem,
quam vocant, implicitam, cum universa Protestantium ecclesia
non agnosco. De cætero, fratres, veritatem colite cum chari-
15 tate; de his, prout Dei spiritus vobis præiverit, ita iudicate:
his mecum utimini, vel ne utimini quidem, nisi fide non
dubia scripturarumque claritate persuasi; in Christo denique
Servatore ac Domino nostro vivite ac valete.

I. M.

the compilation of the New Testament, I maintain that nothing but what is in contradiction to it can properly be called heresy.

For my own part, I adhere to the Holy Scriptures alone;
5 I follow no other heresy or sect. I had not even read any of the works of heretics, so called, when the mistakes of those who are reckoned for orthodox, and their incautious handling of Scripture, first taught me to agree with their opponents whenever those opponents agreed with Scripture. If this be
10 heresy, I confess with St. Paul, Acts xxiv. 14. "that after the way which they call heresy, so worship I the God of my fathers, believing all things which are written in the law and the prophets"; to which I add, whatever is written in the New Testament. Any other judges or paramount interpreters of
15 the Christian belief, together with all implicit faith, as it is called, I, in common with the whole Protestant Church, refuse to recognize.

For the rest, brethren, cultivate truth with brotherly love. Judge of my present undertaking according to the admon-
20 ishing of the Spirit of God, and neither adopt my sentiments, nor reject them, unless every doubt has been removed from your belief by the clear testimony of revelation. Finally, live in the faith of our Lord and Savior Jesus Christ. Farewell.

J. M.

IOANNIS MILTONI

ANGLI

De Doctrina Christiana

EX SACRIS DUNTAXAT LIBRIS PETITA DISQUISITIONUM

LIBRI DUO POSTHUMI.

LIBER PRIMUS.

CAPUT I.

QUID SIT DOCTRINA CHRISTIANA,
QUOTQUE EIUS PARTES.

DOCTRINA Christiana est quam CHRISTUS (licet eo nomine non a principio cognitus) de Deo eiusque cultu ad gloriam Dei salutemque hominum sæculis quibuscunque divinitus tradidit.

5 Scripturis, unde hæc hausimus, credi a Christianis haud inique postulamus; de earum vero auctoritate suo loco tractabimus.

CHRISTUS. Matt. xi. 27. *neque patrem quisquam novit, nisi filius, et cuicunque voluerit filius eum retegere.* Ioan. i. 4. *in*

JOHN MILTON

AN ENGLISHMAN

His Christian Doctrine

COMPILED FROM THE HOLY SCRIPTURES ALONE
IN TWO POSTHUMOUS BOOKS.

BOOK ONE.

CHAPTER I.

OF THE DEFINITION OF CHRISTIAN DOCTRINE, AND THE SEVERAL PARTS THEREOF.

THE Christian Doctrine is that DIVINE REVELATION disclosed in various ages by CHRIST (though he was not known under that name in the beginning) con-cerning the nature and worship of the Deity, for the promo-
5 tion of the glory of God, and the salvation of mankind.

It is not unreasonable to assume that Christians believe in the Scriptures whence this doctrine is derived, but the au-thority of those Scriptures will be examined in the proper place.

10 CHRIST. Matt. xi. 27. "neither knoweth any man the Father, save the Son, and he to whomsover the Son will reveal him."

illo vita erat, et vita illa erat lux hominum. et v. 9. *erat lux illa vera, quæ illuminat omnem hominem venientem in mundum.* 1 Pet. iii. 19. *per quem etiam spiritibus qui sunt in carcere veniens prædicavit.* Christi sub nomine Mosen etiam
5 et prophetas intellige, Christi prænuntios, ab eodemque missos Apostolos. Gal. iii. 24. *Lex pædagogus noster fuit ad Christum ut ex fide iustificaremur.* Heb. xiii. 8. *Iesus Christus heri et hodie idem est et in sæcula.* Col. ii. 17. *quæ sunt umbra rerum futurarum; at corpus est Christi.* 1 Pet. i. 10, 11. *qui*
10 *de ventura in vos gratia prophetarunt: scrutantes in quod aut quale tempus prænuntius ille qui in ipsis erat spiritus Christi, declararet—.* Rom. i. 1. *Paulus servus Iesu Christi.* Sic initio fere cæterarum deinceps epistolarum. 1 Cor. iv. 1. *Sic de vobis reputet homo, ut de ministris Christi.*
15   DIVINITUS. Isa. li. 4. *doctrina a me prodibit.* Matt. xvi. 17. *caro et sanguis hæc non retexit tibi, sed pater meus qui est in cœlis.* Ioan. vi. 45, 46. *erunt omnes docti a Deo.* et ix. 29. *scimus Deum locutum esse Mosi.* Gal. i. 11, 12. *evangelium non est secundum hominem, neque enim ab homine accepi-*
20 *mus.* 1 Thess. iv. 9. *ipsi divinitus docti estis.*

Hæc igitur doctrina, non ex philosophantium scholis, neque ex humanis legibus, sed ex sacris duntaxat literis, præeunte sancto spiritu, petenda est. 2 Tim. i. 14. *præclarum illud depositum custodi per spiritum sanctum, qui inhabitat in*

John i. 4. "in him was life, and the life was the light of men."
v. 9. "that was the true light which lighteth every man that
cometh into the world." 1 Pet. iii. 19. "by which also he went
and preached unto the spirits in prison."

5   Under the name of CHRIST are also comprehended Moses
and the Prophets, who were his forerunners, and the Apostles
whom he sent. Gal. iii. 24. "the law was our schoolmaster to
bring us unto Christ, that we might be justified by faith."
Heb. xiii. 8. "Jesus Christ, the same yesterday, to-day, and
10 for ever." Col. ii. 17. "which are a shadow of things to come:
but the body is of Christ." 1 Pet. i. 10, 11. "who prophesied of the grace that should come unto you: searching what,
or what manner of time the Spirit of Christ which was in
them did signify." Rom. i. 1. "Paul, a servant of Jesus
15 Christ": in which manner he begins nearly all the rest of his
epistles. 1 Cor. iv. 1. "let a man so account of us, as of the
ministers of Christ."

   DIVINE REVELATION. Isa. li. 4. "a law shall proceed from
me." Matt. xvi. 17. "flesh and blood hath not revealed it
20 unto thee, but my father which is in heaven." John vi. 46.
"they shall be all taught of God." ix. 29. "we know that God
spake unto Moses." Gal. i. 11, 12. "the gospel which was
preached of me is not after man; for I neither received it of
man." 1 Thess. iv. 9. "ye yourselves are taught of God."

25   This doctrine, therefore, is to be obtained, not from the
schools of the philosophers, nor from the laws of man, but
from the Holy Scriptures alone, under the guidance of the
Holy Spirit. 2 Tim. i. 14. "that good thing which was com-

nobis. Col. ii. 8. *ne quis sit qui vos deprædetur per philo-*
sophiam—. Dan. iii. 16. *ut respondeamus tibi de hac re, non*
sumus solliciti. Act. iv. 19. *an iustum in conspectu Dei vobis*
potius auscultare, quam Deo, iudicate.

5   Hic autem non novum quicquam docetur, sed memoriæ
tantummodo consulitur; ut quæ sparsim sacris in libris leguntur, commode velut in unum corpus redacta, perque certos
digesta locos, ad manum sint. Quod factum, quanquam Christiana prudentia facile defenditur; divino tamen monitu niti
10   potius videatur. Matt. xiii. 52. *omnis scriba edoctus in regno*
cœlorum, similis est cuipiam patri familias, qui profert e
thesauro suo nova et vetera. Sic etiam Apostolus ad Timotheum, 2 Ep. i. 13. ὑποτύπωσιν ἔχε —. id quod etiam epistolæ
ad Hebræos auctor secum statuisse facere videtur, ut doctrinæ
15   Christianæ capita certo ordine doceret: cap. vi. 1, 2, 3. *de*
resipiscentia, de fide, de Baptismatum doctrina, de manuum
impositione, de resurrectione mortuorum, de iudicio æterno:
atque id faciemus, siquidem promiserit Deus. Quæ methodus
Christiana fidem tum primum suscipientibus in Ecclesia cate-
20   chumenis, accommodatissima erat: idem ostenditur Rom. vi.
17. *ex corde auscultatis in eam formam doctrinæ, quam edocti*
estis. hoc loco vox Græca τύπος ut et illa ex 2 Tim. i. 13.

mitted unto thee keep by the Holy Ghost which dwelleth in us." Col. ii. 8. "lest any man spoil you through philosophy." Dan. iii. 16. "we are not careful to answer thee in this matter." Acts iv. 19. "whether it be right in the sight of God to hearken
5 unto you more than unto God, judge ye."

In this treatise then no novelties of doctrine are taught; but, for the sake of assisting the memory, what is dispersed throughout the different parts of the Holy Scriptures is conveniently reduced into one compact body as it were, and di-
10 gested under certain heads. This method might be easily defended on the ground of Christian prudence, but it seems better to rest its authority on the divine command; Matt. xiii. 52. "every scribe which is instructed unto the kingdom of heaven is like unto a man which is an householder, which
15 bringeth forth out of his treasure things new and old." So also the Apostle says, 2 Tim. i. 13. "hold fast the form," which the author of the Epistle to the Hebrews seems to have determined to adopt as the rule of his own conduct for teaching the heads of Christian doctrine in methodical arrange-
20 ment: vi. 1–3. "of repentance from dead works, and of faith toward God, of the doctrine of baptisms, and of laying on of hands, and of resurrection of the dead, and of eternal judgment; and this will we do, if God permit." This usage of the Christians was admirably suited for catechumens when first
25 professing their faith in the Church. Allusion is made to the same system in Rom. vi. 17. "ye have obeyed from the heart that form of doctrine which was delivered you." In this passage the Greek word $\tau\upsilon\pi\grave{o}\varsigma$, as well as $\dot{\upsilon}\pi\sigma\tau\dot{\upsilon}\pi\omega\sigma\iota\varsigma$ 2 Tim. i. 13.

ὑποτύπωσις, aut partes ipsas evangelicæ scripturæ tum scriptas videtur significare (quemadmodum μόρφωσις illa *cognitionis et veritatis in Lege,* Rom. ii. 20. legem ipsam significabat) aut earum partium, vel etiam totius doctrinæ evangelicæ metho-
5 dicam quandam institutionem. Act. xx. 27. *non subterfugi quo minus annuntiarem vobis omne Dei consilium.* integrum ergo, ut videtur, doctrinæ corpus, et methodo certe aliqua conceptum; nec grande tamen, quod plus minus triennio, quo Paulus Ephesi docuit, totum est annuntiatum; immo aliquo-
10 ties fortasse repetitum.

PARTES DOCTRINÆ CHRISTIANÆ duæ sunt: FIDES seu COG-NITIO DEI, et CHARITAS seu DEI CULTUS. Gen. xvii. 1. *ambula coram me et esto integer.* Psal. xxxvii. 3. *confide et fac.* Luc. xi. 28. *beati qui audiunt et observant.* Act. xxiv. 14. *ut qui*
15 *credam* et v. 6. *me exerceo.* 2 Tim. i. 13. *formam teneto sermonum cum fide et charitate, quæ est in Christo Iesu.* 1 Tim. i. 19. *retinens fidem et bonam conscientiam.* Tit. iii. 8. *qui crediderunt, curent.* 1 Ioan. iii. 23. *ut credamus, et dili-gamus.*

20 Partes hæ duæ, quanquam natura et præcipiendi ratione distinguuntur. usu tamen separari non queunt. Rom. ii. 13. *non qui audiunt sed qui præstant.* Iacob. i. 22. *effectores estote nec auditores solum.* immo obedientia et charitas ad scientiam

seems to signify either that part of the evangelical Scriptures which were then written (as in Rom. ii. 20. μόρφωσις, "the form of knowledge and of the truth in the law," signified the law itself) or some systematic course of instruction derived
5 from them or from the whole doctrine of the gospel. Acts. xx. 27. "I have not shunned to declare unto you all the counsel of God," which must mean some entire body of doctrine, formed according to a certain plan, though probably not of great extent, since the whole was gone through, and perhaps
10 even repeated several times during St. Paul's stay at Ephesus, which was about the space of three years.

Christian doctrine is comprehended under two divisions: FAITH, or THE KNOWLEDGE OF GOD; and LOVE, or THE WORSHIP OF GOD. Gen. xvii. 1. "walk before me, and be thou perfect."
15 Psal. xxxvii. 3. "trust in Jehovah, and do good." Luke xi. 28. "blessed are they that hear the word of God, and keep it." Acts xxiv. 14. "believing all things," and v. 16. "herein do I exercise myself." 2 Tim. i. 13. "hold fast the form of sound words which thou hast heard of me, in faith and in love
20 which is in Christ Jesus." 1 Tim. i. 19. "holding faith and a good conscience." Tit. iii. 8. "that they which have believed might be careful—." 1 John iii. 23. "that we should believe and love."

These two divisions, though they are distinct in their own
25 nature, and put asunder for the convenience of teaching, cannot be separated in practice. Rom. ii. 13. "not the hearers of the law, but the doers of the law shall be justified." James i. 22. "be ye doers of the word, and not hearers only." Besides,

optima semper dux est; eamque ex minima sæpe maiorem et auctiorem reddit. Psal. xxv. 14. *arcanum Iehovæ reverentibus ipsum.* Ioan. vii. 17. *si quis voluerit quod ille vult, cognoscet de doctrina.* et viii. 31, 32. *si manseritis, cognoscetis; et veritas* 5 *vos liberos faciet.* 1 Ioan. ii. 3. *per hoc scimus, quod ipsum novimus, si præcepta eius observemus.*

Fides autem in hac partitione non habitum fidei notat, sed res isto habitu credendas. Act. vi. 7. *auscultabat fidei.* Gal. i. 23. *annuntiat fidem.*

CAPUT II.

DE DEO.

ESSE Deum, quanquam haud pauci sunt qui negent esse, *dicit enim stultus in corde suo, non est Deus,* Psal. xiv. 1. tot tamen clara indicia sui Deus in mente humana, tot per omnem penitus naturam sui vestigia impressit, ut ignorare Deum esse, nemo non insanus possit. 15 Iob. xii. 9. *quid non cognovit ex omnibus istis?* Psal. xix. 2. *cœli enarrant gloriam Dei.* Act. xiv. 17. *non passus est se esse expertem testimonii.* et xvii. 27, 28. *non longe abest ab unoquoque.* Rom. i. 19, 20. *id quod de Deo cognosci potest,*

obedience and love are always the best guides to knowledge, and often lead the way from small beginnings, to a greater and more flourishing degree of proficiency. Psal. xxv. 14. "the secret of Jehovah is with them that fear him." John vii. 17.
5 "if any man will do his will, he shall know of the doctrine." viii. 31, 32. "if ye continue in my word . . . ye shall know the truth, and the truth shall make you free." 1 John ii. 3. "hereby we do know that we know him, if we keep his commandments."

10   It must be observed, that Faith in this division does not mean the habit of believing, but the things to be habitually believed. So Acts vi. 7. "were obedient to the faith." Gal. i. 23. "he preacheth the faith."

CHAPTER II.

OF GOD.

THOUGH there be not a few who deny the existence of God, "for the fool hath said in his heart, There is no God," Psal. xiv. 1. yet the Deity has imprinted upon the human mind so many unquestionable tokens of himself, and so many traces of him are apparent throughout the whole of nature, that no one in his senses can remain igno-
20 rant of the truth. Job xii. 9. "who knoweth not in all these that the hand of Jehovah hath wrought this?" Psal. xix. 1. "the heavens declare the glory of God." Acts xiv. 17. "he left not himself without witness." xvii. 27, 28. "he is not far from every one of us." Rom. i. 19, 20. "that which may be

manifestum est. et ii. 14, 15. *gentes ostendunt opus legis scriptum in cordibus suis; una testimonium reddente ipsorum conscientia.* 1 Cor. i. 21. *postquam in Dei sapientia mundus non cognovit Deum per istam sapientiam, libuit Deo per*
5 *stultitiam prædicationis servare credentes.* Certe quæ in mundo sunt omnia, pulcherrimo ordine, fini alicui bonoque facta, testantur præextitisse summum aliquem efficientem qui finem sibi in his omnibus proposuerit.

Nonnulli naturam aut fatum supremum quoddam in rebus
10 esse argutantur: sed natura natam se fatetur aut proprie rem nullam significat, sed vel rei essentiam, vel communem illam legem, qua nascuntur omnia atque agunt; et fatum quid nisi effatum divinum omnipotentis cuiuspiam numinis potest esse?

15   Quinetiam Natura fieri omnia qui volunt, necesse est fortunam quoque adiungant ei divinitatis participem; atque ita quid aliud assequuntur nisi ut pro uno Deo, quem non ferunt, duas vel inviti Deas perpetuo fere sibi adversantes, rerum dominas inducant. profecto aut Deum, aut malum aliquod
20 summum nominis ignoti rebus mortalium præsidere, multa

known of God is manifest in them." and ii. 14, 15. "the Gentiles . . . show the work of the law written in their hearts, their conscience also bearing witness." 1 Cor. i. 21. "after that in the wisdom of God, the world by wisdom knew

5 not God, it pleased God by the foolishness of preaching to save them that believe." There can be no doubt that every thing in the world, by the beauty of its order, and the evidence of a determinate and beneficial purpose which pervades it, testifies that some supreme efficient Power must have pre-

10 existed, by which the whole was ordained for a specific end.

There are some who pretend that nature or fate is this supreme Power: but the very name of nature implies that it must owe its birth to some prior agent, or, to speak properly, signifies in itself nothing; but means either the essence of a

15 thing, or that general law which is the origin of every thing, and under which every thing acts; on the other hand, fate can be nothing but a divine decree emanating from some almighty power.

Further, those who attribute the creation of every thing to

20 nature, must necessarily associate chance with nature as a joint divinity; so that they gain nothing by this theory, except that in the place of that one God, whom they cannot tolerate, they are obliged, however reluctantly, to substitute two sovereign rulers of affairs, who must almost always be in oppo

25 sition to each other. In short, many visible proofs, the verification of numberless predictions, a multitude of wonderful works have compelled all nations to believe, either that God, or that some evil power whose name was unknown, presided

visa, multa vera prædicta, multa mira edita subegere omnes nationes ut crederent. malum autem bono præpollere summumque verum esse et indignum est et incredibile. Deus igitur est.

5   Quin et Conscientia, sive eadem recta ratio est, quarum vel hæc vel illa ne in pessimis quibusque semper sopita est, esse Deum testificatur. Deus nisi esset, nullum recti, pravique discrimen existeret; virtutis et vitii tota ratio in opinione hominum cæca versaretur; virtutem nemo sequeretur; a vitiis

10 nemo vel pudore vel legum metu se cohiberet, nisi conscientia, sive recta ratio subinde unumquemque vel invitum intus redargueret esse Deum aliquem rerum omnium moderatorem ac Dominum, cui suorum quisque vel recte vel prave factorum rationem sit aliquando redditurus.

15 Probat idem universa etiam scriptura; et nos doctrinæ Christianæ discipulis ut hoc sit prius persuasum, postulamus, iuxta illud Heb. xi. 6. *Qui accedit ad Deum, credat oportet esse Deum.* probat idem antiquissima Gens Iudæorum omnes in terras disiecta, quod Deus præmonuit sæpe ob eorum pec-

20 cata eventurum, in hodiernum usque diem, cæteris tamen gentibus intermixta, nec ad pœnam duntaxat peccatorum suorum exsolvendam per tot sæculorum vicissitudines conservata, sed ad testimonium multo magis Deo scripturarumque veritati vivum atque perpetuum toto orbe terrarum per-

25 hibendum.

over the affairs of the world. Now that evil should prevail over good, and be the true supreme power, is as unmeet as it is incredible. Hence it follows as a necessary consequence, that God exists.

5   Again: the existence of God is further proved by that feeling, whether we term it conscience, or right reason, which even in the worst of characters is not altogether extinguished. If there were no God, there would be no distinction between right and wrong; the estimate of virtue and vice would en-
10 tirely depend on the blind opinion of men; none would follow virtue, none would be restrained from vice by any sense of shame, or fear of the laws, unless conscience or right reason did from time to time convince every one, however unwilling, of the existence of God, the Lord and ruler of all things, to
15 whom, sooner or later, each must give an account of his own actions, whether good or bad.

The whole tenor of Scripture proves the same thing; and the disciples of the doctrine of Christ may fairly be required to give assent to this truth before all others, according to
20 Heb. xi. 6. "he that cometh to God, must believe that he is." It is proved also by the dispersion of the ancient nation of the Jews throughout the whole world, conformably to what God often forewarned them would happen on account of their sins. Nor is it only to pay the penalty of their own guilt that they
25 have been reserved in their scattered state, among the rest of the nations, through the revolution of successive ages, and even to the present day; but also to be a perpetual and living testimony to all people under heaven, of the existence of God, and of the truth of the Holy Scriptures.

Recte autem de Deo sentire, natura vel ratione sola duce sine verbo aut nuntio Dei, potest nemo; Rom. x. 14. *quomodo credent ei de quo non audierint.*

Cognoscitur autem Deus vel ex natura sua, quantum sui nobis cognoscendum præbet, vel ex sua efficientia:

De cognoscendo Deo quod loquimur, id de imperfecto hominum captu intelligi debet; nam Deus, prout in se est humanam cogitationem, nedum sensus longe superat: 1 Tim. vi. 16. *lucem habitans inaccessam.* ideoque tantum sui retexit Deus, quantum vel nostra mens capere, vel naturæ debilitas ferre potest: Exod. xxxiii. 20. 23. *nemo potest videre me et vivere: sed videbis posteriora mea.* Isa. vi. 1. *vidi Dominum insidentem solio celso et elato, cuius fimbriæ complebant templum ipsum.* Ioan. i. 18. *Deum nemo vidit unquam.* et vi. 46. *non quod patrem viderit quisquam, nisi is qui est a Deo; hic vidit patrem.* et v. 37. *neque vocem eius audistis.* 1 Cor. xiii. 12. *per speculum, per ænigma, aliquatenus.*

Nobis tutissimum est, talem nostro animo comprehendere Deum, qualem in sacris literis ipse se exhibet, seque describit. Quamvis enim hoc concedatur, Deum, non qualis in se est, sed qualem nos capere possumus, talem semper vel describi vel adumbrari, nos tamen nihilo minus debebimus talem pror-

No one, however, can have right thoughts of God, with nature or reason alone as his guide, independent of the word, or message of God. Rom. x. 14. "how shall they believe in him of whom they have not heard?"

5   God is known, so far as he is pleased to make us acquainted with himself, either from his own nature, or from his efficient power.

When we speak of knowing God, it must be understood with reference to the imperfect comprehension of man; for to 10 know God as he really is, far transcends the powers of man's thoughts, much more of his perception. 1 Tim. vi. 16. "dwelling in the light which no man can approach unto." God therefore has made as full a revelation of himself as our minds can conceive, or the weakness of our nature can bear. Exod. 15 xxxiii. 20, 23. "there shall no man see me, and live . . . but thou shalt see my back parts." Isa. vi. 1. "I saw the Lord sitting upon a throne, high and lifted up, and his train filled the temple." John i. 18. "no man hath seen God at any time." vi. 46. "not that any man hath seen the Father, save he which 20 is of God, he hath seen the Father." v. 37. "ye have neither heard his voice at any time." 1 Cor. xiii. 12. "we see through a glass, darkly . . . in part."

Our safest way is to form in our minds such a conception of God, as shall correspond with his own delineation and rep-25 resentation of himself in the sacred writings. For granting that both in the literal and figurative descriptions of God, he is exhibited not as he really is, but in such a manner as may be within the scope of our comprehensions, yet we ought to en-

sus mente nostra concipere, qualis ipse se ad captum accom-
modans nostrum, vult concipi: ob id ipsum enim se ad
nos demisit, ne nos elati supra captum humanum supraque
quod scriptum est, vagis cogitationibus atque argutiis locum
5 daremus.

Hic igitur Ἀνθρωποπαθείᾳ (quam figuram Grammatici ad
excusandas poetarum de suo Iove nugas olim excogitarunt)
Theologis, opinor non est opus; scriptura sacra sine dubio, hoc
satis cavit, ne quid vel ipsa indecorum aut indignum Deo scri-
10 beret, vel Deum de semetipso loquentem induceret. Præstat
igitur non ἀνθρωποπαθῶς, id est, more hominum, qui subtilius de Deo comminiscendi finem nullum faciunt, sed more
scripturæ, id est, quo ipse se contemplandum præbuit, ita
Deum contemplari talemque animo concipere; nec ipsum de
15 se quicquam fuisse dicturum aut scriptum voluisse existime-
mus, quod nos de se noluisset cogitare. Quid Deum deceat,
quidve dedeceat, auctorem ipso Deo ne requiramus gravio-
rem. Si *pœnituit Iehovam quod hominem fecisset* Gen. vi.
6. et *propter gemitum eorum* Iudic. ii. 18. pœnituisse cre-
20 damus; modo id in Deo, ut solet in hominibus, ex imprudentia
natum ne putemus: sic enim de se ne nos opinemur, ipse cavit,

tertain such a conception of him, as he, in condescending to accommodate himself to our capacities, has shown that he desires we should conceive. For it is on this very account that he has lowered himself to our level, lest in our flights above 5 the reach of human understanding, and beyond the written word of Scripture, we should be tempted to indulge in vague cogitations and subtleties.

There is no need then that theologians should have recourse here to what they call anthropopathy, a figure invented 10 by the grammarians to excuse the absurdities of the poets on the subject of the heathen divinities. We may be sure that sufficient care has been taken that the Holy Scriptures should contain nothing unsuitable to the character or dignity of God, and that God should say nothing of himself which could 15 derogate from his own majesty. It is better therefore to contemplate the Deity, and to conceive of him, not with reference to human passions, that is, after the manner of men, who are never weary of forming subtle imaginations respecting him, but after the manner of Scripture, that is, in the way wherein 20 God has offered himself to our contemplation; nor should we think that he would say or direct anything to be written of himself, which is inconsistent with the opinion he wishes us to entertain of his character. Let us require no better authority than God himself for determining what is worthy or un-25 worthy of him. If "it repented Jehovah that he had made man," Gen. vi. 6. and "because of their groanings," Judges ii. 18. let us believe that it did repent him, only taking care to remember that what is called repentance when applied to

Num. xxiii. 23. *Deus non est homo qui mentiatur, aut filius hominis, quem pœniteat.* 1 Sam. xv. 29. idem. si *doluisse etiam in corde suo* Gen. vi. 6. et, quod idem est, *imminuta est anima eius* Iudic. x. 16. doluisse credamus. Affectus enim in viro bono boni sunt et virtutibus pares, in Deo sancti: si post sex dierum operam *quieti refici,* Exod. xxxi. 17. si *metuere indignationem ab inimico.* Deut. xxxii. 27. dicitur Deus, credamus dolere quod dolet; credamus eo refici quo refectus est; id metuere quod metuit, non esse infra Deum: longo licet interpretationis ambitu hæc et huiusmodi de Deo dicta lenire tentaveris, eodem res redibit, si *creasse hominem Deus dicitur ad imaginem suam, ad similitudinem suam,* Gen. i. 26. idque non animo solum sed forma etiam externa, nisi eadem verba idem non significant quod postea cap. v. 3. ubi Adam *ad similitudinem suam, ad imaginem suam filium genuit,* et Deus humana membra ac speciem passim sibi tribuit, quid est quod nos quæ ipse sibi tribuit, eadem tribuere vereamur, dummodo quod in nobis imperfectum ac debile est, id Deo sicubi tribuatur, perfectissimum atque pulcherrimum esse credamus: pro certo hoc habentes, Dei maiestatem ac gloriam satis sibi curæ fuisse, ne quid humilius aut demissius Deo, de se un-

God, does not arise from inadvertency, as in men; for so he has himself cautioned us, Num. xxiii. 19. "God is not a man that he should lie, neither the son of man that he should repent." See also 1 Sam. xv. 29. Again, if "it grieved the Lord
5 at his heart," Gen. vi. 6. and if "his soul were grieved for the misery of Israel," Judges x. 16, let us believe that it did grieve him. For the affections which in a good man are good, and rank with virtues, in God are holy. If after the work of six days it be said of God that "he rested and was refreshed,"
10 Exod. xxxi. 17. if it be said that "he feared the wrath of the enemy," Deut. xxxii. 27, let us believe that it is not beneath the dignity of God to grieve in that for which he is grieved, or to be refreshed in that which refresheth him, or to fear in that he feareth. For however we may attempt to soften down
15 such expressions by a latitude of interpretation, when applied to the Deity, it comes in the end to precisely the same. If God be said "to have made man in his own image, after his likeness," Gen. i. 26. and that too not only as to his soul, but also as to his outward form (unless the same words have different
20 significations here and in chap. v. 3. "Adam begat a son in his own likeness, after his image") and if God habitually assign to himself the members and form of man, why should we be afraid of attributing to him what he attributes to himself, so long as what is imperfection and weakness when viewed in
25 reference to ourselves be considered as most complete and excellent when imputed to God? Questionless the glory and majesty of the Deity must have been so dear to him, that he would never say anything of himself which could be humili-

quam loqueretur, ne quid sibi ullo tempore attribuat, quod a nobis attributum sibi esse nolit. Qualis sit Deus, eos optime capere statuamus qui suum accommodant captum Dei verbo; quandoquidem is verbum suum accommodat captui eorum; qualemque esse velit captum de se nostrum, ostendit. ut paucis absolvam, Deus aut in se talis est qualem se dicit esse, aut non est talis: si talis in se est, cur nos aliter sentimus? si talis in se non est, quo id auctore dicimus, quod Deus non dicit? si saltem talis vult concipi, cur noster conceptus alio se vertit? cur id dubitat de Deo cogitare, quod ipse non dubitat Deus de se clare dicere? Quæ enim cognoscenda de Deo ad salutem nostram opus sunt, ea nobis ipse pro bonitate sua abunde revelavit: Deut. xxix. 29. *occulta penes Iehovam; revelata, nobis ut faciamus.* Hæc itaque disserentes, non dicimus Deum singulis partibus ac membris forma esse humana sed, quantum ad nos quidem scire attinet, esse forma, quam in sacris literis ipse sibi tribuit. Quod si Deus, qualem se nobis cognoscendum præbet, talis percipi a nobis vult, nos contra

ating or degrading, and would ascribe to himself no personal
attributes which he would not willingly have ascribed to him
by his creatures. Let us be convinced that those have acquired
the truest apprehension of the nature of God who submit their
5 understandings to his word; considering that he has accom-
modated his word to their understandings, and has shown
what he wishes their notion of the Deity should be.

In a word, God either is, or is not, such as he represents
himself to be. If he be really such, why should we think other-
10 wise of him? If he be not such, on what authority do we say
what God has not said? If it be his will that we should thus
think of him, why does our imagination wander into some
other conception? Why should we hesitate to conceive of
God according to what he has not hesitated to declare explic-
15 itly respecting himself? For such knowledge of the Deity as
was necessary for the salvation of man, he has himself of his
goodness been pleased to reveal abundantly. Deut. xxix. 29.
"the secret things belong unto Jehovah, but those things which
are revealed belong unto us . . . that we may do them."

20 In arguing thus, we do not say that God is in fashion like
unto man in all his parts and members, but that as far as we
are concerned to know, he is of that form which he attributes
to himself in the sacred writings. If therefore we persist in
entertaining a different conception of the Deity than that
25 which it is to be presumed he desires should be cherished, inasmuch as he has himself disclosed it to us, we frustrate the
purposes of God instead of rendering him submissive obedience. As if, forsooth, we wished to show that it was not we

captum alium de Deo captamus, non morem gerimus Deo, sed Deum fine suo frustramur; plane ac si ostendere vellemus, non nos de Deo, sed Deum de nobis demisse nimis cogitare.

Natura autem divina (sic enim dicitur 2 Pet. i. 4. *ut effi-*
5 *ceremini divinæ consortes naturæ;* quanquam hic natura non essentiam, sed imaginem divinam significat, Gal. iv. 8. *Qui natura non sunt Dii,* et Θεοτὴς *Deitas* dicitur, Col. ii. 9. et Θειοτὴς, *divinitas,* Rom. i. 20. et τὸ θεῖον, Act. xvii. 29.) nulla nostra definitione comprehendi potest, ut quæ causas non 10 habeat; cum Deus essentia maximus sit Isa. xxviii. 29. colligi autem descriptio quædam eius ex nominibus et attributis utcunque potest.

Nomina autem et attributa Dei vel naturam eius ostendunt vel vim eius atque virtutem divinam. Tria potissimum 15 Dei nomina eius naturam innuere videntur, יְהֹוָה Iehova, יָהּ Iah, אֶהְיֶה Ehie, et Iehova quidem nomen pronuntiari non vetitum, modo reverenter: Exod. iii. 15. *Iehovah Deus pa-trum vestrorum, hoc est nomen meum et hoc memoriale meum.* et xx. 7. *ne assumito nomen Iehovæ Dei Tui in vanum.* 20 Et pronuntiatum videtur 1 Reg. xvii. 12. *ut vivit Iehova Deus Tuus;* et alibi vulgo. Quod nomen tam in novo testamento quam in versione Græca veteris Κύριος semper redditur: neque id aliam ob causam factum videtur, nisi quod Iehova Græcis literis proferri nequisset. idem est autem fere ac si diceretur, 25 is qui est, vel *qui est, erat, erit,* Apoc. i. idem significat et Iah

who had thought too meanly of God, but God who had thought too meanly of us.

It is impossible to comprehend accurately under any form of definition the "divine nature," for so it is called, 2 Pet. i. 4.
5 "that ye might be partakers of the divine nature"; though nature does not here signify essence, but the divine image, as in Gal. iv. 8. "which by nature are no Gods," and θεοτὴς Col. ii. 9. θειοτὴς Rom. i. 20. τὸ θεῖον Acts xvii. 29. which words are all translated "Godhead." But though the nature of God
10 cannot be defined, since he who has no efficient cause is essentially greatest of all, Isa. xxviii. 29. some description of it at least may be collected from his names and attributes.

The NAMES and ATTRIBUTES of God either show his nature, or his divine power and excellence. There are three names
15 which seem principally to intimate the nature of God: יְהֹוָה "Jehovah," יָה "Jah," אֶהְיֶה "Ehie." Even the name of Jehovah was not forbidden to be pronounced, provided it was with due reverence. Exod. iii. 15. "Jehovah, God of your fathers . . . this is my name for ever, and this is my memorial."
20 xx. 7. "thou shalt not take the name of Jehovah thy God in vain." It seems to be introduced in the same way, 1 Kings xvii. 12. "as Jehovah thy God liveth," and also in many other places. This name both in the New Testament and in the Greek version of the Old is always translated Κύριος, THE
25 LORD, probably for no other reason than because the word Jehovah could not be expressed in Greek letters. Its signification is, "he who is," or, "which is, and which was, and which is to come," Rev. i. 4. Jah, which is a sort of contrac-

quasi contractum quiddam nominis prioris: Exod. xvii. 16.
solium Iah, et alibi Cap. iii. 14. אֶהְיֶה *Ehie qui sum* vel ero,
et persona prima in tertiam affinis verbi mutatur Iehovæ, qui
est vel erit idem quod Iehova ut quidam putant, illisque vo-
5 cabulis rectius prolatum: sed nomen Iehovæ non modo naturæ,
verum etiam promissionum eius existentiam, id est, impletionem, significare videtur: unde illud Exod. vi. 3. *nomine
meo Iehova non cognitus sum illis.* Et quibus vocalibus pronuntiari debeat hoc nomen Iehova, ostendunt ea nomina pro-
10 pria, quæ ex hoc composita, duas eius vocales expressas habent,
ut Iehosaphat, Iehoram, Iehoiada, et multa similia. tertiam
finalem, duo altera divina nomina אֲדֹנָי et יָהּ analogia quadam
suppeditant.

ATTRIBUTA, quæ naturam Dei qualis in se est, ostendunt,
15 sunt, primum, quod sit VERUS DEUS. Ier. x. 10. *Iehova Deus
verus.* Ioan. xvii. 3. *Te esse illum solum verum Deum.* 1 Thess.
v. 9. *Deo vivo et vero.* 1 Ioan. v. 20. *ut cognoscamus verum
illum.*

Secundum, quod Deus sit natura simplicissima SPIRITUS.
20 Exod. iii. 14, 15. *sum qui sum.* Rom. xi. 35, 36. *ex eo et per
eum sunt omnia.* Ioan. iv. 24. *Deus est spiritus.* Quid autem
sit spiritus, vel potius quid non sit, ostenditur. Isa. xxxi. 3. *caro,
non spiritus.* Luc. xxiv. 39. *spiritus carnem et ossa non habet.*
Ex quo intelligitur, essentiam Dei, simplicissima cum sit,
25 nihil compositi in se admittere; hypostasin proinde illam
Heb. i. 3. quam alii vel substantiam vel subsistentiam, vel per-

tion of the former name, has the same signification. Exod. xvii. 16. "Jah hath sworn"—and in other places. Exod. iii. 14. אֶהְיֶה Ehie, "I am that I am," or "will be"; and if the first person be changed into the third of the kindred verb, Jave, "who is," or "will be," meaning the same as Jehovah, as some think, and more properly expressed thus than by the other words; but the name Jave appears to signify not only the existence of his nature, but also of his promises, or rather the completion of his promises; whence it is said, Exod. vi. 3. "by my name JEHOVAH was I not known to them." And with what vowel points this name Jehovah ought to be pronounced, is shown by those proper names into the composition of which two of them enter, as Jehosaphat, Jehoram, Jehoiada, and the like. The third, or final vowel point may be supplied by analogy from the two other divine names, אֲדֹנָי and יָה.

I. The first of those attributes which show the inherent nature of God, is TRUTH. Jer. x. 10. "Jehovah is the true God." John xvii. 3. "that they might know thee the only true God." 1 Thess. i. 9. "the living and true God." 1 John v. 20. "that we may know him that is true."

II. Secondly, God considered in his most simple nature is a SPIRIT. Exod. iii. 14, 15. "I am that I am." Rom. xi. 36. "of him and through him are all things." John iv. 24. "God is a spirit." What a spirit is, or rather what it is not, is shown, Isa. xxxi. 3. "flesh, and not spirit." Luke xxiv. 39. "a spirit hath not flesh and bones." Whence it is evident that the essence of God, being in itself most simple, can admit no compound quality; so that the term *hypostasis* Heb. i. 3. which is

sonam vertunt, nihil esse aliud quam essentiam ipsam perfec-
tissimam, qua Deus a se, in se, et per se est; essentiæ enim
absolutissimæ neque substantia neque subsistentia quicquam
addunt, et persona recentiore usu quodvis individuum intel-
5 lectu præditum significat, cum hypostasis non ipsum ens sed
entis essentiam in abstracto, quod aiunt designet: hypostasis
ergo plane idem quod essentia est, adeoque a multis ita in
supra dicto loco latine redditur: Deus igitur ut essentia, ita
et subsistentia est simplicissima.

10   Tertium, quod sit IMMENSUS et INFINITUS: 1 Reg. viii. 27.
cœli cœlorum non capiunt Te. Iob. xi. 8, 9. *altior altissimis
cœlis, profundior sepulchro imo.* et xxxvi. 26. ita amplus, ut
non cognoscamus.

Quartum, quod sit ÆTERNUS: æternum autem proprie dic-
15 tum id solum omnes esse statuunt, quod nec principium habet
nec finem; quod utrumque de Deo his fere non singulis quidem ex locis, sed multis inter se collatis percipi potest. Iob.
xxxvi. 26. *cuius annorum numero non est pervestigatio.* Gen.
xxi. 33. *Dei æterni;* ad verbum Dei sæculi vel ævi. Psal. xc. 2.
20 *a sæculo et usque in sæculum tu Deus.* vel ab ævo usque in
ævum. et cii. 13. *tu autem Iehova in sæculum permanes.* v. 25.
per generationem et generationem sunt anni tui. et v. 28. *tu
vero idem es, et anni tui non finiuntur.* Psal. cxlv. 13. *regnum*

differently translated *substance,* or *subsistence,* or *person,* can be nothing else but that most perfect essence by which God subsists by himself, in himself, and through himself. For neither *substance* nor *subsistence* makes any addition to what
5 is already a most perfect essence; and the word *person* in its later acceptation signifies any individual thing gifted with intelligence, whereas *hypostasis* denotes not the *ens* itself, but the essence of the *ens* in the abstract. *Hypostasis,* therefore, is clearly the same as essence, and thus many of the Latin com-
10 mentators render it in the passage already quoted. Therefore, as God is a most simple essence, so is he also a most simple subsistence.

III. IMMENSITY and INFINITY. 1 Kings viii. 27. "the heaven and heaven of heavens cannot contain thee." Job xi. 8. "it is
15 as high as heaven . . . deeper than hell." xxxvi. 26. "God is great, and we know him not."

IV. ETERNITY. It is universally acknowledged that nothing is eternal, strictly speaking, but what has neither beginning nor end, both which properties are attributed to God, not
20 indeed in each of the following passages separately, but as a plain deduction from the several texts when compared together. Job xxxvi. 26. "neither can the number of his years be searched out." Gen. xxi. 33. "the everlasting God," literally, "the God of old time" or "ages." Psal. xc. 2. "from ever-
25 lasting to everlasting, thou art God," or "from age to age." cii. 12. "but thou, O Jehovah, shalt endure for ever." v. 24. "thy years are through all generations." v. 27. "but thou art the same, and thy years shall have no end." Psal. cxlv. 13.

tuum omnium sæculorum. Isa. xliii. 10. *ante me non esse for-matum, et post me non futurum quicquam.* et xliv. 6. *ego primus et ultimus.* Abac. i. 12. *nonne tu ab æterno* ad verbum ab antiquitate. Clariora sunt novi fœderis testimonia, eo quod
5 vox Græca semper esse significat. Rom. xvi. 26. *ex imperio æterni Dei.* 1 Tim. i. 17. *Regi æterno.* Apoc. i. 4. *qui est et qui erat et qui venturus est.* Sed quibus verbis ad significan-dam æternitatem scriptura utitur, ea omnia sæculum duntaxat aut antiquitatem sæpe significant. Gen. vi. 4. *qui erant a*
10 *sæculo viri.* Iob. xx. 4. *an hoc nosti: ab æterno,* sive a sæculo, *ex quo posuit Deus hominem super terram.* Isa. xlii. 14. *silui a sæculo.* In sæculum etiam pro longinquo duntaxat tempore dici David ipse intellexit. 2 Sam. vii. 13. *stabiliam solium regni eius in sæculum,* cum v. 19. *adeo ut locutus sis de familia*
15 *servi tui in longinquum.* et 1 Chron. xvii. 12. 14. cum 17. idem. Ioan. ix. 32. *ab sæculo non est auditum aliquem ape-ruisse* &c. Act. iii. 21. *de quibus locutus est Deus a sæculo per os* &c. 2 Tim. i. 9. *ante tempora æterna,* sive sæcularia. Tit. i. 2. idem et Heb. xi. 3. *sæcula* hunc mundum significant: ubi
20 Syrus habet, *quod constructa fuerint sæcula.* his et similibus passim ex locis videtur, quid sit æternum proprie dictum,

"thy kingdom is an everlasting kingdom." Isa. xliii. 10. "before me there was no God formed, neither shall there be after me." xliv. 6. "I am the first, and I am the last." Hab. i. 12. "art thou not from everlasting," literally, "from old
5 time."

The evidence of the New Testament is still clearer, because the Greek word signifies *always existent*. Rom. xvi. 26. "according to the commandment of the everlasting God." 1 Tim. i. 17. "unto the King eternal." Rev. i. 4. "from him which
10 is, and which was, and which is to come."

But all the words used in Scripture to denote eternity, often signify only of old time, or antiquity. Gen. vi. 4. "mighty men which were of old." Job xx. 4. "knowest thou not this of old," or "from eternity, since man was placed upon earth?"
15 Isa. xlii. 14. "I have long time holden my peace." David also seems to have understood that the term "for ever" only intimated "a great while to come." 2 Sam. vii. 13. "I will stablish the throne of his kingdom for ever," compared with v. 19. "thou hast spoken also of thy servant's house for a great while
20 to come." See also 1 Chron. xvii. 12, 14, 17. John ix. 32. "since the world began was it not heard that any man opened the eyes of one that was born blind." Acts iii. 21. "which God hath spoken by the mouth of all his holy prophets since the world began." 2 Tim. i. 9. and Tit. i. 2. "before the world
25 began": and in Heb. xi. 3. the word is also used to signify this world, where the Syriac version translates it, "before the worlds were framed." From these and many similar texts it appears that the idea of eternity, properly so called, is con-

ratione magis quam disertis verbis Hebræorum sermone demonstrari.

Quintum hinc est quod sit IMMUTABILIS. Psal. cii. 28. *tu vero idem es.* Mal. iii. 6. *ego Iehova non mutor.* Iacob. i. 17.
5 *apud quem non est transmutatio aut conversionis obumbratio.*

Sextum inde quoque est quod sit INCORRUPTIBILIS. Psal. cii. 26, 27. *tu permanes.* Rom. i. 23. *Dei, qui non corrumpitur.* 1 Tim. i. 17. *regi incorruptibili.*

Septimum ex infinitate eius est quod sit UBIQUE PRÆSENS.
10 Psal. cxxxix. 8, 9. *si scanderem cœlos, illic es* &c. Prov. xv. 3. *in omni loco oculi Iehovæ.* Ier. xxiii. 24. *cœlos et terram ego impleo.* Eph. iv. 6. *super omnes, et per omnes, et in omnibus.* De omni præsentia autem Dei quæ dicitur, qualiscunque ea sit, id omnino sentiendum erit, quod reverentiæ nostræ Deo
15 debitæ convenire maxime videbitur.

Octavum, quod sit OMNIPOTENS. 2 Chron. xx. 6. *in manu tua vis et potentia.* Iob. xlii. 2. *novi te omnia posse.* Psal. xxxiii. 9. *ipso dicente, est quicquid est.* et cxv. 3. *quicquid placet, facit.* et cxxxv. 6. idem. Matt. xix. 26. *apud Deum omnia*
20 *possibilia.* Luc. i. 37. *apud Deum non erit quicquam quod fieri non potest.* Unde et nomen illud Dei El Shaddai. Gen. xvii. 1. *Ego sum Deus omnipotens,* ad verbum, *sufficiens.* Ruth. i. 21. *cum Omnipotens malis affecerit me.* Ier. xxxii. 18. *Deus iste maximus, potentissimus, et El Elion.* Gen. xiv. 22.

veyed in the Hebrew language rather by comparison and deduction than in express words.

V. The IMMUTABILITY of God has an immediate connection with the last attribute. Psal. cii. 27. "but thou art the same." Mal. iii. 6. "I am Jehovah, I change not." James i. 17. "with whom is no variableness, neither shadow of turning."

VI. His INCORRUPTIBILITY is also derived from the fourth attribute. Psal. cii. 26. "thou shalt endure." Rom. i. 23. "the uncorruptible God." 1 Tim. i. 17. "unto the King immortal."

VII. The OMNIPRESENCE of God, which is his next attribute, is the consequence of his infinity. Psal. cxxxix. 8, 9. "if I ascend up into heaven, thou art there," &c. &c. Prov. xv. 3. "the eyes of Jehovah are in every place." Jer. xxiii. 24. "do not I fill heaven and earth?" Eph. iv. 6. "who is above all, and through all, and in you all." Our thoughts of the omnipresence of God, whatever may be the nature of the attribute, should be such as appear most suitable to the reverence due to the Deity.

VIII. OMNIPOTENCE. 2 Chron. xx. 6. "in thine hand is there not power and might?" Job xlii. 2. "I know that thou canst do every thing." Psal. xxxiii. 9. "he spake, and it was done." cxv. 3. "he hath done whatsoever he hath pleased." See also cxxxv. 6. Matt. xix. 26. "with God all things are possible." Luke i. 37. "with God nothing shall be impossible." Hence the name of El Shaddai, applied to the Deity, Gen. xvii. 1. "I am the Almighty God," literally, "sufficient." Ruth i. 21. "the Almighty hath afflicted me." Jer. xxxii. 18. "the Great, the Mighty God, the Lord of Hosts." Gen. xiv. 22. "Jehovah,

ad Iehovam Deum, excelsum possessorem cœli et terræ, et passim אֲדֹנָי. In novo testamento Κύριος παντοκράτωρ. 2 Cor. vi. 18. Apoc. i. 8. et μόνος δυνάστης, *Rex regum, dominus dominorum.* 1 Tim. vi. 15. Hinc non ita commode, actus purus, ut

5 solet ex Aristotele, dici videtur Deus; Sic enim agere nihil poterit, nisi quod agit; idque necessario; cum tamen omnipotens sit liberrimeque agat. Notandum autem est potentiam Dei non eiusmodi in rebus versari etiam quæ contradictionem, quod aiunt, implicant. 2 Tim. ii. 13. *negare seipsum non po-*

10 *test.* Tit. i. 2. *qui non mentitur Deus.* Heb. vi. 18. *in quibus fieri non potest ut mentiatur Deus.*

Nonum ex octo superioribus velut ex totidem causis existit, quod Deus sit Unus. Verum testes alii non silent: Deut. iv. 35. *Iehovam esse Deum ipsum, nullum esse amplius præter eum.*

15 v. 39. *Iehovam Deum ipsum esse in cœlis superne et in terra inferne; nullum præter eum.* cap. vi. 4. *audi Israel Iehova Deus noster Iehova unus.* et xxxii. 39. *me meipsum esse et nullum esse Deum mecum.* 1 Reg. viii. 60. *ut cognoscant omnes populi terræ, Iehovam esse Deum ipsum, neminem esse*

20 *præter eum.* 2 Reg. xix. 15. *tu es Deus solus omnibus regnis terræ.* Isa. xliv. 1. *præter me nullus est Deus.* v. 3. *an Deus est præter me? utique nulla est rupes, nullam novi,* et xlv. 5. *ego Iehova et nullus præterea; præter me nullus est Deus.* v.

the most high God, the possessor of heaven and earth." Thus
also the name אֲדֹנָי frequently occurs. In the New Testament,
"the Lord Almighty," 2 Cor. vi. 18, and Rev. i. 8. "the only
Potentate, the King of kings and Lord of lords," 1 Tim. vi.
5 15. There seems, therefore, an impropriety in the term of
actus purus, or the active principle, which Aristotle applies to
God, for thus the Deity would have no choice of act, but what
he did he would do of necessity, and could do in no other way,
which would be inconsistent with his omnipotence and free
10 agency. It must be remembered, however, that the power of
God is not exerted in things which imply a contradiction.
2 Tim. ii. 13. "he cannot deny himself." Tit. i. 2. "God, that
cannot lie." Heb. vi. 18. "in which it was impossible for
God to lie."

15 IX. The ninth attribute, or the UNITY of God, may be
considered as proceeding necessarily from all the foregoing
attributes. Separate proof for it, however, is not wanting.
Deut. iv. 35. "Jehovah he is God, there is none else besides
him." v. 39. "Jehovah he is God in heaven above, and upon
20 the earth beneath: there is none else." vi. 4. "hear, O Israel,
Jehovah our God is one Jehovah." xxxii. 39. "I, even I, am
he, and there is no God with me." 1 Kings viii. 60. "that all
the people of the earth may know that Jehovah is God, and
that there is none else." 2 Kings xix. 15. "thou art the God,
25 even thou alone, of all the kingdoms of the earth." Isa. xliv.
6. "besides me there is no God." v. 8. "is there a God besides
me? yea, there is no God; I know not any." xlv. 5. "I am
Jehovah, and there is none else; there is no God besides me."

21. *nullus amplius Deus præter me; nullus præterquam ego.*
22. *ego sum Deus et nullus præterea,* id est, nullus spiritus, nulla persona, nullum ens, præterea est Deus. Nullus enim universe negat. cap. xlvi. 9. *me esse Deum et nullum præterea*
5 *Deum esse et neminem parem mihi.* Quid planius, quid distinctius, quid ad vulgi sensum quotidianumque loquendi usum accommodatius dici potuit? ut intelligeret Dei populus esse unum numero Deum, unum spiritum, et ut quidvis aliud numerando unum esse intelligebat? æquum enim erat et
10 rationi summe consentaneum, sic tradi primum illud adeoque maximum mandatum, in quo Deus ab universo populo etiam infimo religiose coli volebat, ut ne quid in eo ambiguum, ne quid obscurum suos cultores in errorem impelleret, aut dubitatione aliqua suspensos teneret. atque ita prorsus intellexit
15 semper populus ille sub lege atque prophetis, Deum nempe unum numero esse, alium præterea neminem, nedum parem. Enimvero nondum nati erant scholastici qui acuminibus suis, vel potius meris repugnantiis confisi, unitatem Dei quam asserere præ se ferebant, in dubium vocarunt. Quod autem in
20 omnipotentia Dei merito excipi omnes agnoscant, non ea posse Deum quæ contradictionem quod aiunt, implicant, ut supra monuimus, ita hic meminerimus non posse de uno Deo dici quæ unitati eius repugnant, unumque et non unum

v. 21. "there is no God else besides me . . . there is none besides me." v. 22. "I am God, and there is none else"; that is, no spirit, no person, no being besides him is God; for "none" is an universal negative. xlvi. 9. "I am God, and there
5 is none else; I am God, and there is none like me." What can be plainer, what more distinct, what more suitable to general comprehension and the ordinary forms of speech for the purpose of impressing on the people of God that there was numerically one God and one Spirit, in the common acceptation
10 of numerical unity? It was in truth fitting and highly agreeable to reason, that the first and consequently the greatest commandment, to which even the lowest of the people were required to pay scrupulous obedience, should be delivered in so plain a manner, that no ambiguous or obscure expressions
15 might lead his worshippers into error, or keep them in suspense or doubt. Accordingly, the Israelites under the law and the prophets always understood it to mean, that God was numerically one God, besides whom there was none other, much less any equal. For the schoolmen had not as yet ap-
20 peared, who, through their confidence in their own sagacity, or, more properly speaking, on arguments purely contradictory, impugned the doctrine itself of the unity of God which they pretended to assert. But as with regard to the omnipotence of the Deity, it is universally allowed, as has
25 been stated before, that he can do nothing which involves a contradiction; so must it also be remembered in this place, that nothing can be said of the one God, which is inconsistent with his unity, and which assigns to him at the same time the attributes of unity and plurality.

faciunt. Nunc ad novi fœderis testimonia veniamus non minus clara, dum priora repetunt, et hoc insuper clariora, quod Patrem Domini nostri Iesu Christi unum illum Deum esse testantur. Marc. xii. interrogatus Christus quodnam esset primum omnium mandatum, respondit v. 29. ex Deut. vi. 4. supra citato, adeoque non aliter intellecto atque intelligi solebat, *audi Israel. Dominus Deus noster, Dominus unus est.* cui responso scriba illi assensus, v. 32. *bene, inquit, præceptor in veritate dixisti. nam unus est Deus nec alius est præter eum.* Ioan. xvii. 3. *Hæc est vita æterna ut te cognoscant esse illum solum verum Deum.* Rom. iii. 30. *unus est Deus.* 1 Cor. viii. 4. *scimus nullum esse Deum alium, nisi unum.* v. 6. *nobis unus est Deus pater ille a quo omnia.* Gal. iii. 20. *Internuntius autem, unius non est, Deus vero unus est.* Eph. iv. 6. *unus est Deus et pater omnium.* 1 Tim. ii. 5. *unus est Deus.* et nomen אֱלֹהִים etsi plurale sit Hebraice tamen de uno Deo dicitur. Gen. i. 1. אֱלֹהִים בָּרָא. Psal. vii. 10. et lxxxvi. 10. אֱלֹהִים־לְבַדֶּךָ et passim sed et אֱלֹהַּ in singulari dicitur. Psal. xviii. 32. *quis est Deus præter Iehovam, et quis rupes præterquam Dii nostri.* qui versus confirmat singulare et plurale in hoc nomine idem valeri. verum de his plura Cap. v.

Hactenus attributa illa quæ naturam Dei describunt, partim affirmantia, partim negantia, dum creatis in rebus quod

Proceeding to the evidence of the New Testament, we find
it equally clear, so far as it goes over the former ground, and
in one respect even clearer, inasmuch as it testifies that the
Father of our Lord Jesus Christ is that One God. Christ hav-
5 ing been asked, Mark xii. 28. which was the first commandment of all, answers, v. 29. from Deut. vi. 4.—a passage
quoted before, and evidently understood by our Lord in the
same sense which had been always applied to it—"hear, O
Israel, the Lord our God is one Lord." To which answer the
10 scribe assented, v. 32. "well, Master, thou hast said the truth;
for there is one God, and there is none other but he." John
xvii. 3. "this is life eternal, that they might know thee, the
only true God." Rom. iii. 30. "seeing it is one God." 1 Cor.
viii. 4. "we know . . . that there is none other God but
15 one." v. 6. "to us there is but one God, the Father, of whom
are all things." Gal. iii. 20. "a mediator is not a mediator of
one; but God is one." Eph. iv. 6. "one God and Father of all."
1 Tim. ii. 5. "there is one God." So too, though אֱלֹהִים be plural
in the Hebrew, it is used notwithstanding for the One God,
20 Gen. i. 1. אֱלֹהִים בָּרָא. Psal. vii. 10. and lxxxvi. 10. אֱלֹהִים־לְבַדֶּךָ;
and elsewhere. But אֱלֹהַּ is also used in the singular, Psal.
xviii. 31. "who is God save Jehovah, or who is a rock save our
God?" which verse is sufficient to show that the singular and
plural of this word both mean the same thing. More will be
25 found on this subject in the fifth chapter.

Hitherto those attributes only have been mentioned which
describe the nature of God, partly in an affirmative, partly in a
negative sense, inasmuch as they deny the existence of those

imperfectum est, de Deo negant; ut cum immensus, infinitus, immortalis dicitur. sequuntur quæ vim atque virtutem eius divinam ostendunt, sub notione scilicet VITÆ, vel INTELLECTUS, vel VOLUNTATIS.

5   Primum VITÆ, Deut. xxxii. 40. *vivo ego in sæculum.* hinc *Deus vivens* dicitur. Psal. xlii. 3. et passim. Ioan. v. 26. *pater habet vitam in seipso.*

Secundo, sub notione INTELLECTUS Deus est OMNISCIENS. Gen. vi. 5. *vidit cogitationes.* et xviii. 14. *an potest occultari* 10 *ab Iehova quicquam?* 1 Chron. xxviii. 9. *omnia corda exquirit.* 2 Chron. vi. 30. *tu solus nosti animum hominis.* Psal. xxxiii. 15. *formator cordis eorum animadvertit.* et cxxxix. 2. *intelligis cogitationem meam e longinquo.* v. 4. *cum nondum est sermo in lingua, en, o Iehova, nosti ipsum totum.* et cxlvii. 15 5. *cuius intelligentia est innumerabilis.* Iob. xi. 7, 8, 9. *an profunditatem sapientiæ Dei invenias?* et xxvi. 6. *nudum est sepulchrum coram eo.* Prov. xv. 11. *infernus et perditio coram Iehova, quanto magis corda hominum.* et xvi. 2. *perpendit spiritus Iehova.* et xvii. 3. *qui probat corda est Iehova.* 20 Isa. xl. 28. *nulla est pervestigatio prudentiæ eius.* Ier. xvii. 10. *ego scrutator cordis, probator renum.* unde Act. i. 24. appellatur καρδιογνώστης πάντων. Ier. xxiii. 23, 24. *an Deus e propinquo sum ego? dictum Iehovæ annon Deus e longinquo?*

imperfections in the Deity, which belong to created things; as, for instance, when we speak of his immensity, his infinity, his incorruptibility. I now proceed to notice those which show his divine power and excellence under the ideas of VITALITY,
5 INTELLIGENCE, and WILL.

I. VITALITY. Deut. xxxii. 40. "I live for ever," whence he is called "the living God." Psal. xlii. 2. and in many other passages. John v. 26. "the Father hath life in himself."

II. Under the head of the INTELLIGENCE of God must be
10 classed his attribute of OMNISCIENCE. Gen. vi. 5. "God saw . . . every imagination of the thoughts of his heart." Gen. xviii. 14. "is anything too hard for Jehovah?" 1 Chron. xxviii. 9. "Jehovah searcheth all hearts." 2 Chron. vi. 30. "thou only knowest the hearts of the children of men." Psal. xxxiii. 15.
15 "he fashioneth their hearts alike; he considereth all their works." cxxxix. 2. "thou understandest my thought afar off." v. 4. "for there is not a word in my tongue, but, lo, O Jehovah, thou knowest it altogether." cxlvii. 5. "his understanding is infinite." Job xi. 7–9. "canst thou by searching find out
20 God?" &c. xxvi. 6. "hell is naked before him." Prov. xv. 11. "hell and destruction are before Jehovah; how much more then the hearts of the children of men." xvi. 2. "Jehovah weigheth the spirits." xvii. 3. "Jehovah trieth the hearts." Isa. xl. 28. "there is no searching of his understanding." Jer.
25 xvii. 10. "I Jehovah search the heart, I try the reins," whence he is called, Acts i. 24. "the Lord which knoweth the hearts of all men." Jer. xxiii. 23, 24. "am I a God at hand, saith Jehovah, and not a God afar off? can any hide himself in

an delitescere potest quisquam in latebris, ut ego non videam ipsum? Heb. iv. 13. *omnia sunt nuda et ab intimo patentia oculis eius.* hinc *solus sapiens* nominatur. Dan. ii. 10. Rom. xvi. 27. 1 Tim. i. 17. prænovit etiam Deus, quæ eius absoluta
5 præscientia est, et cogitationes et facta hominum libere agentium, etiam nondum natorum, etiam multis post sæculis futura. Deut. xxxi. 16. *Ecce tu cubaturus* &c. *surgens vero populus iste scortabitur.* &c. et v. 20, 21. *avertet se ad Deos alienos* &c. *me cognovisse figmentum eius quid is sit facturus iam hodie*
10 *antequam* &c. 2 Reg. viii. 12. *novi illud malum quo affecturus es filios Israelis* &c.

Tertio, sub notione VOLUNTATIS Deus est SUMME PURUS ET SANCTUS. Exod. xv. 11. *magnificus sanctitate.* Ios. xxiv. 19. *sanctissimus est.* 1 Sam. ii. 2. *nullus est sanctus ut Iehova.* et
15 vi. 20. *coram Iehova Deo sanctissimo.* Iob. xv. 15. *cœlites non sunt mundi in oculis eius.* Isa. vi. 2. *tegebant faciem suam.* v. 3. *sanctus, sanctus, sanctus.* cap. xl. 25. *ait sanctus.* et xli. 20. *sanctum Israelis.* Abac. i. 13. *purior es oculis, quam ut aspicias malum.*
20 Secundo, est SUMME BENIGNUS. Exod. xxxiv. 6. *misericors, gratiosus, longanimis, multus benignitate et fide.* Psal. lxxxvi. 15. et ciii. 8. idem. et v. 5. *non est commoraturum apud Te malum.* et xxv. 6. *benignitates a sæculo.* ciii. 11. *prævalet benignitas eius erga timentes eum.* v. 17. *benignitas Iehovæ a*

secret places that I shall not see him?" Heb. iv. 13. "all things
are naked and opened unto the eyes of him," whence he is
called the "only wise," Dan. ii. 10. Rom. xvi. 27. 1 Tim. i.
17. So extensive is the prescience of God, that he knows be-
5 forehand the thoughts and actions of free agents as yet unborn, and many ages before those thoughts or actions have
their origin. Deut. xxxi. 16. "behold, thou shalt sleep with
thy fathers; and this people will rise up, and go a-whoring
after the gods of the strangers of the land," &c. v. 20, 21.
10 "then will they turn unto other gods," &c. "for I know the
imagination which they go about even now, before I have
brought them into the land which I sware." 2 Kings viii. 12.
"I know the evil that thou wilt do unto the children of Israel."

III. As regards the WILL of God, he is, 1. INFINITELY PURE
15 AND HOLY. Exod. xv. 11. "glorious in holiness." Josh. xxiv. 19.
"he is an holy God." 1 Sam. ii. 2. "there is none holy as
Jehovah." vi. 20. "before this holy God Jehovah." Job xv.
15. "the heavens are not clean in his sight." Isa. vi. 2, 3. "he
covered his face . . . and said, Holy, holy, holy, is the Lord
20 of Hosts." xl. 25. "saith the Holy One." xli. 20. "the Holy
One of Israel." Hab. i. 13. "thou art of purer eyes than to
behold evil."

2. He is MOST GRACIOUS. Exod. xxxiv. 6. "merciful and
gracious, long-suffering, and abundant in goodness and
25 truth." See also Psal. lxxxvi. 15. and ciii. 8. v. 4. "neither
shall evil dwell with thee." xxv. 6. "thy loving-kindnesses
. . . have been ever of old." ciii. 11. "great is his mercy
toward them that fear him." v. 17. "the mercy of Jehovah is

sæculo usque in sæculum. et cxix. 68. *bonus est et beneficus.*
Lam. iii. 22. *summæ benignitatis Iehovæ.* Matt. xix. 17. *nemo*
bonus, nisi Deus. Luc. vi. 36. *estote misericordes, ut etiam*
pater vester est misericors. 2 Cor. i. 3. *pater miserationum.*
5 Eph. ii. 4. *dives misericordia.* 1 Ioan. iv. 8. *Deus est charitas.*
Atque hic rursus ex summa sapientia summaque bonitate intelligitur Deus esse immutabilis; cum summe sapiens summeque bonus statum summe bonum mutare nec velit, nec nisi
negando seipsum possit.

10   Tertio, Deus uti natura est verus, ita ex voluntate VERAX
est et FIDELIS. Psal. xix. 8. *testimonium Iehovæ verax.* et Ioan.
vii. 28. *est verax qui misit me.* Rom. iii. 4. *esto Deus verax,*
omnis autem homo mendax. 2 Tim. ii. 13. *si infidi sumus, ille*
tamen fidus manet. 1 Cor. i. 9. et x. 13. *fidelis est Deus.* Apoc.
15 vi. 10. *est verax.*

    Quarto, IUSTUS. Deut. xxxii. 4. *omnes viæ illius ius, expers*
iniquitatis, iustus est et rectus. Psal. xxxvi. 7. *iustitia tua instar*
montium maximorum. et cxix. 137. *iustus es Iehova et rectus.*
Isa. v. 16. *sanctificatur iustitia.* de iustitia autem Dei, quid
20 possit aut non possit, nihil attinet hic latius dissertare; cum
aut per se planum sit, aut aliis pro re nata locis opportunius
reservandum. Quin et severitas attribuitur Deo. Rom. xi. 22.
præcisam severitatem in eos qui exciderunt.

from everlasting to everlasting." cxix. 68. "thou art good,
and doest good." Lam. iii. 22. "it is of the mercies of Jehovah
that we are not consumed." Matt. xix. 17. "there is none good
but one, that is, God." Luke vi. 36. "be ye merciful, as your
Father also is merciful." 2 Cor. i. 3. "the Father of mercies."
Eph. ii. 4. "rich in mercy." 1 John iv. 8. "God is love." Another proof of the immutability of God may be also derived
from the consideration of his infinite wisdom and goodness;
since a being infinitely wise and good would neither wish to
change an infinitely good state for another, nor would be able
to change it without contradicting his own attributes.

3. As God is true in respect of his nature, so is he also TRUE
and FAITHFUL in respect of his will. Psal. xix. 7. "the testimony
of Jehovah is sure." John vii. 28. "he that sent me is true."
Rom. iii. 4. "let God be true, but every man a liar." 2 Tim.
ii. 13. "if we believe not, yet he abideth faithful." 1 Cor. i. 9.
and x. 13. "God is faithful." Rev. vi. 10. "O Lord, holy and
true."

4. He is also JUST. Deut. xxxii. 4. "all his ways are judgment, a God of truth and without iniquity, just and right is
he." Psal. xxxvi. 6. "thy righteousness is like the great mountains." cxix. 137. "righteous art thou, O Jehovah, and upright are thy judgments." Isa. v. 16. "God . . . shall be
sanctified in righteousness." There is no need for discussing
at large in this place what is consistent or inconsistent with
the justice of God, since it is either plain in itself, or where any
remarks are necessary, they will be introduced as the occasion
requires in other parts of this work. Severity also is attributed
to God. Rom. xi. 22. "on them which fell, severity."

Ex his omnibus attributis efflorescit illa summa Dei excellentia qua vere est perfectus, et in summa gloria vere beatus, et iure quidem summo et merito suo dominus omnium supremus, ut passim nominatur. Psal. xvi. 11. *satietas gaudiorum* in *conspectu tuo.* et civ. 1. *gloriam et maiestatem induisti.* Dan. vii. 10. *cui millies mille ministrabant.* Matt. v. 48. *sicut pater perfectus est.* 1 Tim. i. 11. *beatus Deus.* et vi. 15. *ille beatus.*

Huius divinæ gloriæ quantum capere mortales possunt, extat aliqua descriptio. Exod. xix. 18, &c. *mons Sinai fumabat*—. et xxiv. 10. &c. *aspexerunt Deum Israelis, et sub pedibus eius velut opus pavimentatum sapphiro, et velut corpus ipsum cœli nitore.* et xxxiii. 9, 10. *ut descendens columna illa nubis*—&c. et amplius, v. 18. 1 Reg. xix. 11 *ecce autem Iehova transibat*—. cap. viii. 10, 11. *ut nubes impleret domum Iehovæ*—. et xxii. 19. *vidi Iehovam insidentem solio*—. Psal. xviii. 8. &c. et civ. Mic. i. 3. &c. Nahum. i. 3. &c. Isa. vi. Ezech. i. et viii. 1, 2, 3. et x. 1. &c. et xliii. 2, 3. Abac. iii. 3. &c. Dan. vii. 9. Apoc. iv.

Unde nobis denique MIRABILIS et INCOMPREHENSIBILIS dicendus est. Iud. xiii. 18. *quid rogitas de nomine meo, cum sit mirificum?* Psal. cxlv. 3. *magnitudinis eius non est pervestigatio.* Isa. xl. 28. *nulla est pervestigatio prudentiæ eius.*

From all these attributes springs that infinite excellence
which constitutes the true perfection of God, and causes him
to abound in glory, and to be most deservedly and justly the
supreme Lord of all things, as he is so often called. Psal. xvi.
5 11. "in thy presence is fulness of joy." civ. 1. "thou art
clothed with honor and majesty." Dan. vii. 10. "thousand
thousands ministered unto him." Matt. v. 48. "as your Father
which is in heaven is perfect." 1 Tim. i. 11. "the blessed
God." vi. 15. "who is the blessed . . . potentate."

10   Some description of this divine glory has been revealed, as
far as it falls within the scope of human comprehension. Exod.
xix. 18, &c. "mount Sinai was altogether on a smoke—."
xxiv. 10, &c. "they saw the God of Israel, and there was under
his feet as it were a paved work of a sapphire stone, and as it
15 were the body of heaven in his clearness." xxxiii. 9, 10. "the
cloudy pillar descended," &c. &c.— and v. 18, &c. 1 Kings
xix. 11. "behold, Jehovah passed by." viii. 10, 11. "the cloud
filled the house of Jehovah." xxii. 19. "I saw Jehovah sitting
on his throne." Psal. xviii. 8, &c. and civ. Micah i. 3, &c.
20 Nahum i. 3, &c. Isa. vi. Ezek. i. and viii. 1–3. and x. 1, &c.
and xliii. 2, 3. Hab. iii. 3, &c. Dan. vii. 9. Rev. iv.

    It follows, finally, that God must be styled by us WONDERFUL
and INCOMPREHENSIBLE. Judges xiii. 18. "why askest thou thus
after my name, seeing it is secret?" Psal. cxlv. 3. "his greatness
25 is unsearchable." Isa. xl. 28. "there is no searching of his
understanding."

CAPUT III.

DE DIVINO DECRETO.

HACTENUS ex natura sua cognoscitur Deus: nunc ex efficientia sua cognoscendus.

EFFICIENTIA DEI est INTERNA, vel EXTERNA.

5 INTERNA est quæ intra Deum terminatur: qualia sunt eius decreta: Eph. i. 9. *quod præstituerat in se.*

DECRETUM DEI est GENERALE vel SPECIALE.

GENERALE est quo DEUS OMNIA AB ÆTERNO QUÆ QUIDEM VOLEBAT AUT FACTURUS IPSE ERAT, LIBERRIME, SAPIENTISSIME, SANC-

10 TISSIMEQUE DECREVIT.

OMNIA QUÆ, &c. Eph. i. 11. *qui agit omnia ex consilio voluntatis suæ.* Nimirum quæ ipse quidem solus agit, et vult; non quæ agunt cæteri omnes, aut ipse cum iis quibus libere agendi naturam ac potestatem concessit. Sic decrevit mun-

15 dum creare; sic se non amplius terræ maledicturum, Gen. viii. 21.

AB ÆTERNO. Act. xv. 28. *nota sunt Deo a sæculo omnia opera eius.* 1 Cor. ii. 7. *sapientiam occultam illam, quam præfinivit Deus ante sæcula.*

CHAPTER III.

OF THE DIVINE DECREES.

HITHERTO I have considered that knowledge of God which his nature affords. That which is derived from his efficiency is the next subject of inquiry:

5   The EFFICIENCY OF GOD is either INTERNAL or EXTERNAL.

The INTERNAL EFFICIENCY of God is that which is independent of all extraneous agency. Such are his decrees. Eph. i. 9. "which he hath purposed in himself."

The DECREES OF GOD are GENERAL or SPECIAL. GOD'S GENERAL
10 DECREE is that WHEREBY HE HAS DECREED FROM ALL ETERNITY OF HIS OWN MOST FREE AND WISE AND HOLY PURPOSE, WHATEVER HE HIMSELF WILLED, OR WAS ABOUT TO DO.

WHATEVER, &c. Eph. i. 11. "who worketh all things after the counsel of his own will"; that is, whatever he himself
15 works or wills singly, not what is done by others, or by himself in co-operation with those to whom he has conceded the natural power of free agency. The creation of the world, and the removal of the curse from the ground, Gen. viii. 21. are among his sole decrees.

20   FROM ALL ETERNITY. Acts xv. 18. "known unto God are all his works from the beginning of the world." 1 Cor. ii. 7. "even the hidden wisdom which God ordained before the world."

LIBERRIME. id est, non coactus, nulla necessitate impulsus, sed prout voluit. Eph. i. 11. ut supra.

SAPIENTISSIME. id est, secundum perfectam rerum omnium creandarum præscientiam. Act. ii. 23. *definito consilio et* 5 *præcognitione Dei.* et iv. 28. *quæcunque manus tua et con-silium tuum prædefiniit, ut fierent.* et xv. 28. *nota sunt Deo a sæculo omnia opera eius.* 1 Cor. ii. 7. *sapientiam occultam illam, quam prædefinivit Deus.* Eph. iii. 10, 11. *multiformis illa sapientia Dei secundum præstitutum æternum.*

10 Qui igitur decretum seu voluntatem Dei ab eius æterno consilio et præcognitione seiungunt, aut ordine prius ponunt, absurde faciunt. præcognitio enim Dei, mutato solum no-mine, sapientia eius est, sive illa rerum omnium idea quam, ut humanitus loquar, prius in mente habuit quam quicquam 15 decerneret.

Nihil itaque Deus decrevisse absolute censendus est, quod in potestate libere agentium reliquit: id quod scripturæ totius series ostendit. Gen. xix. 17. cum 21. *ad montem fuge, ne perimaris. ecce, rationem habeo tui etiam in hac re; ut non* 20 *subvertam civitatem istam quam dixisti.* Exod. iii. 8, 17. *inde descendi, ut liberem eum—, et educam eum in regionem bonam—,* qui tamen in deserto periit. Decreverat etiam po-pulum per Mosen educere. at illum Mosen occidisset, cap.

OF HIS OWN MOST FREE—; that is, without control, impelled by no necessity, but according to his own will. Eph. i. 11. as before.

MOST WISE—; that is, according to his perfect foreknowl-
5 edge of all things that were to be created. Acts ii. 23. "by the determinate counsel and foreknowledge of God." iv. 28. "for to do whatsoever thy hand and thy counsel determined before to be done." xv. 18. "known unto God are all his works from the beginning of the world." 1 Cor. ii. 7. "the hidden wisdom
10 which God ordained before the world." Eph. iii. 10, 11. "the manifold wisdom of God, according to the eternal purpose which he purposed."

Hence it is absurd to separate the decrees or will of the Deity from his eternal counsel and foreknowledge, or to give
15 them priority of order. For the foreknowledge of God is nothing but the wisdom of God, under another name, or that idea of every thing, which he had in his mind, to use the language of men, before he decreed anything.

We must conclude, therefore, that God decreed nothing
20 absolutely, which he left in the power of free agents, a doctrine which is shown by the whole canon of Scripture. Gen. xix. 17, 21. "escape to the mountain, lest thou be consumed . . . see, I have accepted thee concerning this thing also, that I will not overthrow this city for the which thou hast spoken."
25 Exod. iii. 8, 17. "I am come down to deliver them . . . and to bring them up unto a good land"—though these very individuals actually perished in the wilderness. God also had determined to deliver his people by the hand of Moses, whom

iv. 24. nisi is statim circumcidisset filium. 1 Sam. ii. 30. *dixeram quidem; at nunc absit mihi.* ratione etiam adiecta. *nam honorantes me honorabo.* et xiii. 13, 14. *iam certe sta-bilivisset regnum tuum Iehova; nunc autem regnum tuum* 5 *non stabit.* 2 Reg. xx. 1. dixerat Deus Ezechiam statim moriturum: quod non est factum tamen; ergo nec simplici-ter decretum. Mors Iosiæ præcise non est decreta; sed ipse non auscultavit verbis Neconis ex verbo Dei, monentis ne egrederetur. 2 Chron. xxxv. 22. Ier. xviii. 8, 9, 10. *quo mo-* 10 *mento loquar de gente et regno me ædificaturum et planta-turum esse; si fecerit quod malum videtur in oculis meis, non auscultando voci meæ, vicissim pœnitebit me illius boni quod dixero me benefacturum ei.* id est, rescindam decretum meum ob non servatam ab illo populo decreti conditionem. En regu-15 lam ab ipso Deo traditam! quo pacto ipsius decreta intelligi semper velit; cum intellecta nimirum decreti semper condi-tione. Ier. xxvi. 3. *si forte auscultantes revertantur quisque a via sua mala ut pœniteat me mali quod ego cogito facere illis propter pravitatem actionum illorum.* Itaque ne excidium 20 quidem Hierosolymæ absolute decreverat Deus. Ier. xxxviii. 17. &c. *sic ait Iehova, si egressus fueris ad principes regis*

he would nevertheless have put to death, Exod. iv. 24. if he had not immediately circumcised his son. 1 Sam. ii. 30. "I said indeed . . . but now Jehovah saith, Be it far from me"; —and the reason for this change is added—"for, them that honor me I will honor." xiii. 13, 14. "now would Jehovah have established thy kingdom . . . but now thy kingdom shall not continue." Again, God had said, 2 Kings xx. 1. that Hezekiah should die immediately, which event however did not happen, and therefore could not have been decreed without reservation. The death of Josiah was not decreed peremptorily, but he would not hearken to the voice of Necho when he warned him according to the word of the Lord, not to come out against him; 2 Chron. xxxv. 22. Again, Jer. xviii. 9, 10. "at what instant I shall speak concerning a nation, and concerning a kingdom, to build and to plant it; if it do evil in my sight, that it obey not my voice, then I will repent of the good wherewith I said I would benefit them"; that is, I will rescind the decree, because that people hath not kept the condition on which the decree depended. Here then is a rule laid down by God himself, according to which he would always have his decrees understood; namely, that regard should be paid to the conditionate terms attached to them. Jer. xxvi. 3. "if so be they will hearken, and turn every man from his evil way, that I may repent me of the evil, which I purpose to do unto them because of the evil of their doings." So also God had not even decreed absolutely the burning of Jerusalem. Jer. xxxviii. 17, &c. "thus saith Jehovah . . . if thou wilt assuredly go forth unto the king of Babylon's princes, then

Babyloniæ, utique vivet anima tua et civitas hæc non comburetur igne—. Ionæ iii. 5. *adhuc quadraginta dies, et subvertetur Nineve.* at v. 11. cum vidit eos reversos esse, pœnituit eum: quamvis irato Iona, et id minime decere Deum sen-
5 tiente. Act. xxvii. 24. 31. *dono dedi tibi omnes. at nisi isti manserint in navi*—. hic prolatam divinitus sententiam revocat Paulus: donum Paulo datum revocat Deus, nisi ipsi pro sua quisque virili parte sibimet consulant.

Ex his itaque scripturæ locis et quæ istiusmodi occurrunt
10 plurima, quorum in auctoritate nobis acquiescendum imprimis est, constat non omnia absolute a summo Deo decerni.

Sin ad humanam rationem divina exigere decreta fas est, quoniam de iis multi multa in utramque partem subtilius fere quam solidius disputant, defendi hæc non absoluta decer-
15 nendi ratio, ut sapientissima Deoque nullo modo indigna, humanis etiam argumentis breviter potest. Hæc enim decreta Dei, quæ supra attulimus, et quæ istiusmodi passim occurrunt, si absolute sine ullis conditionibus intellectis accipiantur, sibi contradicere videbitur Deus, et mutabilis esse.

20   At inquiunt, in eiusmodi locis, cum finis tum etiam ipsa

thy soul shall live, and this city shall not be burned with fire."
Jonah iii. 4. "yet forty days, and Nineveh shall be over-
thrown," whereas it appears from the tenth verse, that when
God saw that they turned from their evil way, he repented of
5 his purpose, notwithstanding the anger of Jonah who thought
the change unworthy of God. Acts xxvii. 24, 31. "God hath
given thee all them that sail with thee"—and again—"except
these abide in the ship, ye cannot be saved," where Paul revokes the declaration he had previously made on the authority
10 of God; or rather, God revokes the gift he had made to Paul,
except on condition that they should consult for their own
safety by their own personal exertions.

It appears, therefore, from these passages of Scripture, as
well as from many others of the same kind, to which we must
15 bow, as to a paramount authority, that the most high God has
not decreed all things absolutely.

If, however, it be allowable to examine the divine decrees
by the laws of human reason, since so many arguments have
been maintained on this subject by controvertists on both sides
20 with more of subtlety than of solid argument, this theory of
contingent decrees may be defended even on the principles of
men, as most wise, and in no respect unworthy of the Deity.
For if those decrees of God which have been referred to above,
and such others of the same class as occur perpetually, were to
25 be understood in an absolute sense, without any implied con-
ditions, God would contradict himself, and appear inconsistent.

It is argued, however, that in such instances not only was

media prædestinabantur ad finem. Aiunt illi quidem; Scriptura nusquam ait: et hoc solum per se satis est, cur hanc regulam reiiciamus: et tamen hoc amplius accedit incommodi, quod omnem ex humanis rebus libertatem, omnem bene
5 agendi conatum ac studium hac ratione funditus tollere necesse erit. Quid enim? si salutem mihi omnino decrevit Deus, quicquid ego contra fecero, non interibo. at medium quoque decrevit ad salutem ut faceres bene. non possum ergo non facere aliquando bene, siquidem id quoque Deus decrevit:
10 faciam interim quod libet: si nunquam benefecero, nunquam destinatum fuisse me saluti comperero; et quicquid benefecissem operam fuisse perditurum. plura vide infra cap. sequenti.

Nec iuvat respondisse, immutabilitatis eam esse necessita-
15 tem, qua omnia decernuntur, aut infallibilitatis, sive præscientiæ qua omnia præcognoscuntur, non coactionis, nam et de his duabus necessitatibus scholasticis infra satisfaciemus, et nullam interim agnoscimus necessitatem aliam, nisi quam Logica, id est, ratio docet; cum efficiens vel interna propen-
20 sione sua unum quiddam determinate agit, quæ necessitas naturæ dicitur, ut cum ignis urit, vel externa vi cogitur efficere,

the ultimate purpose predestinated, but even the means themselves were predestinated with a view to it. So indeed it is asserted, but not on the authority of Scripture; and the silence of Scripture would alone be a sufficient reason for rejecting
5 the doctrine. But it is also attended by this additional inconvenience, that it would entirely take away from human affairs all liberty of action, all endeavor and desire to do right. For we might argue thus: If God have at all events decreed my salvation, however I may act, I shall not perish. But God has also
10 decreed as the means of salvation that you should act rightly. I cannot, therefore, but act rightly at some time or other, since God has so decreed; in the mean time I will do as I please; if I never act rightly, it will be seen that I was never predestinated to salvation, and that whatever good I might have done
15 would have been to no purpose. See more on this subject in the following chapter.

Nor is it sufficient to affirm in reply, that it is not compulsory necessity which is here intended, but a necessity arising from the immutability of God, whereby all things are decreed,
20 or a necessity arising from his infallibility or prescience, whereby all things are foreknown. I shall dispose hereafter of this twofold necessity of the schools; in the meantime no other law of necessity can be admitted than what logic, or in other words, what sound reason teaches; that is to say, when
25 the efficient either causes some determinate and uniform effect by its own inherent propensity, as for example, when fire burns, which kind is denominated physical necessity; or when the efficient is compelled by some extraneous force to operate

quæ coactionis; qua quicquid agit efficiens, agit per accidens. Nulla igitur necessitas extrinsecus adveniens non aut determinat aut cogit; horum autem utrovis modo, tolli funditus libertatem non est obscurum. Quod si in Deo immutabilis 5 quædam et interna necessitas bene agendi, aliunde non pendens, cum libertate summa potest consistere, quorum utraque in eadem natura divina ad idem fertur, non ideo sequitur de duabus disparatis naturis, nempe Dei et hominis, idem esse concedendum, ubi hinc externa immutabilitas, inde libertas 10 interna adversari sibi possunt, et non idem velle. Verum nec in Deo necessitatem agendi ullam concedimus: sed esse quidem necessario Deum; decernere autem adeoque agere liberrime quicquid agit, scriptura ipsa testatur.

At inquiunt, necessitas divina sive causæ primæ, liberta-15 tem libere agentium non cogit. Respondeo. si non cogit, certe aut determinat, aut adiuvat, aut agit nihil. si determinat aut adiuvat, causa vel sola vel socia et principalis est earum rerum omnium quæ libere agentes bene aut male agunt: si nihil agit, causa omnino nulla est, nedum necessitas dicenda.

20 Neque indignum quicquam affingitur Deo, si quos even-

the effect, which is called compulsory necessity, and in the latter case, whatever effect the efficient produces, it produces *per accidens*. Now any necessity arising from external causes influences the agent either determinately or compulsorily; and

5 it is apparent that in either alternative his liberty must be wholly annihilated. But though a certain immutable and internal necessity of acting rightly, independent of all extraneous influence whatever, may exist in God conjointly with the most perfect liberty, both which principles in the same

10 divine nature tend to the same point, it does not therefore follow that the same thing can be conceded with regard to two different natures, as the nature of God and the nature of man, in which case the external immutability of one party may be in opposition to the internal liberty of the other, and may

15 prevent unity of will. Nor is it admitted that the actions of God are in themselves necessary, but only that he has a necessary existence; for Scripture itself testifies that his decrees, and therefore his actions, of what kind soever they be, are perfectly free.

20 But it is objected that divine necessity, or a first cause, imposes no constraint upon the liberty of free agents. I answer, if it do not constrain, it either determines, or co-operates, or is wholly inefficient. If it determine or co-operate, it is either the sole or the joint and principal cause of every action,

25 whether good or bad, of free agents. If it be wholly inefficient, it cannot be called a cause in any sense, much less can it be termed necessity.

Nor do we imagine anything unworthy of God, when we

tus, quas conditiones in potestate hominis libera sitas esse Deus ipse voluit, eas ab arbitrio hominis pendere affirmemus; quandoquidem addixit Deus iis conditionibus decreta ipse sua, ut causas liberas ex ea libertate agere sineret, quam ipse iis indidit.

5 Illud indignius Deo esset, verbo ostendi, re adimi libertatem homini, quæ necessitate quadam sophistica immutabilitatis videlicet aut infallibilitatis non coactionis, vel urgeatur, vel saltem obumbretur: id quod multos mortales in fraudem impulit, etiamque impellit.

10 Quamquam proprie loquendo, nulla ab re alia divinum pendere dicimus consilium, nisi ab ipsa Dei sapientia, qua omnia perfecte apud se olim præcognovit, cuiusmodi futura essent, qualemque suo tempore eventum habitura.

At isti, inquis, rerum eventus, propter humanum arbitrium 15 incerti, cum certissimo Dei decreto consistere qui possunt? scriptum est enim Psal. xxxiii. 11. *consilium Iehovæ in sæculum stabit.* idem Prov. xix. 21. Isa. xlvi. 10. Heb. vi. 17. *immutabilitatem consilii sui.* Respondeo primum, eventus rerum istos non esse Deo incertos, sed certissimos; nec tamen 20 esse necessarios, ut infra videbimus: deinde, his omnibus in locis, stare dicitur divinum consilium contra vim omnem et

assert that those conditional events depend on the human will, which God himself has chosen to place at the free disposal of man; since the Deity purposely framed his own decrees with reference to particular circumstances, in order that he might
5 permit free causes to act conformably to that liberty with which he had endued them. On the contrary, it would be much more unworthy of God, that man should nominally enjoy a liberty of which he was virtually deprived, which would be the case were that liberty to be oppressed or even
10 obscured under the pretext of some sophistical necessity of immutability or infallibility, though not of compulsion, a notion which has led, and still continues to lead many individuals into error.

However, properly speaking, the divine counsels can be
15 said to depend on nothing, but on the wisdom of God himself, whereby he perfectly foreknew in his own mind from the beginning what would be the nature and event of every future occurrence when its appointed season should arrive.

But it is asked how events, which are uncertain, inasmuch
20 as they depend on the human will, can harmonize with the decrees of God, which are immutably fixed? for it is written, Psal. xxxiii. 11. "the counsel of Jehovah standeth for ever." See also Prov. xix. 21. and Isa. xlvi. 10. Heb. vi. 17. "the immutability of his counsel." To this objection it may be
25 answered, first, that to God the issue of events is not uncertain, but foreknown with the utmost certainty, though they be not decreed necessarily, as will appear hereafter. Secondly, in all the passages referred to, the divine counsel is said to

consilium humanum; non contra libertatem arbitrii, quibus
in rebus ipse Deus hominem suæ spontis fecerat, et ita facere
ab æterno decreverat; alioqui enim decretum decreto repug-
naret; et sequeretur id quod tu aliis obiectas, mutabilem fieri
5 Deum, dum arbitraria quæ is esse iusserat, tu necessaria reddis.
sed non est mutabilis Deus, si præcise nihil decernit quod per
libertatem homini decretam aliter se habere potest: mutabilis
tum esset, tum consilium eius non staret, si libertati semel
decretæ per aliud decretum officeret, aut vel minimam neces-
10 sitatis umbram induceret.

Omnis igitur a libertate necessitas removenda est; et ne illa
quidem immutabilitatis aut præscientiæ umbratica et externa
admittenda. Si ulla manet necessitas, ut supra dixi, aut liberos
determinat ad hoc unum, aut nolentes cogit, aut volentes ad-
15 iuvat, aut agit nihil: si liberos determinat ad hoc unum,
reddetur omnium actionum adeoque peccatorum suorum
homo causa naturalis, et quasi in propensione ad peccandum
conditus: si nolentes cogit, reddetur homo sub illa decreti

stand against all human power and counsel, but not against liberty of will in things which God himself has placed at man's disposal, and had determined so to place from all eternity. For otherwise one of God's decrees would be in direct opposition to another, which would lead to the very consequence imputed by the objector to the doctrines of his opponents, inasmuch as by considering those things as necessary which the Deity has left to the uncontrolled decision of man, God would be rendered mutable. But God is not mutable, so long as he decrees nothing absolutely which could happen otherwise through the liberty assigned to man; he would indeed be mutable, neither would his counsel stand, if he were to obstruct by another decree that liberty which he had already decreed, or were to darken it with the least shadow of necessity.

It follows, therefore, that the liberty of man must be considered entirely independent of necessity, nor can any admission be made in favor of that modification of the principle which is founded on the doctrine of God's immutability and prescience. If there be any necessity at all, as has been stated before, it either determines free agents to a particular line of conduct, or it constrains them against their will, or it cooperates with them in conjunction with their will, or it is altogether inoperative. If it determine free agents to a particular line of conduct, man will be rendered the natural cause of all his actions, and consequently of his sins, and formed as it were with an inclination for sinning. If it constrain them against their will, man being subject to this compulsory de-

coactione causa peccatorum tantum per accidens, Deus causa
per se: si adiuvat, reddetur tamen cum homine Deus eorun-
dem causa vel principalis vel socia: si agit denique nihil,
necessitas nulla est, seque ipsa removet, agendo nihil. Decrevisse enim id Deum necessario, quod homini tamen scimus
integrum fuisse, et immutabile id esse quod postea fieri aut
non fieri potuit, impossibile omnino est.

Quod itaque primo homini arbitrium erat, id ab æterno
immutabile aut decretum absolute esse non poterat. et certe
in potestate hominis aut nihil unquam fuit, aut si fuit quicquam, de eo simpliciter statuisse Deum non est dicendum.

Quæ absurda hinc sequi aiunt, aut absurda non sunt, aut
non sequuntur. quarundam enim rerum sive eventuum
ideam in Deo aliunde advenire, neque impium est dictu neque
ineptum. nam cum ab æterno statuisset Deus, hominem ita
sui arbitrii futurum, ut posset labi vel non labi idea certe
eventus istius mali sive lapsus, in Deo aliunde erat; quod
omnes fatentur.

Neque hinc sequitur, temporale causam esse aut limitatio-

cree becomes the cause of sins only *per accidens,* God being
the cause of sins *per se*. If it co-operate with them in conjunction with their will, then God becomes either the principal or
the joint cause of sins with man. If finally it be altogether
inoperative, there is no such thing as necessity, it virtually
destroys itself by being without operation. For it is wholly
impossible, that God should have fixed by a necessary decree
what we know at the same time to be in the power of man;
or that that should be immutable which it remains for subsequent contingent circumstances either to fulfil or frustrate.

Whatever, therefore, was left to the free will of our first
parents, could not have been decreed immutably or absolutely
from all eternity; and questionless, the Deity must either have
never left anything in the power of man, or he cannot be said
to have determined finally respecting whatever was so left
without reference to possible contingencies.

If it be objected, that this doctrine leads to absurd consequences, we reply, either the consequences are not absurd, or
they are not the consequences of the doctrine. For it is neither
impious nor absurd to say, that the idea of certain things or
events might be suggested to God from some extraneous
source; since inasmuch as God had determined from all
eternity, that man should so far be a free agent, that it remained with himself to decide whether he would stand or fall,
the idea of that evil event, or of the fall of man, was suggested
to God from an extraneous source, a truth which all confess.

Nor does it follow from hence, that what is temporal becomes the cause of, or a restriction upon what is eternal, for

nem æterni: non enim temporale quidpiam, sed sapientia æterna divino consilio causam præbuit.

Qualis itaque materia sive obiectum divini consilii erat, nempe angelus vel homo libera voluntate impertiendus, qui posset labi, vel non labi, tale procul dubio decretum ipsum erat, ut omnia quæ exinde consecuta sunt mala, potuissent sequi, vel non sequi: si steteris, manebis; non steteris, eiiciere: si non comederis, vives; comederis, moriere.

Perperam igitur, qui decreto absoluto libertatem agendi subiiciunt, decretum Dei causam esse eius præscientiæ, et ordine præcedere, statuunt. Etenim si pro nostro more et captu loquendum de Deo est, præscisse prius, tum decrevisse, rationi magis consentaneum videtur; immo vero scripturæ, ipsique Deo; quippe qui ex præscientia, quod modo probavimus, sapientissime omnia decreverit.

Voluntatem quidem Dei primam esse rerum causam, non negamus; præscientiam tamen et sapientiam eius a voluntate non secernimus, multo minus posteriorem existimamus. postremo, voluntas Dei non minus prima rerum omnium causa est, si quædam ab ipso arbitraria decernuntur, quam si omnia decernerentur necessaria.

it was not any thing temporal, but the wisdom of the eternal mind that gave occasion for framing the divine counsel.

Seeing, therefore, that in assigning the gift of free will God suffered both men and angels to stand or fall at their own uncontrolled choice, there can be no doubt that the decree itself bore a strict analogy to the object which the divine counsel regarded, not necessitating the evil consequences which ensued, but leaving them contingent; hence the covenant was of this kind: If thou stand, thou shalt abide in Paradise; if thou fall, thou shalt be cast out; if thou eat not the forbidden fruit, thou shalt live; if thou eat, thou shalt die.

Hence, those who contend that the liberty of actions is subject to an absolute decree, erroneously conclude that the decree of God is the cause of his foreknowledge, and antecedent in order of time. If we must apply to God a phraseology borrowed from our own habits and understanding, to consider his decrees as consequent upon his foreknowledge seems more agreeable to reason, as well as to Scripture, and to the nature of the Deity himself, who, as has just been proved, decreed every thing according to his infinite wisdom by virtue of his foreknowledge.

That the will of God is the first cause of all things is not intended to be denied, but his prescience and wisdom must not be separated from his will, much less considered as subsequent to the latter in point of time. The will of God, in fine, is not less the universal first cause, because he has himself decreed that some things should be left to our own free will, than if each particular event had been decreed necessarily.

Ut multa paucis complectar, summatim sic se res habet, rationi summe consentanea. decrevit Deus pro sua sapientia, angelos atque homines rationis, adeoque liberæ voluntatis compotes creare: prævidit simul quam illi in partem, sua in-
5 tegerrima libertate utentes, suopte arbitrio essent inclinaturi. Quid ergo? num hac Dei providentia sive præscientia imposi- tam esse iis necessitatem ullam dicemus? profecto non magis, quam si mortalium quisquam hoc idem prævidisset. Quod enim quivis mortalium certo prævidit eventurum, id non
10 minus certo eveniet, quam quod Deus ipse prædixit. Sic præ- vidit Elisæus, quanta mala Rex Hazael illaturus Israelitis ali- quot post annos esset. 2 Reg. viii. 12. Nec tamen id propter Elisæi præscientiam necessario evenisse quisquam affirma- verit: eventus enim ille nihilo minus ab arbitrio semper libero
15 certissime nascetur. neque enim quicquam evenit, quia Deus prævidit, sed unumquodque prævidit Deus, quia ex causis propriis ipsius decreto libere agentibus, ipsique notissimis, ita est unumquodque eventurum: et eventus quidem ille non est in Deo qui prævidet, sed in eo solo qui prævidetur. Cum igitur
20 decretum divinum in libere agentes, ut supra demonstravi- mus, absolutum esse queat nullum, certe præscientia divina, cum nihilo plus agat in agentibus libere, quam præscientia hominis, id est, omnino nihil, ut quæ utrobique pariter actio

To comprehend the whole matter in a few words, the sum of the argument may be thus stated in strict conformity with reason. God of his wisdom determined to create men and angels reasonable beings, and therefore free agents; foresee-
ing at the same time which way the bias of their will would incline, in the exercise of their own uncontrolled liberty. What then? shall we say that this foresight or foreknowledge on the part of God imposed on them the necessity of acting in any definite way? No more than if the future event had been
foreseen by any human being. For what any human being has foreseen as certain to happen, will not less certainly happen than what God himself has predicted. Thus Elisha foresaw how much evil Hazael would bring upon the children of Israel in the course of a few years, 2 Kings viii. 12. Yet no one
would affirm that the evil took place necessarily on account of the foreknowledge of Elisha; for had he never foreknown it, the event would have occurred with equal certainty, through the free will of the agent. In like manner nothing happens of necessity because God has foreseen it; but he foresees the event
of every action, because he is acquainted with their natural causes, which, in pursuance of his own decree, are left at liberty to exert their legitimate influence. Consequently the issue does not depend on God who foresees it, but on him alone who is the object of his foresight. Since therefore, as has before
been shown, there can be no absolute decree of God regarding free agents, undoubtedly the prescience of the Deity (which can no more bias free agents than the prescience of man, that is, not at all, since the action in both cases is intransitive, and

sit immanens et in se terminetur, neque necessitatem ullam imponere per se potest, neque causa est omnino ulla liberarum actionum statuenda. Si statuitur, tollenda prorsus ex rebus inanissima vox ista libertas erit; non modo ex religione, verum
5 etiam ex moribus, etiam ex adiaphoris: nihil non necessario fiet, cum nihil non præsciscat Deus.

Ut aliquando succincte finiamus tenendum est, Deum præscire quidem futura omnia, non autem omnia absolute decrevisse, ne peccata omnia Deo imputentur, Dæmonesque, et
10 quicunque impii culpa eximantur: tu hoc arripis satisque concessum putas quo evincas, aut Deum non omnia præscire, aut idcirco futura omnia necessario fore, quia Deus præscivit: et certo quidem fore quæ Deus futura præviderit fateor, necessario non item: certo futura sunt, eo quod divina præsci-
15 entia falli non potest, non necessario tamen, quia præscientia, cum actio tantum immanens sit, in obiectum nihil agit: quod igitur contingenter et libere futurum est, non ex præscientia Dei tandem producitur, sed ex causis suis libere agentibus quæ Deum non latent quam in partem sponte sua inclinaturæ
20 sint; sic novit Adamum sua sponte lapsurum; certo igitur

has no external influence) can neither impose any necessity of itself, nor can it be considered at all as the cause of free actions. If it be so considered, the very name of liberty must be altogether abolished as an unmeaning sound; and that not only
5 in matters of religion, but even in questions of morality and indifferent things. There can be nothing but what will happen necessarily, since there is nothing but what is foreknown by God.

That this long discussion may be at length concluded by a
10 brief summary of the whole matter, we must hold that God foreknows all future events, but that he has not decreed them all absolutely: lest the consequence should be that sin in general would be imputed to the Deity, and evil spirits and wicked men exempted from blame. Does my opponent avail himself
15 of this, and think the concession enough to prove either that God does not foreknow every thing, or that all future events must therefore happen necessarily, because God has foreknown them? I allow that future events which God has foreseen, will happen certainly, but not of necessity. They will
20 happen certainly, because the divine prescience cannot be deceived, but they will not happen necessarily, because prescience can have no influence on the object foreknown, inasmuch as it is only an intransitive action. What therefore is to happen according to contingency and the free will of man, is
25 not the effect of God's prescience, but is produced by the free agency of its own natural causes, the future spontaneous inclination of which is perfectly known to God. Thus God foreknew that Adam would fall of his own free will; his fall was

lapsurus erat; non necessario, quia sponte sua, contraria enim hæc duo sunt; sic præscivit Deus fore ut deficerent Israelitæ a vero cultu ad alienos Deos, Deut. xxxi. 16. Si propter hanc Dei præscientiam necessario erant defecturi, immerito sane

5 minatus est, se multa mala iis immissurum. v. 17. frustra canticum illud scribi iusserit quod sibi testis loco esset contra filios Israelis, quippe necessario peccantes; verum præscientia Dei non magis quam illa Mosis v. 27. quicquam egit extra se; et testatur Deus, prænosse se eos impetu proprio, suaque sponte

10 peccaturos, v. 16. *surgens vero populus iste scortabitur,* &c. et v. 18. *quod averterit se ad Deos alienos.* non ergo desciverunt Israelitæ quia Deus hoc prænovit, sed inde Deus prænovit quod ex causis sibi notis, quamvis libere agentes, certo tamen erant defecturi. v. 20. *comedens saturabitur ac sagina-*

15 *bitur: sed avertet se,* &c. v. 21. *me cognovisse figmentum eius quid is sit facturus iam hodie antequam introducam eum in terram,* &c. ex his omnibus quæ dicta sunt satis tandem liquet neque decretum Dei neque præscientiam causas liberas necessitate ulla præpedire. Quod tamen nonnulli dum per

20 fas nefasque oppugnare moliuntur, non dubitant Deum asse-

therefore certain, but not necessary, since it proceeded from his own free will, which is incompatible with necessity. Thus also God foreknew that the Israelites would turn from the true worship to strange gods, Deut. xxxi. 16. If they were to be led to revolt necessarily on account of this prescience on the part of God, it was unjust to threaten them with the many evils which he was about to send upon them, v. 17. it would have been to no purpose that a song was ordered to be written, which should be a witness for him against the children of Israel, because their sin would have been of necessity. The truth is that the prescience of God, like that of Moses, v. 27. had no extraneous influence, and God testifies, v. 16. that he foreknew they would sin from their own voluntary impulse, and of their own accord—"this people will rise up," &c. and v. 18. "I will surely hide my face in that day . . . in that they are turned unto other gods." Hence the subsequent revolt of the Israelites was not the consequence of God's foreknowledge, but his foreknowledge led him to know that, although they were free agents, they would certainly revolt, owing to causes with which he was well acquainted. v. 20, 21. "when they shall have eaten and filled themselves, and waxen fat, then will they turn unto other gods . . . I know their imagination which they go about, even now before I have brought them into the land which I sware."

From what has been said it is sufficiently evident, that free causes are not impeded by any law of necessity arising from the decree or prescience of God. There are some who in their zeal to oppose this doctrine, do not hesitate even to assert that

verare causam per se peccati et auctorem: hos equidem nisi per errorem non malitiose hoc dicere putarem blasphemorum omnium perditissimos crederem; quos refellere si coner, idem agam, ac si prolixe disputem Deum non esse Diabolum. Hac-
5 tenus DECRETUM Dei GENERALE.

DECRETUM Dei SPECIALE omnium primum ac præstantissi-mum est de FILIO SUO: unde et PATER primario dicitur. Psal. ii. 7. *decretum enarraturus sum; Iehova dixit mihi, Filius meus es, ego hodie genui te.* Heb. i. 5. *nam cui dixit unquam*
10 *angelorum, Filius meus es, ego hodie genui te.* ac rursum, *Ego ero ei Pater, et ipse erit mihi Filius.* 1 Pet. i. 19, 20. *Christi, præcogniti quidem ante iacta mundi fundamenta.* Isa. xlii. 1. *electus meus, quem benigne accipit anima mea.* 1 Pet. ii. 4. *apud Deum electus et pretiosus.* Ex his cunctis
15 locis apparet, Filium Dei decreto Patris fuisse genitum.

DECRETUM Dei SPECIALE de ANGELIS diserte nusquam legi-tur: intelligitur autem ex 1 Tim. v. 21. *electorum angelorum.* Eph. i. 9, 10. *mysterium voluntatis suæ* &c. *ut recolligeret sub unum caput omnia in Christo, tum quæ in cœlis* &c.

God is himself the cause and origin of sin. Such men, if they are not to be looked upon as misguided rather than mischievous, should be ranked among the most abandoned of all blasphemers. An attempt to refute them, would be nothing more than an argument to prove that God was not the evil spirit.

Thus far of the GENERAL DECREE of God. Of his SPECIAL DECREES the first and most important is that which regards his SON, and from which he primarily derives his name of FATHER. Psal. ii. 7. "I will declare the decree: Jehovah hath said unto me, Thou art my Son, this day have I begotten thee." Heb. i. 5. "unto which of the angels said he at any time, Thou art my son, this day have I begotten thee? And again, I will be to him a Father, and he shall be to me a Son." 1 Pet. i. 19, 20. "Christ . . . who verily was fore-ordained before the foundation of the world." Isa. xlii. 1. "mine elect, in whom my soul delighteth." 1 Pet. ii. 4. "chosen of God, and precious." From all these passages it appears that the Son of God was begotten by the decree of the Father.

There is no express mention made of any SPECIAL DECREE respecting THE ANGELS, but its existence seems to be implied, 1 Tim. v. 21. "the elect angels." Eph. i. 9, 10. "the mystery of his will . . . that he might gather together in one all things in Christ, both which are in heaven, and which are on earth."

CAPUT IV.

DE PRÆDESTINATIONE.

DECRETUM Dei SPECIALE de HOMINIBUS præcipuum, PRÆDESTINATIO nominatur: qua DEUS, ANTE IACTA MUNDI FUNDAMENTA, GENERIS HUMANI, QUAMVIS SUA SPONTE LAPSURI, MISERTUS, AD GLORIAM MISERICORDIÆ, GRATIÆ, 5 SAPIENTIÆQUE SUÆ PATEFACIENDAM, IUXTA PRÆSTITUTUM, sive propositum SUUM IN CHRISTO, EOS QUI CREDITURI ESSENT ATQUE IN FIDE PERMANSURI, AD SALUTEM ÆTERNAM PRÆDESTINAVIT.

Solet quidem vox prædestinationis non ad electionem solum, sed etiam ad reprobationem significandam in scholis 10 usurpari: temere nimis in re tam ardua, cum scriptura diserte ad unam electionem referat, quoties hac de re verba facit: Rom. viii. 29, 30. *prædestinavit conformandos imagini filii sui: quos vero prædestinavit, eos etiam vocavit, iustificavit, glorificavit.* I Cor. ii. 7. *sapientiam, quam prædestinavit Deus* 15 *ante sæcula ad gloriam nostram.* Eph. i. 5. *prædestinavit nos ad adoptionem.* v. 11. *in quo etiam in sortem adsciti sumus, cum essemus prædestinati secundum præstitutum eius.* Act. ii. 23. *hunc definito consilio et præscientia Dei deditum.* cum iv. 28. *ut facerent quæcunque manus tua et consilium tuum*

CHAPTER IV.

OF PREDESTINATION.

THE principal SPECIAL DECREE of God RELATING TO MAN is termed PREDESTINATION, whereby GOD IN PITY TO MANKIND, THOUGH FORESEEING THAT THEY WOULD FALL OF THEIR OWN ACCORD, PREDESTINATED TO ETERNAL SALVATION
5 BEFORE THE FOUNDATION OF THE WORLD THOSE WHO SHOULD BELIEVE AND CONTINUE IN THE FAITH; FOR A MANIFESTATION OF THE GLORY OF HIS MERCY, GRACE, AND WISDOM, ACCORDING TO HIS PURPOSE IN CHRIST.

It has been the practice of the schools to use the word pre-
10 destination, not only in the sense of election, but also of repro-
bation. This is not consistent with the caution necessary on so momentous a subject, since wherever it is mentioned in Scripture, election alone is uniformly intended. Rom. viii. 29, 30. "whom he did predestinate to be conformed to the image of
15 his Son . . . moreover whom he did predestinate, them he also called: and whom he called, them he also justified: and whom he justified, them he also glorified." 1 Cor. ii. 7. "the hidden wisdom, which God ordained before the world unto our glory." Eph. i. 5. "having predestinated us unto the
20 adoption." v. 11. "in whom also we have obtained an inheri-
tance, being predestinated according to his purpose." Acts ii. 23. compared with iv. 28. "him being delivered by the determinate counsel and foreknowledge of God they have taken . . . for to do whatsoever thy hand and thy counsel deter-

prædestinavit ut fierent, nempe ad salutem hominum pro-
curandam.

Aliis loquendi modis eodem sensu prædestinatio electionem
semper unam spectat: Rom. viii. 28. *qui ex præstituto,* vel
5 proposito *vocati sunt* et ix. 23, 24. *vasa misericordiæ quæ
præparavit ad gloriam; quos etiam vocavit.* Eph. iii. 11. *secundum præstitutum æternum quod constituit in Christo
Iesu.* 2 Tim. i. 9. *ex præstituto suo et gratia.* Nam ex illo loco.
1 Thess. v. 9. *non constituit nos Deus ad iram, sed ad salutem
10 obtinendam per Dominum nostrum Iesum Christum,* non
sequitur, ex negatione scilicet affirmatio, aliquos esse ad iram
constitutos. neque ex illo. 1 Pet. ii. 8. *ad quod etiam constituti
erant,* significatur præstitutos fuisse ab æterno, sed quovis
tempore post defectionem; ut in tempore electi et constituti a
15 Christo ad suum munus apostoli dicuntur. Ioan. xv. 16.

Et de ascriptione quidem ad vitam (si metaphoris et alle-
goriis in re tam controversa nitendum est) crebra fit mentio
et libri vitæ, libri mortis nulla usquam. Isa. iv. 3. *ascriptus
vitæ.* Dan. xii. 1. *tempore illo eripietur populus quisquis in-
20 ventus fuerit in libro illo.* Luc. x. 20. *gaudete potius quod
nomina vestra scripta sunt in cœlis.* Philipp. iv. 3. *quorum nomina sunt in libro vitæ.* quamquam hoc scriptionis tropo non

mined before to be done," namely, as a means of procuring the salvation of man.

In other modes of expression, where predestination is alluded to, it is always in the same sense of election alone. Rom.
5 viii. 28. "to them who are the called according to his purpose." ix. 23, 24. "the vessels of mercy which he had afore prepared unto glory, even us, whom he hath called." Eph. iii. 11. "according to the eternal purpose which he purposed in Christ Jesus." 2 Tim. i. 9. "according to his own purpose
10 and grace." For when it is said negatively, 1 Thess. v. 9. "God hath not appointed us to wrath, but to obtain salvation by our Lord Jesus Christ," we are not obliged to imply that there are others who are appointed to wrath. Nor does the expression in 1 Pet. ii. 8. "whereunto also they were appointed," signify
15 that they were appointed from all eternity, but from some time subsequent to their defection, as the Apostles are said to be "chosen" in time, "and ordained" by Christ to their office, John xv. 16.

Again, if an argument of any weight in the discussion of
20 so controverted a subject can be derived from allegorical and metaphorical expressions, mention is frequently made of those who are written among the living, and of the book of life, but never of the book of death. Isa. iv. 3. "written among the living." Dan. xii. 1. "at that time thy people shall be
25 delivered, every one that shall be found written in the book." Luke x. 20. "rather rejoice, because your names are written in heaven." Philipp. iv. 3. "whose names are in the book of life." Enrolment in the book of life, however, does not appear to

praedestinatio æterna quæ generalis est, sed temporanea quædam et particularis Dei sententia de quibusvis hominibus
secundum opera ipsorum significari videtur. Psal. lxix. 29.
deleantur de libro vitæ, et cum iustis ne conscribantur: non
5 ergo ab æterno adscripti sunt. Isa. lxv. 6. *ecce scriptum est
coram me; non tacebo, nisi rependero.* Apoc. xx. 12. *iudicati
sunt mortui ex iis quæ scripta erant in libris secundum opera
ipsorum.* ergo sane liber ille non erat prædestinationis æternæ,
sed operum ipsorum. Itaque nec illi ab æterno præscripti, qui
10 Iudæ 4. *olim præscripti ad hoc iudicium.* Quid enim necesse
est *olim* sic extendere? sed ex quo in peccatis iam invetera-
verant et obduruerant. Quid enim, inquam necesse est *olim*
sic retro extendere vel hoc loco vel illo. 2 Pet. ii. 3. unde hic
locus desumptus videtur; *quibus iam olim damnatio non
15 cessat, et quorum exitium non dormitat:* ex quo nimirum
apostatæ sunt facti, tametsi id diu dissimularunt.

Obiicitur et illud Prov. xvi. 4. *omnia fecit Iehova propter
se, etiam improbum ad diem mali.* atqui Deus non fecit improbum, nedum propter se, quid ergo fecit? denuntiavit im-
20 probo, ut par erat, pœnam meritam, non immerenti prædestinavit. planius Eccles. vii. 29. *Deum ipsum fecisse hominem*

signify eternal predestination, which is general, but some
temporary and particular decision of God applied to certain
men, on account of their works. Psal. lxix. 28. "let them be
blotted out of the book of the living, and not be written with
5 the righteous"; whence it appears that they had not been
written from everlasting. Isa. lxv. 6. "behold it is written
before me; I will not keep silence, but will recompense."
Rev. xx. 12. "the dead were judged out of those things which
were written in the books, according to their works"; where-
10 by it is evident that it was not the book of eternal predestination, but of their works. Nor were those ordained from everlasting who are said, Jude 4. to have been "before of old
ordained to this condemnation." For why should we give so
extensive a signification to the term "of old," instead of defin-
15 ing it to mean, from the time when they had become invet-
erate and hardened sinners? Why must we understand it to
imply so remote a period, either in this text, or in the passage
whence it seems to be taken? 2 Pet. ii. 3. "whose judgment
now of a long time lingereth not, and their damnation slum-
20 bereth not"; that is, from the time of their apostasy, however long they had dissembled it.

The text, Prov. xvi. 4. is also objected, "Jehovah hath made
all things for himself; yea, even the wicked for the day of
evil." But God did not make man wicked, much less did he
25 make him so "for himself." All that he did was to sentence
the wicked to deserved punishment, as was most fitting, but
he did not predestinate him who was innocent to the same
fate. It is more clearly expressed, Eccles. vii. 29. "God hath

rectum, ipsos autem quærere ratiocinia plurima. unde sequitur tam certo dies mali, ac si improbus ad eam esse factus.

PRÆDESTINATIO itaque ad electionem referenda semper est, et pro eodem sæpe sumi videtur. Quod dixit Paulus, Rom. viii. 29. *quos prænovit, prædestinavit;* eodem sensu dicitur, 1 Pet. i. 2. *electis iuxta prænotionem.* Rom. ix. 11. *propositum Dei quod est secundum electionem.* et xi. 5. *secundum electionem gratuitam.* Eph. i. 4. *elegit nos in ipso.* Col. iii. 12. *ut electi Dei, sancti et dilecti.* 2 Thess. ii. 13. *quod elegerit vos Deus ab initio ad salutem.* in prædestinatione igitur nihil reprobationis esse potuit: 1 Tim. ii. 4. *qui omnes homines vult servari et ad agnitionem veritatis venire.* 2 Pet. iii. 9. *patiente est in nos animo, nolens ullos perire, sed omnes ad resipiscentiam tendere. In nos,* id est, omnes homines: non solum electos, ut volunt nonnulli, sed præsertim improbos, ut Rom. ix. 22. *pertulit vasa iræ.* Quod si Petrus, ut disputant, vix se infidelibus annumerasset, certe neque electis iis, qui nondum resipuissent. deinde non tardat Deus propter electos, sed accelerat potius. Matt. xxiv. 22. *decurtabuntur dies illi.*

Electionem autem intelligimus, non generalem illam, sive ut ita dicam, nationalem, qua Deus totam Israelis nationem

made man upright; but they have sought out many inventions," whence the day of evil ensues as certainly, as if the wicked had been made for it.

PREDESTINATION, therefore, must always be understood with reference to election, and seems often to be used instead of the latter term. What St. Paul says, Rom. viii. 29. "whom he did foreknow, he also did predestinate," is thus expressed 1 Pet. i. 2. "elect according to the foreknowledge." Rom. ix. 11. "the purpose of God according to election." xi. 5. "according to the election of grace." Eph. i. 4. "he hath chosen us in him." Col. iii. 12. "as the elect of God, holy and beloved." 2 Thess. ii. 13. "because God hath from the beginning chosen you to salvation." Reprobation, therefore, could not be included under predestination. 1 Tim. ii. 4. "who will have all men to be saved, and to come unto the knowledge of the truth." 2 Pet. iii. 9. "the Lord . . . is long-suffering to us-ward, not willing that any should perish, but that all should come to repentance": to us-ward; that is, towards all men, not towards the elect only, as some interpret it, but particularly towards the wicked, as it is said, Rom. ix. 22. "God endured . . . the vessels of wrath." For if, as some object, Peter would scarcely have included himself among the unbelievers, much less would he have numbered himself among such of the elect as had not yet come to repentance. Nor does God delay, but rather hastens the times on account of the elect. Matt. xxiv. 22. "for the elect's sake those days shall be shortened."

I do not understand by the term election, that general or national election, by which God chose the whole nation of

in populum sibi elegit, Deut. iv. 37. *propterea quod dilexit*
maiores vestros, elegitque semen eorum post eos, et vii. 6, 7,
8. *te selegit Iehova, ut sis ei populus peculiaris,* et passim,
Isa. xlv. 4. *propter Israelem electum meum,* vel contra, qua
5 reiectis Iudæis, omnes gentes elegit, quibus annuntiari potius
evangelium voluerit, de qua præcipue Rom. ix. et xi. nec qua
ad munus aliquod eligitur, 1 Sam. x. 24. *videtisne quem*
elegit Iehova. Ioan. vi. 70. *nonne ego vos duodecim elegi et*
unus ex vobis est Diabolus; unde electi nonnunquam dicun-
10 tur quicunque cæteris re aliqua præstant, ut 2 Ioan. 1. *electæ*
Dominæ, quasi diceret, lectissimæ, et 13. *sororis tuæ electæ.*
1 Pet. ii. 6. *lapidem electum, pretiosum.* 1 Tim. v. 21. *elec-*
torum angelorum. sed illam hic specialem electionem intelligimus, quæ cum æterna prædestinatione idem fere est. electio
15 igitur pars prædestinationis non est multoque minus Reprobatio. Cum enim prædestinatio proprie finis notionem in se
contineat, hominum saltem credentium salutem, rem quidem
per se expetibilem; reprobatio autem non credentium interitum, rem per se ingratam et odiosam; reprobationem, certe
20 ut finem, haudquaquam sibi proposuit Deus aut prædestinavit. Ezech. xviii. 32. *non delector morte morientis.* et
xxxiii. 11. *ne vivam.* &c. *si delector morte improbi, sed* &c.

Israel for his own people, Deut. iv. 37. "because he loved thy fathers, therefore he chose their seed after them," and vii. 6–8. "Jehovah thy God hath chosen thee to be a special people unto himself," Isa. xlv. 4. "for Israel mine elect." Nor do I
5 mean that sense of the word election in which God, after rejecting the Jews, is said to have chosen that the Gospel should be announced to the Gentiles, to which the apostle particularly alludes, Rom. ix. and xi.; nor that in which an individual is said to be selected for the performance of some office, as
10 1 Sam. x. 24. "see ye him whom the Lord hath chosen?" John vi. 70. "have not I chosen you twelve, and one of you is a devil?" whence those are sometimes called elect who are eminent for any particular excellence, as 2 John 1. "the elect lady," that is, most precious, and v. 13. "thy elect sister."
15 1 Pet. ii. 6. "a chief corner stone, elect and precious." 1 Tim. v. 21. "the elect angels." But that special election is here intended, which is nearly synonymous with eternal predestination. Election, therefore, is not a part of predestination; much less then is reprobation. For, speaking accurately, the
20 ultimate purpose of predestination is salvation of believers, a thing in itself desirable, whereas the object which reprobation has in view is the destruction of unbelievers, a thing in itself ungrateful and odious; whence it is clear that God could never have predestinated reprobation, or proposed it to himself as
25 an end. Ezek. xviii. 32. "I have no pleasure in the death of him that dieth." xxxiii. 11. "as I live, said the Lord God, I have no pleasure in the death of the wicked, but that the wicked should turn from his way and live." If therefore the

Si neque peccatum neque mortem peccantis voluit Deus, hoc est, neque causam neque effectum reprobationis, certe ipsam noluit. reprobatio igitur prædestinationis divinæ pars nulla est.

5   QUA DEUS. nimirum Pater. Luc. xii. 32. *libuit patri vestro.* Sic ubicunque divini decreti aut consilii mentio fit. Ioan. xvii. 2. *quot dedisti ei.* v. 6. *quos dedisti mihi selectos e mundo.* xi. 24. idem. Eph. i. 4. *elegit nos in ipso.* v. 5. *prædestinavit nos.* 11. *prædestinati secundum præstitutum eius.*

10   ANTE IACTA MUNDI FUNDAMENTA. Eph. i. 4. 2 Tim. i. 9. *ante tempora sæculorum.* Tit. i. 2. idem.

GENERIS HUMANI, QUAMVIS SUA SPONTE LAPSURI, MISERTUS. materia seu obiectum prædestinationis, non erat simpliciter homo creandus, sed sua sponte lapsurus: misericordiæ enim 15 et gratiæ divinæ patefactio, quem Deus finem sibi prædestinationis proposuit, peccatum et miseriam prius in homine, ab ipsoque solo homine profectam, necessario ponit. et fatentur quidem omnes, potuisse hominem non labi. at si per decretum Dei non potuit non labi (quæ duo contradicentia ab iisdem 20 simul dicuntur) profecto iam non ad gratiam, sed ad iustitiam Dei pertinuit necessario lapsu lapsum restituere. Quamvis

Deity have no pleasure either in sin, or in the death of the sinner, that is, either in the cause or the effect of reprobation, certainly he cannot delight in reprobation itself. It follows, that reprobation forms no part of what is meant by the divine
5 predestination.

WHEREBY GOD, &c. that is, God the Father. Luke xii. 32. "it is your Father's good pleasure." Thus, also, wherever mention is made of the divine decrees or counsel: John xvii. 2. "as many as thou hast given him." v. 6, 11, 24. "the men which
10 thou gavest me out of the world." Eph. i. 4. "he hath chosen us in him." v. 5. "having predestinated us." v. 11. "being predestinated according to his purpose."

BEFORE THE FOUNDATION OF THE WORLD, Eph. i. 4. 2 Tim. i. 9. "before the world began." See also Tit. i. 2.

15 IN PITY TO MANKIND, THOUGH FORESEEING THAT THEY WOULD FALL OF THEIR OWN ACCORD. It was not simply man as a being who was to be created, but man as a being who was to fall of his own accord, that was the matter or object of predestination; for that manifestation of divine grace and mercy which
20 God designed as the ultimate purpose of predestination, presupposes the existence of sin and misery in man, originating from himself alone. That the fall of man was not necessary is admitted on all sides; but if such, nevertheless, was the nature of the divine decree, that his fall became really inevitable,
25 both which opinions, however contradictory, are sometimes held by the same persons, then the restoration of man, after he had lapsed of necessity, became no longer a matter of grace on the part of God, but of simple justice. For if it be granted

enim non invitum, sed necessario duntaxat lapsum esse demus,
illa tamen necessitas voluntatem vel vi quadam tacita flexisse,
vel ductu quodam rexisse semper videbitur. Quod si prævidit
Deus hominem sua sponte lapsurum, decreto nil opus erat
5 quod ad lapsum attinebat, sed tantum quod ad hominem lapsurum, quid ei fieret. Cum itaque defectio primi hominis
præcognita duntaxat sapientissimo Deo fuit, non decreta;
sequitur, prædestinationem quoque ante lapsum hominis decretum absolutum non fuisse: immo etiam post lapsum, non
10 tam ex ipso decreto, quam ex immutabili conditione decreti,
expendi prædestinatio ac definiri semper debebit.

PRÆDESTINAVIT. id est designavit, elegit. et quasi scopum et
finem salutem hominum sibi proposuit. Atque hinc præteri-
tionis ab æterno, derelictionisque commenta illa redarguun-
15 tur; quod contra plane idque sæpe testatus est Deus velle se
omnium salutem, nullius interitum, ut supra citatum est, nihil
odisse quod fecit, nihil omisisse quod ad salutem omnium
sufficeret.

AD GLORIAM MISERICORDIÆ, GRATIÆ, SAPIENTIÆQUE SUÆ PATE-
20 FACIENDAM. hic summus prædestinationis finis est. Rom. ix. 23.
ut notas faceret divitias gloriæ suæ erga vasa misericordiæ.
Eph. i. 6. *ad laudem gloriosæ suæ gratiæ.* I Cor. ii. 7. *loqui-*
mur sapientiam Dei in mysterio, quæ abscondita est, quam
prædestinavit Deus ante sæcula ad gloriam nostram.

that he lapsed, though not against his own will, yet of necessity, it will be impossible not to think that the admitted necessity must have overruled or influenced his will by some secret force or guidance. But if God foresaw that man would
5 fall of his own free will, there was no occasion for any decree relative to the fall itself, but only relative to the provision to be made for man, whose future fall was foreseen. Since then the apostasy of the first man was not decreed, but only foreknown by the infinite wisdom of God, it follows that pre-
10 destination was not an absolute decree before the fall of man; and even after his fall, it ought always to be considered and defined as arising, not so much from a decree itself, as from the immutable condition of a decree.

PREDESTINATED; that is, designated, elected: proposed to
15 himself the salvation of man as the scope and end of his counsel. Hence may be refuted the notion of a preterition and desertion from all eternity, in direct opposition to which God explicitly and frequently declares, as has been quoted above, that he desires not the death of any one, but the salvation of
20 all; that he hates nothing that he has made; and that he has omitted nothing which might suffice for universal salvation.

FOR A MANIFESTATION OF THE GLORY OF HIS MERCY, GRACE, AND WISDOM. This is the chief end of predestination. Rom. ix. 23. "that he might make known the riches of his glory on the
25 vessels of mercy." 1 Cor. ii. 7. "we speak the wisdom of God in a mystery, even the hidden wisdom which God had ordained before the world unto our glory." Eph. i. 6. "to the praise of the glory of his grace."

IUXTA PRÆSTITUTUM sive propositum SUUM IN CHRISTO. Eph.
iii. 10, 11. *multiformis illa sapientia Dei; secundum præsti-*
tutum æternum, quod constituit in Christo Iesu Domino
nostro. cap. i. 4. *elegit nos in ipso.* v. 5. *prædestinavit nos in*
5 *adoptionem per Iesum Christum.* 11. *in ipso, in quo etiam in*
sortem adsciti sumus, cum essemus prædestinati secundum
præstitutum eius. Hinc illa dilectio Dei, in Christo nobis
declarata: Ioan. iii. 16. *ita Deus dilexit mundum, ut filium*
suum unigenitum dederit. Eph. ii. 4, 5. *propter multam*
10 *charitatem, gratia estis servati.* 1 Ioan. iv. 9, 10. *per hoc mani-*
festa facta est charitas Dei in nos, quod filium suum &c. Sine
Christo igitur præcognito, nulla cum hominibus lapsuris re-
conciliatio Dei, nulla gratia decreta est. et prædestinationem
quidem cum Deus effectum esse misericordiæ, dilectionis,
15 gratiæ, sapientiæque suæ in Christo tam aperte declaraverit,
eam non debemus voluntati eius, ut fere fit, absolutæ atque
arcanæ attribuere, ne in iis quidem locis ubi solius voluntatis
fit mentio. Exod. xxxiii. 19. *gratiam faciam cui faciam.* id
est, ne nunc latius causas enarrem. Rom. ix. 18. *cuius vult*
20 *miseretur.* ea nempe ratione, quam constituit in Christo;
vel etiam de gratia sua et misericordia extraordinaria loqui
huiusmodi locis solitum esse Deum, expendenti singula apparebit. Sic Luc. xii. 32. *libuit patri vestro.* Eph. i. 5. *per*

ACCORDING TO HIS PURPOSE IN CHRIST. Eph. iii. 10, 11. "the
manifold wisdom of God, according to the eternal purpose
which he purposed in Christ Jesus our Lord." i. 4, 5. "he
hath chosen us in him; having predestinated us unto the
5 adoption of children by Jesus Christ." v. 11. "in him, in
whom also we have obtained an inheritance, being predestinated according to his purpose." This is the source of that love
of God, declared to us in Christ. John iii. 16. "God so loved
the world, that he gave his only begotten Son." Eph. ii. 4, 5.
10 "for his great love wherewith he loved us . . . by grace ye
are saved." 1 John iv. 9, 10. "in this was manifested the love
of God towards us, because that God sent his only begotten
Son into the world," &c. Hence there was no grace decreed
for man who was to fall, no mode of reconciliation with God,
15 independently of the foreknown sacrifice of Christ; and since
God has so plainly declared that predestination is the effect of
his mercy, and love, and grace, and wisdom in Christ, it is to
these qualities that we ought to attribute it, and not, as is
generally done, to his absolute and secret will, even in those
20 passages where mention is made of his will only. Exod. xxxiii.
19. "I will be gracious to whom I will be gracious"; that is,
not to enter more largely into the causes of this graciousness
at present, Rom. ix. 18. "he hath mercy on whom he will
have mercy," by that method, namely, which he had ap-
25 pointed in Christ. It will appear, moreover, on examination
of the particular texts, that in passages of this kind God is
generally speaking of some extraordinary manifestation of his
grace and mercy. Thus Luke xii. 32. "it is your Father's good

Iesum Christum in sese, pro bene placito voluntatis suæ. v.
11. *in ipso—ex consilio voluntatis suæ.* Iacob. i. 18. *quia
voluit*—nempe in Christo, qui scilicet sermo illi et veritas est—
progenuit nos sermone veritatis.

5   EOS QUI CREDITURI ESSENT ATQUE IN FIDE PERMANSURI. Hæc
decreti conditio immutabilis est; nullam neque Deo neque
decretis eius mutabilitatem attribuit; *hoc solidum Dei fundamentum stat, habens hoc sigillum,* 2 Tim. ii. 19. *novit Dominus eos qui sunt sui.* Nempe, *quisquis abscedit ab inius-*
10 *titia nominans nomen Christi,* id est, quisquis credit. Muta-
bilitas tota in iis est, qui a fide deficiunt; iuxta illud 2 Tim.
ii. 13. *Si non credimus, ille tamen fidus manet, negare seipsum non potest.* Prædestinatio itaque et electio videtur nulla
esse singularis, sed duntaxat generalis; id est, eorum omnium
15 qui ex animo credunt et credere persistunt; prædestinari
neminem aut eligi qua Petrus est aut Ioannes, sed quatenus
credit credensque perseverat: atque tum demum generale
electionis decretum credenti unicuique singulatim applicari
et perseverantibus ratum fieri.

20   Hoc ipsum tota Scriptura disertissime declarat, dum salutem atque vitam æternam sub conditione obedientiæ in veteri
testamento, fidei in novo æque omnibus proponit. Tale autem

pleasure." Eph. i. 5, 11. "by Jesus Christ to himself, according to the good pleasure of his will: in whom also we have
obtained an inheritance . . . after the counsel of his own
will." James i. 18. "of his own will"—that is, in Christ, who
5 is the word and truth of God—"begat he us with the word
of truth."

THOSE WHO SHOULD BELIEVE, AND CONTINUE IN THE FAITH. →
This condition is immutably attached to the decree; nor does
it attribute mutability, either to God or to his decrees; 2 Tim.
10 ii. 19, "the foundation of God standeth sure, having this seal,
The Lord knoweth them that are his": or according to the
explanation in the same verse, all who "name the name of
Christ, and depart from iniquity"; that is, whoever believes:
the mutability is entirely on the side of them who renounce
15 their faith, as it is said, 2 Tim. ii. 13. "if we believe not, yet
he abideth faithful; he cannot deny himself." It seems then
that there is no particular predestination or election, but only
general—or in other words, that the privilege belongs to all
who heartily believe and continue in their belief—that none
20 are predestinated or elected irrespectively; for example, that
Peter is not elected as Peter, or John as John, but inasmuch as
they are believers, and continue in their belief, and that thus
the general decree of election becomes personally applicable
to each particular believer, and is ratified to all who remain
25 steadfast in the faith.

This is most explicitly declared by the whole of Scripture,
which offers salvation and eternal life equally to all, under
the condition of obedience in the Old Testament, and of faith

procul dubio erat decretum qualis est decreti promulgatio:
sin minus, improbitatem quandam affingeremus Deo, qui
aliud ore loqueretur, aliud sub pectore celaret. Quod facit illa
scholastica distinctio, quæ duplicem Dei voluntatem ponit;
5 alteram signi, qua præcipit quid a nobis fieri velit; alteram
bene placiti, qua decernit nos id nunquam esse facturos;
idemque prorsus valet ac si sic distinguerent, duplicem esse in
Deo voluntatem, unam, qua vult, alteram, qua non vult. Atqui
in scripturis aiunt eadem de re sic reperiri: vult Deus Pha-
10 raonem dimittere populum, quia iubet; non vult, propterea
quod Pharaonem indurat. Immo vero volebat solum Deus,
nolebat Pharao; ut magis nollet, induravit eum Deus: ipse,
quod voluit, invito Pharaone, perficere distulit, ut nolentem
eo gravioribus pœnis afficeret. Non sic egit cum parente nostro
15 Adamo, non sic cum iis quos ad gratiam vocat atque invitat,
ut cum recte facere nos iubeat, ne recte faciamus decernat.
sed quid potest cogitari absurdius istiusmodi opinione, ad
quam stabiliendam confingenda est necessitas quæ non cogit,
est voluntas quæ non vult.
20   Promulgatio autem decreti, quod alterum est probandum,

in the New. There can be no doubt that the tenor of the decree as promulgated was in conformity with the decree itself, otherwise the integrity of God would be impugned, as expressing one intention, and concealing another within his
5 breast. Such a charge is in effect made by the scholastic distinction which ascribes a two-fold will to God; his revealed will, whereby he prescribes the way in which he desires us to act, and his hidden will, whereby he decrees that we shall never so act: which is much the same as to attribute to the
10 Deity two distinct wills, whereof one is in direct contradiction to the other. It is, however, asserted that the Scriptures contain two opposite statements respecting the same thing: it was the will of God that Pharaoh should let the people go, for such was the divine command; but it was also not his will, for he
15 hardened Pharaoh's heart. The truth however is, that it was God alone who willed their departure, and Pharaoh alone who was unwilling; and that he might be the more unwilling, God hardened his heart, and himself deferred the execution of his own pleasure, which was in opposition to that of Pharaoh,
20 that he might afflict him with heavier punishment on account of the reluctance of his will. Neither in his mode of dealing with our common father Adam, nor with those whom he calls and invites to accept of grace, can God be charged with commanding righteousness, while he decrees our disobedience to
25 the command. What can be imagined more absurd than a necessity which does not necessitate, and a will without volition?

The tenor of the decree as promulgated, which was the

passim conditionalis est: Gen. ii. 17. *de isto ne comedas: nam quo die comederis, moriturus es.* plane quasi dixisset, nolo te de isto comedere; sane ergo non decrevi te comesurum: nam si comederis, moriere; si non comederis, vives: conditionale igitur decretum ipsum ante lapsum erat: quod idem post lapsum aliis innumeris ex locis demonstratur: Gen. iv. 7. *nonne si bene egeris, remissio? si vero non bene egeris, præ foribus est peccatum,* sive pœna peccati excubans. Exod. xxxii. 32, 33. *dele me nunc de libro tuo quem scripsisti. eum qui peccat in me, delebo de libro meo.* hic Moses præ amore gentis suæ non meminerat fideles deleri non posse, quamdiu tales sunt; aut emollienda vox ista est ad illud Rom. ix. 1. &c. *optarim equidem, si fieri posset:* sed responsum Dei prædestinationis rationem conditione fundatam, quamvis metaphorice, satis tamen dilucide exponit, *peccantem delebo.* Declaratur hoc amplius in ipso legis fœdere inculcato, Deut. vii. 6, 7, 8. ubi Deus maxime declarat se gratis populum suum elegisse ac dilexisse. et v. 9. ubi vult agnosci se *Deum fidelissimum observantem fœderis sui et benignitatis suæ,* addit tamen conditionem, *erga diligentes* videlicet *ipsum, et observantes mandata eius.* et apertissime, v. 12. *erit propterea, quod audientes iudicia*

other point to be proved, is uniformly conditional. Gen. ii.
17. "thou shalt not eat of it; for in the day that thou eatest
thereof thou shalt surely die," which is the same as if God had
said, I will that thou shalt not eat of it; I have not therefore
5 decreed that thou shalt eat of it; for if thou eatest, thou shalt
die; if thou eatest not, thou shalt live. Thus the decree itself
was conditional before the fall; which from numberless other
passages appears to have been also conditional after the fall.
Gen. iv. 7. "if thou doest well, shalt thou not be accepted?
10 and if thou doest not well, sin lieth at the door," or "the punishment of sin watcheth for thee." Exod. xxxii. 32, 33. "blot
me, I pray thee, out of thy book which thou hast written . . .
whosoever hath sinned against me, him will I blot out of my
book." Such was the love of Moses for his nation, that he
15 either did not remember that believers, so long as they continued such, could not be blotted out, or the prayer must be
understood in a modified sense, as in Rom. ix. 1, &c. "I could
wish, if it were possible—." The reply of God, however, although metaphorical, explains with sufficient clearness that
20 the principle of predestination depends upon a condition,
"whosoever hath sinned, him will I blot out." This is announced more fully in the enforcement of the legal covenant,
Deut. vii. 6–8. where God pointedly declares his choice and
love of his people to have been gratuitous; and in v. 9. where
25 he desires to be known as "a faithful God which keepeth his
covenant and mercy," yet he adds as a condition, "with them
that love him and keep his commandments." Again, it is said
still more clearly, v. 12. "it shall come to pass, if ye hearken

ista, observaveritis ac feceritis ea, ut observet Iehova Deus tuus tibi fœdus illud et benignitatem quam iuramento promiserat maioribus tuis. Hæc et similia loca, tametsi de electione vel universali populi ad cultum Dei publicum vel unius cuius-
5 piam hominis aut familiæ ad munus aliquod, verba facere potissimum videantur, (vix enim est ut de electione proprie dicta, id est, ad vitam æternam, in veteri fœdere verbum ullum aut vestigium expressum reperias) divini tamen decreti ratio utrobique eadem est. Sic de Solomone quasi de Christo altero;
10 1 Chron. xxviii. 6. *elegi ipsum mihi in filium, et ego futurus sum ei in patrem.* At quo pacto? *si firmus fuerit in exercendis præceptis meis et iudiciis meis sicut hoc tempore.* v. 7. et 9. *si exquisiveris eum, præsto erit tibi; sed si dereliqueris eum, reiiciet te in perpetuum.* posterorum quoque eius electio ea-
15 dem lege stetit, 2 Chron. vi. 16. *dummodo* vel duntaxat *si observaverint filii tui* &c. et xxxiii. 8. idem. et cap. xv. v. 1, 2. *si requiritis eum, præsto erit vobis; sin derelinquitis* &c. unde Isaias, cap. xiv. 1. dicere non veretur, *eliget rursus Israelitas.* Zech. i. 16. idem. et quinam sint electi ostendit Isaias cap. lxv.
20 9, 10. *possidebunt hæreditatem istam electi mei* &c. *eritque Saronis regio—pro populo meo qui requisierint me.* Ier. xxii. 24. *etiamsi esset Conia sigillum in manu dextera mea, tamen inde evellerem.*

Idem attendendum est in fœdere gratiæ, sicubi conditio non
25 adiungitur, sed fere adiungitur. Marc. xvi. 16. *qui crediderit*

to these judgments, and keep and do them, that Jehovah thy God shall keep unto thee the covenant and the mercy which he sware unto thy fathers." Though these and similar passages seem chiefly to refer either to the universal election of
5 a nation to the service of God, or of a particular individual or family to some office (for in the Old Testament scarcely a single expression can be discovered referring to election properly so called; that is, election to eternal life), yet the principle of the divine decree is in all cases the same. Thus it is said of
10 Solomon, as of another Christ, 1 Chron. xxviii. 6, 7, 9. "I have chosen him to be my son, and I will be his father." But what are the terms of the covenant?—"if he be constant to do my commandments and my judgments, as at this day . . . if thou seek him, he will be found of thee; but if thou forsake
15 him, he will cast thee off for ever." The election of his posterity also depended on the same stipulation. 2 Chron. vi. 16. "so that thy children take heed to their way, to walk in my law." See also xxxiii. 8. and xv. 2. "the Lord is with you, while ye be with him . . . but if ye forsake him, he will
20 forsake you"; whence Isaiah does not scruple to say, xiv. 1, "the Lord will yet choose Israel." See also Zech. i. 16. Isaiah also shows who are the elect; lxv. 9, 10. "mine elect shall inherit it . . . and Sharon shall be . . . for my people that have sought me." Jer. xxii. 24. "though Coniah were the
25 signet upon my right hand, yet would I pluck thee hence."

The same must be remembered with respect to the covenant of grace, as often as the condition itself is not expressly added. It is, however, rarely omitted. Mark xvi. 16. "he that

et baptizatus fuerit, servabitur; qui vero non crediderit, con-
demnabitur. cogitate audire sic olim præstinantem Deum;
controversias infinitas hac una sententia sustuleris: vel hac
etiam, Ioan. iii. 16. *ita Deus dilexit mundum, ut filium suum*
5 *unigenitum dederit, ut omnis qui credit in eum, non pereat.*
et xv. 6. *nisi quis in me manserit, abiectus extra vineam* &c.
et v. 10. *si præcepta mea observaveritis, manebitis* &c. *sicut*
ego. et cap. xvii. 20. *non tantum pro istis rogo, sed et pro iis,*
qui per sermonem eorum credituri sunt in me. tales ergo præ-
10 destinavit pater. Itaque Pharisæi et Legis interpretes, Luc.
vii. 30. *irritum reddiderunt consilium Dei adversus seme-*
tipsos, non baptizati ab eo. præstinati ergo et ipsi olim, si
credidissent. Quis Petro certius electus est? interpositam
tamen audis conditionem, Ioan. xiii. 8. *nisi te lavero, partem*
15 *non habes mecum.* Quid ergo? assensus est Petrus; et libenter
quidem, partem habuit: non assensisset, partem non habuis-
set. Nam Iudas alter quamvis non modo electus, id enim ad
munus referri potest, verum etiam a patre datus Christo esse
dicatur, partem suam amisit. Ioan. xvii. 12. *quos dedisti mihi*
20 *ego custodivi; et nemo ex iis periit nisi filius perditionis, ut*
scriptura impleretur. Sic cap. i. v. 11, 12. *ad sua venit, et sui*
eum non exceperunt. quotquot autem eum exceperunt, dedit

believeth and is baptized shall be saved; but he that believeth —
not shall be damned." If we figure to ourselves that God
originally predestinated mankind on such conditional terms
as these, endless controversies might be decided by this single
5 sentence, or by John iii. 16. "God so loved the world that he
gave his only begotten Son, that whosoever believeth in him
should not perish, but have everlasting life." xv. 6. "if a man
abide not in me, he is cast forth as a branch." v. 10. "if ye
keep my commandments, ye shall abide in my love, even as I
10 have kept my Father's commandment." xvii. 20. "neither
pray I for these alone, but for them also which shall believe
on me through their word"; that is, for those whom the Father
had predestinated. So also, Luke vii. 30. "the Pharisees and
lawyers rejected the counsel of God against themselves, being
15 not baptized of him"; whence it appears that even they had
been predestinated, on condition of belief. No man was more
evidently one of the elect than Peter, and yet a condition is
expressly reserved, John xiii. 8. "if I wash thee not, thou hast
no part with me." What then ensued? Peter readily com-
20 plied, and consequently had part with his Lord: had he not
complied, he would have had no part with him. For though
Judas is not only said to have been chosen, which may refer
to his apostleship, but even to have been given to Christ by the
Father, he yet attained not salvation. John xvii. 12. "those
25 that thou gavest me I have kept, and none of them is lost, but
the son of perdition; that the Scripture might be fulfilled."
i. 11, 12. "he came unto his own, and his own received him
not. But as many as received him, to them gave he power,"

eis &c. Nempe iis qui credunt in nomen eius. non ante dedit iis quam recepissent, quam credidissent. ne suis quidem nominatis. Sic Paulus Eph. i. 13. *in quo posteaquam credidistis, obsignati estis spiritu illo* &c. Sane qui non nisi postea obsignati erant quam credidissent, non erant antea nominatim prædestinati, quos initio epistolæ sanctos vocat, 2 Cor. vi. 1. *hortamur,* inquit, *ne frustra gratiam Dei receperitis.* Apoc. iii. 5. *qui vicerit, amicietur* &c. *neque unquam delebo nomen eius de libro vitæ.* at xxii. 19. *si quis abstulerit aliquid ex verbis libri prophetiæ huius, auferet Deus partem eius de libro vitæ.*

Porro, si in Christo, ut iam supra demonstratum est, prædestinavit Deus, certe per fidem in Christo: 2 Thess. ii. 13. *quod elegerit vos Deus ab initio ad salutem per sanctificationem spiritus et fidem habitam veritatis.* Non ergo nisi credituros. Tit. i. 1. *secundum fidem electorum Dei, et agnitionem veritatis, quæ est secundum pietatem.* Heb. xi. 6. *fieri non potest, ut absque fide quisquam Deo sit gratus.* adeoque ut sit electus. unde electos et credentes ubique eosdem et esse et dici crediderim; ut cum dicitur, *multi sunt vocati, pauci vero electi.* Matt. xx. 16. idem valeat, ac si diceretur, pauci vero credentes. Rom. viii. 33. *quis intentabit crimina adversus electos Dei,* id est, credentes: ne electionem a fide, ac

&c., that is, to those who believed in his name; to whom he did not give power before they had received and believed in him, not even to those who were specially called his own. So St. Paul, Eph. i. 13. "in whom also after that ye believed, ye were sealed with that holy spirit of promise." Undoubtedly those whom in the beginning of his epistle he calls holy, were not sealed till after that they had believed, were not individually predestinated before that period. 2 Cor. vi. 1. "we beseech you also that ye receive not the grace of God in vain." Rev. iii. 5. "he that overcometh, the same shall be clothed in white raiment, and I will not blot out his name out of the book of life." On the other hand it is said, xxii. 19. "if any man shall take away from the words of the book of this prophecy, God shall take away his part out of the book of life."

Again, if God have predestinated us "in Christ," as has been proved already, it certainly must be on condition of faith in Christ. 2 Thess. ii. 13. "God hath from the beginning chosen you to salvation through sanctification of the Spirit, and belief of the truth," whence it appears that it is only those who will believe that are chosen. Tit. i. 1. "according to the faith of God's elect, and the acknowledging of the truth which is after godliness." Heb. xi. 6. "without faith it is impossible to please God," and thus become one of the elect; whence I infer that believers are the same as the elect, and that the terms are used indiscriminately. So Matt. xx. 16. "many be called, but few chosen," only signifies that they which believe are few. Rom. viii. 33. "who shall lay anything to the charge of God's elect?" that is, of believers: otherwise

proinde a Christo separantes, durioribus doctrinis, immo
odiosis et ratione carentibus, implicemur. Sic cap. xi. 7. *electi*
id est, credentes, *assecuti sunt;* ex v. 20. *tu,* nempe electus, *per*
fidem stas. et 22. *si permanseris in benignitate; alioquin et*
5 *tu excideris.* Sic de semetipso interpretatur Paulus, 1 Cor. ix.
27. *ne quo modo cum aliis prædicarim, ipse reiectaneus fiam.*
Philipp. iii. 12. *non quod iam metam apprehenderim aut iam*
sim consummatus, sed persequor experiens an ipse quoque
apprehendam, cuius etiam rei causa apprehensus fui a Christo
10 *Iesu.* 2 Tim. ii. 10, 12. *omnia tolero propter electos, ut et ipsi*
salutem consequantur, quæ est in Christo Iesu. at v. 13. *si*
non credimus &c.

Restant duo quidem difficiles loci ex analogia tot clariorum
explicandi: non enim clara obscuris, sed obscura claris illus-
15 trantur. Locus prior est Act. xiii. 48. alter Rom. viii. 28, 29,
30. posterior prius tractabitur, ut mea quidem sententia
minus difficilis: verba hæc sunt; *novimus autem iis qui dili-*
gunt Deum, omnia cooperari ad bonum; iis qui iuxta pro-
positum sunt vocati. nam quos prænovit, etiam prædestinavit
20 *conformandos imagini filii sui* &c. *quos vero prædestinavit,*
eos etiam vocavit; et quos vocavit, eos etiam iustificavit, quos
autem iustificavit, eos etiam glorificavit.

by separating election from faith, and therefore from Christ, we should be entangled in hard, not to say detestable and absurd doctrines. So also, Rom. xi. 7. "the election have obtained it"; that is, believers, as is clear from the twentieth
5 verse, "thou," that is, thou that art elect, "standest by faith"; and v. 22. "if thou continue in his goodness; otherwise thou also shalt be cut off." Such is St. Paul's interpretation of the doctrine in his own case; 1 Cor. ix. 27. "lest that by any means when I have preached to others, I myself should be a
10 castaway." Philipp. iii. 12. "not as though I had already attained, either were already perfect; but I follow after, if that I may apprehend that for which also I am apprehended of Christ Jesus." 2 Tim. ii. 10, 12. "I endure all things for the elect's sake, that they may also obtain the salvation which is
15 in Christ Jesus," &c. yet it is said in the next verse, "if we believe not, yet he abideth faithful," &c.

Two difficult texts remain to be explained from analogy by the aid of so many plainer passages; for what is obscure must be illustrated by what is clear, not what is clear by what is
20 obscure. The first passage occurs Acts xiii. 48. the other Rom. viii. 28–30. which, as being in my judgment the least difficult of the two, I shall discuss first. It is as follows: "we know that all things work together for good to them that love God, to them who are the called according to his purpose: for whom
25 he did foreknow, he also did predestinate to be conformed to the image of his Son," &c. "moreover whom he did predestinate, them he also called; and whom he called, them he also justified; and whom he justified, them he also glorified."

Primum hoc animadvertendum est ex v. 28. *Qui diligunt Deum* et *qui iuxta propositum vocati sunt eosdem esse:* eosdem igitur *quos prænovit, quos prædestinavit, eos enim vocavit,* v. 30. unde facile perspicitur generalis hic prædestinationis rationem atque ordinem proponi, non quorundam præter cæteros; perinde ac si diceretur, novimus quod iis qui diligunt Deum, id est, qui credunt (qui diligunt enim credunt) omnia cooperantur ad bonum: et ostenditur quo ordine. primum Deus credituros prænovit, id est, decrevit vel approbavit eos fore duntaxat quos in Christo respiceret, omnes utique si credidissent; eos ad salutem prædestinavit; adeoque omnes variis modis vocavit, ut crederent, id est, Deum vere agnoscerent; ita credentes iustificavit, perseverantes demum glorificavit. Quinam autem sint quos prænovit Deus, ut planius fiat, sciendum est Deum dici trifariam aliquem vel aliquid nosse. primum, notitia universali; quemadmodum Act. xv. 18. *nota sunt Deo ab omni ævo omnia opera sua.* Secundo, notitia approbationis aut gratiæ, qui Hebraicus idiotismus est; eoque magis explanandus. Exod. xxxiii. 12. *novi te nominatim, atque etiam invenisti gratiam in oculis meis.* Psal. i. 6. *novit Iehova viam iustorum.* Matt. vii. 23. *nunquam*

In the first place it must be remarked, that it appears from v. 28, that those "who love God" are the same as those "who are the called according to his purpose," and consequently as those "whom he did foreknow," and "whom he did predesti-
5 nate," for "them he also called," as is said in v. 30. Hence it is apparent that the apostle is here propounding the scheme and order of predestination in general, not of the predestination of certain individuals in preference to others. As if he had said, We know that all things work together for good to
10 those who love God, that is, to those who believe, for those who love God believe in him. Further, as regards the order, God originally foreknew those who should believe; that is, he decreed or announced it as his pleasure that it should be those alone who should find grace in his sight through Christ, that
15 is, all men, if they would believe. These he predestinated to salvation, and to this end he, in various ways, called all mankind to believe, or in other words, to acknowledge God in truth; those who actually thus believed he justified; and those who continued in the faith unto the end he finally glorified.
20 But that it may be more clear who those are whom God has foreknown, it must be observed that there are three ways in which any person or thing is said to be known to God. First, by his universal knowledge, as Acts xv. 18. "known unto God are all his works from the beginning of the world." Secondly,
25 by his approving or gracious knowledge, which is an Hebraism, and therefore requires more explanation. Exod. xxxiii. 12. "I know thee by name, and thou hast also found grace in my sight." Psal. i. 6. "Jehovah knoweth the way of the right-

novi vos. tertia est notitia displicentiæ; Deut. xxxi. 21. *me nosse figmentum eius* &c. 2 Reg. xix. 27. *incessum tuum novi, etiam furorem tuum contra me.* Apoc. iii. 1. *novi opera tua, quod dicaris vivere, sed mortuus es.* Approbationis tantum
5 notitiam hic posse intelligi, palam est: prænovit autem sive approbavit, nisi in Christo, neminem; in Christo neminem nisi credentem. Qui igitur dilecti dilecturi erant, id est, credituri, eos prænovit Deus, sive approbavit, in genere scilicet omnes si credidissent: quos ita prænovit, eos prædestinavit,
10 et ut crederent vocavit; credentes iustificavit. Quod si credentes iustificavit et solos quidem, siquidem sola fides iustificat, solos profecto credituros prænovit; quos enim prænovit, eos iustificavit, quos ergo iustificavit, eosdem prænovit; credituros nemirum solos. Sic cap. xi. 2. *non abiecit Deus popu-*
15 *lum suum quem prænovit,* id est, credentes, v. 20. 2 Tim. ii. 19. *novit Dominus eos qui sunt sui:* nempe *omnes qui abscedunt ab iniustitia, nominantes nomen Christi,* scilicet credentes. 1 Pet. i. 2. *electis iuxta prænotionem Dei patris in sanctificatione spiritus ad obedientiam et aspersionem sangui-*
20 *nis Iesu Christi.* Quid est hoc totum nisi credentibus? quos elegit pater iuxta prænotionem sive approbationem eorum in

eous." Matt. vii. 23. "I never knew you." Thirdly, by a
knowledge attended with displeasure. Deut. xxxi. 21. "I
know their imagination which they go about," &c. 2 Kings
xix. 27. "I know . . . thy coming in, and thy rage against
5 me." Rev. iii. 1. "I know thy works, that thou hast a name
that thou livest, and art dead." In the passage under discussion it is evident that the approving knowledge of God can
be alone intended; but he foreknew or approved no one, except in Christ, and no one in Christ except a believer. Those
10 therefore who were about to love, that is, to believe in God,
God foreknew or approved; or in general all men, if they
should believe; those whom he thus foreknew, he predestinated, and called them that they might believe; those who
believed, he justified. But if God justified believers, and
15 believers only, inasmuch as it is faith alone that justifieth,
he foreknew those only who would believe, for those whom
he foreknew he justified; those therefore whom he justified he
also foreknew, namely, those alone who were about to believe.
So Rom. xi. 2. "God hath not cast away his people which he
20 foreknew," that is, believers, as appears from v. 20. 2 Tim.
ii. 19. "the Lord knoweth them that are his," that is, "all who
name the name of Christ, and depart from iniquity"; or in
other words, all believers. 1 Pet. i. 2. "elect according to the
foreknowledge of God the Father, through sanctification of
25 the Spirit, unto obedience and sprinkling of the blood of
Jesus Christ." This can be applicable to none but believers,
whom the Father has chosen, according to his foreknowledge
and approbation of them, through the sanctification of the

sanctificatione spiritus et fide, sine qua aspersio sanguinis
Christi nihil erat iis profutura. Incommode itaque videntur
plerique his in locis prænotionem Dei præscientiam interpretari; cum præscientia Dei ad rationem sive essentiam prædes-
5 tinationis nihil pertinere videatur. omnis qui credit ac perseverat, eum prædestinavit atque elegit Deus. Quid ad nos
attinet scire, præscieritne quinam essent, quinam non essent
credituri? Neque enim credit quisquam quia Deus præscivit,
sed idcirco Deus præscivit, quia crediturus quis erat. Neque
10 sane præscientia sive prænotio Dei de certis aut singulis hominibus in prædestinationis doctrina quid faciat, intelligi potest,
nisi ut quæstiones inutiles et prorsus inexplicabiles pariat.
Cur enim singulos aut certos homines prænosceret Deus, aut
quid in iis prænosse potuit quod eum induceret ad certos illos
15 potius quam omnes prædestinandos, communi conditione
fidei sancita? Satis sit nobis hac in re nihil aliud indagare,
quam Deum ex misericordia summaque sua gratia in Christo,
omnes credituros, ad salutem prædestinasse.

Alter locus est Act. xiii. 48. *audientes autem gentes, gaude-*
20 *bant; et glorificabant verbum Domini; et crediderunt quot*
erant ordinati ad vitam æternam. Difficultatem affert iniecta

Spirit and faith, without which the sprinkling of the blood of Christ would avail them nothing. Hence it seems that the generality of commentators are wrong in interpreting the foreknowledge of God in these passages in the sense of pre-
5 science; since the prescience of God seems to have no connection with the principle or essence of predestination; for God has predestinated and elected whoever believes and continues in the faith. Of what consequence is it to us to know whether the prescience of God foresees who will, or will not, subse-
10 quently believe? for no one believes because God has foreseen his belief, but God foresees his belief because he was about to believe. Nor is it easy to understand how the prescience or foreknowledge of God with regard to particular persons can be brought to bear at all upon the doctrine of predestination,
15 except for the purpose of raising a number of useless and utterly inapplicable questions. For why should God foreknow particular individuals, or what could he foreknow in them which should induce him to predestinate them in particular, rather than all in general, when the condition of faith,
20 which was common to all mankind, had been once laid down. Without searching deeper into this subject, let us be contented to know nothing more than that God, out of his infinite mercy and grace in Christ, has predestinated to salvation all who should believe.

25   The other passage is Acts xiii. 48. "when the Gentiles heard this, they were glad, and glorified the word of the Lord; and as many as were ordained to eternal life, believed." The difficulty is caused by the abrupt manner in which the sacred his-

subito historici sententia reliquæ scripturæ etiam a seipso
scriptæ nequaquam primo aspectu consentanea: qui dictum
modo narraverat a Petro, cap. x. 34, 35. *in veritate percipio,*
Deum non esse personæ, seu faciei *acceptorem; sed in omni*
5 *gente qui timet eum et operatur iustitiam, acceptus est illi:*
Acceptus certe est electus. et ne proselytum iam ante fuisse
dicas Cornelium, dicit idem Paulus etiam de iis qui legem non
norant, Rom. ii. 10, 11, 14. *non est personarum acceptio*
apud Deum. qui legem non habeat &c. 1 Pet. i. 17. *qui sine*
10 *personarum acceptione iudicat secundum cuiusque opus.* Sin
credit unusquisque propterea quod ordinatus erat, non ordinatus quia crediturus, effugere non poterunt, qui sic docent,
quin id esse Deum statuant, quod ipse se haberi nolle toties
testatur, personarum acceptorem. Deinde, si crediderunt
15 gentes eo quod erant ordinatæ, eadem erit prima causa cur
Iudæi non crediderint, v. 46. id quod et illos magnopere excu-
sabit; cum non oblata, sed ostentata solum vita æterna fuisse
videretur; et ad reliquas gentes cohortandas minime erat accommodatum, qui inde statim arbitrarentur, nulla sua volun-
20 tate aut opera opus esse ad vitam æternam, sed fatali nescio
qua ordinatione. cum alioqui tota scriptura manifestissimum
sit, credere quidem omnes quot ordinati sunt ad vitam æter-

torian introduces an assertion which appears at first sight to contradict himself as well as the rest of Scripture; for he had before attributed to Peter this saying, chap. x. 34, 35. "of a truth I perceive that God is no respecter of persons; but in
5 every nation he that feareth him, and worketh righteousness, is accepted with him." "Accepted" certainly means chosen; and lest it should be urged that Cornelius was a proselyte previously, St. Paul says the same even of those who had never known the law, Rom. ii. 10, 14. "there is no respect of per-
10 sons with God," &c. "when the Gentiles which have not the law," &c. 1 Pet. i. 17. "the Father, who without respect of persons judgeth according to every man's work." Now those who hold the doctrine that a man believes because he is or-dained to eternal life, not that he is ordained to eternal life
15 because he will believe, cannot avoid attributing to God the character of a respecter of persons, which he so constantly disclaims. Besides, if the Gentiles believed because they were ordained to eternal life, the same must have been the primary cause of the unbelief of the Jews, v. 46. which will plead
20 greatly in their excuse, since it would seem that eternal life had only been placed in their view, not offered to their accep-tance. Nor would such a dispensation be calculated to en-courage the other nations, who would immediately conclude from it that there was no occasion for any will or works of
25 their own in order to obtain eternal life, but that the whole depended on some appointed decree, whereas, on the con-trary, Scripture uniformly shows in the clearest manner, that as many as have been ordained to eternal life believe, not

nam non eo simpliciter quod ordinati, sed quod ea conditione ordinati sunt. Quocirca sagaciores meo quidem iudicio interpretes aliquam in verbo græco τεταγμένοι, quod *ordinati* vertitur, subesse ambiguitatem existimant, et idem valere

5 τεταγμένοι, quod εὖ ἤτοι μετρίως διατεθειμένοι, bene aut mediocriter dispositi sive affecti, animo composito, attento, erecto, et non inordinato; contra atque illi Iudæi fuerunt, ad vitam æternam, qui sermonem Dei repulerant, seque indignos vita æterna ostenderant. Significatio affinis huius vocis *Ordinati*

10 inusitata Græcis non est; ut apud Plutarchum in Pompeio. et erant *qui ambulabant inordinate.* 2 Thess. iii. 6, 11. certe quidem ad vitam æternam. Sensus et res ipsa, quam hic volumus, in scripturis haud raro aliis verbis reperitur. Luc. ix. 62. εὔθετος, bene dispositus, sive aptus ad regnum Dei. Marc.

15 xii. 34. *non longe a regno Dei.* 2 Tim. ii. 21. *vas ad decus accommodatum usibus Domini, et ad omne opus bonum præparatum.* Quædam enim in homine reliquiæ sunt imaginis divinæ, ut infra ostendemus: quarum ex concursu hic illo ad regnum Dei fit aptior et quasi dispositior. Cur itaque hanc

20 gratiam alii amplectantur, alii reiiciant, in ipsa hominis natura (neque enim stipites plane sumus) quærenda saltem aliqua causa est. compertum hoc est atque imprimis constat, omnes homines, quamvis in peccato mortuos iræque filios, alios tamen aliis deteriores esse: id et in natura, ingenio ac mori-

25 bus eorum qui a gratia Dei alienissimi sunt, animadvertere

simply because they have been so ordained, but because they have been ordained on condition of believing.

For these reasons other interpreters of more sagacity, according to my judgment, have thought that there is some
5 ambiguity in the Greek word which is translated "ordained," and that it has the same force as "well or moderately disposed or affected," of a composed, attentive, upright, and not disorderly mind; of a different spirit from those Jews, as touching eternal life, who had put from them the word of God,
10 and had shown themselves unworthy of everlasting life. The Greeks use the word in a similar sense, as in Plutarch, and 2 Thess. iii. 6, 11. "there are some which walk disorderly," certainly with reference to eternal life. This sense of the word, and even the particular application which is here intended,
15 frequently occurs in Scripture in other terms. Luke ix. 62. "well disposed" or "fit for the kingdom of God." Mark xii. 34. "not far from the kingdom of God." 2 Tim. ii. 21. "a vessel . . . meet for the master's use, and prepared for every good work." For, as will be shown hereafter, there are some rem-
20 nants of the divine image left in man, the union of which in one individual renders him more fit and disposed for the kingdom of God than another. Since therefore we are not merely senseless stocks, some cause at least must be discovered in the nature of man himself, why divine grace is rejected by some
25 and embraced by others. One thing appears certain, that though all men be dead in sin and children of wrath, yet some are worse than others; and this difference may not only be perceived daily in the nature, disposition, and habits of those

licet non solum quotidie, verum etiam ex parabola illa Matt. xiii. in illa quadruplici vel saltem triplici natura soli, partim petrosi, partim spinosi, partim quodammodo boni saltem præ lapideo ac spinoso, cum nondum ullum semen receperat: et

5 Matt. x. 11. &c. *exquirite quis in ea sit dignus &c. et siquidem fuerit domus digna, venito pax vestra super eam.* Qua potuit ratione quisquam esse dignus ante evangelium auditum, nisi eo quod esset ordinatus, id est, bene animatus ac dispositus ad vitam æternam? id quod cæteros in ipsorum pœna post

10 mortem esse sensuros docet Christus: Matt. xi. 22. *Tyro et Sidoni tolerabilior erit* &c. Luc. xii. 47, 48. *cædetur multis plagis cædetur paucis.* ad postremum omnes ratione insita satis instructi sunt, qua pravis affectibus obsistere per se queant, ne quis pravitatem suæ naturæ præ aliis causetur impor-

15 tunius, aut conqueratur. At, inquis, Deus non id spectat ut ex improbis eligat minus improbum, sed præponi sæpius deteriorem. Deut. ix. 5. *nequaquam propter iustitiam tuam aut propter rectum animum tuum ingressurus es ad possidendum terram eorum.* et Luc. x. 13. *si in Tyro et Sidone*

20 *editæ fuissent virtutes quæ editæ sunt apud vos, olim cum sacco et cinere sedentes resipuissent.* Respondeo, neque posse statui ex his locis quid spectet Deus in iis quos eligit: primum

who are most alienated from the grace of God, but may also be inferred from the expressions used in the parable, Matt. xiii. where the nature of the soil is variously described in three or four ways, part as stony ground, part overrun with thorns,
5 part good ground, at least in comparison of the rest, before it had as yet received any seed. See also Matt. x. 11, &c. "inquire who in it is worthy," &c. . . . "and if the house be worthy, let your peace come upon it." How could any one be worthy before the Gospel had been preached, unless on ac-
10 count of his being *ordained,* that is, well inclined or disposed, to eternal life? a truth which Christ teaches will be made evident to others by the measure of their own punishment after death; Matt. xi. 22. "it shall be more tolerable for Tyre and Sidon at the day of judgment, than for you." Luke xii. 47,
15 48. "that servant which knew his Lord's will . . . shall be beaten with many stripes: but he that knew not . . . shall be beaten with few stripes." And, lastly, the gift of reason has been implanted in all, by which they may of themselves resist bad desires, so that no one can complain of, or allege in excuse,
20 the depravity of his own nature compared with that of others.

But, it is objected, God has no regard to the less depraved among the wicked in his choice, but often selects the worse rather than the better. Deut. ix. 5. "not for thy righteousness, or for the uprightness of thine heart, dost thou go to possess
25 their land." Luke x. 13. "if the mighty works had been done in Tyre and Sidon, which have been done in you, they had a great while ago repented, sitting in sackcloth and ashes." I answer, that it cannot be determined from these passages,

enim iustitiam spectasse vel minimam non disputavimus; deinde in priore loco non agitur de electione ad vitam æternam, sed de terra Cananæa Israelitis danda, quæ alias ob causas data est iis, quam ob quas vita æterna data fuisset; 5 partim propter scelera incolarum, partim ut præstaretur quod iuramento promissum erat maioribus eorum, quorum nihil nostræ sententiæ adversatur. Posteriore loco non electi cum reprobis, sed inter se reprobi conferuntur, Tyrii cum Iudæis incredulis, quorum neutri resipuerunt: neque vero Tyrii vere 10 unquam resipuissent, etiamsi illa apud eos edita miracula fuissent; id enim si prævidisset Deus, nunquam iis defuisset: sed hoc ita dicitur ut illud Matt. xxi. 31. *publicani et meretrices præeunt vos in regnum Dei.* Postremo inquies *non volentis, neque currentis, sed miserentis Dei,* Rom. ix. 16. At, 15 inquam, nos neque volentem neque currentem inducimus; sed minus nolentem, minus cessantem, minus obnitentem; Deum nihilominus miserentem, simulque summe sapientem summeque iustum. Interim qui ait non esse volentis neque

what God regards in those whom he chooses; for in the first place, I have not argued that he has regarded righteousness even in the least degree. Secondly, in the former passage the question is not respecting election to life eternal, but concern-
5 ing the gift of the land of Canaan to the Israelites, a gift assigned them for other reasons than those for which eternal life would have been given: partly on account of the wickedness of the original inhabitants, and partly that the promise might be fulfilled which had been ratified by an oath to their
10 forefathers; wherein there is nothing that contradicts my doctrine. In the latter passage, it is not the elect who are compared with the reprobate, but the reprobate who are compared with each other, the Tyrians with the unbelieving Jews, neither of which nations had repented. Nor would the
15 Tyrians ever have truly repented, even if those mighty works had been wrought among them, for if God had foreseen that they would have repented, he would never have forsaken them; but the expression is to be understood in the same sense as Matt. xxi. 31. "the publicans and the harlots go into the
20 kingdom of God before you."

Lastly, it will be objected that "it is not of him that willeth, nor of him that runneth, but of God that showeth mercy," Rom. ix. 16. I answer, that my argument does not presuppose one that willeth or that runneth, but one that is less re-
25 luctant, less backward, less resisting than another; though it is God, nevertheless, that showeth mercy, and is at once infinitely wise and just. On the other hand, whoever affirms that "it is not of him that willeth nor of him that runneth,"

currentis, ponit certe volentem, ponit currentem; sed hoc solum agit, ut neque volenti neque currenti laudis quicquam tribuat aut meriti. Cum autem statuisset Deus homines restituere, decrevit etiam sine dubio (quid enim erat æquius?)

5 amissam libertatem, aliqua saltem ex parte restituere voluntati. Quos itaque pro illo arbitrio vel ante vel in ipsa vocatione utcunque liberato, volentes quoquo modo aut currentes vidit, quos ordinatos hic vocari verisimile est, dedit iis amplius ut vellent atque currerent, id est, ut crederent. iuxta illud 1 Sam.

10 xvi. 7. *Iehova ad cor spectat,* nempe sive naturali indole ut se habet, sive post vocantis gratiam. et illud notissimum *habenti dabitur.* Exempla esse possunt. Centurio Matt. viii. 10. *ne in Israele quidem tantam fidem inveni.* et mulier Cananæa cap. xv. 28. *O mulier, magna est fides tua.* et Marc. ix. 24.

15 *credo Domine: succurre incredulitati meæ.* et Zacchæus, Luc. xix. 3. *quærebat videre Iesum quis esset.* itaque v. 9. *dixit ei Iesus, hodie salus huic domui facta est.* Non igitur ab æterno ordinatus est Zacchæus, sed ex quo Christi se cupidum monstrarat. Nec minus idcirco miserentis est Dei, cum principalis

20 causa pro sola, merito, non in sermone solum communi,

admits that there is one who wills, and one who runs, but only guards against assigning him any portion of merit or praise. When, however, God determined to restore mankind, he also without doubt decreed that the liberty of will which they had lost should be at least partially regained, which was but reasonable. Whomsoever therefore in the exercise of that degree of freedom which their will had acquired either previously to their call, or by reason of the call itself, God had seen in any respect willing or running (who it is probable are here meant by the ordained), to them he gave a greater power of willing and running, that is, of believing. Thus it is said, I Sam. xvi. 7. "Jehovah looketh on the heart," namely, on the disposition of men either as it is by nature, or after grace has been received from him that calleth them. To the same purport is that well known saying, "to him that hath shall be given." This may be illustrated by example, as in the case of the centurion, Matt. viii. 10. "I have not found so great faith, no, not in Israel"—in that of the woman of Canaan, Matt. xv. 28. "O woman, great is thy faith"—in that of the father of the demoniac, Mark ix. 24. "Lord, I believe; help thou mine unbelief"—and in that of Zaccheus, Luke xix. 3. "he sought to see Jesus who he was," whence, v. 9. "Jesus said unto him, This day is salvation come to this house." Zaccheus therefore had not been ordained from all eternity, but from the time when he had shown himself eagerly desirous of knowing Christ.

Nor is it less on this account "of God that showeth mercy," since the principal is often not improperly put for the sole

verum apud dialecticos etiam habeatur. et certe nisi prior misertus esset Deus, nemo prorsus neque voluisset neque cucurrisset. Philipp. ii. 13. *Deus enim est qui efficit in vobis et velle et agere, pro benevolentia sua.* 2 Cor. iii. 5. *non quod sufficientes simus per nos ipsos ad cogitandum quicquam, sed sufficientia nostra ex Deo est:* et miserente quidem sine quo, neque volens neque currens quicquam promovisset. Atque hic satis intellectum puto ex analogia reliquarum omnium scripturarum quinam illi sint qui ordinati ad vitam æternam ex illo Actorum loco fuisse dicuntur. Quæ omnia simul reputans existimarim Lucam nihil hic novi sic subito inseruisse; illud tantummodo Petri dictum de Cornelio Act. x. 34, 35. alio nunc exemplo confirmare voluisse credidit Cornelius gentesque cum eo, quotquot nempe timebant Deum, dabantque operam iustitiæ; tales enim in omni gente accepti Deo sunt: crediderunt hic etiam gentes, quotquot res serias et homini dignas cogitabant, seque faciles ad discendum præbuerunt, gaudentes, et verbum Domini glorificantes; tales in omni gente Deo acceptos Petrus declaravit: tales hic Lucas quamvis gentes, ordinatos tamen, id est, idoneos ad vitam æternam ex Petri sententia confirmat.

Verum adhuc fortassis obiicietur, si sic statuis Deum prædestinasse homines, hac nempe conditione duntaxat, si credi-

cause by logicians themselves as well as in common discourse; and it is certain that unless God had first shown mercy, it would have been in the power of no one either to will or to run. Philipp. ii. 13. "for it is God that worketh in you both to will and to do of his good pleasure." 2 Cor. iii. 5. "not that we are sufficient of ourselves to think any thing as of ourselves; but our sufficiency is of God," without whose mercy he that willeth or he that runneth would gain nothing.

Reasoning, therefore, from the analogy of all the other passages of Scripture, I think there can be no difficulty in determining who those are that are said in the verse quoted from the Acts to have been ordained to eternal life. On a review of the whole subject, I should conclude that Luke did not intend to advance in so abrupt a manner any new doctrine, but simply to confirm by a fresh example the saying of Peter respecting Cornelius, Acts x. 34, 35. Cornelius and the Gentiles with him believed, as many at least as feared God and worked righteousness, for such were accepted of God in every nation. So in the other passage, those of the Gentiles whose thoughts were already devoted to serious subjects, worthy the attention of men, believed, and gave themselves up to instruction with docility and gladness of heart, glorifying the word of the Lord. Such Peter declared were accepted of God in every nation, and such Luke in conformity with Peter's opinion asserts to be ordained to, that is, qualified for eternal life, even though they were Gentiles.

But an objection of another kind may perhaps be made. If God be said to have predestinated men only on condition

dissent atque in fide permansissent, praedestinatio non erit
tota gratiae; ex voluntate ac fide hominum pendebit: unde
gratiae divinae sua laus in solidum non constabit. Immo inquam constabit optime; nihiloque minus, immo vero multo
5 magis longeque clarius quam ex doctrina ipsorum, qui haec
nobis impingunt. Summa enim Dei gratia agnoscitur, primum, quod omnino nos culpa nostra lapsuros miseratus est:
deinde, quod usque eo mundum dilexit, ut pro eo filium
unigenitum dederit; quod dedit denique, ut libertate arbitrii
10 per renovationem spiritus recuperata, velle rursus queamus,
id est, libere agere. quemadmodum aperuit cor Lydiae, Act.
xvi. 14. Quod si conditio decreti, voluntas nempe ab ipso libe-
rata, et fides, quae ab hominibus postulatur, in potestate hominum libere agentium relinquitur, id, cum aequissimum est,
15 tum gratiae nihil derogat: quandoquidem velle et credere aut
donum Dei est, aut, quantum eius est in homine situm,
nullam boni operis aut meriti, sed facultatis duntaxat naturalis rationem habet. Neque idcirco Deus voluntate pendet humana, sed voluntatem ipse exsequitur suam, qua voluit ho-
20 mines in amore atque cultu Dei, adeoque in salute sua, suo
semper uti arbitrio; quo nisi utantur, quem cultum, quem
amorem praebemus Deo, nihili profecto est, nullius pretii;

that they believe and continue in the faith, predestination will not be altogether of grace, but must depend on the will and belief of mankind; which is derogatory to the exclusive efficacy of divine grace. I maintain on the contrary that, so far 5 from the doctrine of grace being impugned, it is thus placed in a much clearer light than by the theory of those who make the objection. For the grace of God is seen to be infinite, in the first place, by his showing any pity at all for man whose fall was to happen through his own fault. Secondly, by his 10 "so loving the world, that he gave his only begotten Son" for its salvation. Thirdly, by his granting us again the power of volition, that is, of acting freely, in consequence of recovering the liberty of the will by the renewing of the Spirit. It was thus that he opened the heart of Lydia, Acts xvi. 14. Admit-15 ting, however, that the condition whereon the decree depends (that is to say, the will enfranchised by God himself, and that faith which is required of mankind) is left in the power of free agents, there is nothing in the doctrine either derogatory to grace, or inconsistent with justice; since the power of will-20 ing and believing is either the gift of God, or, so far as it is inherent in man, partakes not of the nature of merit or good works, but only of a natural faculty. Nor does this reasoning represent God as depending upon the human will, but as fulfilling his own pleasure, whereby he has chosen that man 25 should always use his own will with a regard to the love and worship of the Deity, and consequently with a regard to his own salvation. If this use of the will be not admitted, whatever worship or love we render to God is entirely vain and of

omnis officii gratia, necessitate imposita languet, immo omnis
evanescit: arbitrium autem cui decretum quodvis impendet
atque imminet, liberum esse non potest.

Quæ itaque toties declamitant nonnulli et queruntur, hoc
5 modo prædestinationem operibus, pœnitentia fideque prævisa poni ordine posteriorem; ab hominibus voluntate sus-
pendi; Deum solida salutis nostræ gloria spoliari; hominem
superbia inflari; consolationem Christianam in vita et morte
labefactari; iustificationem gratuitam abnegari; nihil horum
10 huic sententiæ obiici merito potest: ratio interim, adeoque
laus divinæ non solum gratiæ, verum etiam sapientiæ ac iustitiæ aliquanto clarius elucet; quem finem prædestinationis
Deus proposuit sibi primarium.

Cum itaque tam perspicuum sit prædestinasse Deum om-
15 nes ab æterno qui credidissent atque in fide permansissent,
sequitur, nisi non credentium aut non permanentium reprobationem esse nullam; eamque potius consecutione quam decreto esse; nullam deinde ab æterno esse hominum singu-
lorum. Deus enim omnes libero arbitrio utentes communi
20 conditione proposita, ad salutem prædestinavit; ad interitum
neminem, nisi sua culpa et quodammodo per accidens; quemadmodum et Evangelium offendiculo esse et exitio quibus-

no value; the acceptableness of duties done under a law of necessity is diminished, or rather is annihilated altogether, inasmuch as freedom can no longer be attributed to that will over which some fixed decree is inevitably suspended.

5   The objections, therefore, which some urge so vehemently against this doctrine, are of no force whatever; namely, that the repentance and faith of the predestinated having been foreseen, predestination becomes posterior in point of time to works, that it is rendered dependent on the will of man,
10 that God is defrauded of part of the glory of our salvation, that man is puffed up with pride, that the foundations of all Christian consolation in life and in death are shaken, that gratuitous justification is denied. On the contrary, the scheme, and consequently the glory, not only of the divine grace, but
15 also of the divine wisdom and justice, is thus displayed in a clearer manner than on the opposite hypothesis; and consequently the principal end is effected which God proposed to himself in predestination.

Seeing, then, that God has predestinated from eternity all
20 those who should believe and continue in the faith, it follows that none can be reprobated, except they do not believe or continue in the faith, and even this rather as a consequence than a decree; there can therefore be no reprobation of individuals from all eternity. For God has predestinated to salvation, on
25 the proviso of a general condition, all who enjoy freedom of will; while none are predestinated to destruction, except through their own fault, and as it were *per accidens,* in the same manner as the gospel itself is said to be a stumbling-

dam dicitur. Hoc non minus clare quam quod capitis parte
superiore disputatum est, scripturarum testimoniis demon-
strabitur. Isa. l. 1. *ubi est libellus repudii?* &c. *en, iniquita-*
tibus vestris venditis vos. Hos. iv. 6. *quia tu sprevisti scien-*
5 *tiam, spernam quoque te* &c. *quia oblitus es legis Dei Tui,*
obliviscar filiorum tuorum ego quoque. Apoc. xiii. 8. *adora-*
bunt eam omnes incolæ terræ, quorum non sunt scripta no-
mina in libro vitæ agni illius mactati iam inde a iacto mundi
fundamento. Et quinam sunt isti nisi non credentes? quos
10 idcirco deseruit Deus quia *bestiam sunt secuti.* v. 3. Illud
sane Zephan. ii. 1, 2, 3. decretum reprobationis non dixerim,
sed pœnarum potius temporalium; utcunque non absolutum,
quod verba ipsa indicant: *excutite vos,* &c. *antequam pariat*
decretum, &c. *fortasse abscondemini die iræ Iehovæ.*

15   Si enim Deus reprobandos absolute aliquos decrevit, quod
non legimus, ex ipsorum regula qui statuunt reprobationem
decretum esse absolutum, decrevit quoque causas medias, sine
quibus decretum illud suum exsequi non potest: causa autem
media peccatum solum est. Nec valet hoc effugium quo
20 solent uti, non decrevit Deus peccatum, sed permittere peccatum; immo hoc repugnat; sic non permittit duntaxat: qui
autem permittit, non decernit, sed liberum relinquit.

block and a savor of death to some. This shall be proved on the testimony of Scripture no less explicitly than the doctrine asserted in the former part of the chapter. Isa. l. 1. "where is the bill of your mother's divorcement, whom I have put away? . . . behold for your iniquities have ye sold yourselves." Hos. iv. 6. "because thou hast rejected knowledge, I will also reject thee . . . seeing thou hast forgotten the law of thy God, I will also forget thy children." Rev. xiii. 8. "all that dwell upon the earth shall worship him, whose names are not written in the book of life of the Lamb slain from the foundation of the world"; those, namely, who have not believed, whom God has expressly deserted because they "wandered after the beast," v. 3. Nor should I call the decree in Zephaniah ii. 1–3. a decree of eternal reprobation, but rather of temporal punishment, and at any rate not an absolute decree, as the passage itself is sufficient to show: "gather yourselves together," &c. "before the decree bring forth . . ." &c. &c. "it may be ye shall be hid in the day of the anger of Jehovah."

If God had decreed any to absolute reprobation, which we nowhere read in Scripture, the system of those who affirm that reprobation is an absolute decree, requires that he should have decreed also the means whereby his own decree might be fulfilled. Now these means are neither more nor less than sin. Nor will it avail to reply that God did not decree sin, but only permitted it; for there is a fatal objection to this common subterfuge; namely, that it implies more than simple permission. Further, he who permits a thing does not decree it, but leaves it free.

Quod si reprobationis decretum ullum est, quemadmodum electionem fide fundari atque constitui, ita reprobationem resipiscentia rescindi scriptura passim declarat. Ier. vi. 30. *argentum reprobum vocantur illi, quia reprobat Iehova illos;* et tamen cap. sequentis v. 3. ad eosdem, *bonas efficite vias vestras et actiones vestras; tum faciam ut habitetis in loco hoc.* Sic cap. xviii. 6. &c. ubi ius suum Deus cum iure figuli confert (unde hausisse Paulus videtur Rom. ix.) *si convertatur gens illa a malo suo, contra quam loquutus fuero, pœnitebit quoque me eius mali quod cogitaveram facere ei.* Sic ubi Deus æquitatem viarum suarum dilucide exponit: Ezech. xviii. 25, 26, 27. *cum revertet improbus ab improbitate sua quam faciebat, exercet ius et iustitiam, hic animam suam vivam conservat.* et xxxiii. 14, 15. *quum dixero improbo, omnino moriturus es; si conversus a peccato suo exercuerit iudicium et iustitiam, &c. omnino vivet, non morietur.* et inculcatum illud duobus proxime citatis capitibus, illius v. 31, 32. huius v. 11. *Quare moreremini O Domus Israelis! non enim delector morte morientis, dictum Domini Iehovæ, avertite itaque vos et vivite. Dic iis, ne vivam ego, dictum Domini Iehovæ, si delector morte improbi; sed delector cum revertitur improbus a via sua, ut vivat: revertimini, revertimini a viis vestris pessimis, cur enim moreremini domus Israelis?* Luc. xiii. 5. *nisi resipiscatis, omnes similiter peribitis.* ergo si

But even if there be any decree of reprobation, Scripture everywhere declares, that as election is established and confirmed by faith, so reprobation is rescinded by repentance. Jer. vi. 30. "reprobate silver shall men call them, because Jehovah hath rejected them"; and yet in the third verse of the following chapter God addresses the same people—"amend your ways and your doings, and I will cause you to dwell in this place." So too in chap. xviii. 6, &c. where God compares his own right with that of the potter, whence St. Paul seems to have taken his metaphor, Rom. ix. "if that nation, against whom I have pronounced, turn from their evil, I will repent of the evil that I thought to do unto them." So too, where God enters into an explicit vindication of the justice of his ways, Ezek. xviii. 25–27. "when the wicked man turneth away from the wickedness that he hath committed, and doeth that which is lawful and right, he shall save his soul alive." xxxiii. 14, 15. "when I say unto the wicked, Thou shalt surely die, if he turn from his sin, and do that which is lawful and right," &c. &c. "he shall surely live, he shall not die." The same is inculcated in other parts of the chapters just quoted: xviii. 31, 32. "why will ye die, O house of Israel? for I have no pleasure in the death of him that dieth, saith the Lord Jehovah; wherefore turn yourselves, and live ye." xxxiii. 11. "say unto them, As I live, saith the Lord Jehovah, I have no pleasure in the death of the wicked; but that the wicked turn from his way and live; turn ye, turn ye from your evil ways, for why will ye die, O house of Israel?" Luke xiii. 5. "except ye repent, ye shall all likewise perish": therefore, if ye repent,

resipiscitis, non peribitis. Resipiscentia igitur si absit, quid
prodest electio: si adsit, quid obest reprobatio? Itaque Paulus
de iis ipsis quos electis oppositos dicit occaluisse Rom. xi. 7.
electi assecuti sunt, reliqui occaluerunt, subiungit statim v. 11.
num impegerunt ut exciderent? absit. et v. 23. &c. *sed et
illi, si non permanserint in incredulitate, inserentur: potens
enim est Deus rursum eos inserere* &c. Tandem v. 32. *con-
clusit enim Deus eos omnes in contumacia, ut omnium eorum
misereretur.*

Quod si Deus neminem nisi non obedientem, non credentem reiicit, certe gratiam etsi non parem attamen sufficientem
omnibus impertit, qua possint ad agnitionem veritatis et salutem pervenire: non parem; quia ne reprobis quidem, quos
vocant, parem gratiam largitus est Matt. xi. 21, 23. *væ Tibi
&c. nam si Tyri et Sidoni editæ fuissent virtutes, quæ editæ
sunt apud vos* &c. Luc. x. 13. idem. hoc enim iuris vendicat
sibi Deus, ut quivis alius in res suas, ut statuat de iis pro arbitrio suo, nec rationem reddere cogatur, quamvis iustissimam
reddere, si velit, possit: Rom. ix. 20, 21. *immo vero, O homo,
tu quis es, qui ex adverso responsas Deo? num dicet figmentum fictori, cur me tale fecisti? annon habet ius figulus in
lutum?* Causa igitur cur Deus non omnes pari gratia dignetur,

ye shall not perish. If then there be no repentance, of what advantage is election; or if there be repentance, of what injury is reprobation? Accordingly St. Paul, after speaking of those whom he describes as blinded, who are opposed to the elect,
5 Rom. xi. 7. "the election hath obtained it, and the rest were blinded," subjoins immediately, v. 11. "have they stumbled that they should fall? God forbid"; and v. 23, &c. "and they also, if they abide not in unbelief, shall be graffed in; for God is able to graff them in again," &c. lastly, he adds, v. 32. "God
10 hath concluded them all in unbelief, that he might have mercy upon all."

If then God reject none but the disobedient and unbelieving, he undoubtedly gives grace to all, if not in equal measure, at least sufficient for attaining knowledge of the truth and final
15 salvation. I have said, not in equal measure, because not even to the reprobate, as they are called, has he imparted uniformly the same degree of grace. Matt. xi. 21, 23. "woe unto thee, Chorazin," &c. "for if the mighty works which have been done in you, had been done in Tyre and Sidon," &c. See also
20 Luke x. 13. For God, as any other proprietor might do with regard to his private possessions, claims to himself the right of determining concerning his own creatures according to his pleasure, nor can he be called to account for his decision, though, if he chose, he could give the best reasons for it. Rom.
25 ix. 20, 21. "nay but, O man, who art thou that repliest against God? shall the thing formed say to him that formed it, Why hast thou made me thus? hath not the potter power over the clay?" That an equal portion of grace should not be extended

est suprema ipsius voluntas; quod sufficienti tamen omnes, est iustitia eius. Isa. v. 4. *quid faciendum amplius vineæ meæ, quod non fecerim in ea?* hæc enim dicuntur de Iudæis universis, non de electis tantum. et xxvi. 10. *cum gratia fit im-* 5 *probo, non discit iustitiam.* Ezech. xii. 2. *quibus sunt oculi ad videndum, nec viderunt; quibus aures ad audiendum, nec audierunt, quia domus rebellis sunt.* 2 Reg. xvii. 13. &c. *cumque contestaretur Iehova in Israelem et in Iudam per omnes prophetas, dicendo, revertimini* &c. *non auscultave-* 10 *rant sed obduraverant cervices suas.* 2 Chron. xxxvi. 15, 16. idem. Ioan. i. 9. *erat lux illa vera, quæ illuminat omnem hominem venientem in mundum.* et ix. 41. *si cæci essetis, non haberetis peccatum; nunc vero dicitis, videmus; itaque peccatum vestrum manet:* quia scilicet non ignorantia pec- 15 catis sed arrogantia. et xv. 22. *si non venissem, et locutus essem iis; peccatum non haberent; nunc autem non habent quod prætexant peccato suo.* et cap. xii. a v. 34. ad 41. *adhuc parvo tempore lux vobiscum est: ambulate dum lucem habetis, ne vos tenebræ deprehendant.* &c. *dum lucem habetis* 20 *credite in lucem, ut filii lucis fiatis.* Act. xiii. 46. *vobis necesse fuit primum exponi sermonem Dei: postquam autem illum repellitis, et indignos vos ipsos decernitis æterna vita, ecce, convertimus nos ad gentes.* et xiv. 16, 17. *qui præteritis ætatibus sivit omnes gentes suis ipsarum viis incedere. quam-*

to all, is attributable to the supreme will of God alone; that
there are none to whom he does not vouchsafe grace sufficient
for their salvation, is attributable to his justice. Isa. v. 4.
"what could have been done more in my vineyard, that I have
5 not done in it?" which is said of the whole nation of the Jews,
not of the elect only. xxvi. 10. "let favor be showed to the
wicked, yet will he not learn righteousness." Ezek. xii. 2.
"which have eyes to see, and see not, they have ears to hear,
and hear not; for they are a rebellious house." 2 Kings xvii.
10 13. "Jehovah testified against Israel, and against Judah, by
all the prophets, and by all the seers, saying, Turn ye from
your evil ways," &c. . . . "notwithstanding they would not
hear, but hardened their necks." See also 2 Chron. xxxvi.
15, 16. John i. 9. "that was the true light, which lighteth
15 every man that cometh into the world." ix. 41. "if ye were
blind, ye should have no sin; but now ye say, We see, therefore your sin remaineth"; namely, because your sin is the
fruit of pride, not of ignorance. xv. 22. "if I had not come
and spoken unto them, they had not had sin: but now they
20 have no cloak for their sin." xii. 34–41. "yet a little while is
the light with you: walk while ye have the light, lest darkness
come upon you," &c. "while ye have light, believe in the
light, that ye may be the children of light." Acts xiii. 46. "It
was necessary that the word of God should first have been
25 spoken to you, but seeing ye put it from you, and judge yourselves unworthy of everlasting life, lo, we turn to the Gentiles." xiv. 16, 17. "who in times past suffered all nations to
walk in their own ways: nevertheless he left not himself with-

quam non passus est se expertem esse testimonii. Rom. x. 20,
21. *inventus sum ab iis qui me non quærebant; manifestus
factus sum iis qui de me non interrogabant. adversus Israelem
autem dicit, toto die expandi manus meas ad populum non*
5 *obedientem et contradicentem.* 2 Cor. vi. 1, 2. *ecce nunc est
præstitutum illud tempus acceptum, ecce nunc dies salutis.*
Heb. iii. 7, 8. cum Psal. xcv. 7, 9. *hodie si vocem eius audie-
ritis, ne obdurate corda vestra.* Sane si peccatores tantummodo vult reverti, Ezech. xxxiii. 11. ut supra, si omnes vult
10 salvos, 1 Tim. ii. 4. si nullos perire, 2 Pet. iii. 9. quod satis sit
gratiæ, vult idem nemini deesse: ni velit, quo pacto veritatem
suam hominibus probare possit, non liquet. Neque vero ad
excusationem duntaxat eripiendam sufficientem esse sufficit
gratiam: inexcusabiles enim, etiamsi omnis gratiæ expertes,
15 periissemus. Verum ostentata semel gratia atque oblata, nisi
ea plane et revera sufficiens ad salutem sit, excusabiles profecto semper erunt qui pereunt, et iniuria peribunt. Quod
itaque a Mose pro concione ad Israelitas, Deut. xxix. 4. dictum est, *non dedit vobis Iehova mentem ad cognoscendum et*
20 *oculos ad videndum et aures ad audiendum usque in diem
hunc,* interpretandum est, id dici a Mose humanius et indul-
gentius, ne quid in tanto conventu populi fœdus iamiamque
cum Deo inituri, gravius aut asperius dixisse iudicaretur, si

out witness." Rom. x. 20, 21. "I was found of them that sought me not; I was made manifest unto them that asked not after me: but to Israel he saith, All day long I have stretched forth my hands unto a disobedient and gainsaying people."
5 2 Cor. vi. 1, 2. "behold, now is the accepted time; behold, now is the day of salvation." Heb. iii. 7, 8. compared with Psal. xcv. 7, 9. "to-day if ye will hear his voice, harden not your hearts." Undoubtedly if he desire that the wicked should turn from their way and live, Ezek. xxxiii. 11.—if he would
10 have all men to be saved, 1 Tim. ii. 4.—if he be unwilling that any should perish, 2 Pet. iii. 9. he must also will that an adequate proportion of saving grace shall be withholden from no man; for if otherwise, it does not appear how his truth towards mankind can be justified. Nor is it enough that only
15 so much grace shall be bestowed, as will suffice to take away all excuse; for our condemnation would have been reasonable, even had no grace at all been bestowed. But the offer of grace having been once proclaimed, those who perish will always have some excuse, and will perish unjustly, unless it be evi-
20 dent that the grace imparted is actually sufficient for salvation. So that what Moses said in his address to the Israelites, Deut. xxix. 4. "Jehovah hath not given you an heart to perceive, and eyes to see, and ears to hear, unto this day," must be understood as having been dictated by the kindness and tenderness
25 of his feelings, which led him to avoid the appearance of harshness and asperity in selecting that particular time for openly reproving the hardness of the hearts of so large an assembly of the people, who were then on the point of enter-

duritiam cordis eo præsertim tempore palam iis exprobrasset. Cum igitur eorum impœnitentiæ duæ dici causæ poterant, aut nondum data mens a Deo, cui liberum est, quandocunque vult, dare; aut Deo non reddita eorum obedientia, liberæ Dei
5 voluntatis mentionem fecit; eorum duritiam intelligendam reliquit. Certe enim quivis potuit hoc facile intelligere, si Deus mentem iis non dederat ad illum usque diem, in causa fuisse maxime duritiam ipsorum: vel dedisse quidem Deum (qui tot miracula eorum causa edidisset) et mentis et ocu-
10 lorum et aurium quod satis esset; ipsos autem datis uti noluisse.

Teneatur hoc itaque firmumque maneat: Deus neminem nisi post gratiam, eamque sufficientem, repudiatam ac spretam, idque sero, ad gloriam longanimitatis atque iustitiæ suæ patefaciendam, pœnitentiæ ac salutis æternæ aditu excludit.
15 Neque enim simpliciter et præcise usquam declaravit Deus voluntatem suam esse causam reprobationis, sed rationes voluntatis hac in re suæ passim exponit; gravissima nimirum reproborum peccata prius commissa aut prævisa, pœnitentiam nullam, spretam gratiam, Deum sæpius vocantem non au-
20 ditum. Non enim ut electio gratiæ, sic reprobatio soli assignanda est divinæ voluntati: Deut. ix. 5. *nequaquam propter iustitiam aut propter rectum animum tuum ingressurus es;*

ing into covenant with God. Since, therefore, there were two causes to which their impenitence might be ascribed—either, that a heart had not yet been given by God, who was at liberty to give it when he pleased, or, that they had not yielded obe-
5 dience to God—he made mention only of God's free will, leaving their hardness of heart to be suggested silently by their own consciences; for no one could be at a loss to perceive either that their own stubbornness must have been the principal cause, if to that day God had not given them an understand-
10 ing heart, or, on the contrary, that God, who had wrought so many miracles for their sakes, had abundantly given them a heart to perceive, and eyes to see, and ears to hear, but that they had refused to make use of these gifts.

Thus much, therefore, may be considered as a certain and
15 irrefragable truth: that God excludes no one from the pale of repentance and eternal salvation, till he has despised and re-jected the propositions of sufficient grace, offered even to a late hour, for the sake of manifesting the glory of his long-suffering and justice. So far from God having anywhere de-
20 clared in direct and precise terms that reprobation is the effect of his arbitrary will, the reasons which influence him in cases of this kind, are frequently stated: namely, the grievous sins of the reprobate previously committed, or foreseen before actual commission; want of repentance; contempt of grace;
25 deafness to the repeated calls of God. For reprobation must not be attributed, like the election of grace, to the divine will alone. Deut. ix. 5. "not for thy righteousness, or for the up-rightness of thine heart, dost thou go to possess their land: but

sed propter improbitatem gentium istarum Iehova expellit eas. Nam misericordiæ causam ullam aut rationem reddi necesse non est, nisi ipsam voluntatem misericordem; reprobationis autem, quam pœna sequitur, ut iusta esse possit, non

5 Dei voluntas, sed peccatum hominis causa sola esse debet, peccatum, inquam, aut commissum aut prævisum, gratia aut semper spreta aut sero nimis et pœnæ tantum formidine petita, cum iam tempus definitum gratiæ præteriit. Neque vero ob aliam causam reprobavit Deus, ob aliam condemnavit mor-

10 tique addixit, ut vulgo distinguunt; sed quos propter peccatum condemnavit, eos propter peccatum quemadmodum in tempore, ita etiam ab æterno reprobavit. Atque hæc non tam in voluntate divina, quam in ipsorum obstinato animo reprobatio est posita; non tam est decretum Dei quam ipso-

15 rum decretum reproborum de non agenda pœnitentia dum licet: Act. xiii. 46. *postquam illum repellitis, et indignos vos ipsos decernitis æterna vita.* Matt. xxi. 43. *lapidem reprobarunt* &c. *propterea tolletur a vobis regnum Dei.* 1 Pet. ii. 7, 8. idem. Matt. xxiii. 37. *quoties volui* &c. *et noluistis?* Neque

20 enim minus iniustum esset reprobationem decernere nisi propter peccatum quam condemnare. Quemadmodum igitur nulla condemnatio est nisi propter incredulitatem aut peccatum, Ioan. iii. 18, 19. *Qui non credit, iam condemnatus est, quia non credidit* &c. *hæc est condemnatio, quod lux venit in*

for the wickedness of these nations Jehovah thy God doth drive them out before thee." For the exercise of mercy requires no vindication; it is unnecessary to assign any cause for it, except God's own merciful will; whereas before reproba-
5 tion, which is followed by punishment, can be looked upon as just, the sin of the individual, not the arbitrary will of God must be its primary cause—sin, that is to say, either committed or foreseen, grace having been repeatedly rejected, or sought at length too late, and only through fear of punish-
10 ment, when the prescribed time was already past. For God does not reprobate for one cause, and condemn or assign to death for another, according to the distinction commonly made; but those whom he has condemned on account of sin, he has also reprobated on account of sin, as in time, so from
15 all eternity. And this reprobation lies not so much in the divine will, as in the obstinacy of their own minds; nor is it the decree of God, but rather of the reprobate themselves, by their refusal to repent while it is in their power. Acts xiii. 46. "ye put it from you, and judge yourselves unworthy of everlasting
20 life." Matt. xxi. 43. "the stone which the builders rejected," &c. "therefore the kingdom of God shall be taken from you." See also 1 Pet. ii. 7, 8. Matt. xxiii. 37. "how often would I have gathered thy children together," &c. "and ye would not." Nor would it be less unjust to decree reprobation, than
25 to condemn for any other cause than sin. Inasmuch, therefore, as there is no condemnation except on account of unbelief or of sin (John iii. 18, 19. "he that believeth not is condemned already, because he hath not believed," &c. "this is

mundum, sed dilexerunt homines potius tenebras quam lucem,
et xii. 48. *qui aspernatur me, nec recipit verba mea, habet qui*
iudicet ipsum, sermo quem locutus sum &c. 2 Thess. ii. 12.
ut damnentur omnes qui non crediderint; ita ex omnibus iis
5 locis quæ ad sanciendum reprobationis decretum afferuntur,
demonstrabimus neminem Dei decreto, nisi post gratiam repudiatam ac spretam, idque sero, pœnitentiæ ac salutis æternæ
aditu excludi. Ab illo Iacobi et Esaui exemplo Rom. ix. quoniam in eo ut permultis visum est, cardo huius quæstionis
10 vertitur, initium ducamus. Nec tam hic de prædestinatione
quam de immerita vocatione gentium ex merita Iudæorum
reiectione agi ostendemus.

Ostendit Paulus v. 6. non ideo excidisse verbum Dei Abra-
hamo factum quod eius posteri non omnes Christum rece-
15 perunt, sed plures ex Gentibus quam ex Iudæis; quia promissio non facta est in omnibus Abrahami filiis, sed in Isaaco,
v. 7. hoc est, *non qui filii carnis, ii filii Dei; sed qui sunt filii*
promissionis, reputantur in semine, v. 8. Non ergo filiis Abrahami carnalibus facta promissio est, sed filiis Dei, qui hinc
20 filii promissionis dicuntur. Quinam autem sint filii Dei,
quoniam hoc loco Paulus non dicit, petamus ab Ioan. i. 11, 12.

the condemnation, that light is come into the world, and men loved darkness rather than light": xii. 48. "he that rejecteth me, and receiveth not my words, hath one that judgeth him; the word that I have spoken," &c. 2 Thess. ii. 12. "that they
5 all might be damned who believed not the truth), the texts themselves which are produced in confirmation of the decree of reprobation will prove that no one is excluded by any decree of God from the pale of repentance and eternal salvation, unless it be after the contempt and rejection of grace, and that
10 at a very late hour.

I will begin with the case of Jacob and Esau, Rom. ix. because many are of opinion that it is decisive respecting the question at issue. It will be seen that predestination is not so much the subject of discussion in this passage as the unmer-
15 ited calling of the Gentiles after the Jews had been deservedly rejected.

St. Paul shows in the sixth verse that the word which God spake to Abraham, had not been frustrated, though so far from the whole of his posterity having received Christ, more
20 had believed among the Gentiles than among the Jews. For the promise was not made in all the children of Abraham, but in Isaac, v. 7; that is to say, "they which are the children of the flesh, these are not the children of God, but the children of the promise are counted for the seed," v. 8. The
25 promise therefore was not made to the children of Abraham according to the flesh, but to the children of God, who are therefore called the children of the promise. But since Paul does not say in this passage who are the children of God, an

ubi hanc ipsam multo licet brevius, tractat: *ad sua venit, et sui eum non receperunt, dedit iis hoc ius, ut filii Dei sint facti; nempe iis qui credunt in nomen eius.* promissum ergo est non carnis Abrahami, sed fidei eius filiis qui Christum

5 receperunt, Dei nempe et promissionis filiis, id est, credentibus: ubi enim promissio, ibi et fides esse debet. Altero exemplo ostendit, ne Isaaci quidem omnibus posteris Deum eandem gratiam largiri, sed filiis promissionis, id est, credentibus, longe potiorem; idque pro voluntate sua, ut nequis

10 possit quicquam suis meritis attribuere: v. 11, 12. *nondum enim natis pueris, cum nihil fecissent boni vel mali, ut, quod est secundum electionem, propositum Dei maneret non ex operibus sed ex vocante, dictum est ei, maior serviet minori:* propositum autem iuxta quam electionem? sane iuxta elec-

15 tionem ad quodvis beneficium, ad quodvis privilegium, et speciatim hic ad primogenituræ ius minoris, sive pueri sive populi: unde est, ut nunc Gentes præferat Iudæis. Et electionis quidem propositum hic audio, reprobationis nullum. Sat habet ab hoc exemplo Paulus electionis propositum ad

20 quamcunque gratiam aut beneficium stabilire. Quid nos am-

explanation must be sought from John i. 11, 12. where this very promise is briefly referred to; "he came unto his own, and his own received him not: but as many as received him, to them gave he power to become the sons of God, even to
5 them that believe on his name." The promise therefore is not to the children of Abraham in the flesh, but to as many of the children of his faith as received Christ, namely, to the children of God and of the promise, that is, to believers; for where there is a promise, there must be also a faith in that promise.
10   St. Paul then shows by another example, that God did not grant mercy in the same degree to all the posterity even of Isaac, but much more abundantly to the children of the promise, that is, to believers; and that this difference origi- nates in his own will: lest any one should arrogate any thing
15 to himself on the score of his own merits. v. 11, 12. "for the children being not yet born, neither having done any good or evil, that the purpose of God according to election might stand, not of works, but of him that calleth, it was said unto her, The elder shall serve the younger." The purpose of God,
20 according to what election? Doubtless according to the elec- tion to some benefit, to some privilege, and in this instance specially to the right of primogeniture transferred from the elder to the younger of the sons or of the nations; whence it arises that God now prefers the Gentiles to the Jews. Here
25 then I acknowledge that his *purpose of election* is expressly mentioned, but not of reprobation. St. Paul contents himself with establishing the general principle of election to any mercy or benefit whatever from this single example. Why

plius ex his verbis acerbum et truculentum, quod non habent, exprimere conamur? Non, si *maior,* sive puer sive populus, de populo certe hoc potius dicitur, *serviet minori,* maior continuo reprobus decernitur: non, si minor, maiore gratia, maior continuo nulla dignatus. Id enim neque de Esauo qui in domo patris verum Dei cultum edoctus est, neque de eius posteris, quos constat cum cæteris Gentibus ad fidem vocatos, dici potest. unde illud additum in benedictione Esaui Gen. xxvii. 42. *erit tamen cum planxeris, ut rumpendo excutias iugum eius e collo tuo.* certe si Esaui servitus reprobationem eius significavit, significant et hæc verba eam non fuisse sempiternam. At hoc iugulat; *Iacobum dilexi, Esauum autem odio habui,* v. 13. in quo autem dilexit aut odit Deus? interrogatus ipse ostendit, Mal. i. 2, 3. *odisse se in eo Esauum, quod disposuit montes eius desolationi:* dilexit ergo in eo Iacobum quod eum in Patriam ex Babylonia reduxit; iuxta eandem electionem qua nunc gentes invitat, Iudæos relinquit. Utcunque ne hinc quidem reprobationis decretum statuitur, quamvis hoc a Paulo ad illustrandum illud dictum, *maior serviet minori,* quasi obiter adiiciatur: non enim hoc, ut superius illud, pueris nondum natis, sed iamdiu mortuis, Mal. i. 2, 3. cum alter gratiam Dei arripuisset, alter sprevisset. Nec

should we endeavor to extort from the words a harsh and severe meaning, which does not belong to them? If the elder shall serve the younger, whether the individual or the people be intended (and in this case it certainly applies best to the people), it does not therefore follow that the elder shall be reprobated by a perpetual decree; nor, if the younger be favored with a larger amount of grace, that the elder shall be favored with none. For this cannot be said of Esau, who was taught the true worship of God in the house of his father, nor of his posterity, whom we know to have been called to the faith with the rest of the Gentiles. Hence this clause is added in Esau's blessing, Gen. xxvii. 40. "it shall come to pass when thou shalt have the dominion, that thou shalt break his yoke from off thy neck"; which, if the servitude of Esau implies his reprobation, must certainly imply that it was not to last for ever. There is, however, an expression in the same chapter which is alleged as decisive: "Jacob have I loved, but Esau have I hated," v. 13. But how did God evince his love or hatred? He gives his own answer, Mal. i. 2, 3. "I hated Esau, and laid his mountains and his heritage waste." He evinced his love therefore to Jacob, by bringing him back again into his country from the land of Babylon; according to the purpose of that same election by which he now calls the Gentiles, and abandons the Jews. At the same time even this text does not prove the existence of any decree of reprobation, though St. Paul subjoins it incidentally, as it were, to illustrate the former phrase, "the elder shall serve the younger"; for the text in Mal. i. 2, 3. differs from the present passage, inasmuch

tamen hinc gratia minuitur, cum Iacobus immeritum plane
se fassus sit, Gen. xxxiii. 10. Asserit itaque Paulus ius Dei
etiam immerentibus gratiam quamcunque largientis, v. 14,
15. et confirmat, *neque volentis esse neque currentis* (ne
5 Iacobi quidem qui immeritum plane se fassus est; nec Iudæorum, qui legis iustitiam sectabantur) *sed miserentis Dei,*
v. 16. Sic asseruit ius Dei Paulus in electione quacunque
etiam immerentium; quales videbantur tunc esse gentes.

Nunc pergit idem demonstrare in abdicatione Iudæorum,
10 ex iustitia quam exercere summo iure potest in quosvis peccatores; nec tamen in reprobatione et odio nondum natorum,
sed in obduratione et pœna iam insigniter impiorum, v. 17,
18. *dicit enim scriptura Pharaoni, ad hoc ipsum excitavi te*
&c. neque enim *excitavi* est decrevi; sed excitando eliciebat
15 solum duritiem Pharaonis iam sibi notam, dum æquissima
imperabat; iuxta illud Exod. iii. 19. *ego novi non esse vobis*
permissurum regem. Sic 1 Pet. ii. 7, 8. (in quod caput multa

as it does not speak of the children yet unborn, but of the children when they had been long dead, after the one had eagerly accepted, and the other had despised the grace of God. Nor does this derogate in the least from the freedom of grace, 5 because Jacob himself openly confesses that he was undeserving of the favor which he had obtained; Gen. xxxiii. 10. St. Paul therefore asserts the right of God to impart whatever grace he chooses even to the undeserving, v. 14, 15. and concludes—"so then it is not of him that willeth, or of him that 10 runneth" (not even of Jacob, who had openly confessed himself undeserving, nor of the Jews who followed after the law of righteousness), "but of God that showeth mercy," v. 16. Thus St. Paul establishes the right of God with respect to any election whatever, even of the undeserving, such as the Gen- 15 tiles then seemed to be.

The apostle then proceeds to prove the same with regard to the rejection of the Jews, by considering God's right to exercise justice upon sinners in general; which justice, however, he does not display by reprobation, and hatred towards 20 the children yet unborn, but by judicially hardening the heart, and punishing flagrant offenders. v. 17, 18. "the Scripture saith unto Pharaoh, Even for this same purpose have I raised thee up," &c. He does not say, "I have decreed," but, "I have raised up"; that is, in raising up Pharaoh he only called into 25 action, by means of a most reasonable command, that hardness of heart, with which he was already acquainted. So Exod. iii. 19. "I am sure that the king of Egypt will not let you go." So too 1 Pet. ii. (in which chapter much has been borrowed

ex hoc capite traducta sunt) *ad quod etiam constituti fuerant;
inobedientes nimirum qui lapidem illum angularem reprobaverant; qui non parendo sermoni, impingunt.* ante igitur
reprobantes hi quidem, quam reprobati erant; tum demum
5　ad pœnam constituti, ex quo immorigeri esse perstiterunt.
Sequentibus porro versibus 19, 20, 21. (ut ad Romanos re-
deamus) *dices ergo mihi, quid adhuc succenset* &c.? *cur me
fecisti sic?* durum scilicet et ad dedecus, cum aliorum mise-
rearis? non decreti reprobationis, sed pœnæ obdurationis, quæ
10　sera post longam Dei tolerantiam et extrema fere maximorum pœna peccatorum est, rationem exponit: v. 21. *annon
habet potestatem figulus in lutum?* id est, idoneam sibi ma-
teriam, ut quos vult, non immorigeros tamen, honore afficiat;
iuxta illud 2 Tim. ii. 21. *si quis sese ab his expurgarit, erit vas
15　ad decus* &c. contumaces autem adhuc magis obduret, id est,
pœna afficiat, iuxta versum huius capitis sequentem: *pertulit
multa longanimitate vasa iræ, compacta ad interitum.* a quo
autem compacta, nisi a propria duritie? a qua et iniquitas
eorum completa est, Gen. xv. 16. iuxta et illud Eph. v. 6.
20　*propter hæc venit ira Dei in filios contumaciæ.* passiva autem

from the ninth of Romans), v. 7, 8. "unto them which be disobedient, the stone which the builders disallowed" . . . &c. "even to them that stumble at the word, being disobedient; whereunto also they were appointed." They therefore
5 first disallowed Christ, before they were disallowed by him; they were then finally appointed for punishment, when they persisted in disobedience.

To return, however, to the chapter in Romans. We read in the next verses, 19–21. "thou wilt say then unto me, Why
10 doth he yet find fault?" &c. "why hast thou made me thus"; that is, hard-hearted, and a vessel unto dishonor, whilst thou showest mercy to others? In answer to which the apostle proves the reasonableness, not indeed of a decree of reprobation, but of that penal hardness of heart, which, after much
15 long-suffering on the part of God, is generally the final punishment reserved for the more atrocious sins. v. 21. "hath not the potter power over the clay?" that is, the material fitted for his own purposes, to put honor upon whom he chooses, provided it be not on the disobedient; as it is said 2 Tim. ii. 21.
20 "if a man purge himself from these, he shall be a vessel unto honor," &c. whilst he hardens still more the hearts of the contumacious, that is, he punishes them, according to the next verse of this chapter—"he endured with much long-suffering the vessels of wrath fitted to destruction." Whence
25 then were they fitted, except from their own hardness of heart, whereby the measure of their iniquity was completed! See Gen. xv. 16. and Eph. v. 6. "because of these things cometh the wrath of God upon the children of disobedience." Nor

non semper externam vim notant: sic deditum vitiis, sic pro-
pensum ad hoc vel illud dicimus, quem suopte solum ingenio
sic se habere tamen intelligimus. Postremo nihil hic aliud
fuisse propositum Paulo, nisi ut liberam atque gratuitam Dei
5 misericordiam ostenderet in gentibus vocandis atque ser-
vandis, qui audientes fidei fuissent, iustum iudicium in ob-
durandis Iudæis atque aliis, qui legem operum obstinate sec-
tarentur, evincunt tres ultimi versus capitis, quibus totius
quæstionis conclusio continetur; [Rom. ix.] v. 30, 31, 32.
10 *Quid igitur dicemus? nempe gentes—apprehendisse—ex*
fide. non ergo ex electione absque fide. *Israelem—non per-*
venisse—Quare? quia non ex fide. non ergo ex decreto reprobationis absque incredulitate.

Prætervecti hunc scopulum, in reliquis vix hærebimus.
15 Psal. xcv. 10, 11. *quadraginta annis fastidio habui genera-*
tionem illam, &c. *quibus in ira mea eos non ingressuros in*
requiem meam. Hic vide quam sero decreverit Deus; nec
nisi tentatores sui et obduratos (siquidem his typis metienda
spiritualia sunt, quod supra in Esauo factum est) æterna
20 requie exclusisse. 2 Chron. xxxvi. 15, 16. *cumque mitteret*
Iehova &c. *eo quod clementer amplecteretur populum suum,*
subsannabant nuntios Dei &c. *donec accensus est æstus iræ*

does the use of the passive voice always imply the sufferance
of some external force; for we speak of one being given up to
vice, or inclined to this or that propensity, meaning only that
such is the bias of his own disposition. Finally, the three last
5 verses of the chapter, which contain the conclusion of the
whole question, are a convincing proof that St. Paul only intended to show on the one hand, the free and gratuitous mercy
of God in calling the Gentiles to salvation, who would be
obedient to the faith, and, on the other, the justice of his
10 judgments in hardening the hearts of the Jews and others,
who obstinately adhered to the law of works. v. 30–32. "what
shall we say then? that the Gentiles . . . have attained to
righteousness which is of faith"—not therefore of election
independent of faith: "but Israel . . . hath not attained:
15 wherefore? because they sought it not by faith"—not therefore of a decree of reprobation independent of unbelief.

After having passed this difficulty, those which remain
will scarcely interrupt our course. Psal. xcv. 10, 11. "forty
years long was I grieved with this generation," &c. "unto
20 whom I sware in my wrath that they should not enter into
my rest." Here we must observe how long it was before God
passed his decree, and that (if we may reason by analogy respecting spiritual things, from types of this kind, as was done
before in the case of Esau) he excluded from his eternal rest
25 only those who tempted him, and whose hearts were hardened. 2 Chron. xxxvi. 15, 16. "Jehovah God of their fathers
sent to them by his messengers," &c. "because he had com-
passion on his people and on his dwelling-place: but they

Iehovæ in populum suum, adeo ut non esset curatio. Isa.
xxviii. 12, 13. *cum dixerit iis, hæc est ipsa requies* &c. *et
noluerint auscultare: sed fuit iis verbum Iehovæ præceptum
præcepto* &c. *ut pergerent, et corruentes* &c. *idcirco audite
verbum Iehovæ, viri irrisores* &c. *et* xxix. 10. *nam perfudit
vos Iehova spiritu soporis, et obstipavit oculos vestros* &c.
ratio redditur, non decretum Dei, sed ipsorum peccata gravissima v. 13, 14. *propterea quod appropinquans populus iste
ore suo* &c. *cor autem suum procul* &c. *idcirco peribit sapientia sapientum* &c. Sic Matt. xi. 25, 26. gloriam tibi tribuo
*Pater, quod hæc occultaveris sapientibus et intelligentibus, et
ea detexeris infantibus: etiam Pater, quia ita libuit apud Te.*
Verum cur hoc ita libuerit, ne in libitu solo positum hoc putemus, cur etiam idcirco Patri gloriam Christus tribuerit,
superiores versus 21, 22, 23. docebunt; in quibus ostenditur,
quales illi sapientes prius fuerint; nempe contemptores gratiæ divinæ. et cap. xiii. 11. *vobis datum est: illis non est datum.*
cur autem? sequens versus ostendit: *quisquis enim habet,
dabitur ei, et amplius habebit; quisquis autem non habet,
etiam quod habet, tolletur ab eo.* Quis hæc non de aspernan-

mocked the messengers of God," &c. "until the wrath of Jehovah arose against his people, till there was no remedy."
Isa. xxviii. 12, 13. "to whom he said, This is the rest wherewith ye may cause the weary to rest," &c. "yet they would not
5 hear: but the word of Jehovah was unto them precept upon
precept," &c. "that they might go, and fall backward," &c.
"wherefore hear the word of Jehovah, ye scornful men," &c.
xxix. 10. "for Jehovah hath poured out upon you the spirit of
deep sleep, and hath closed your eyes." The reason is given,
10 v. 13, 14. where it appears that it was not on account of God's
decree, but of their own grievous wickedness: "forasmuch as
this people draw near me with their mouth," &c. "but have
removed their heart far from me . . . therefore the wisdom
of their wise men shall perish," &c. Matt. xi. 25, 26. "I thank
15 thee, O Father, because thou hast hid these things from the
wise and prudent, and hast revealed them unto babes: even
so, Father, for so it seemed good in thy sight." Lest we should
attribute this solely to the arbitrary will of God, the verses preceding will explain why *it seemed good,* and why Christ
20 ascribes glory to the Father on this account, v. 21–23; where
it is disclosed what those wise men had first shown themselves
to be, namely, despisers of the divine grace. See also xiii. 11.
"it is given unto you to know the mysteries of the kingdom of
heaven, but to them it is not given." Do we ask why? the next
25 verse subjoins the reason: "whosoever hath, to him shall be
given, and he shall have more abundance; but whosoever hath
not, from him shall be taken away even that he hath." This
can be applied only to those who have first voluntarily re-

tibus prius divinam gratiam interpretatur, sicut et eadem pene verba cap. xxv. 29. de negligentibus? itaque et v. 13. cap. xiii. ut supra, eandem porro rationem persequitur: *propterea per parabolas loquar iis, quia conspicientes non vident* &c. Hinc facile solvuntur illa loca: Ioan. viii. 43. *non potestis audire sermonem meum.* Nempe quia cum possetis noluistis, per incredulitatem vestram non potestis, in qua obdurescitis; non per decretum Dei; vel saltem per arrogantiam audire non sustinetis, vel denique, ut v. sequente 44. *quia ex patre Diabolo estis, et cupiditates patris vestri vultis exsequi.* et v. 46. *si veritatem dico, quare non creditis vos mihi?* Ipse pro iis respondet v. 47. *propterea vos non auditis, quia ex Deo non estis.* Quid hoc est *non estis ex Deo!* an scilicet, non estis electi? immo vero idem est quod esse ex Diabolo, v. 44. id est, Diabolum sequi potius quam Deum. Sic x. 26. *vos non creditis; non enim estis ex ovibus meis.* Quare non ex ovibus meis? an quia sic decretum erat? minime: sed quia non auditis, quia me non sequimini: *oves meæ vocem meam audiunt, et sequuntur me,* v. 27. vos quod etiam atque etiam inculco, non creditis. v. 25, 26. *dixi vobis, nec creditis: opera quæ ego facio in nomine patris mei, hæc testantur de me: sed vos non creditis; non enim estis ex ovibus meis.* Ordo sic est: non creditis, quia non estis ex ovibus meis; non estis ex ovibus meis, quia me non auditis, me non sequimini. Certe cur non crederent, causam aliquam edere Christus voluit, quæ incredulitatis culpam in ipsos conferret, non culpa eximeret: at si

jected divine grace, in the sense in which nearly the same words are addressed to the slothful servant, xxv. 29. In the same manner must be explained xiii. 13. "therefore speak I to them in parables, because they seeing see not," &c. Hence
5 an easy solution is afforded for other texts. John viii. 43. "ye cannot hear my word";—because when ye were able, ye would not, ye are now unable, not on account of any decree of God, but through unbelief in which you are hardened, or through pride, on account of which you cannot endure to
10 hear the word; or lastly, as it is expressed in the following verse, because "ye are of your father the devil, and the lusts of your father ye will do." Again, v. 46. "if I say the truth, why do ye not believe me?" Christ himself answers the question, v. 47. "ye therefore hear not, because ye are not of God."
15 Not to be of God cannot signify not elect, but means, as it is said in v. 44. "to be of the devil," that is, to follow the devil rather than God. So too, x. 26. "ye believe not, because ye are not of my sheep." Why "not of my sheep?" Because it was so decreed? By no means, but because ye do not hear the
20 word; because ye do not follow me; "my sheep hear my voice, and they follow me," v. 27. Ye, as I repeatedly tell you, do not believe. v. 25, 26. "I told you, and ye believed not; the works that I do in my Father's name, they bear witness of me: but ye believe not, because ye are not of my sheep, as I said
25 unto you." The argument runs thus: ye do not believe, because ye are not of my sheep; ye are not of my sheep, because ye neither hear my word, nor follow me. Christ certainly intended to give such a reason for their unbelief as would

ex ovibus eius non esse, idem est quod non esse electos, id
quod in eorum potestate non fuit, excusavit profecto eos potius quam inculpavit, quod minime videtur voluisse. Sic xii.
39, 40. ex Isa. vi. 10. *propterea non poterant credere quia*
5 *iterum dixit Esaias, excæcavit oculos eorum* &c. Non quo
facultatem aut gratiam credendi vel verba Esaiæ iis ademerint,
vel decretum Dei Esaiæ ore promulgatum præripuerit, sed
quod prophetæ verba declarent, quid causæ esset, cur credere
non potuerint; quia nempe Deus excæcaverat oculos eorum:
10 cur autem excæcaverat, antecedens caput exponit, a v. 4: quia
nempe nihil aliud restabat faciendum vineæ suæ infrugiferæ,
quam ut eam exscinderet. Quod adhuc etiam clarius est Luc.
xiii. 24, 25. *multi studebunt intrare, et non poterunt, ex quo*
videlicet surrexerit paterfamilias, et occluserit ostium. et xiv.
15 24. *dico vobis, neminem virorum illorum qui vocati fuerant*
gustaturum cœnam meam. et xix. 42. *si vel tu nosses hoc*
saltem tuo die quæ ad pacem tuam pertinent, sed ea nunc
occulta sunt oculis tuis. Rom. i. 21. cum 24. et 26. *propterea*
quod cum Deum cognoverint, ut Deum non glorificaverunt
20 &c. *Quapropter etiam tradidit* &c. *propter hoc tradidit eos*
&c. 2 Thess. ii. 10, 11, 12. *cum omni seductione iniustitiæ*
in iis qui pereunt, propterea quod amorem veritatis non re-
ceperunt, ut salvi fierent: et propter hoc mittet iis Deus effi-

throw the fault of it upon themselves, not as would exempt them from blame; whereas if not to be of his sheep, be interpreted to mean not to be of the elect, a privilege which had never been within their option, his words would contain an
5 excuse for their conduct, rather than a reproof, which would be contrary to his obvious purpose. Again, xii. 39, 40, compared with Isa. vi. 10. "therefore they could not believe, because that Esaias saith again, He hath blinded their eyes," &c. Not because the words of Isaiah, or the decree of God deliv-
10 ered by his mouth, had previously taken away from them the grace or power of believing irrespectively; but, as the prophet declares, alleging the reason why they could not believe, because God had blinded their eyes. Why he had blinded their eyes the preceding chapter explains, v. 4, &c. because nothing
15 more remained to be done to his unfruitful vineyard, but to cut it down. This appears still more clearly Luke xiii. 24, 25. "many will seek to enter in, and shall not be able: when once the master of the house is risen up, and hath shut to the door." xiv. 24. "I say unto you, that none of those men that were
20 bidden shall taste of my supper." xix. 42. "if thou hadst known, at least in this thy day, the things which belong unto thy peace! but now they are hid from thine eyes." Rom. i. 21, 24, 26. "because that when they knew God, they glorified him not as God," &c. "wherefore God also gave them up,"
25 &c. "for this cause God gave them up," &c. 2 Thess. ii. 10-12. "with all deceivableness of unrighteousness in them that perish; because they received not the love of the truth, that they might be saved: and for this cause God shall send

caciam erroris, ut credant mendacio; ut damnentur omnes qui non crediderint veritati, sed acquieverint in iniustitia. et iii. 2. *non enim omnium est fides.* non est nimirum obstinate et absurde sceleratorum, ut ex verbis antecedentibus eodem
5 sensu percipitur. Sic 1 Pet. ii. 7, 8. *lapis quem reprobaverunt &c. et lapis ad quem impingitur, et petra offendiculi nempe iis qui impingunt ad sermonem non assentientes ad quod etiam constituti fuerant.* ad non assentiendum scilicet; quare? quia lapidem illum reprobaverant et ad eum impegerant, re-
10 probantes ipsi priusquam reprobati. Hæc qui attenderit, facile perspiciet, in hac potissimum doctrina esse toties offensum, dum pœna obdurationis a decreto reprobationis non distinguitur. iuxta illud Prov. xix. 3. *stultitia hominis pervertit viam ipsius, et adversus Iehovam indignatur animus eius.* Accusant
15 enim revera Deum, tametsi id vehementer negant: et ab Homero etiam ethnico egregie redarguuntur, Odyss. I. 7.

> Αὐτῶν γὰρ σφετέρῃσιν ἀτασθαλίῃσιν ὄλοντο.

> Suis enim ipsorum flagitiis perierunt.

Et rursus, inducta Iovis persona: Lib. I. 32.

20
> Ὦ πόποι, οἶον δή νυ θεοὺς βροτοὶ αἰτιόωνται!
> Ἐξ ἡμέων γάρ φασι κάκ᾽ ἔμμεναι· οἱ δὲ καὶ αὐτοὶ
> σφῆσιν ἀτασθαλίῃσιν, ὑπὲρ μόρον, ἄλγε᾽ ἔχουσιν.

> Papæ, ut scilicet Deos, mortales accusant!
> Ex nobis enim dicunt mala esse: illi vero ipsi
25
> Suismet flagitiis, præter fatum, dolores patiuntur.

them strong delusion, that they should believe a lie: that they all might be damned who believed not the truth, but had pleasure in unrighteousness." iii. 2. "for all men have not faith"; that is, obstinate and unreasonable sinners have it not;
5 which the context shows is the sense intended. 1 Pet. ii. 7, 8. "the stone which the builders disallowed," &c. "and a stone of stumbling and rock of offence, even to them which stumble at the word, being disobedient; whereunto also they were appointed"—that is, to be disobedient. And why? Because they
10 had disallowed that stone, and had stumbled upon it, disallowing Christ themselves before they were disallowed by him. Attention to these points will show that mistakes arise on the doctrine in question as often as the proper distinction between the punishment of hardening the heart and the de-
15 cree of reprobation is omitted to be made; according to Prov. xix. 3. "the foolishness of man perverteth his way, and his heart fretteth against Jehovah." For such do in effect impugn the justice of God, however vehemently they may disclaim the intention; and might justly be reproved in the words of the
20 heathen Homer, *Odyssey*, I. 7:

> "they perish'd self-destroy'd
> By their own fault."

And again, in the person of Jupiter, I. 32:

> "Perverse mankind! whose wills, created free,
25 > Charge all their woes on absolute decree:
> All to the dooming gods their guilt translate,
> And follies are miscall'd the crimes of fate."

CAPUT V.

PRÆFATIO.

DE FILIO DEI SANCTOQUE SPIRITU hoc loco dicturus, non, nisi denuo præfatus aggrediendum esse opus tam arduum existimavi. Equidem si Romanæ Ecclesiæ, quæ credi sibi propter se in omnibus fidei capitibus
5 postulat, alumnum me esse profiterer, quamquam illa negat Trinitatis doctrinam hodie receptam ullo ex loco scripturarum probari posse, tamen, sic edoctus vel saltem assuefactus, in illius solo decreto atque auctoritate acquievissem: nunc cum eorum ex numero sim, qui solum Dei verbum pro norma fidei
10 agnoscant, id libere expromo, quod multo mihi quam recepta opinio liquere clarius ex sacris literis videtur, cur quisquam, qui vel Protestantis vel Reformati nomen eandemque mecum fidei normam præ se ferat; eam ob rem offendi in me possit non video: præsertim cum imponam nemini quicquam;
15 quod credibilius esse arbitror tantummodo proponam; hoc unicum obtestatus qui ista legerit, ut animo veritatis duntaxat studioso, minimeque præiudiciis occupato singula velit æstimare atque expendere. Neque enim scripturæ auctoritatem, quæ sacrosancta est, sed hominum interpretationes humano

CHAPTER V.

PREFATORY REMARKS.

I CANNOT enter upon subjects of so much difficulty as the SON OF GOD and the HOLY SPIRIT, without again premising a few introductory remarks. If indeed I were a member of the Church of Rome, which requires implicit obedience to its creed on all points of faith, I should have acquiesced from education or habit in its simple decree and authority, even though it denies that the doctrine of the Trinity, as now received, is capable of being proved from any passage of Scripture. But since I enrol myself among the number of those who acknowledge the word of God alone as the rule of faith, and freely advance what appears to me much more clearly deducible from the Holy Scriptures than the commonly received opinion, I see no reason why any one who belongs to the same Protestant or Reformed Church, and professes to acknowledge the same rule of faith as myself, should take offence at my freedom, particularly as I impose my authority on no one, but merely propose what I think more worthy of belief than the creed in general acceptation. I only entreat that my readers will ponder and examine my statements in a spirit which desires to discover nothing but the truth, and with a mind free from prejudice. For without intending to oppose the authority of Scripture, which I consider inviolably sacred, I only take upon myself to refute human interpretations as often as the occasion requires, con-

iure immo vero officio quoties ita facto est opus, suscepi re-
darguendas. Quod si cum iis controversia hæc esset, qui voce
ipsa divina explicatam sibi cœlitus quam tuentur doctrinam
præstare nobis possent, impius plane sit, qui contra vel mutire
5 nedum obstrepere ausit: Sin ii sunt, qui supra vires humanas,
communemque spiritum nihil vendicare sibi queant, Quid est
æquius quam ut permittant alteri eandem atque ipsi ratione
ac via veritatem indaganti, et prodesse aliis æque cupienti, suas
quemque sedulo inquirendi, libereque disserendi partes obti-
10 nere. nunc divina ope subnixi rem ipsam aggrediamur.

DE FILIO DEI.

Hactenus efficientia Dei INTERNA fuit in decretis.

EXTERNA est decretorum executio, qua aliquid apud se
decretum, extra se efficit.

15 Estque vel GENERATIO vel CREATIO vel RERUM OMNIUM GUBER-
NATIO.

GENERATIO est qua Filium ex decreto suo genuit Deus unicum. unde et Pater primario dicitur.

formably to my right, or rather to my duty as a man. If indeed those with whom I have to contend were able to produce direct attestation from heaven to the truth of the doctrine which they espouse, it would be nothing less than impiety to venture to raise, I do not say a clamor, but so much as a murmur against it. But inasmuch as they can lay claim to nothing more than human powers, assisted by that spiritual illumination which is common to all, it is not unreasonable that they should on their part allow the privileges of diligent research and free discussion to another inquirer, who is seeking truth through the same means and in the same way as themselves, and whose desire of benefiting mankind is equal to their own.

In reliance, therefore, upon the divine assistance, let us now enter upon the subject itself.

OF THE SON OF GOD.

Hitherto I have considered the INTERNAL EFFICIENCY of God, as manifested in his decrees.

His EXTERNAL EFFICIENCY, or the execution of his decrees, whereby he carries into effect by external agency whatever decrees he has purposed within himself, may be comprised under the heads of GENERATION, CREATION, and the GOVERNMENT OF THE UNIVERSE.

First, GENERATION, whereby God, in pursuance of his decree, has begotten his only Son; whence he chiefly derives his appellation of Father.

Generation must be an external efficiency, since the Father

Externam autem esse efficientiam generationem necesse est, cum Filius sit a Patre persona altera; et fatentur idem Theologi, cum emanationem quandam esse Filii a Patre ipsi tradunt; id quod clarius in doctrina de sancto spiritu appa-
5 rebit; quem cum eiusdem essentiæ cum Patre esse doceant, emanare tamen et egredi et procedere et spirari a Patre, quæ omnia externam efficientiam testantur, non negant. addunt etiam eiusdem essentiæ cum Patre esse Filium; et ab æterno generatum. Unde hic locus et per se difficilis omnino est, et
10 receptam methodum sectanti implicatissimus: cum enim Pater duplici sensu genuisse Filium in sacris literis dicatur, uno proprio, altero metaphorico, nempe vel producendo, vel exaltando; quæ loca ad exaltationem Filii, munusque media-torium pertinent, ea plerique ad generationem eius eamque
15 æternam asserendam adhibuerunt; excusandi quidem, si ex-cusatio hic ullum habet locum, cum versiculum tota scriptura quo generationem Filii æternam probarent, reperire potuerint nullum. hoc constat, quicquid moderni quidam contra argu-tantur, Filium, verbi sive Sermonis sub nomine, in principio
20 extitisse, rerum creatarum primum fuisse, per quem deinde cætera omnia tam in cœlo quam in terra sunt facta. Ioan. i. 1, 2, 3. *in principio erat Sermo et Sermo ille erat apud Deum, eratque ille Sermo Deus* &c. et xvii. 5. *nunc igitur glorifica*

and Son are different persons; and the divines themselves acknowledge this, who argue that there is a certain emanation
of the Son from the Father (which will be explained when the
doctrine concerning the Holy Spirit is under examination);
5 for though they teach that the Spirit is co-essential with the
Father, they do not deny its emanation, procession, spiration,
and issuing from the Father, which are all expressions de-
noting external efficiency. In conjunction with this doctrine
they hold that the Son is also co-essential with the Father, and
10 generated from all eternity. Hence this question, which is
naturally very obscure, becomes involved in still greater diffi-
culties if the received opinion respecting it be followed; for
though the Father be said in Scripture to have begotten the
Son in a double sense, the one literal, with reference to the
15 production of the Son, the other metaphorical, with reference
to his exaltation, many commentators have applied the passages which allude to the exaltation and mediatorial functions of Christ as proof of his generation from all eternity.
They have indeed this excuse, if any excuse can be received in
20 such a case, that it is impossible to find a single text in all
Scripture to prove the eternal generation of the Son. Certain,
however, it is, whatever some of the moderns may allege to
the contrary, that the Son existed in the beginning, under the
name of the logos or word, and was the first of the whole
25 creation, by whom afterwards all other things were made
both in heaven and earth. John i. 1–3. "in the beginning was
the Word, and the Word was with God, and the Word was
God," &c. xvii. 5. "and now, O Father, glorify me with thine

me tu Pater apud temetipsum ea gloria quam habui apud te priusquam mundus esset. Col. i. 15, 18. *primogenitus omnis rei creatæ.* Apoc. iii. 14. *principium creationis Dei.* 1 Cor. viii. 6. *Iesus Christus per quem omnia.* Eph. iii. 9. *qui omnia hæc condidit per Iesum Christum.* Col. i. 16. *per eum condita sunt omnia* &c. Heb. i. 2. *per quem etiam mundum condidit.* hinc v. 10. *tu creasti.* de quo plura vide infra, Cap. vii. de creatione. hæc omnia existentiam quidem Filii ante mundum conditum testantur, generationem eius æternam non item. cætera quæ afferuntur loca metaphoricam tantum generationem indicant, id est, suscitationem a mortuis aut ad mediatoris munera unctionem, ipso Paulo Psalmi secundi interprete. Psal. ii. 7. *decretum enarraturus sum. Iehova dixit mihi, Filius meus es, ego hodie genui te.* Quod sic interpretatur Paulus, Act. xiii. 32, 33. *suscitato Iesu, uti etiam in Psalmo secundo scriptum est, Filius meus es, ego hodie genui te.* Rom. i. 4. *definito Filio Dei potenter secundum spiritum sanctitatis per resurrectionem ex mortuis.* hinc Col. i. 18. Apoc. i. 5. *primogenitus ex mortuis.* deinde Heb. i. 5. ubi de exaltatione Filii supra Angelos loquitur. *Nam cui dixit unquam angelorum, Filius meus es, ego hodie genui te. Ac*

own self with the glory which I had with thee before the world was." Col. i. 15, 18. "the first-born of every creature." Rev. iii. 14. "the beginning of the creation of God." 1 Cor. viii. 6. "Jesus Christ, by whom are all things." Eph. iii. 9. 5 "who created all things by Jesus Christ." Col. i. 16. "all things were created by him and for him." Heb. i. 2. "by whom also he made the worlds," whence it is said, v. 10, "thou, Lord, in the beginning hast laid the foundation of the earth"; respecting which more will be said in the seventh 10 chapter, on the Creation.

All these passages prove the existence of the Son before the world was made, but they conclude nothing respecting his generation from all eternity. The other texts which are produced relate only to his metaphorical generation, that is, to 15 his resuscitation from the dead, or to his unction to the mediatorial office, according to St. Paul's own interpretation of the second Psalm: "I will declare the decree; Jehovah hath said unto me, Thou are my Son; this day have I begotten thee," which the apostle thus explains, Acts xiii. 32, 33. "God 20 hath fulfilled the promise unto us their children, in that he hath raised up Jesus again; as it is also written in the second Psalm, Thou art my Son; this day have I begotten thee." Rom. i. 4. "declared to be the Son of God with power, according to the Spirit of holiness, by the resurrection from the 25 dead." Hence, Col. i. 18. Rev. i. 4. "the first begotten of the dead." Heb. i. 5, speaking of the exaltation of the Son above the angels; "for unto which of the angels said he at any time, Thou art my Son, this day have I begotten thee? and again,

rursum ego ero illi in Patrem, et ille erit mihi in Filium. et v.
5, 6. ubi de sacerdotio Christi. *Ita et Christus non ipse sibi
hunc honorem tribuit ut fieret pontifex, sed is qui dixit ei,
Filius meus es tu, ego hodie genui te. Sicut et in alio Psalmo*
5 *dicit, tu es sacerdos in æternum* &c. quin et genuisse Deus,
id est, regem creasse Filium ex Psalmo secundo intelligetur,
v. 6, 7. *ego inungens regem meum præfeci Sioni monti sanctitatis meæ;* tum sequente versu postquam inunxerat regem
suum, unde et *Christus* dicitur, *ego,* inquit, *hodie genui te.*
10 Sic Heb. i. 4, 5. *tanto præstantior factus angelis, quanto excellentius præ illis sortitus est nomen.* Quod autem nomen nisi
Filii? ut sequens versus declarat. *Nam cui dixit unquam angelorum, Filius meus es tu, ego hodie genui te.* idem ipse de
se profitetur Filius. Ioan. x. 35, 36. *mene quem Pater sancti-*
15 *ficavit et misit in mundum, vos dicitis blasphemare quia dixi,
Filius Dei sum.* Eodem loquendi tropo sanctos etiam homines
genuisse Deus dicitur ratione licet longe inferiore.

Ex omnibus autem superius citatis locis præsertim cum toto
Psalmo secundo collatis et diligentissime animadversis facile
20 apparet, non necessitate naturæ, quod contendi solet, sed decreto et voluntate Patris tam fuisse Filium quocunque modo
genitum quam pontificem et regem constitutum atque ex
mortuis suscitatum. Neque vero hoc obstat quo minus vel

I will be to him a Father, and he shall be to me a Son." Again,
v. 5, 6, with reference to the priesthood of Christ; "so also
Christ glorified not himself to be made an High Priest, but
he that said unto him, Thou art my Son, this day have I be-
5 gotten thee: as he saith also in another place, Thou art a priest
for ever," &c. Further, it will be apparent from the second
Psalm, that God has begotten the Son, that is, has made him
a king: v. 6. "yet have I set my King upon my holy hill of
Sion"; and then in the next verse, after having anointed his
10 King, whence the name of *Christ* is derived, he says, "this
day have I begotten thee." Heb. i. 4, 5. "being made so much
better than the angels, as he hath by inheritance obtained a
more excellent name than they." No other name can be intended but that of Son, as the following verse proves: "for
15 unto which of the angels said he at any time, Thou art my
Son; this day have I begotten thee?" The Son also declares
the same of himself. John x. 35, 36. "say ye of Him whom
the Father hath sanctified, and sent into the world, Thou
blasphemest, because I said, I am the Son of God?" By a sim-
20 ilar figure of speech, though in a much lower sense, the saints
are also said to be begotten of God.

It is evident however upon a careful comparison and examination of all these passages, and particularly from the
whole of the second Psalm, that however the generation of
25 the Son may have taken place, it arose from no natural necessity, as is generally contended, but was no less owing to the
decree and will of the Father than his priesthood or kingly
power, or his resuscitation from the dead. Nor is it any ob-

quovis modo genitus vel *proprius* Dei *Filius* dicatur. Rom.
viii. 32. proprius enim Dei Filius non alia ratione est dictus,
nisi quod non alium habuerit Patrem præter unum Deum;
itaque et Deum ipse proprium dixit Patrem. Ioan. v. 18. Nam
5 Adami ex pulvere facti opifex erat Deus, potius quam Pater;
Filii autem ex substantia eius producti proprius erat Pater:
nec tamen inde sequitur eiusdem esse cum Patre essentiæ;
Sic enim maxime omnium improprie Filius nominaretur:
proprius enim Filius non est Patri coævus, multo minus eius-
10 dem numero essentiæ cum Patre, ne idem sit Pater et Filius
eiusdem; proprius Pater non necessitate naturæ, sed libera
voluntate gignit; quod et perfectius, et ad honorem pater-
num accommodatius est, Dei præsertim qui omnia iam sæpius
ex libris sacris ostenditur ex consilio voluntatis suæ liberrime
15 agere; sic ergo genuisse.

Poterat enim Deus certe salva essentia sua non genuisse;
cum ad essentiam Dei, qui propagatione prorsus non indiget,
generatio nihil pertineat: quod autem ad essentiam suam
sive naturam nihil pertinet, id utique naturæ necessitate tan-
20 quam naturalis agens non agit; si natura necessario egit,

jection to this that he bears the title of begotten, in whatever sense that expression is to be understood, or of God's *own Son,* Rom. viii. 32. For he is called the own Son of God merely because he had no other Father besides God, whence 5 he himself said, that *God was his Father,* John v. 18. For to Adam God stood less in the relation of Father, than of Creator, having only formed him from the dust of the earth; whereas he was properly the Father of the Son made of his own substance. Yet it does not follow from hence that the 10 Son is co-essential with the Father, for then the title of Son would be least of all applicable to him, since he who is properly the Son is not coeval with the Father, much less of the same numerical essence, otherwise the Father and the Son would be one person; nor did the Father beget him from any 15 natural necessity, but of his own free will, a mode more perfect and more agreeable to the paternal dignity; particularly since the Father is God, all whose works, and consequently the works of generation, are executed freely according to his own good pleasure, as has been already proved from 20 Scripture.

For questionless, it was in God's power consistently with the perfection of his own essence not to have begotten the Son, inasmuch as generation does not pertain to the nature of the Deity, who stands in no need of propagation; but what- 25 ever does not pertain to his own essence or nature, he does not effect like a natural agent from any physical necessity. If the generation of the Son proceeded from a physical necessity, the Father impaired himself by physically begetting a co-equal;

parem sibi natura gignendo se imminuit: id quod non magis potuit Deus facere, quam seipsum negare; non igitur nisi decreto ac libera voluntate sua gignere potuit.

Decreto itaque suo adeoque in tempore genuit Deus Filium;
5 decretum enim præcesserit decreti executionem necesse fuit, id quod adiecta vox *hodie* satis declarat. quo proinde scripturarum loco, qui generationem Filii æternam statuunt, se tueantur nusquam reperio: Nam illud Micæ. v. 2. non generationem sed opera eaque a principio tantum edita præ se fert.
10 sed de his infra fusius. *Unigenitus* etiam Filius dicitur. Ioan. i. 14. (*et spectavimus gloriam eius, gloriam, inquam ut unigeniti egressi a Patre*) et v. 18. *unigenitus Dei qui est in sinu Patris*. c. iii. 16. *ut filium suum unigenitum dederit.* v. 18. idem. 1 Ioan. iv. 9. *filium suum unigenitum misit.* Non tamen
15 essentia cum Patre unum, quippe visibilem, datum, missum, egressum a Patre, sed per eminentiam unigenitum dictum aliorum multorum ratione quos itidem Deus genuisse dicitur. Ioan. i. 13. *ex Deo geniti:* 1 Ioan. iii. 9. *Quisquis natus est ex Deo* &c. Iacob. i. 18. *Is quia voluit, progenuit nos sermone*
20 *veritatis, ut* &c. 1 Ioan. v. 1. *quisquis credit* &c. *ex Deo genitus est.* 1 Pet. i. 3. *qui ex multa sua misericordia genuit nos in*

which God could no more do than he could deny himself; therefore the generation of the Son cannot have proceeded otherwise than from a decree, and of the Father's own free will.

5 Thus the Son was begotten of the Father in consequence of his decree, and therefore within the limits of time, for the decree itself must have been anterior to the execution of the decree, as is sufficiently clear from the insertion of the word *to-day*. Nor can I discover on what passage of Scripture the 10 assertors of the eternal generation of the Son ground their opinion, for the text in Micah v. 2. does not speak of his generation, but of his works, which are said only to have been wrought *from of old*. But this will be discussed more at large hereafter.

15 The Son is also called *only begotten*. John i. 14. "and we beheld his glory, the glory as of the only begotten of the Father." v. 18. "the only begotten Son which is in the bosom of the Father." iii. 16, 18. "he gave his only begotten Son." 1 John iv. 9. "God sent his only begotten Son." Yet he is not 20 called one with the Father in essence, inasmuch as he was visible to sight, and given by the Father, by whom also he was sent, and from whom he proceeded; but he enjoys the title of only begotten by way of superiority, as distinguished from many others who are also said to have been born of God. 25 John i. 13. "which were born of God." 1 John iii. 9. "whosoever is born of God, doth not commit sin." James i. 18. "of his own will begat he us with the word of truth." 1 John v. 1. "whosoever believeth," &c. "is born of God." 1 Pet. i. 3.

spem. &c. verum cum genitus nusquam in sacris libris Filius dicatur nisi sensu, ut supra, metaphorico, credibile est Filium dici unigenitum, eo potissimum quod unus sit mediator Dei atque hominum.

5   Itaque et *primogenitus* dicitur Filius Rom. viii. 29. *ut is sit primogenitus inter multos fratres.* Col. i. 15. *primogenitus omnis rei creatæ.* v. 18. *primogenitus ex mortuis.* Heb. i. 6. *cum inducit primogenitum.* Apoc. iii. 14. *principium creationis Dei.* Quæ loca omnia et unam eius cum Patre essentiam,
10 et generationis æternitatem excludunt. quin et de Israele, Exod. iv. 22. *sic dicit Iehova, Filius meus, primogenitus meus est Israel:* etiam de Ephraimo, Ier. xxxi. 9. *primogenitus meus est.* et de piis omnibus, Heb. xii. 23. *ad conventum primogenitorum.*

15   Atque hactenus fere metaphorica generatio fuit: cum autem proprie qui gignit alium a se nondum existentem, efficiat ut sit; Deusque si natura necessario gignit non nisi Deum sibi parem gignere; nec Deus gigni possit; quorum altero sequeretur duos esse Deos infinitos, altero causam primam effectum
20 fieri, quod nemo sanus concesserit. quærendum est quo sensu quove modo Deus Pater Filium genuerit, id quoque Scriptura

"which according to his abundant mercy hath begotten us again unto a lively hope." But since throughout the Scriptures the Son is never said to be begotten, except, as above, in a metaphorical sense, it seems probable that he is called *only begotten* principally because he is the one mediator between God and man.

So also the Son is called the *first born*. Rom. viii. 29. "that he might be the first born among many brethren." Col. i. 15. "the first born of every creature." v. 18. "the first born from the dead." Heb. i. 6. "when he bringeth in the first begotten into the world." Rev. iii. 14. "the beginning of the creation of God"—all which passages preclude the idea of his co-essentiality with the Father, and of his generation from all eternity. Thus it is said of Israel, Exod. iv. 22. "thus saith Jehovah, Israel is my son, even my first born"; and of Ephraim, Jer. xxxi. 9. "Ephraim is my first born"; and of all the saints, Heb. xii. 23. "to the general assembly of the first born."

Hitherto only the metaphorical generation of Christ has been considered; but since to generate another who had no previous existence, is to give him being, and that if God generate by a physical necessity, he can generate nothing but a co-equal Deity, which would be inconsistent with self-existence, an essential attribute of Divinity; (so that according to the one hypothesis there would be two infinite Gods, or according to the other the *first* or *efficient* cause would become the *effect,* which no man in his senses will admit) it becomes necessary to inquire how or in what sense God the Father can have begotten the Son. This point also will be easily explained

sacra facile expediet. Cum enim Filius dicitur *primogenitus omnis rei creatæ,* et Apoc. iii. 14. *principium creationis Dei,* quid aliud planius intelligi potest, quam quod Deus Filium rerum omnium primum divina natura præditum sua volun-
5 tate creavit sive generavit aut produxit, sicut in plenitudine temporis humanam naturam ex Maria virgine mirifice pro-creavit. Divinæ autem naturæ generationem nemo neque sub-limius neque disertius declarat, quam Apostolus ille Heb. i. 2, 3. *quem constituit hæredem omnium per quem etiam*
10 *mundum condidit. Qui cum sit effulgentia gloriæ et character subsistentiæ illius* &c. Ex quo quid aliud intelligi potest quam Deum divinæ naturæ quantum voluit Filio impertisse, immo etiam substantiæ divinæ, modo ne substantia pro essentia tota accipiatur, quam Pater et Filio dederit et eandem numero sibi
15 retinuerit; hoc enim non est gignere sed repugnantia loqui. Hæc sunt quæ de Filii Dei generatione divinitus traduntur: Qui sapere vult altius, revera non sapit, sed inani captus phi-losophia vel potius sophistica implicat se statim et tenebris circumdat.
20   Verum cum Christus non solum Dei Filius unigenitus sed etiam Deus aliquoties in Scripturis nominetur, unumque om-nino esse Deum omnes doceamur, plerisque hæc stare simul non posse persuasis acutioribus, ut sibi videbantur, in men-tem venit res sane inaudita, et ab omni ratione alienissima,

by reference to Scripture. For when the Son is said to be *the first born of every creature,* and *the beginning of the creation of God,* nothing can be more evident than that God of his own will created, or generated, or produced the Son before all things, endued with the divine nature, as in the fulness of time he miraculously begat him in his human nature of the Virgin Mary. The generation of the divine nature is described by no one with more sublimity and copiousness than by the apostle to the Hebrews, i. 2, 3. "whom he hath appointed heir of all things, by whom also he made the worlds; who being the brightness of his glory, and the express image of his person," &c. It must be understood from this, that God imparted to the Son as much as he pleased of the divine nature, nay of the divine substance itself, care being taken not to confound the substance with the whole essence, which would imply, that the Father had given to the Son what he retained numerically the same himself; which would be a contradiction of terms instead of a mode of generation. This is the whole that is revealed concerning the generation of the Son of God. Whoever wishes to be wiser than this, becomes foiled in his pursuit after wisdom, entangled in the deceitfulness of vain philosophy, or rather of sophistry, and involved in darkness.

Since, however, Christ not only bears the name of the only begotten Son of God, but is also several times called in Scripture God, notwithstanding the universal doctrine that there is but one God, it appeared to many, who had no mean opinion of their own acuteness, that there was an inconsistency in this; which gave rise to an hypothesis no less strange than

Filium, quamvis persona atque numero alterum, essentia tamen cum Patre esse unum adeoque Deum unum.

Verum nisi ratio saltem unius et duorum apud Deum atque homines eadem semper sit, frustra nobis mandatum illud 5 primum toties intonaverit Deus, unum atque solum se esse Deum, si alter praeterea existere dicatur, qui et ipse unus Deus credi debeat. Unus et alter unius essentiae esse non possunt; Deus est unum ens, non duo; una essentia unius est entis, una etiam subsistentia, quae nihil aliud quam essentia substantialis 10 est; si uni essentiae duas subsistentias dederis sive personas, repugnantia dixeris; essentiam unam et non unam. si una essentia divina communis est duorum, habebit se illa essentia sive Deitas aut ut totum ad partes, aut ut genus ad species, aut denique ut subiectum commune ad accidentia sua. nihil 15 horum concesseris, quae absurdissima sequantur quo alio modo una tertia possit duorum pluriumve esse, nunquam ex-pediverint.

Quod si verba ipsius Dei reges et magnates alloquentis satis expendissent, Psal. lxxxii. 6. *ego dico, Dii quidem estis, et* 20 *filii altissimi vos omnes* et ipsius Christi. Ioan. x. 35. *si illos dixit deos ad quos sermo Dei factus est, et non potest solvi*

repugnant to reason, namely, that the Son, although personally and numerically another, was yet essentially one with the Father, and that thus the unity of God was preserved.

But unless the terms unity and duality mean the same with God as with man, it would have been to no purpose that God had so repeatedly inculcated that first commandment, that he was the one and only God, if another could be said to exist besides, who also himself ought to be believed in as the one God. Unity and duality cannot consist of one and the same essence. God is one ens, not two; one essence and one subsistence, which is nothing but a substantial essence, appertain to one ens; if two subsistences or two persons be assigned to one essence, it involves a contradiction of terms, by representing the essence as at once simple and compound. If one divine essence be common to two persons, that essence or divinity will either be in the relation of a whole to its several parts, or of a genus to its several species, or lastly of a common subject to its accidents. If none of these alternatives be conceded, there is no mode of escaping from the absurd consequences that follow, such as that one essence may be the third part of two or more.

There would have been no occasion for the supporters of these opinions to offer such violence to reason, nay even to so much plain scriptural evidence, if they had duly considered God's own words addressed to kings and princes, Psal. lxxxii. 6. "I have said, Ye are gods, and all of you are children of the Most High"; or those of Christ himself, John x. 35. "if he called them Gods, unto whom the word of God

scriptura, et Pauli, 1 Cor. viii. 5, 6. *etiamsi sint qui dicantur Dii, et in cœlo et in terra: (sicut sunt Dii multi et Domini multi) nobis tamen unus est Deus Pater ille a quo omnia* &c. Petri denique 2. Ep. i. 4. *ut per hæc efficeremini divinæ con-*
5 *sortes vel participes naturæ:* quod longe maius est quam esse deos, quo sensu reges dii dicti sunt, nec tamen sanctos quisquam eiusdem cum Deo essentiæ fore idcirco crediderit; hæc, inquam, si satis expendissent, tantam vim inferre rationi, immo Scripturarum tot testimoniis luculentissimis necesse
10 non habuissent.

Nos itaque in sacris rationi renuntiemus; quod divina scriptura docet, id unice sequamur. expectet igitur nemo dum hic longum ex metaphysicis apparatum præmittam, et personalitatum illud totum drama advocem, cum hoc primum ex
15 plurimis sacræ scripturæ locis clarissimum sit, unum esse vere ac proprie atque a seipso summum Deum: et unus cum dicitur, quandoquidem unam duntaxat personam, quod aiunt, id est, unam numero, humana ratio et loquendi usus, Deique populus Iudaicus semper intellexit, ex sacris libris quæramus,
20 quis ille unus, ille verus atque summus Deus sit: idque imprimis ex evangelio: hoc enim apertissimum esse oportet, quod Christus ipse suos Apostolos, quod ipsi Apostoli suos discipulos de uno Deo explanate et copiose docuerunt: hac in parte obscurum aut ambiguum esse evangelium, minime est
25 credendum. Neque enim ad id datum est evangelium, ut de

came, and the Scripture cannot be broken—"; or those of St. Paul, 1 Cor. viii. 5, 6. "for though there be that are called gods, whether in heaven or earth (for there be gods many and lords many), but to us there is but one God, the Father, of whom are all things," &c. or lastly of St. Peter, ii. 1, 4. "that by these ye might be partakers of the divine nature," which implies much more than the title of gods in the sense in which that title is applied to kings; though no one would conclude from this expression that the saints were co-essential with God.

Let us then discard reason in sacred matters, and follow the doctrine of Holy Scripture exclusively. Accordingly, no one need expect that I should here premise a long metaphysical discussion, and advocate in all its parts the drama of the personalities in the Godhead: since it is most evident, in the first place, from numberless passages of Scripture, that there is in reality but one true independent and supreme God; and as he is called one (inasmuch as human reason and the common language of mankind, and the Jews, the people of God, have always considered him as one person only, that is, one in a numerical sense), let us have recourse to the sacred writings in order to know who this one true and supreme God is. This knowledge ought to be derived in the first instance from the gospel, since the clearest doctrine respecting the one God must necessarily be that copious and explanatory revelation concerning him which was delivered by Christ himself to his apostles, and by the apostles to their followers. Nor is it to be supposed that the gospel would be ambiguous or obscure on this subject; for it was not given for the purpose of promul-

natura Dei incredibilia et nova, Deique populo antea prorsus inaudita expromeret, sed ut promissam a Deo Abrahami salutem Gentium per Dei filium Messiam annuntiaret: *Deum nemo vidit unquam: unigenitus Filius qui est in sinu Patris,*
5 *ille nobis exposuit.* Ioan. i. 18. Filium itaque imprimis De Deo consulamus.

Filii apertissimo testimonio, Pater est ille unus verus Deus, a quo omnia. Marc. xii. 28, 29, 32. interrogatus a Scriba quodnam esset primum omnium mandatum, respondit ex
10 Deut. vi. 4. *primum omnium mandatum est, audi Israel, Dominus Deus noster, Dominus unus est:* vel ut est Hebraice, *Iehova Deus noster, Iehova unus.* Assensit Scriba; *unus est Deus, nec alius est præter eum.* Assensum illum Christus approbavit v. 34. Scribam autem ut et omnes Iudæos sic intel-
15 lexisse, unum esse Deum ut qui una duntaxat, nunc vulgo quod aiunt persona sit, manifestissimum est; eumque fuisse solum Deum Patrem probatur ex Ioan. viii. 41. 54. *unum Patrem habemus Deum. Pater meus is est qui glorificat me; quem vos dicitis Deum vestrum esse.* et iv. 21. *neque in monte*
20 *hoc neque Hierosolymis adorabitis Patrem.* Convenit igitur Christo cum universo populo Dei, Patrem esse unum illum atque solum Deum. tam enim obscurum fuisse, perque tot

gating new and incredible doctrines respecting the nature of God, hitherto utterly unheard of by his own people, but to announce salvation to the Gentiles through Messiah the Son of God, according to the promise of the God of Abraham.

5 "No man hath seen God at any time; the only begotten Son, which is in the bosom of the Father, he hath declared him," John i. 18. Let us therefore consult the Son in the first place respecting God.

According to the testimony of the Son, delivered in the 10 clearest terms, the Father is that one true God, by whom are all things. Being asked by one of the scribes, Mark xii. 28, 29, 32. which was the first commandment of all, he answered from Deut. vi. 4. "the first of all the commandments is. Hear, O Israel, the Lord our God is one Lord"; or as it is in the 15 Hebrew, "Jehovah our God is one Jehovah." The scribe assented; "there is one God, and there is none other one but he"; and in the following verse Christ approves this answer. Nothing can be more clear than that it was the opinion of the scribe, as well as of the other Jews, that by the unity of God 20 is intended his oneness of person. That this God was no other than God the Father, is proved from John viii. 41, 54. "we have one Father, even God. It is my Father that honoreth me; of whom ye say that he is your God." iv. 21. "neither in this mountain, nor yet at Jerusalem, shall ye worship the Father." 25 Christ therefore agrees with the whole people of God, that the Father is that one and only God. For who can believe it possible for the very first of the commandments to have been so obscure, and so ill understood by the Church through such a

sæcula non intellectum prorsus in Ecclesia primum omnium mandatum, duasque alteras personas ignotas plane in populo Dei, divino honore ad illam usque ætatem caruisse, quis credat? cum Deus de evangelico etiam cultu docens populum
5 suum, Iehovam unum quem semper habuerint pro Deo præmoneat habiturum, et Davidem, id est, Christum pro rege ac Domino. Ier. xxx. 9. *servient Iehovæ Deo suo, et Davidi regi suo, quem excitabo ipsis.* Sane hic Christus, qualem eum a populo suo sub evangelio vel nosci vel coli Deus volebat, a
10 Iehova uno Deo et natura et titulo distinguitur. Itaque nec ipse Christus Dei Filius in Evangelio aliud nos docet de uno Deo atque lex docuerat; eumque Patrem esse suum clarissime ubique asserit. Ioan. xvii. 3. *hæc est vita æterna, ut cognoscant te illum solum verum Deum, et quem misisti, Iesum Chris-*
15 *tum.* et xx. 17. *ascendo ad patrem meum et patrem vestrum, et ad Deum meum et Deum vestrum.* certe si Pater est Deus Christi et Deus noster, Deusque est unus, Quis est Deus præter Patrem?

Hoc etiam Christi Apostolus et interpres Paulus, tam clare
20 tamque perspicue et quasi id unum agens nos docet, ut nemo in Ecclesia Pastor catechumenum de uno Deo, quemadmodum humana omnis ratio unum numero intelligit, disertius

succession of ages, that two other persons, equally entitled to
worship, should have remained wholly unknown to the people of God, and debarred of divine honors even to that very
day? especially as God, where he is teaching his own people
5 respecting the nature of their worship under the gospel, fore-
warns them that they would have for their God the one
Jehovah whom they had always served, and David, that is,
Christ, for their King and Lord. Jer. xxx. 9. "they shall serve
Jehovah their God, and David their King, whom I will raise
10 up unto them." In this passage Christ, such as God willed
that he should be known or worshipped by his people under
the gospel, is expressly distinguished from the one God Jehovah, both by nature and title. Christ himself therefore, the
Son of God, teaches us nothing in the gospel respecting the
15 one God but what the law had before taught, and everywhere
clearly asserts him to be his Father. John xvii. 3. "this is life
eternal, that they might know thee, the only true God, and
Jesus Christ whom thou hast sent." xx. 17. "I ascend unto
my Father and your Father; and to my God and your God":
20 if therefore the Father be the God of Christ, and the same be
our God, and if there be none other God but one, there can
be no God besides the Father.

Paul, the apostle and interpreter of Christ, teaches the same
in so clear and perspicuous a manner, that one might almost
25 imagine the inculcation of this truth to have been his sole
object. No teacher of catechumens in the Church could have
spoken more plainly and expressly of the one God, according
to the sense in which the universal consent of mankind has

et planius docere potuerit. 1 Cor. viii. 4, 5, 6. *scimus ido-*
lum nihil esse in mundo, et nullum esse Deum alium nisi
unum: nam etiamsi sint qui dicantur dii et in cœlo et in terra
(sicut sunt dii multi et domini multi) nobis tamen unus est
5 *Deus, Pater ille, a quo omnia, et nos in ipso, et unus Dominus*
Iesus Christus, per quem omnia et nos per ipsum. Hic *nullum*
esse Deum alium vel alterum, *nisi unum,* non essentiam solum
sed personam etiam alteram quamcunque excludit; diserte
enim v. 6. *ille unus est Pater;* non alia igitur persona nisi una.
10 quemadmodum esse alium ad asserendam sancti spiritus personam Theologi ex Ioan. xiv. 16. argumentari solent: et *Diis*
dictis sive in cœlo sive in terra, solus *Deus pater ille a quo*
omnia, et *multis unus* numero opponitur: Filius etsi alius
Deus, hic *Dominus* tantum appellatur: is *a quo omnia* ab eo
15 *per quem omnia* clare, et siquidem diversitas causandi diver-
sitatem essentiæ arguit, essentia distinguitur. Numerica porro
differentia cum ab essentia fluat, qui duo sunt numero, duo
sint etiam essentia necesse est. Unus Dominus, nempe factus
a Deo patre Act. ii. 36. magis ergo Dominus Pater, qui fecit:
20 etiamsi hic Dominus non dicatur: Nam qui Patrem *Deum*
unum dicit, dicit eundem unum summum Dominum; ut est

agreed to understand unity of number. 1 Cor. viii. 4–6. "we know that an idol is nothing in the world, and that there is none other God but one: for though there be that are called gods, whether in heaven or in earth (as there be gods many and lords many), but to us there is but one God, the Father, of whom are all things, and we in him; and one Lord Jesus Christ, by whom are all things, and we by him." Here the expression "there is none other God but one" excludes not only all other essences, but all other persons whatever; for it is expressly said in the sixth verse, that "the Father is that one God": wherefore there is no other person but one; at least in that sense which is intended by divines, when they argue from John xiv. 16. that there is *another,* for the sake of asserting the personality of the Holy Spirit. Again, to those "who are called gods, whether in heaven or in earth, God the Father of whom are all things" is opposed singly; he who is numerically "one God," to "many gods." Though the Son be another God, yet in this passage he is called merely "Lord"; he "of whom are all things" is clearly distinguished from him "by whom are all things," and if a difference of causation prove a difference of essence, he is distinguished also in essence. Besides, since a numerical difference originates in difference of essence, those who are two numerically, must be also two essentially. There is "one Lord," namely he whom "God the Father hath made," Acts ii. 36. much more therefore is the Father Lord, who made him, though he be not here called Lord. For he who calls the Father "one God," also calls him one Lord above all, as Psal. cx. 1. "the Lord saith unto my

Psal. cx. 1. *dixit Dominus Domino meo.* de quo loco infra uberius. Qui *unum Dominum Iesum Christum* dicit, non dicit eundem unum Deum, præsertim cum et Dominus et Christus a Deo Patre sit factus Act. ii. 36. quem itaque hic
5 dicit *unum Dominum Iesum Christum,* eiusdem alibi et Deum et Dominum dicit Patrem. Eph. i. 17. *Deus Domini nostri Iesu Christi.* 1 Cor. xi. 3. *caput Christi Deum.* et xv. 28. *ipse Filius subiicietur ei.* Sane pater si *pater Christi,* si *Deus Christi,* si *caput Christi,* si is cui Christus Dominus
10 immo ipse Filius subiicitur et subiicietur, quid abest quin Pater sit eiusdem Christi Domini etiam Dominus, eiusdem Christi Dei etiam Deus; cum Christus quo modo est Dominus, quo modo Filius, eodem esse Deum necesse sit? postremo Pater is est *a quo* et *ex quo,* et *per quem,* et *in quem*
15 *sunt omnia,* Rom. xi. 36. Heb. ii. 10. Filius non *a quo,* sed *per quem* duntaxat; idque addita exceptione, *omnia,* nempe *quæ facta sunt,* Ioan. i. 3. *omnia, excepto eo qui subiecit ei omnia,* 1 Cor. xv. 27. Clarum est igitur intelligi debere *per quem* nempe secundaria ac delegata vi *sunt omnia.* et par-
20 ticulam *per* cum ad Patrem refertur, principem notare causam, ut Ioan. vi. 57. *vivo per Patrem;* cum ad Filium, secundariam et instrumentalem: de quo infra clarius.

Lord," a passage which will be more fully discussed hereafter. He who calls Jesus Christ "one Lord," does not call him one God, for this reason among others, that "God the Father hath made him both Lord and Christ," Acts ii. 36. Elsewhere

5 therefore he calls the Father both God and Lord of him whom he here calls "one Lord Jesus Christ." Eph. i. 17. "the God of our Lord Jesus Christ." 1 Cor. xi. 3. "the head of Christ is God." xv. 28. "the Son also himself shall be subject unto him." If in truth the Father be called "the Father of Christ,"

10 if he be called "the God of Christ," if he be called "the head of Christ," if he be called the God to whom Christ described as the Lord, nay, even as "the Son himself, is subject, and shall be subjected," why should not the Father be also the Lord of the same Lord Christ, and the God of the same God Christ;

15 since Christ must also be God in the same relative manner that he is Lord and Son? Lastly, the Father is he "of whom," and "from whom," and "by whom" and "for whom are all things"; Rom. xi. 36. Heb. ii. 10. The Son is not he "of whom," but only "by whom"; and that not without an ex-

20 ception, namely, "all things which were made." John i. 3. "all things, except him which did put all things under him," 1 Cor. xv. 27. It is evident therefore that when it is said "all things were by him," it must be understood of a secondary and delegated power; and that when the particle "by" is used

25 in reference to the Father, it denotes the primary cause, as John vi. 57. "I live by the Father"; when in reference to the Son, the secondary and instrumental cause: which will be explained more clearly on a future occasion.

Sic Eph. iv. 4, 5, 6. *unum est corpus et unus spiritus, sicut et vocati estis in unam spem vocationis vestræ: unus Dominus, una fides, unum baptisma: unus est Deus et pater omnium, qui est supra omnes, et per omnes, et in omnibus vobis.* Hic unus est spiritus, unus Dominus, at unus est Pater: et ita unus Deus, quemadmodum cætera illa omnia una sunt, id est numero, adeoque ipsa persona. 1 Tim. ii. 5. *unus est Deus, unus etiam mediator Dei et hominum, homo Christus Iesus.* hic a natura inferiori, homo potius nominatur totus mediator, ne vel par Patri, vel idem existimetur Deus, cum de Uno Deo distincte et accurate agitur. Et sane quemadmodum sui mediator ad se aliquis esse queat, expediri nulla ratione potest: iuxta illud Gal. iii. 20. *mediator unius non est: Deus vero unus est.* mediator igitur Dei quo pacto Deus? Quid quod ipse de se constanter testatus est Ioan. viii. 28. a seipso nihil facere, et v. 42. a seipso non venire. Certe ergo ad seipsum non agit mediatorem; ad seipsum mediator non redit. Rom. v. 10. *reconciliati sumus Deo per mortem Filii eius.* Cui Deo reconciliati sumus, is si unus est, non erit Deus is per quem reconciliamur, cum alter sit; nam si est idem, ipse medius inter se et nos, reconciliabit nos sibi per se; quod prorsus inextricabile est.

Cum hæc omnia per se tam clara sint, ut nulla explana-

Again, Eph. iv. 4–6. "there is one body and one Spirit, even as ye are called in one hope of your calling; one Lord, one faith, one baptism; one God and Father of all, who is above all, and through all, and in you all." Here there is one Spirit, and one Lord; but the Father is one, and therefore God is one in the same sense as the remaining objects of which unity is predicated, that is, numerically one, and therefore one also in person. 1 Tim. ii. 5. "there is one God, and one mediator between God and men, the man Christ Jesus." Here the mediator, though not purely human, is purposely named man, by the title derived from his inferior nature, lest he should be thought equal to the Father, or the same God, the argument distinctly and expressly referring to one God. Besides, it cannot be explained how any one can be a mediator to himself on his own behalf; according to Gal. iii. 20. "a mediator is not a mediator of one, but God is one." How then can God be a mediator of God? Not to mention that he himself uniformly testifies of himself, John viii. 28. "I do nothing of myself," and v. 42. "neither came I of myself." Undoubtedly therefore he does not act as a mediator to himself; nor return as a mediator to himself. Rom. v. 10. "we were reconciled to God by the death of his Son." To whatever God we were reconciled, if he be one God, he cannot be the God by whom we are reconciled, inasmuch as that God is another person; for if he be one and the same, he must be a mediator between himself and us, and reconcile us to himself by himself; which is an insurmountable difficulty.

Though all this be so self-evident as to require no explana-

tione indigeant, unum Patrem a seipso esse Deum, quod qui
non est, Deus esse non potest, mirum quam putidis argutiis,
ne dicam præstigiis, claritatem horum locorum obscurare
atque eludere conati sint nonnulli, omnem lapidem movendo,
5 omnia diverticula quærendo, omnia tentando, non ut evangelii simplicissimam veritatem simplicibus et pauperibus annuntiare, sed paradoxum aliquod absurdissimum ne plane
corruat, adscitis e media scholarum barbarie miris quibusdam vocabulorum ac sophismatum falsis adminiculis, summa
10 contentione et pertinacia fulcire videantur.

At scripturarum aliarum causa hæc sese commentari de-
fendunt, utcunque rationi videantur minus consentanea; cæ-
teroqui scripturas inter se consentire non videri: rationis
igitur nulla ratio habeatur; scripturam rursus audiamus.

15 Duo duntaxat loci sunt. Primus est Ioan. x. 30. *ego et
pater unum sumus,* id est, unum essentia, ut vulgo interpretantur. At per Deum immortalem nihil temere agamus de
Deo. Non uno modo unum duæ res dici possunt. *Ego et
pater unum sumus* ait Filius, ait scriptura. acquiesco. Unum
20 essentia divinavit nescio quis. commentum humanum reiicio.
Quemadmodum enim unum cum Patre sit Filius, non nobis
divinandum Filius reliquit, (quisquis id primus in ecclesia
sibi arrogavit) sed ipse docet clarissime quantum quidem

tion; namely, that the Father alone is a self-existent God, and that a being which is not self-existent cannot be God, it is wonderful with what futile subtleties, or rather with what juggling artifices, certain individuals have endeavored to
5 elude or obscure the plain meaning of these passages; leaving no stone unturned, recurring to every shift, attempting every means, as if their object were not to preach the pure and unadulterated truth of the gospel to the poor and simple, but rather by dint of vehemence and obstinacy to sustain some
10 absurd paradox from falling, by the treacherous aid of sophisms and verbal distinctions, borrowed from the barbarous ignorance of the schools.

They defend their conduct, however, on the ground, that though these opinions may seem inconsistent with reason,
15 they are to be received for the sake of other passages of Scripture, and that otherwise Scripture will not be consistent with itself. Setting aside reason therefore, let us have recourse again to the language of Scripture.

The passages in question are two only. The first is John x.
20 30. "I and my Father are one"; that is, one in essence, as it is commonly interpreted. But God forbid that we should decide rashly on any point relative to the Deity. Two things may be called one in more than one way. Scripture saith, and the Son saith, "I and my Father are one"; I bow to their authority.
25 Certain commentators conjecture that they are one in essence; I reject what is merely man's invention. For the Son has not left us to conjecture in what manner he is one with the Father (whatever member of the Church may have first arrogated

nostra interest scire. Unum sunt Pater et Filius non utique essentia, ipse enim contra versu superiore dixerat, *Pater meus qui dedit mihi eas, maior omnibus est* (immo cap. xiv. 28. *maior me est*) et in sequentibus diserte negat fecisse seipsum
5 Deum; eo quod dixisset, *ego et pater unum sumus.* hoc tantum dixisse confirmat, quod longe minus est, v. 36. *me quem Pater sanctificavit et misit in mundum, vos dicitis blasphemare, quia dixi, Filius Dei sum?* Hæc de duobus essentia disparatis dici necesse est, et quidem non æqualibus. Quod
10 si de una duorum divina essentia hæc docet Filius, cur non potius de una trium? cur individuam dividit trinitatem? Quod non est totum, non est unum. Ex ipsorum igitur sententia qui affirmant, Filius et Pater sine Spiritu, essentia non sunt unum. Quemadmodum igitur unum sunt? Ipse solus
15 docere potest; et docet. primum, quia unum loquuntur, unum agunt; atque ita se explicat eodem capite cum Iudæi dictum illud perperam intelligerent; v. 38. *operibus credite, ut cognoscatis et credatis Patrem in me esse, et me in eo.* Sic cap. xiv. 10. *non credis me in Patre et Patrem in me esse? verba*

to himself the merit of the discovery), but explains the doctrine himself most fully, so far as we are concerned to know it. The Father and the Son are one, not indeed in essence, for he had himself said the contrary in the preceding verse, "my
5 Father, which gave them me, is greater than all" (see also xiv. 28. "my Father is greater than I"), and in the following verses he distinctly denies that he made himself God in saying, "I and my Father are one"; he insists that he had only said as follows, which implies far less, v. 36. "say ye of him
10 whom the Father hath sanctified, and sent into the world, Thou blasphemest; because I said, I am the Son of God?" This must be spoken of two persons not only not co-essential, but not co-equal. Now if the Son be laying down a doctrine respecting the unity of the divine essence in two persons of
15 the Trinity, how is it that he does not rather attribute the same unity of essence to the three persons? Why does he divide the indivisible Trinity? For there cannot be unity without totality. Therefore, on the authority of the opinions holden by my opponents themselves, the Son and the Father
20 without the Spirit are not one in essence. How then are they one? It is the province of Christ alone to acquaint us with this, and accordingly he does acquaint us with it. In the first place, they are one, inasmuch as they speak and act with unanimity; and so he explains himself in the same chapter,
25 after the Jews had misunderstood his saying, x. 38. "believe the works; that ye may know and believe that the Father is in me, and I in him." xiv. 10. "believest thou not that I am in the Father, and the Father in me? the words that I speak

quæ ego loquor vobis, a meipso non loquor; sed Pater qui in me manet, ipse facit opera: hic Patrem a seipso toto evidenter distinguit, sed Patrem in se manere quidem ait; quod non essentiam eorum unam sed communionem tantum arctissi-
5 mam declarat. Secundo, declarat se et Patrem esse unum quomodo nos cum eo unum sumus: id utique non est essentia, sed dilectione, communione, consensu, charitate, animo, gloria denique: Ioan. xiv. 20, 21. *in illo die vos cognoscetis me esse in Patre meo, et vos in me, et me in vobis. Qui habet*
10 *mandata mea et observat illa, is est qui diligit me; qui autem diligit me, diligetur a Patre meo.* et xvii. 21. *ut omnes unum sint, sicut tu Pater in me et ego in te; ut et ipsi in nobis unum sint* &c. et v. 23. *ego in iis, et tu in me, ut sint consummati in unum; et ut cognoscat mundus quod tu me miseris, et eos*
15 *diligas prout me dilexisti.* et 22. *ego gloriam quam dedisti mihi dedi iis, ut sint unum sicut et nos unum sumus.* Cum tot modis Filius Patrem et se esse unum clare doceat, ego eos omnes modos posthabeam? modum alium, nempe illud essentia unum, adversa atque invita ratione, ratiocinando ex-
20 cogitem, aut ab nescio quo primum homine excogitatum præponam? Quo fideiussore? Ecclesia? Ego vero, docente ipsa Ecclesia orthodoxa, recte aliter instituor; Christum prius esse audiendum.

unto you, I speak not of myself, but the Father that dwelleth in me, he doeth the works." Here he evidently distinguishes the Father from himself in his whole capacity, but asserts at the same time that the Father remains in him; which does not denote unity of essence, but only intimacy of communion. Secondly, he declares himself to be one with the Father in the same manner as we are one with him; that is, not in essence, but in love, in communion, in agreement, in charity, in spirit, in glory. John xiv. 20, 21. "at that day ye shall know that I am in the Father, and ye in me, and I in you: he that hath my commandments, and keepeth them, he it is that loveth me; and he that loveth me, shall be loved of my Father." xvii. 21. "that they all may be one, as thou, Father, art in me, and I in thee; that they also may be one in us." v. 23. "I in them, and thou in me, that they may be made perfect in one, and that the world may know that thou hast sent me, and hast loved them as thou hast loved me." v. 22. "the glory which thou gavest me I have given them, that they may be one, even as we are one." When the Son has shown in so many modes how he and the Father are one, why should I set them all aside? why should I, on the strength of my own reasoning, though in opposition to reason itself, devise another mode, which makes them one in essence; or why, if already devised by some other person, adopt it, in preference to Christ's own mode? If it be proposed on the single authority of the Church, the true doctrine of the orthodox Church herself teaches me otherwise; inasmuch as it instructs me to listen to the words of Christ before all other.

Alter locus, omnium ut putatur vulgo evidentissimus, quo
recepta sententia de unitate trium personarum essentiali fundata est, 1 Ioan. v. 7. *Tres sunt qui testificantur in cœlo,
Pater, Sermo, et spiritus sanctus, et hi tres unum sunt*, præ-
5 terquam quod et in Syro et duabus reliquis Orientalium ver-
sionibus, Arabica nimirum et Æthiopica, et in plerisque
Græcis codicibus antiquis non reperiatur hic versus, et in
quibus reperitur, mira varietate descriptus est, non magis
probat, qui unum esse dicuntur, eos necessario essentia unum
10 esse in cœlo, quam quæ sequente versu in terra unum esse
dicuntur. certe de unitate consensus et testimonii itidem ut
loco proxime citato, duntaxat hic agi ab Ioanne, siquidem
Ioannis hæc vere sunt, non vidit modo Erasmus, sed Beza
etiam vel invitus agnovit; quos ipsos adire licet. deinde tres
15 illi quinam sunt? tres Deos esse pernegabis; ergo nec est unus
Deus, sed una trium testium testificatio, unum testimonium.
Qui autem unus essentia cum Deo Patre non est, par esse Patri
non potest. sed de hoc loco infra amplius capite sequente.

At, inquiunt, ut verbis disertis non ponat scriptura unum
20 essentia esse Patrem et Filium; ratio tamen ex scripturæ vel
his vel aliis locis id efficit atque evincit. primum, ut hoc con-

The other passage, which, according to the general opinion affords the clearest foundation for the received doctrine of the essential unity of the three persons, is 1 John v. 7. "there are three that bear record in heaven, the Father, the
5 Word, and the Holy Ghost, and these three are one." But not to mention that this verse is wanting in the Syriac and the other two Oriental versions, the Arabic and the Ethiopic, as well as in the greater part of the ancient Greek manuscripts, and that in those manuscripts which actually contain it many
10 various readings occur, it no more necessarily proves those to be essentially one, who are said to be one in heaven, than it proves those to be essentially one, who are said in the following verse to be one on earth. And not only Erasmus, but even Beza, however unwillingly, acknowledged (as may be seen
15 in their own writings) that if John be really the author of the verse, he is only speaking here, as in the last quoted passage, of an unity of agreement and testimony. Besides, who are the three who are said to bear witness? That they are three Gods, will not be admitted; therefore neither is it the one God, but
20 one record or one testimony of three witnesses, which is implied. But he who is not co-essential with God the Father, cannot be co-equal with the Father. This text however will be discussed more at large in the following chapter.

But, it is objected, although Scripture does not say in express words that the Father and Son are one in essence, yet
25 reason proves the truth of the doctrine from the texts quoted above, as well as from other passages of Scripture.

In the first place, granting (which I am far from doing)

cedam quod nullo modo concedo, tamen in re tam sublimi supraque rationem posita, in ipsis fidei elementis et quasi primis postulatis, solo Dei verbo, eoque clarissimo ac disertissimo, non sola ratione, fides niti potest. Verum hic ratio voce maxima reclamat. Quid enim obsecro evincere hic potest ratio? an sententiam rationi contrariam? certe ratio rationem parit, non notiones absurdas et ab omni humano intellectu remotissimas. Concludendum est igitur, hanc sententiam neque scriptura neque ratione constare. Reliquum est ex duobus necessario consequentibus, si Deus est unus isque Pater, et tamen Filius quoque Deus dicitur; uti is decreto, ut antedictum est, et voluntate Patris et nomen et naturam divinam a Deo Patre acceperit. Hoc neque ratio ulla redarguit, et scriptura innumeris testimoniis docet.

Sed quoniam qui Filium volunt unum esse cum Patre Deum, tametsi superioribus illis duobus locis destituantur, quibus omnes etiam non nituntur, id tamen liquido satis demonstrare se posse confidunt, si scripturarum crebris auctoritatibus probare poterunt, Filio et nomen et attributa et opera Dei, divinum denique honorem passim attribui, eandem et nos insistamus viam: neque alio postulamus ut credatur pacto unum esse Deum Patrem et præterea neminem, nisi demon-

that this is the case, yet on a subject so sublime, and so far above our reason, where the very elements and first postulates, as it were, of our faith are concerned, belief must be founded, not on mere reason, but on the word of God exclusively,
5 where the language of the revelation is most clear and particular. Reason itself, however, protests strongly against the doctrine in question; for how can reason establish (as it must in the present case) a position contrary to reason? Undoubtedly the product of reason must be something consistent with
10 reason, not a notion as absurd as it is removed from all human comprehension. Hence we conclude, that this opinion is agreeable neither to Scripture nor reason. The other alternative therefore must be adopted, namely, that if God be one God, and that one God be the Father, and if notwithstand-
15 ing the Son be also called God, the Son must have received the name and nature of Deity from God the Father, in conformity with his decree and will, after the manner stated before. This doctrine is not disproved by reason, and Scripture teaches it in innumerable passages.
20   But those who insist that the Son is one God with the Father, consider their point as susceptible of ample proof, even without the two texts already examined (on which indeed some admit that no reliance is to be placed), if it can be demonstrated from a sufficient number of Scripture testi-
25 monies that the name, attributes, and works of God, as well as divine honors, are habitually ascribed to the Son. To proceed therefore in the same line of argument, I do not ask them to believe that the Father alone and none else is God,

stramus atque evincimus, primum, hæc omnia omnibus in
locis cum ab ipso Filio, tum ab eius Apostolis uni duntaxat Deo
Patri verbis disertis attribui; deinde, sicubi hæc Filio tribuuntur, id ita fieri, ut primario ac proprie Patri soli attribuenda
5 hæc esse omnia facile possit intelligi; quicquid Filio Deitatis
tribuitur, id omne Filium fateri, se Patris dono singulari ac
beneficio possidere, idemque Apostolos testari; maiorem
proinde rebus omnibus Patrem Filio et ipsum Filium et Apostolos eius, dictis suis omnibus et scriptis agnoscere.

10   Scio quid hic sint responsuri, qui unum esse Deum, non
unum tamen Patrem Deum esse credunt. Occurram itaque
initio semel, ne ad loca singula molesti sint atque obstrepant.
duo petunt principia, quod dici solet, vel emendicant potius
ut sibi gratis demus; primum ut Dei nomen Patri soli passim
15 attributum, οὐσιωδῶς intelligatur non ὑποστατικῶς, id est, ut
unius Patris nomen tres personas significet, vel totam Trinitatis essentiam, non unam Patris personam. Quæ distinctio
cum multis modis absurda est, tum ad eorum duntaxat exco-
gitata sententiam sustentandam; cum re quidem vera non eam
20 sustentet, sed ab ea sustentetur; adeoque sententiam ipsam
si infirmaveris, id est, negaveris modo, inanis illa distinctio

unless I shall have proved, first, that in every passage each of
the particulars above-mentioned is attributed in express terms
only to one God the Father, as well by the Son himself as by
his apostles. Secondly, that wherever they are attributed to
5 the Son, it is in such a manner that they are easily understood
to be attributable in their original and proper sense to the
Father alone; and that the Son acknowledges himself to
possess whatever share of Deity is assigned to him, by virtue
of the peculiar gift and kindness of the Father; as the apostles
10 also testify. And lastly, that the Son himself and his apostles
acknowledge throughout the whole of their discourses and
writings, that the Father is greater than the Son in all things.

I am aware of the answer which will be here made by those
who, while they believe in the unity of God, yet maintain that
15 the Father alone is not God. I shall therefore meet their objection in the outset, lest they should raise a difficulty and
outcry at each individual passage. They twice beg the question, or rather require us to make two gratuitous concessions.
In the first place, they insist, that wherever the name of God
20 is attributed to the Father alone, it should be understood
οὐσιωδῶς, not ὑποστατικῶς, that is to say, that the name of
the Father, who is unity, should be understood to signify the
three persons, or the whole essence of the Trinity, not the
single person of the Father. This is on many accounts a ridic-
25 ulous distinction, and invented solely for the purpose of supporting their peculiar opinion; although in reality, instead of
supporting it, it will be found to be dependent on it, and
therefore if the opinion itself be invalidated, for which pur-

simul cadit: quæ non inanis modo, sed omnino nulla distinctio
est, immo idem per idem, græcis adverbiis ad præstringendos
novitiorum oculos callide vibratum. Cum enim essentia et
hypostasis, ut secundo capite ostendimus, idem sit, coniugata
5 certe adverbia essentialiter et hypostatice nihil distinguunt.
Si igitur Dei nomen soli Patri essentialiter attribuitur, hypostatice etiam soli Patri attribuetur; cum una essentia substantialis nihil aliud quam hypostasis una sit, et contra; Quæsi-
verim itaque ab adversariis velintne Deum Patrem ens esse an
10 non? Ens certe entium. ergo, inquam, ut hypostasin unam,
ita essentiam quoque sibi propriam, et maxime omnium in-
communicabilem habebit, nemini, id est, nulli præterea personæ communem. nec propriam hypostasin sine propria
essentia habere potest. Enti enim æque omni impossibile est
15 essentiam suam, per quam est id quod est, et ab aliis omnibus
numero differt, cum alia re quavis habere communem; Filius
igitur ut propriam hypostasin, ita et propriam sibi essentiam
si non habet, sed Patris, profecto eorum sententia aut non ens
efficitur, aut cum Patre plane idem. Quæ quidem doctrina
20 religionem Christianam funditus evertit. quod autem respon-

pose a simple denial is sufficient, the futile distinction falls to
the ground at the same time. For the fact is, not merely that
the distinction is a futile one, but that it is no distinction at
all; it is a mere verbal quibble, founded on the use of synonymous words, and cunningly dressed up in terms borrowed
from the Greek to dazzle the eyes of novices. For since *essence*
and *hypostasis* mean the same thing, as has been shown in the
second chapter, it follows that there can be no real difference
of meaning between the adverbs *essentially* and *substantially*,
which are derived from them. If then the name of God be
attributed to the Father alone *essentially*, it must also be attributed to the Father alone *substantially;* since one substantial essence means nothing else than one hypostasis, and vice
versa. I would therefore ask my adversaries, whether they
hold the Father to be an abstract ens or not? Questionless they
will reply, the primary ens of all. I answer, therefore, that as
he has one hypostasis, so must he have one essence proper to
himself, incommunicable in the highest degree, and partici-
pated by no one, that is, by no person besides, for he cannot
have his own proper hypostasis, without having his own
proper essence. For it is impossible for any ens to retain its
own essence in common with any other thing whatever, since
by this essence it is what it is, and is numerically distinguished
from all others. If therefore the Son, who has his own proper
hypostasis, have not also his own proper essence, but the essence of the Father, he becomes on their hypothesis either no
ens at all, or the same ens with the Father; which strikes at the
very foundation of the Christian religion. The answer which

deri solet, essentiæ quidem unius finitæ unam duntaxat posse
esse personam, infinitæ essentiæ posse esse personas plures,
ridiculum est; eo enim ipso quod infinita essentia est, tanto
magis nonnisi unius personæ esse potest; Patris cum essentiam
5 tum personam omnes infinitam esse agnoscunt; communicari
igitur Patris essentia personæ alteri non potest: sic enim duo
infiniti esse possent, immo millies milleni.

Alterum petunt, ut quicquid Divinitatis Filius Patri soli et
quasi maiori tribuit, id vel tanquam homo vel tanquam me-
10 diator tribuisse existimetur: quod quoties locus et res ipsa
postulat, ultro idque sine ullo nostro incommodo facile da-
bimus; contendant enim quantum volent, Filium ut hominem duntaxat aut mediatorem Patri soli tribuisse omnia, nunquam ea ratione probaverint Deum esse cum Patre unum:
15 quoties non ipsa res sed eorum duntaxat theses flagitant uti
hoc sibi gratis demus, facile negabimus; Filiumque maxime
ut Filium, etiam ut Deum, Patri tanquam Dei Deo, non sibi
quocunque nomine aut ratione tribuere quæ tribuit, ostendemus.

20 Ad nomen igitur quod attinet Dei, id, ubi etiam Patris et
Filii simul fit mentio, tenore perpetuo Patri soli tribuitur, si
eos tantummodo excipias locos de quibus infra singulatim

is commonly made, is ridiculous; namely, that although one finite essence can pertain to one person only, one infinite essence may pertain to a plurality of persons; whereas in reality the infinitude of the essence affords an additional reason why it can pertain to only one person. All acknowledge that both the essence and the person of the Father are infinite; therefore the essence of the Father cannot be communicated to another person, for otherwise there might be two, or any imaginable number of infinite persons.

The second postulate is, that wherever the Son attributes Deity to the Father alone, and as to one greater than himself, he must be understood to speak in his human character, or as mediator. Wherever the context and the fact itself require this interpretation, I shall readily concede it, without losing anything by the concession; for however strongly it may be contended, that when the Son attributes every thing to the Father alone, he speaks in his human or mediatorial capacity, it can never be inferred from hence that he is one God with the Father. On the other hand I shall not scruple to deny the proposition, whenever it is to be conceded not to the sense of the passage, but merely to serve their own theory; and shall prove that what the Son attributes to the Father, he attributes in his filial or even in his divine character to the Father as God of God, and not to himself under any title or pretence whatever.

With regard to the name of God, wherever simultaneous mention is made of the Father and the Son, that name is uniformly ascribed to the Father alone, except in such passages

videbimus; cæteros longe plures, priore nunc loco, et quamvis longo, firmo tamen agmine plerosque proferemus. Ioan. iii. 16. *ita Deus dilexit mundum, ut filium suum* &c. et vi. 27. *hunc pater obsignavit Deus.* et v. 29. *hoc illud est opus Dei,* 5 *ut credatis in eum quem ille misit.* et xiv. 1. *creditis in Deum? etiam in me credite.* credere autem in aliquem quid valeat, infra dicemus: interim hic duo disparata manifesta sunt, *in Deum* et *in me.* Sic omnes simul Apostoli. Act. iv. 24. *sustulerunt vocem ad Deum dixeruntque, Domine tu es Deus ille* 10 *qui fecisti cœlum ac terram—qui spiritu sancto per os Davidis pueri tui dixisti, cur fremuerunt gentes adversus Dominum et Christum eius?* Rom. viii. 3. *Deus suo ipsius Filio misso.* 1 Thess. iii. 11. *ipse vero Deus et Pater noster, et dominus noster Iesus Christus dirigat* &c. Col. ii. 2. *ad agnitionem* 15 *mysterii Dei ac Patris et Christi.* et iii. 3. *vita vestra abscondita est cum Christo in Deo.* 2 Tim. iv. 1. *obtestor te in conspectu* τοῦ Θεοῦ καὶ τοῦ Κυρίου &c. 1 Ioan. iv. 9. *charitas Dei, quod Filium suum* &c. Sic etiam ubi Christus prior nominatur. Gal. i. 1. *per Iesum Christum ac Deum Patrem qui suscitavit* 20 *eum ex mortuis.* 2 Thess. ii. 16. *ipse vero Dominus noster Iesus Christus, et Deus ac Pater noster.* Idem ex omnibus Pauli cæterorumque Apostolorum epistolis, ipso statim initio, ubi

as shall be hereafter separately considered. I shall quote in
the first place the texts of the former class, which are by far
the more considerable in point of number, and form a large
and compact body of proofs. John iii. 16. "so God loved the
5 world, that he gave his own Son," &c. vi. 27. "him hath God
the Father sealed." v. 29. "this is the work of God, that ye
believe on him whom he hath sent." xiv. 1. "ye believe in
God, believe also in me." What is meant by believing in any
one, will be explained hereafter; in the mean time it is clear
10 that two distinct things are here intended—"in God" and "in
me." Thus all the apostles in conjunction, Acts iv. 24. "lifted
up their voice to God with one accord, and said, Lord, thou
art God which hast made heaven and earth . . . who by the
mouth of thy servant David hast said, Why did the heathen
15 rage . . . against the Lord, and against his Christ?" Rom.
viii. 3. "God sending his own Son." 1 Thess. iii. 11. "now
God himself, and our Father, and our Lord Jesus Christ,
direct our way unto you." Col. ii. 2. "to the acknowledgment
of the mystery of God, and of the Father, and of Christ." iii.
20 3. "your life is hid with Christ in God." 2 Tim. iv. 1. "I
charge thee therefore before God and the Lord Jesus Christ."
1 John iv. 9. "the love of God toward us, because that God
sent his only begotten Son." So also where Christ is named
first in order. Gal. i. 1. "by Jesus Christ, and God the Father,
25 who raised him from the dead." 2 Thess. ii. 16. "now our
Lord Jesus Christ himself, and God, even our Father." The
same thing may be observed in the very outset of all the Epistles of St. Paul and of the other apostles, where, as is natural,

maxime quisnam is sit cuius divina auctoritate sint missi, explicate, ut par est, atque distincte asseverare solent; animad-
vertas licet. Rom. i. 7, 8. 1 Cor. i. 1, 2, 3. 2 Cor. i. 1, 2, 3.
et sic deinceps ad Apocalypsin usque. et Marc. i. 1.

5   Attributa etiam divina solius esse Patris docet Filius, ex-
cluso etiam seipso. Omniscientiam. Matt. xxiv. 36. *de die
autem illo et hora nemo novit, ne angeli quidem cœlorum sed
pater meus solus.* et clarius Marc. xiii. 32. *ne angeli quidem,
nec ipse filius, sed pater.* Supremum in cœlo ac terra impe-
10 rium, summam auctoritatem, summam decernendi potestatem pro liberrima voluntate sua. Matt. vi. 13. *tuum est regnum, potentia ac gloria in sæcula.* Et xviii. 35. *ita et pater
meus cœlestis faciet vobis; nisi remiseritis* &c. et xxvi. 29. *in
regno patris mei.* et cap. xx. 23. *sedere ad dexteram meam
15 et sinistram meam, non est meum dare, sed quibus paratum
est a patre meo. Non est meum,* mediatoris nimirum, ut
vulgo interpretantur: At dubium non est, quin mater et filii
tantam rem ambitiose petentes, totum Christum, quantuscunque esset, orarent, ut, quanto maxima vel hominis vel
20 Dei potentia valebat, daret quod petebant. v. 20. *adorans et
petens.* et 21. *dic ut sedeant.* His Christus etiam totus re-

it is their custom to declare in express and distinct terms who he is by whose divine authority they have been sent. Rom. i. 7, 8. 1 Cor. i. 1–3. 2 Cor. i. 1–3. and so throughout to the book of Revelation. See also Mark i. 1.

5   The Son likewise teaches that the attributes of divinity belong to the Father alone, to the exclusion even of himself. With regard to omniscience. Matt. xxiv. 36. "of that day and hour knoweth no man, no not the angels of heaven, but my Father only"; and still more explicitly, Mark xiii. 32. "not 10 the angels which are in heaven, neither the Son, but the Father."

With regard to supreme dominion both in heaven and earth, the unlimited authority and full power of decreeing according to his own independent will. Matt. vi. 13. "thine 15 is the kingdom and the power and the glory for ever." xviii. 35. "so likewise shall my heavenly Father do also unto you, if ye from your hearts forgive not," &c. xxvi. 29. "in my Father's kingdom." xx. 23. "to sit on my right hand and on my left, is not mine to give, but it shall be given to them for 20 whom it is prepared of my Father. It is not mine—," in my mediatorial capacity, as it is commonly interpreted. But questionless when the ambition of the mother and her two sons incited them to prefer this important demand, they addressed their petition to the entire nature of Christ, how exalted so-25 ever it might be, praying him to grant their request to the utmost extent of his power whether as God or man; v. 20. "worshipping him, and desiring a certain thing of him," and v. 21. "grant that they may sit." Christ also answers with

spondit, *non est meum;* et ne aliqua tamen ratione suum hoc esse putarent, non in sua quacunque sed in Patris potestate solius hoc esse testatur: Si ut mediator duntaxat respondisset, Sophistam sane, quod absit, egisse videretur, matremque et filios ea captione elusisse, quam Logici pravam expositionem vel æquivocam vocant, cum alio quis respectu, aut animi sensu respondet quam interrogatus est. Idem de aliis huiusmodi locis est dicendum, quoties Christus de se verba facit. postquam enim duæ naturæ in unam personam hypostatice coaluere, quicquid de se loquitur Christus, non alterutram naturam, sed totam Christi personam de se toto loqui necesse est, nisi ipse dintinguit. Qui unionem, quam vocant, hypostaticam arbitratu suo divellunt, nihil profecto sincerum sermonibus aut responsis Christi relinquunt; ambigua et incerta, vera et non vera omnia, non Christum, sed pro Christo nescio quem, nunc hunc nunc illum sermocinantem nobis exhibent; ut Horatianum illud in eos probe conveniat

Quo teneam vultus mutantem Protea nodo?

Luc. xxiii. 34. *Pater, remitte hoc ipsis* &c. Ioan. xiv. 2. *in domo Patris mei.* Etiam ipse Christus Matt. xxvi. 39. *Pater mi, si possibile est, abeat a me poculum istud; veruntamen non ut ego volo, sed ut tu.* Certe quibus voluntas non eadem,

reference to his whole nature—"it is not mine to give"; and
lest for some reason they might still believe the gift belonged
to him, he declares that it was altogether out of his province,
and the exclusive privilege of the Father. If his reply was
5 meant solely to refer to his mediatorial capacity, it would have
bordered on sophistry, which God forbid that we should attribute to him; as if he were capable of evading the request of
Salome and her sons by the quibble which the logicians call
expositio prava or *æquivoca,* when the respondent answers in
10 a sense or with a mental intention different from the meaning of the questioner. The same must be said of other passages
of the same kind, where Christ speaks of himself; for after
the hypostatical union of two natures in one person, it follows that whatever Christ says of himself, he says not as the
15 possessor of either nature separately, but with reference to the
whole of his character, and in his entire person, except where
he himself makes a distinction. Those who divide this hypostatical union at their own discretion, strip the discourses and
answers of Christ of all their sincerity; they represent every
20 thing as ambiguous and uncertain, as true and false at the
same time; it is not Christ that speaks, but some unknown
substitute, sometimes one, and sometimes another; so that the
words of Horace may be justly applied to such disputants:
"With what noose shall I hold this Proteus, who is ever chang-
25 ing his form?" Luke xxiii. 34. "Father, forgive them," &c.
John xiv. 2. "in my Father's house." So also Christ himself
says, Matt. xxvi. 39. "O my Father, if it be possible, let this
cup pass from me; nevertheless not as I will, but as thou wilt."

iis nec essentia eadem. At nec intellectum nec voluntatem numero eandem esse Patris et Filii, multis ex locis docetur. Matt. xxiv. 36. *nemo novit* &c. *sed Pater meus solus.* et Marc. xiii. 32. *nec ipse filius, sed pater.* Ioan. vi. 38. *descendi e cœlo*

5 *non ut facerem voluntatem meam, sed voluntatem mittentis me.* quibus igitur nec intellectus, nec voluntas numero eadem, iis essentia esse eadem non potest. nec tergiversandi ullus hic locus, cum de natura etiam divina Filii hæc ipse Filius protulerit. et v. 42. idem. et 53. *an putas me non posse nunc pre-*

10 *cari patrem meum, qui huc sistat mihi plures quam duodecim legiones angelorum.* Marc. xiv. 36. *Abba, Pater, omnia fieri abs te possunt: transfer a me poculum istud* &c. Luc. xxii. 29. *disposuit mihi pater meus regnum.* et xxiii. 46. *pater, in manus tuas depono spiritum meum.* Ioan. xii. 27. *Pater,*

15 *libera me ab hora hac.* Si solus homo petiit hæc omnia (quod solet responderi) cur a solo Patre omnia, non a seipso, siquidem ipse etiam est Deus? Si homo et summus ipse Deus, cur omnino petiit quod penes se erat? Quid divina natura cum humana in unam personam coniuncta opus fuit, si ipsa par

20 Patri, omnia tamen Patre accepta retulit? Bonitatem sum-

Now it is manifest that those who have not the same will, cannot have the same essence. It appears however from many passages, that the Father and Son have not, in a numerical sense, the same intelligence or will. Matt. xxiv. 36. "no man
5 knoweth . . . but my Father only." Mark xiii. 32. "neither the Son, but the Father." John vi. 38. "I came down from heaven, not to do mine own will, but the will of him that sent me." Those therefore whose understanding and will are not numerically the same, cannot have the same essence. Nor is
10 there any mode of evading this conclusion, inasmuch as this is the language of the Son himself respecting his own divine nature. See also Matt. xxvi. 42. and v. 53. "thinkest thou that I cannot now pray to my Father, and he shall presently give me more than twelve legions of angels?" Mark xiv. 36.
15 "Abba, Father, all things are possible unto thee; take away this cup from me," &c. Luke xxii. 29. "I appoint unto you a kingdom, as my Father hath appointed unto me." xxiii. 46. "Father, into thy hands I commend my spirit." John xii. 27. "Father, save me from this hour." If these prayers be uttered
20 only in his human capacity, which is the common explanation, why does he petition these things from the Father alone instead of from himself, if he were God? Or rather, supposing him to be at once man and the supreme God, why does he ask at all for what was in his own power? What need was
25 there for the union of the divine and human nature in one person, if he himself, being equal to the Father, gave back again into his hands every thing that he had received from him?

mam. Matt. xix. 17. *cur me dicis bonum? nullus est bonus*
nisi unus, nempe Deus. Si blandientium titulos Pharisæis dari
solitos Christus noluit sibi sumere, eamque ob rem iuvenem
illum paulo severius accepit, mirum non est; hoc utique pla-
5 num, cum ait, nullus est bonus nisi unus, nempe Deus, noluisse se eundem essentia cum uno illo Deo haberi: sic enim
quid aliud nisi bonitatis laudem a se removisset, ut in se conferret. Ioan. vi. 32. *Pater meus dat vobis panem illum cœle-*
stem verum. v. 65. *neminem posse venire ad me* (et hominem
10 scilicet et Deum) *nisi fuerit ei datum a patre meo.* Gloriam
summam. Matt. xviii. 10. *angelos eorum in cœlis per omne*
tempus cernere faciem Patris mei qui in cœlis est. Ioan. xvii.
4. *ego te glorificavi in terra* &c. Quid? quod et promissio veræ
sapientiæ, etiam in ipso Christo cognoscendo (id ipsum quod
15 nunc quærimus) fit obedientibus patri. Ioan. vii. 17. 18. *si*
quis voluerit quod ille vult facere, cognoscet de doctrina,
utrum ex Deo sit, an ego ex meipso loquar. Qui a semetipso
loquitur, gloriam propriam quærit: qui autem quærit glo-
riam eius qui misit ipsum, hic verax est, et iniustitia in eo non
20 *est.* et xv. 8. *in hac re glorificatus fuerit pater meus, ut fruc-*
tum multum feratis, et eritis mei discipuli. Matt. vii. 21. *Nam*
quisquis dicit mihi Domine Domine, non introibit in regnum
cœlorum; sed qui facit quod vult pater meus qui in cœlis est.

With regard to his supreme goodness. Matt. xix. 17. "why callest thou me good? there is none good but one, that is, God." We need not be surprised that Christ should refuse to accept the adulatory titles which were wont to be given to the
5 Pharisees, and on this account should receive the young man with less kindness than usual; but when he says, "there is none good but one, that is, God," it is evident that he did not choose to be considered essentially the same with that one God; for otherwise this would only have been disclaiming
10 the credit of goodness in one character, for the purpose of assuming it in another. John vi. 32. "my Father giveth you the true bread from heaven." v. 65. "no man can come unto me"—that is, to me, both God and man—"except it were given unto him of my Father."

15   With regard to his supreme glory. Matt. xviii. 10. "their angels do always behold the face of my Father which is in heaven." John xvii. 4. "I have glorified thee on the earth." Nay, it is to those who obey the Father that the promise of true wisdom is made even with regard to the knowing Christ himself, which is the very point now in question. John vii.
20 himself, which is the very point now in question. John vii. 17, 18. "if any man will do his will, he shall know of the doctrine whether it be of God, or whether I speak of myself: he that speaketh of himself seeketh his own glory; but he that seeketh his glory that sent him, the same is true, and no un-
25 righteousness is in him." xv. 8. "herein is my Father glorified, that ye bear much fruit; so shall ye be my disciples." Matt. vii. 21. "not every one that saith unto me, Lord, Lord, shall enter into the kingdom of heaven, but he that doeth the will

et xii. 50. *quisquis fecerit quod vult pater meus qui est in cœlis, is est meus frater et soror et mater.* Sic divina omnia Christus ipse tribuit soli Patri. Sic itidem ubique tribuunt Apostoli. Rom. xv. 5, 6. *Deus auctor tolerantiæ et consolationis, det* 5 *vobis &c. secundum Christum Iesum.* et xvi. 25, 26, 27. *ei vero qui potest vos stabilire* &c. *ex imperio æterni Dei* &c. *soli inquam sapienti Deo gloria esto per Iesum Christum.* Iudæ 25. *soli sapienti Deo servatori nostro gloria esto per Iesum Christum Dominum nostrum,* ut vetus interpres et nonnulli 10 codices Græci habent. 1 Tim. vi. 13, 14, 15, 16. *denuntio tibi coram Deo qui vivificat omnia, et Iesu Christo qui testatam fecit* &c. *usque ad illustrem illum adventum Domini nostri Iesu Christi; quem præstitutis temporibus ostendet ille beatus, Rex ille Regum et Dominus Dominorum: qui solus habet im-* 15 *mortalitatem; lucem habitans inaccessam; quem vidit nemo hominum, neque videre potest; cui honor et robur in æternum. Amen.*

Opera. Rom. xvi. 25, 26, 27. ut supra. 1 Tim. vi. 13, 14, 15, 16. ut supra. 2 Cor. i. 21, 22. *porro qui nos confirmat* 20 *vobiscum in Christum, Deus est; qui etiam obsignavit nos.* Deus autem qui confirmat est unus. 1 Pet. i. 2. *electis ex præcognitione Dei patris ad sanctificationem spiritus per obedientiam et aspersionem sanguinis Iesu Christi.* Etiam erga ipsum filium opera vel in ipso filio. Act. v. 30, 31, 32, 33.

of my Father that is in heaven." xii. 50. "whosoever shall do the will of my Father which is in heaven, the same is my brother, and sister, and mother."

Thus Christ assigns every attribute of the Deity to the Father alone. The apostles uniformly speak in a similar manner. Rom. xv. 5, 6. "the God of patience and consolation grant you to be like minded one toward another, according to Christ Jesus." xvi. 25–27. "to him that is of power to stablish you . . . according to the commandment of the everlasting God . . . to God only wise, be glory through Jesus Christ—our Lord," as the *Vetus Interpres* and some of the Greek manuscripts read it. 1 Tim. vi. 13–16. "I give thee charge in the sight of God, who quickeneth all things, and before Christ Jesus, who witnessed a good confession . . . until the appearing of our Lord Jesus Christ, which in his times he shall show, who is the blessed and only Potentate, the King of kings and Lord of lords; who alone hath immortality, dwelling in the light which no man can approach unto, whom no man hath seen, nor can see; to whom be honor and power everlasting. Amen."

With regard to his works. See Rom. xvi. 25–27. 1 Tim. vi. 13–16. as quoted above. 2 Cor. i. 21, 22. "now he which stablisheth us with you in Christ, and hath anointed us, is God; who hath also sealed us." Now the God which stablisheth us, is one God. 1 Pet. i. 2. "elect according to the foreknowledge of God the Father, through sanctification of the Spirit unto obedience and sprinkling of the blood of Jesus Christ." Even those works which regard the Son himself, or

Deus ille patrum nostrorum suscitavit Iesum, quem—. *hunc,
inquam, Deus dextra sua evectum, constituit principem ac
servatorem, ut det resipiscentiam Israeli, et remissionem peccatorum.* Gal. i. 1. *per Iesum Christum ac Deum patrem, qui*
5 *suscitavit eum ex mortuis.* Rom. x. 9. *si credideris in corde
tuo quod Deus eum suscitavit ex mortuis, servaberis.* 1 Cor.
vi. 14. *Deus et Dominum suscitavit, et nos suscitabit potentia
sua.* 1 Thess. i. 9, 10. *ad expectandum filium eius e cœlis
quem suscitavit ex mortuis.* Heb. x. 5. *sacrificium et oblatio-*
10 *nem noluisti, corpus autem adaptasti mihi.* 1 Pet. i. 21. *per
eum credentes in Deum qui suscitavit eum ex mortuis.* En
quot locis a patre solo suscitatus filius dicitur; quibus unus
ille Ioan. ii. 19. *destruite templum hoc, et intra triduum excitabo illud,* præponderare non debet; ubi ad non suos, pleniore
15 responso indignos, breviter et ænigmatice non explanate locutus est, adeoque paternæ potentiæ mentionem facere necesse
non habuit.

Honorem Divinum. Quemadmodum enim filius patrem
solum passim adorat ac veneratur, ita et nos docet. Matt. vi.
20 6. *ora patrem tuum.* v. 9. *vos igitur orate, pater noster qui es
in cœlis.* cap. xviii. 19. *de omni re quam petierint, fiet iis a
patre meo qui in cœlis est.* Luc. xi. 1, 2. *doce nos orare &c.
dixit autem iis, quum oratis dicite, pater noster* &c. Ioan. ii.

which were done in him. Acts v. 30–33. "the God of our fathers raised up Jesus . . . him hath God exalted with his right hand to be a Prince and a Savior, for to give repentance to Israel, and forgiveness of sins." Gal. i. 1. "by Jesus Christ, 5 and God the Father, who raised him from the dead." Rom. x. 9. "if thou shalt believe in thine heart that God hath raised him from the dead, thou shalt be saved." 1 Cor. vi. 14. "God hath both raised up the Lord, and will also raise us up by his own power." 1 Thess. i. 10. "to wait for his Son from heaven, 10 whom he raised from the dead." Heb. x. 5. "sacrifice and offering thou wouldst not, but a body hast thou prepared me." 1 Pet. i. 21. "who by him do believe in God that raised him up from the dead." So many are the texts wherein the Son is said to be raised up by the Father alone, which ought to have 15 greater weight than the single passage in St. John, ii. 19. "destroy this temple, and in three days I will raise it up," where he spake briefly and enigmatically, without explaining his meaning to enemies who were unworthy of a fuller answer, on which account he thought it unnecessary to mention 20 the power of the Father.

With regard to divine honors. For as the Son uniformly pays worship and reverence to the Father alone, so he teaches us to follow the same practice. Matt. vi. 6. "pray to thy Father." v. 9. "after this manner therefore pray ye; Our 25 Father, which art in heaven," &c. xviii. 19. "as touching any thing that they shall ask, it shall be done for them of my Father which is in heaven." Luke xi. 1, 2. "teach us to pray," &c. "and he said unto them, When ye pray, say, Our Father,

16. *ne facite domum patris mei* &c. *et* iv. 21, 23. *venit tempus et nunc est, quum veri adoratores adorabunt patrem spiritu ac veritate: etenim pater tales quærit qui ipsum adorent.* et xv. 16. *ut quicquid petieritis a patre in nomine meo, det vobis.* et xvi. 23. *illo die me non interrogabitis quicquam: quæcunque petieritis a patre in nomine meo, dabit vobis.* Rom. i. 8, 9. *primum quidem gratias ago Deo meo per Iesum Christum super omnibus vobis, quod—testis enim mihi est Deus, quem colo spiritu meo in Evangelio filii sui* &c. et v. 11. *gloriamur in Deo per Dominum nostrum Iesum Christum.* et vii. 25. *gratias ago Deo meo per Iesum Christum.* et xv. 6. *ut concorditer uno ore glorificetis Deum ac patrem Domini nostri Iesu Christi.* 1 Cor. i. 4. *gratias ago Deo meo semper de vobis ob gratiam Dei quæ data est vobis in Christo Iesu.* 2 Ep. i. 3. *benedictus est Deus ac pater Domini nostri Iesu Christi; pater ille miserationum, et Deus omnis consolationis.* Gal. i. 4, 5. *qui dedit semetipsum* &c. *secundum voluntatem Dei ac patris nostri; cui sit gloria in sæcula sæculorum.* Eph. i. 3. *benedictus Deus et pater Domini nostri Iesu Christi* &c. et ii. 18. *quoniam utrique per ipsum habemus aditum per unum spiritum ad patrem.* et iii. 14. *flecto genua mea ad patrem Domini nostri.* et v. 20, 21. *ei vero qui summa cum exsuperantia potest omnia facere supra ea quæ petimus aut cogitamus, pro illa vi agente in nobis, ei sit gloria in ecclesia per Christum Iesum, in omnes ætates sæculi sæculorum.* Philipp. i. 2, 3. *gratia vobis et pax a Deo patre nostro, et Domino Iesu Christo.*

which art in heaven." John ii. 16. "make not my Father's house an house of merchandise." iv. 21–23. "the hour cometh, and now is, when the true worshippers shall worship the Father in spirit and in truth; for the Father seeketh such to worship him." xv. 16. "that whatsoever ye shall ask of the Father in my name, he may give it you." xvi. 23. "in that day ye shall ask me nothing; . . . whatsoever ye shall ask the Father in my name, he will give it you." Rom. i. 8, 9. "first, I thank my God through Jesus Christ for you all . . . for God is my witness, whom I serve with my spirit in the gospel of his Son," &c. v. 11. "we also joy in God through our Lord Jesus Christ." vii. 25. "I thank God, through Jesus Christ our Lord." xv. 6. "that ye may with one mind and one mouth glorify God, even the Father of our Lord Jesus Christ." 1 Cor. i. 4. "I thank my God always on your behalf, for the grace of God which is given you by Jesus Christ." 2 Cor. i. 3. "blessed be God, even the Father of our Lord Jesus Christ, the Father of mercies, and the God of all comfort." Gal. i. 4, 5. "who gave himself . . . according to the will of God and our Father; to whom be glory for ever and ever." Eph. i. 3. "blessed be the God and Father of our Lord Jesus Christ," &c. ii. 18. "for through him we both have access by one Spirit unto the Father." iii. 14. "for this cause I bow my knees unto the Father of our Lord Jesus Christ." v. 20, 21. "now unto him that is able to do exceeding abundantly, above all that we ask or think, according to the power that worketh in us, unto him be glory in the Church by Christ Jesus, throughout all ages, world without end." Philipp. i. 2, 3. "grace be unto you

gratias ago Deo meo &c. Col. i. 3. idem. et iii. 17. *quicquid feceritis* &c. *in nomine Domini* &c. *gratias agentes Deo et patri per eum.* 1 Thess. i. 2, 3. *gratias agimus Deo semper de omnibus vobis, mentionem vestri facientes in precibus nostris,*
5 *indesinenter commemorantes efficacem vestram fidem et laboriosam charitatem, et patientem illam expectationem in Domino nostro Iesu Christo coram Deo et patre nostro.* et v. 9, 10. *ad serviendum Deo vivo et vero, et ad expectandum filium eius e cœlis, quem suscitavit ex mortuis* &c. 2 Thess.
10 i. 2, 3. idem. 2 Tim. i. 3. *gratiam habeo Deo, quem colo a maioribus.* Maiores autem Pauli Deum patrem solum colebant. Philem. iv. 5. et 1 Pet. i. 3. idem. et iv. 11. *si quis* &c. *ut eloquia Dei, ex viribus Dei, ut in omnibus glorificetur Deus per Iesum Christum.* Iacob. i. 27. *religiosus autem cultus pure*
15 *apud Deum et patrem, hic est* &c. 1 Ioan. ii. 1. *advocatum apud patrem habemus, Iesum Christum, iustum.* 2 Ep. iv. 5, 6. *qui sincere ambulent, sicut mandatum accepimus a patre. hæc est charitas; ut ambulemus secundum præcepta ipsius.* Apoc. i. 6. *qui fecit nos Reges et sacerdotes Deo ac*
20 *patri suo, ei gloria et robur in sæcula sæculorum.* Matt. xxi. 12. *introivit Iesus in templum Dei.* At inquiunt qui adversantur, scriptum est Mal. iii. 1. *veniet in templum suum ille Dominus, quem vos quæritis, et angelus* &c. Respondeo, his verbis more prophetico adventum Domini in carnem signi-

and peace from God our Father, and from the Lord Jesus Christ. I thank my God upon every remembrance of you." See also Col. i. 3. and iii. 17. "whatsoever ye do . . . do all in the name of the Lord Jesus, giving thanks to God and the Father by him." 1 Thess. i. 2, 3. "we give thanks to God for you all, making mention of you in our prayers; remembering without ceasing your work of faith, and labor of love, and patience of hope in our Lord Jesus Christ, in the sight of God and our Father." v. 9, 10. "to serve the living and true God; and to wait for his Son from heaven, whom he raised from the dead." See also 2 Thess. i. 2, 3. and 2 Tim. i. 3. "I thank God, whom I serve from my forefathers." Now the forefathers of Paul served God the Father alone. See also Philem. 4, 5. and 1 Pet. i. 3. and iv. 10. "as every man hath received the gift . . . let him speak as the oracles of God . . . as of the ability which God giveth, that God in all things may be glorified through Jesus Christ." James i. 27. "pure religion and undefiled before God and the Father, is this." 1 John ii. 1. "we have an advocate with the Father, Jesus Christ the righteous." 2 John 4–6. "walking in truth, as we have received a commandment from the Father . . . this is love, that we walk after his commandments." Rev. i. 6. "who made us kings and priests unto God and His Father; to him be glory and dominion for ever and ever." Matt. xxi. 12. "Jesus went into the temple of God." Here however my opponents quote the passage from Malachi, iii. 1. "the Lord whom ye seek shall suddenly come to his temple, even the messenger of the covenant." I answer, that in prophetical

ficari, sive in templum corporis, ut Ioan. ii. 21. Alium enim
in templo neque quærebant ullum Iudæi quem colerent præter
patrem, et templum ipse patris domum, non suam, eodem
capite nominavit: et illum quidem Dominum et angelum, id
5 est, missum a Deo fœderis mediatorem, non Deum, quærebant: veniet denique in ecclesiam suam, quod templi nomine
apud prophetas adumbrari solet. Sic ubi Deus et homines
quasi per antithesin ponuntur, solus pater pro uno Deo est.
Iacob. iii. 9. *per ipsam benedicimus Deo et patri, et per ipsam*
10 *execramur homines, ad similitudinem Dei factos.* 1 Ioan. ii.
15, 16. *Si quis diligit mundum, non est charitas patris in eo;*
non est ex patre, sed ex mundo.

At Filius aliquoties Deus, immo Iehova dicitur; divina
etiam omnia filio quoque attribuuntur, ut multis cum veteris
15 tum novi fœderis ex locis acriter disputant.

Hoc itaque alterum ex iis est quod initio demonstrandum
suscepi; quoniam ex analogia scripturæ iam satis ostendi ubi
Patris et filii mentio simul fit, nomen, attributa, opera Dei,
divinum denique honorem uni ac soli Deo Patri semper attri-
20 bui, ut nunc ostendam, sicubi hæc filio tribuuntur, id ita fieri

language these words signify the coming of the Lord into the flesh, or into the temple of the body, as it is expressed in John ii. 21. For the Jews sought no one in the temple as an object of worship, except the Father; and Christ himself in the same chapter has called the temple his Father's house, and not his own. Nor were they seeking God, but "that Lord and messenger of the covenant"; that is, him who was sent from God as the mediator of the covenant; he it was who should come to his Church, which the prophets generally express figuratively under the image of the temple. So also where the terms God and man are put in opposition to each other, the Father stands exclusively for the one God. James iii. 9. "therewith bless we God, even the Father; and therewith curse we men, which are made after the similitude of God." 1 John ii. 15, 16. "if any man love the world, the love of the Father is not in him: for all that is in the world . . . is not of the Father, but of the world."

But it is strenuously urged on the other hand, that the Son is sometimes called God, and even Jehovah; and that all the attributes of the Deity are assigned to him likewise in many passages both of the Old and New Testament. We arrive therefore at the other point which I originally undertook to prove; and since it has been already shown from the analogy of Scripture, that where the Father and the Son are mentioned together, the name, attributes, and works of the Deity, as well as divine honors, are always assigned to the one and only God the Father, I will now demonstrate, that whenever the same properties are assigned to the Son, it is in such

ut primario ac proprie patri soli attribuenda hæc esse omnia, facile possit intelligi.

Notandum enim imprimis est Dei nomen, Dei patris voluntate atque concessione, etiam angelis, etiam hominibus 5 (quanto magis unigenito filio, patris imagini;) haud raro impertiri.

Angelis. Psal. viii. 6. *minorem diis.* et xcvii. 7, 9. cum Heb. i. 6. Iudicibus. Exod. xxi. 6. *sistet eum Dominus eius coram diis* vel magistratibus. et xxii. 8, 9, 28. idem. Psal. 10 lxxxii. 1, 6. *ego dixi, dii estis et filii excelsi vos omnes.* et toti domui Davidis, sive omnibus sanctis, Zech. xii. 8. *erit domus Davidis ut dii, et angelus coram illis.*

Attribuitur etiam vox אֱלֹהִים pluralis numeri cum sit, (ne plurali plures personas in Deo significari putemus) uni an-15 gelo. Iudic. xiii. 21. cum 22. *tunc novit Manoa eum angelum Iehovæ esse, quapropter dixit Manoa uxori suæ, omnino morituri sumus, nam Deum vidimus.* Uni Deo falso. Exod. xx. 3. *non erunt tibi Dii alii.* Dagoni. Iudic. xvi. 23. et singulis idolis. 1 Reg. xi. 33. et Mosi. Exod. iv. 16. et vii. 1. 20 Et soli Deo Patri. Psal. ii. 7. et xlv. 8. et sæpissime.

Eadem est ratio vocis אֲדֹנִים Domini, numero quidem plurali, sensu autem singulari; et cum affixis pluralibus Hebræorum

a manner as to make it easily intelligible that they ought all primarily and properly to be attributed to the Father alone.

It must be observed in the first place, that the name of God is not unfrequently ascribed, by the will and concession of God the Father, even to angels and men, how much more then to the only begotten Son, the image of the Father. To angels. Psal. xcvii. 7, 9. "worship him all ye gods . . . thou art high above all the earth; thou art exalted far above all gods," compared with Heb. i. 6. See also Psal. viii. 5. To judges. Exod. xxii. 28. "thou shalt not revile the gods, nor curse the ruler of thy people." See also, in the Hebrew, Exod. xxi. 6. xxii. 8, 9. Psal. lxxxii. 1, 6. "he judgeth among the gods. I have said, Ye are gods, and all of you are children of the Most High." To the whole house of David, or to all the saints. Zech. xii. 8. "the house of David shall be as God, as the angel of the Lord before them." The word אלהים, though it be of the plural number, is also employed to signify a single angel, in case it should be thought that the use of the plural implies a plurality of persons in the Godhead: Judges xiii. 21. "then Manoah knew that he was an angel of Jehovah: and Manoah said unto his wife, We shall surely die, because we have seen God." The same word is also applied to a single false god. Exod. xx. 3. "thou shalt have no other gods before me." To Dagon. Judges xvi. 23. To single idols. 1 Kings xi. 33. To Moses. Exod. iv. 16. and vii. 1. To God the Father alone. Psal. ii. 7. xlv. 7. and in many other places. Similar to this is the use of the word אדנים, "the Lord," in the plural number with a singular meaning; and with a plural affix

more. et אֲדֹנִי cum vocali Patha, de uno homine; cum vocali Kamets, de uno Deo, aut uno angelo Dei personam gerente, passim occurrit.

Hæc sedulo ab ipsis Grammaticis et Lexicographis annota-
5 ta fere sunt, ut etiam in voce בַּעַל appellative sumpta. idem fortasse de propriis nominibus בְּעָלִים et עַשְׁתָּרוֹת censendum. Nam
et apud Græcos vox δεσπότης, id est, Dominus, numero itidem
plurali, sensu singulari reverentiæ nimirum et honoris causa
usurpari solet. Sic apud Euripidem Iphigen. in Aulid. λίαν
10 δεσπόταισι πιστὸς εἶ, pro δεσπότῃ. et rursus, εὐκλεές τοι δεσποτῶν
θνήσκειν ὕπερ, pro δεσπότου. Sic nuntius in Rheso et nuntius
in Bacchis.

Hæc omnia idcirco attendenda, ne quis imperitia longua-
rum hallucinatus, voce Elohim cum singulari adiungitur,
15 plurium personarum unam essentiam significari, continuo
sibi persuadeat. Etenim in eo siquid est, quot illa vox personas,
totidem Deos innuit. Quid! quod voci Elohim nunc adiecti-
vum nunc verbum plurale adiunctum reperitur; quod non
personas tantum, sed etiam naturas significaret plures, si quid
20 huiusmodi in Syntaxi positum esset: Deut. v. 32. *Deorum
viventium.* Ios. xxiv. 19. *Dii sancti Ille.* Sic Ier. x. 10. Gen.
xx. 13. *cum me errare facerent Dii.* Quid! quod occurrit
etiam nonnunquam singularis אֱלֹהַּ Deut. xxxii. 18. et sæpe
alias. Et nomen singulare אָדוֹן Dominus Iehovæ adiungitur,
25 Exod. xxiii. 17. Et cum affixo singulari tribuitur Christo,
Psal. cx. 1. *dictum Iehovæ* לַאדֹנִי *Domino meo.* quibus verbis

according to the Hebrew mode. The word אֲדֹנָי also with the
vowel *Patha* is frequently employed to signify one man, and
with the vowel *Kamets* to signify one God, or one angel
bearing the character of God. This peculiarity in the above
5 words has been carefully noticed by the grammarians and
lexicographers themselves, as well as in בַּעַל used appellatively.
The same thing may perhaps be remarked of the proper
names בְּעָלִים and עַשְׁתָּרֹת. For even among the Greeks the
word δεσπότης, that is, Lord, is also used in the plural number
10 in the sense of the singular, when extraordinary respect and
honor are intended to be paid. Thus in the *Iphigenia in Aulis*
of Euripides, λίαν δεσπόταισι πιστὸς εἶ, for δεσπότῃ, and again
εὐκλεές τοι δεσποτῶν θνῄσκειν ὕπερ for δεσπότου. It is also used
in the *Rhesus* and the *Bacchæ* in the same manner.

15 Attention must be paid to these circumstances, lest any
one through ignorance of the language should erroneously
suppose, that whenever the word Elohim is joined with a
singular, it is intended to intimate a plurality of persons in
unity of essence. But if there be any significance at all in this
20 peculiarity, the word must imply as many Gods, as it does
persons. Besides, a plural adjective or a plural verb is sometimes joined to the word Elohim, which, if a construction of
this kind could mean anything, would signify not a plurality
of persons only, but also of natures. See in the Hebrew Deut.
25 v. 26. Josh. xxiv. 19. Jer. x. 10. Gen. xx. 13. Further, the
singular אֱלֹהַּ also sometimes occurs, Deut. xxxii. 18. and elsewhere. It is also attributed to Christ with the singular affix.
Psal. cx. 1. לַאדֹנִי "Jehovah said unto my Lord," in which

propheta Christum etiam summi honoris causa Dominum hic
nominatum, et alterum ab Iehova, et, si qua affixo fides,
minorem dicit. At cum patrem alloquitur, v. 5. mutato affixo
אֲדֹנִי inquit, *Dominus qui sedet ad dexteram tuam franget* &c.

5   Nomen autem Dei videtur attributum angelis fuisse, propterea quod divinitus missi, divinæ speciem gloriæ atque personæ, immo verba ipsa Dei præ se tulerunt. ut Gen. xxi. 17,
18. et xxii. 11, 12, 15. *per meipsum iuro, dictum Iehovæ.*
Nempe quæ vox prophetis in ore tam crebro erat, alibi quidem
10 intelligitur, hic exprimitur, ut intelligamus tandem angelos
sive nuntios, tametsi loquentis Dei nomen atque personam
sustinere videntur, non sua tamen verba sed mittentis Dei
iussa annuntiare. Sic ipse credidit patriarcha Iacobus. Gen.
xxxi. 11, 12, 13. *dixit mihi angelus Dei, vidi quicquid Laban*
15 *facit tibi. Ego sum Deus ille Bethelis* &c. et xxxii. 30. *Deum*
vidi hisce oculis in os. cum Hos. xii. 4, 5. *principem se gessit*
cum Deo, cum angelo. Exod. xxiv. 10, 11. *aspexerunt Deum*
Israelis; postquam intuiti essent Deum ipsum. Deut. iv. 33.
num audierit ullus populus vocem Dei loquentis e medio ignis,
20 *ut tu audisti, et vixerit?* et tamen Exod. xxxiii. 20. *non potest*
homo videre me et vivere. Et Ioan. i. 18. *Deum nemo vidit*
unquam. et v. 37. *neque vocem eius unquam audivistis, neque*

passage the Psalmist speaks of Christ (to whom the name of "Lord" is assigned as a title of the highest honor) both as distinct from Jehovah, and, if any reliance can be placed on the affix, as inferior to Jehovah. But when he addresses the
5 Father, the affix is changed, and he says, v. 5. אֲדֹנָי, "the Lord at thy right hand shall strike through kings in the day of his wrath."

The name of God seems to be attributed to angels, because as heavenly messengers they bear the appearance of the divine
10 glory and person, and even speak in the very words of the Deity. Gen. xxi. 17, 18. xxii. 11, 12, 15, 16. "by myself have I sworn, saith Jehovah." For the expression so frequently in the mouth of the prophets, and which is elsewhere often omitted, is here inserted, for the purpose of showing that
15 angels and messengers do not declare their own words, but the commands of God who sends them, even though the speaker seem to bear the name and character of the Deity himself. So believed the patriarch Jacob, Gen. xxxi. 11–13. "the angel of God spake unto me, saying . . . I have seen all that
20 Laban doeth unto thee. I am the God of Bethel," &c. xxxii. 30. "I have seen God face to face"; compared with Hos. xii. 4, 5. "he had power with God, yea, he had power over the angel." Exod. xxiv. 10, 11. "they saw the God of Israel . . . also they saw God." Deut. iv. 33. "did ever people hear the
25 voice of God speaking out of the midst of the fire, as thou hast heard, and live?" Yet it is said, Exod. xxxiii. 20. "there shall no man see me, and live." John i. 18. "no man hath seen God at any time." v. 37. "ye have neither heard his

speciem eius vidistis. 1 Tim. vi. 16. *lucem habitans inaccessam, quem vidit nemo hominum, neque videre potest.* Qui
igitur auditus quique visus fuit, sequitur Deum non fuisse; ne
ubi Dei quidem, immo Iehovæ et angelorum simul fit mentio.
5 Gen. xxviii. 12, 13. *ecce angelos. ecce Iehovam.* 1 Reg. xxii.
19. *vidi Iehovam* &c. *et totum exercitum cœli* &c. Isa. vi. 1, 2.
vidi Dominum &c. *Seraphim astantes* &c. Non ipsum, inquam, Deum vidit, sed quempiam puta angelum parte aliqua
indutum divinæ gloriæ, vel ipsum Dei filium, paternæ gloriæ
10 imaginem; ut Ioan. xii. 41. *quum vidit gloriam eius.* Si enim
eiusdem fuisset essentiæ, non magis potuisset aspici, ne audiri
quidem magis quam ipse pater. ut infra uberius ostendetur.
Hinc examinati erant homines etiam sanctissimi viso angelo
quasi vidissent ipsum Deum. Gen. xxxii. 30. *Deum vidi,*
15 cum Iudic. vi. 22. *quum vidit Gideon angelum Iehovæ eum
esse, dixit, Aha Domine Iehova, quandoquidem vidi angelum
Iehovæ in os.* et cap. xiii. 21, 22. ut supra. Iudicibus idcirco
impertitum est Dei nomen, quod ii vices Dei in iudiciis exercendis quodammodo gerant. Utroque hoc modo, sive ut
20 angelus, sive ut Iudex, filius, et longe quidem præstantiore
Deus, ea ipsa defensione apud Iudæos pro se uti haud alienum

voice at any time, nor seen his shape." 1 Tim. vi. 16. "dwelling in the light which no man can approach unto, whom no man hath seen, nor can see." It follows therefore that whoever was heard or seen, it was not God; not even where mention is made of God, nay even of Jehovah himself, and of the angels in the same sentence. Gen. xxviii. 12. 13. "behold the angels of God . . . and behold, Jehovah stood above them." 1 Kings xxii. 19. "I saw Jehovah sitting on his throne, and all the host of heaven standing by him." Isa. vi. 1, 2. "I saw the Lord sitting upon a throne . . . above it stood the seraphim." I repeat, it was not God himself that he saw, but perhaps one of the angels clothed in some modification of the divine glory, or the Son of God himself, the image of the glory of his Father, as John understands the vision, xii. 41. "these things said Esaias, when he saw his glory." For if he had been of the same essence, he could no more have been seen or heard than the Father himself, as will be more fully shown hereafter. Hence even the holiest of men were troubled in mind when they had seen an angel, as if they had seen God himself. Gen. xxxii. 30. "I have seen God." Judges vi. 22. "when Gideon perceived that he was an angel of Jehovah, Gideon said, Alas, O Lord Jehovah, for because I have seen an angel of Jehovah face to face." See also xiii. 21, 22. as before.

The name of God is ascribed to judges, because they occupy the place of God to a certain degree in the administration of judgment. The Son, who was entitled to the name of God both in the capacity of a messenger and of a judge, and indeed in virtue of a much better right, did not think it foreign to his

est arbitratus, cum ab iis blasphemiæ accusaretur quod se fecisset Deum. Ioan. x. 34, 35, 36. *respondit Iesus nonne scriptum est* &c. *ego dixi, dii estis? si illos dixit deos ad quos sermo Dei factus est, et non potest solvi scriptura, me quem*
5 *pater sanctificavit et misit in mundum, vos dicitis blasphemare quia dixi, filius Dei sum?* præsertim cum Iudices filios Excelsi Deus ipse dixerit ut supra. Hinc 1 Cor. viii. 4, 5. *etiamsi sint qui dicantur dii et in cœlo et in terra (sicut sunt dii multi et domini multi) nobis tamen unus est deus, pater ille a quo*
10 *omnia, et nos in ipso, et unus Dominus Iesus Christus per quem omnia, et nos per ipsum.*

Hac ratione filium esse Deum, loca ipsa præcipua quæ ad asserendam eius deitatem afferuntur, perpensa diligenter et considerata satis declarant. Ioan. i. 1. *in principio erat Sermo,*
15 *et sermo erat ad* vel apud *Deum, eratque sermo Deus. In principio,* inquit, non ab æterno. *Sermo;* audibilis ergo: at Deus, ut invisibilis est, ita et est inaudibilis, Ioan. v. 37. non igitur eiusdem essentiæ sermo cum Deo. *Apud Deum, eratque Deus:* nimirum quia apud Deum, in sinu videlicet patris, ut infra,
20 v. 18. Num ergo unus essentia cum eo ad vel apud quem est? Certe non magis quam discipulus ille unus erat essentia cum

character, when the Jews accused him of blasphemy because he made himself God, to allege in his own defence the very reason which has been advanced. John x. 34–36. "Jesus answered them, Is it not written in your law, I said, Ye are gods? If he called them gods unto whom the word of God came, and the Scripture cannot be broken; say ye of him whom the Father hath sanctified and sent into the world, Thou blasphemest; because I said, I am the Son of God?" especially when God himself had called the judges children of the Most High, as has been stated before. Hence 1 Cor. viii. 4, 5. "for though there be that are called gods, whether in heaven or in earth (as there be gods many, and lords many), but to us there is but one God, the Father, of whom are all things, and we in him; and one Lord Jesus Christ, by whom are all things, and we by him."

Even the principal texts themselves which are brought forward to prove the divinity of the Son, if carefully weighed and considered, are sufficient to show that the Son is God in the manner which has been explained. John i. 1. "in the beginning was the Word, and the Word was with God, and the Word was God." It is not said, from everlasting, but "in the beginning." "The Word"— therefore the Word was audible. But God, as he cannot be seen, so neither can he be heard; John v. 37. The Word therefore is not of the same essence with God. "The Word was with God, and was God"; namely, because he was with God, that is, in the bosom of the Father, as it is expressed v. 18. Does it follow therefore that he is one in essence with him with whom he was? It no more follows,

Christo cuius in sinu recumbebat, Cap. xiii. 23. Respuit enim hoc ratio: scriptura nusquam dicit; humana igitur commenta relinquamus. Ipsum Evangelistam sui interpretem sequamur. Apoc. xix. 13. *vocatur nomen eius, Sermo ille Dei:* Nempe
5 unius Dei, persona ipse distincta. A quo distincta? a Deo videlicet eoque uno. Quo pacto igitur et ipse Deus? eodem nimirum quo sermo dictus est, quo filius unigenitus; voluntate unius Dei. Quæ ratio videtur esse, cur versu secundo repetat, *hic erat in principio ad* vel apud *Deum:* inculcans id quod
10 maxime nos velit animadvertere, non fuisse eum in principio Deum, sed fuisse eum in principio ad vel apud Deum; ut ostenderet eum proximitate solum et dilectione, non essentia Deum fuisse: id quod evangelista innumeris infra locis evangelii sui sic explanat.

15   Alter locus est vox illa Thomæ Ioan. xx. 28. *Domine mi et Deus mi.* Credulus plus nimio sit is oportet, qui ex hac Thomæ abrupta exclamatione, novam fidei confessionem cæteris discipulis incognitam elicere conetur, præ admiratione non modo Christum Dominum suum sed et Deum
20 maiorum suorum, Deum scilicet patrem inclamantis, ac si dixisset, Domine! Quid video, quid audio, quid manibus tracto? is, quem hic Deum Thomæ dici volunt, ipse paulo ante fassus de se erat v. 17. *ascendo ad Deum meum et Deum*

than that the disciple "who was lying on Jesus' breast," John
xiii. 23. was one in essence with Christ. Reason rejects the
doctrine; Scripture nowhere asserts it; let us therefore aban-
don human devices, and follow the evangelist himself; who
5 is his own interpreter. Rev. xix. 13. "his name is called The
Word of God"; that is, of the one God: he himself is a distinct
person. If therefore he be a distinct person, he is distinct from
God, who is unity. How then is he himself also God? By
the same right as he enjoys the title of the Word, or of the only
10 begotten Son, namely, by the will of the one God. This seems
to be the reason why it is repeated in the second verse—"the
same was in the beginning with God"; which enforces what
the apostle wished we should principally observe, not that he
was in the beginning God, but in the beginning with God;
15 that he might show him to be God only by proximity and
love, not in essence; which doctrine is consistent with the subsequent explanations of the evangelist in numberless passages
of his gospel.

Another passage is the speech of Thomas, John xx. 28. "my
20 Lord and my God." He must have an immoderate share of
credulity who attempts to elicit a new confession of faith,
unknown to the rest of the disciples, from this abrupt exclamation of the apostle, who invokes in his surprise not only
Christ his own Lord, but the God of his ancestors, namely,
25 God the Father;—as if he had said, Lord! what do I see—
what do I hear—what do I handle with my hands? He whom
Thomas is supposed to call God in this passage, had acknowledged respecting himself not long before, v. 17. "I ascend

vestrum. Dei autem Deus essentia unus esse non potest cum
eo cuius Deus est. nunc utrius ex voce fidem nostram tutius
informabimus, Christi diserte docentis, an Thomæ novitii,
modo increduli, nunc subito præ admiratione et ecstasi qua-
5 dam abrupte exclamantis, siquidem Christum Deum suum
appellavit. Illatis enim digitis, quem tetigit, nempe hominem, quasi nescius quid diceret, Deum dixit. Neque enim
credibile est, unionem hypostaticam in eius personæ sic repente intellexisse, cuius surrectionem modo non credidit.
10 Laudatur itaque Petri fides, qui duntaxat *filium Dei viventis*
dixerat: *beatus es Simon* Matt. xvi. 16, 17. Fides Thomæ,
quamvis ad deitatem Christi asserendam, ut vulgo volunt,
multo illustrior, non laudatur, immo extenuatur, et tantum
non reprehenditur versu sequente; *quia vidisti me Thoma,*
15 *credidisti; beati qui non viderunt, et crediderunt.* Et tamen,
quamvis tarditas credentis meruerit culpam, testimonii certe
tanta quanta nusquam alias de Christo Deo, si plerique recte
interpretantur, perspicuitas aliquam profecto laudem tulisset;
tulit nullam. Quid igitur vetat hoc loco, quod dixi supra,
20 *Domine mi* de Christo, *Deus mi,* de Deo Patre intelligi, qui

unto my God and your God." Now the God of God cannot
be essentially one with him whose God he is. On whose word
therefore can we ground our faith with most security; on that
of Christ, whose doctrine is clear, or of Thomas, a new
5 disciple, first incredulous, then suddenly breaking out into
an abrupt exclamation in an ecstasy of wonder, if indeed he
really called Christ his God? For having reached out his
fingers, he called the man whom he touched, as if uncon-
scious of what he was saying, by the name of God. Neither
10 is it credible that he should have so quickly understood the
hypostatic union of that person whose resurrection he had just
before disbelieved. Accordingly the faith of Peter is commended—"blessed art thou, Simon"—for having only said
—"thou art the Son of the living God," Matt. xvi. 16, 17.
15 The faith of Thomas, although as it is commonly explained,
it asserts the divinity of Christ in a much more remarkable
manner, is so far from being praised, that it is undervalued,
and almost reproved in the next verse—"Thomas, because
thou hast seen me, thou hast believed; blessed are they that
20 have not seen, and yet have believed." And yet, though the
slowness of his belief may have deserved blame, the testimony
borne by him to Christ as God, which, if the common interpretation be received as true, is clearer than occurs in any other
passage, would undoubtedly have met with some commenda-
25 tion; whereas it obtains none whatever. Hence there is nothing to invalidate that interpretation of the passage which has
been already suggested, referring the words "my Lord" to
Christ; "my God" to God the Father, who had just testified

Christum tam mirifice suscitando a mortuis iam suum esse filium testatus esset.

Sic Heb. i. 8. *ad filium,* vel, de filio, *thronus tuus Deus in sæculum.* At v. 9. *dilexisti iustitiam* &c. *propterea unxit* 5 *te Deus, Deus tuus, oleo exultationis ultra consortes tuos.* ubi singula pene verba indicant, qua ratione Christus Deus sit; et ad quidvis aliud potius citari ab hoc auctore verba illa Iehovæ, Ps. xlv. per os amasiarum, quam ad æqualitatem filii cum patre ostendendam, cum et hæc de Solomone etiam 10 ibidem dicta sint; qui et Deus dici potuit utpote re annuente etiam scriptura.

Atque hæc tria, eorum quæ afferuntur, certissima propemodum sunt loca: nam ex illo Matt. i. 23. *vocabunt,* sic enim plerique Græci codices, *nomen eius Immanuel; quod est si* 15 *interpreteris, nobiscum Deus,* non sequitur eum quem sic vocent necessario esse Deum, sed duntaxat a Deo missum, quaemadmodum cecinit Zacharias Luc. i. 68, 69. *benedictus Dominus Deus Israelis quod inviserit et redemerit populum suum, et erexerit* &c. Neque ex illo Act. xvi. 31, 24. *Crede in* 20 *Dominum Iesum Christum. Exultavit cum tota domo quod credidisset Deo.* Non enim hinc sequitur, ergo Christus est

that Christ was his Son, by raising him up from the dead in so wonderful a manner.

So too Heb. i. 8. "unto the Son"—or "of the Son"—"he saith, Thy throne, O God, is for ever and ever." But in the next verse it follows, "thou hast loved righteousness," &c. "therefore God, even thy God, hath anointed thee with the oil of gladness above thy fellows," where almost every word indicates the sense in which Christ is here termed God; and the words of Jehovah put into the mouth of the bridal virgins, Psal. xlv. might have been more properly quoted by this writer for any other purpose than to prove that the Son is co-equal with the Father, since they are originally applied to Solomon, to whom, as appropriately as to Christ, the title of God might have been given on account of his kingly power, conformably to the language of Scripture.

These three passages are the most distinct of all that are brought forward; for the text in Matt. i. 23. "they shall call (for so the great majority of the Greek manuscripts read it) his name Immanuel, which being interpreted is, God with us," does not prove that he whom they were so to call should necessarily be God, but only a messenger from God, according to the song of Zacharias, Luke i. 68, 69. "blessed be the Lord God of Israel; for he hath visited and redeemed his people, and hath raised up an horn of salvation for us." &c. Nor can anything certain be inferred from Acts xvi. 31, 34. "believe on the Lord Jesus Christ, and he rejoiced, believing in God with all his house." For it does not follow from hence that Christ is God, since the apostles have never distinctly

Deus. neque enim Christum esse ultimum fidei obiectum apostoli explanate usquam tradiderunt: sed verba sunt historici succincte loquentis id quod apostoli sine dubio explicatius docuerunt, ut crederent Deo patri per Christum. neque ex
5 illo cap. xx. 28. *ecclesiam Dei, quam per proprium sanguinem acquisivit.* Nam id est, per proprium filium, ut alibi: Deus enim proprie sanguinem non habet. et quid frequentius quam sanguis pro sobole dicitur. verum Syriaca versio non *Dei,* sed *Christi ecclesiam* scribit; ut nostra recens *Do-*
10 *mini ecclesiam.* Neque vero Græcorum codicum certa hic fides est; quorum quinque teste Beza, legunt τοῦ Κυρίου καὶ Θεοῦ; et suspicatur is τοῦ Κυρίου ex margine irrepsisse; cum proclivius sit suspicari irrepsisse, quod additum est, καὶ Θεοῦ. Neque ex illo Rom. ix. 5. *qui est supra omnes Deus bene-*
15 *dictus in sæcula, Amen.* Primum enim apud Hilarium et Cyprianum hoc loco *Deus* non legitur; uti nec apud alios patres nonnullos, si qua Erasmo fides: qui etiam ex varia interpunctione, in dubium vocari huius loci sententiam posse ostendit, utrum de filio, an potius de patre intelligenda hæc
20 clausula sit. Sed fac illibata hæc esse; fac de filio dici; essentiam non attingunt, honorem duntaxat divinum a Patre cum filio communicatum innuunt; et primum quod sit Deus

pointed out Christ as the ultimate object of faith; but these are merely the words of the historian, expressing briefly what the apostles doubtless inculcated in a more detailed manner, faith in God the Father through Christ. Nor is the passage in
5 Acts xx. 28. more decisive, "the Church of God, which he hath purchased with his own blood"; that is, with his own Son, as it is elsewhere expressed, for God properly speaking has no blood; and no usage is more common than the substitution of the figurative term blood for offspring. But the
10 Syriac version reads, not "the Church of God," but "the Church of Christ"; and in our own recent translation it is, "the Church of the Lord." Nor can any certain dependence be placed on the authority of the Greek manuscripts, five of which read τοῦ Κυρίου καὶ Θεοῦ, according to Beza, who sus-
15 pects that the words τοῦ Κυρίου have crept in from the margin, though it is more natural to suppose the words καὶ Θεοῦ to have crept in, on account of their being an addition to the former. The same must be said respecting Rom. ix. 5. "who is over all, God blessed for ever. Amen." For in the first place,
20 Hilary and Cyprian do not read the word "God" in this passage, nor do some of the other Fathers, if we may believe the authority of Erasmus; who has also shown that the difference of punctuation may raise a doubt with regard to the true meaning of the passage, namely, whether the clause in
25 question should not rather be understood of the Father than of the Son. But waiving these objections, and supposing that the words are spoken of the Son; they have nothing to do with his essence, but only intimate that divine honor is communi-

dictus ut supra copiose ostendimus. At interpellant, quæ
verba habentur de Patre. Rom. i. 25. *præterito creatore, qui
est benedictus in sæcula, Amen.* eadem nunc de filio repe-
tuntur; filius ergo est patri æqualis; immo vero inquam su-
5 perior quam pater si hæc ratio ullius est usus. Hic enim ad-
ditur *supra omnes:* sed meminerunt intelligi sic debere, ut
Ioan. iii. 31, 32. *qui superne venit, supra omnes est, qui e
cœlo venit, supra omnes est.* his verbis natura etiam divina
diserte significatur, et tamen *quod vidit et audivit hoc testatur.*
10 Quæ verba non a seipso venisse, sed missum et obsequentem
Patri declarant; mediatorem nempe dices. At inquam mediator esse non potuit, mitti et obsequi non potuit, nisi natura
minor Deo et Patre. Itaque deposito etiam mediatoris munere,
quantus quantus demum erit, aut unquam fuit, subiiciendus
15 est Deo ac Patri. Ita igitur *supra omnes* est, ut is semper exci-
piendus sit, *qui subiecit ei omnia* 1 Cor. xv. 27. adeoque supra
eum ipsum est cui omnia subiecit: *benedictus* denique si est,
benedictionem etiam tam ut homo quam ut Deus, divinum-

cated to the Son by the Father, and particularly that he is
called God; which is nothing more than what has been already
fully shown by other arguments. But, it is said, the same
words which were spoken of the Father, Rom. i. 25. "more
5 than the Creator, who is blessed for ever. Amen," are here
repeated of the Son; therefore the Son is equal to the Father.
If there be any force in this reasoning, it will rather prove
that the Son is greater than the Father; for according to the
ninth chapter, he is "over all," which however, they remind
10 us, ought to be understood in the same sense as John iii. 31,
32. "he that cometh from above, is above all; he that cometh
from heaven is above all." In these words even the divine
nature is clearly implied, and yet, "what he hath seen and
heard, that he testifieth," which language affirms that he
15 came not of himself, but was sent from the Father, and was
obedient to him. It will be answered, that it is only his mediatorial character which is intended. But he never could
have become a mediator, nor could he have been sent from
God, or have been obedient to him, unless he had been in-
20 ferior to God and the Father as to his nature. Therefore also
after he shall have laid aside his functions as mediator, whatever may be his greatness, or whatever it may previously have
been, he must be subject to God and the Father. Hence he is
to be accounted above all, with this reservation, that he is
25 always to be excepted "who did put all things under him,"
1 Cor. xv. 27. and who consequently is above him under
whom he has put all things. If lastly he be termed "blessed,"
it must be observed that he received blessing as well as divine

que honorem accepit: Apoc. v. 12. *dignus est agnus ille mactatus, qui accipiat potestatem et divitias et vires et honorem et gloriam et benedictionem,* inde v. 13. *ei qui insidet throno et agno benedictio et honor et gloria et robur, in sæcula sæcu-*
5 *lorum.* Et ille locus 1 Tim. iii. 16. *Deus conspicuus factus in carne,* incerta lectione gravius etiam laborat: apud Ambrosium enim et veterem interpretem Deus hic non legitur, cum magno vetustorum exemplarium consensu; teste rursus Erasmo. utcunque hæc sint, obscurum non est, locum hunc
10 totum De Deo Patre simul cum filio intelligi oportere, si recte attendatur. summum enim pietatis mysterium non est Christus, sed Deus pater in Christo, ut patet Col. ii. 2. *ad cognitionem mysterii Dei ac Patris et Christi.* 2 Cor. v. 18, 19. *hæc autem omnia sunt ex Deo, qui reconciliavit nos sibi per*
15 *Iesum Christum: nempe quia Deus erat in Christo mundum reconcilians sibi, non imputando eis offensas eorum.* Quidni igitur per omnia reconciliationis munera, quæ hoc ad Timotheum loco recensentur, Deus pater in Christo fuerit? *Deus conspicuus factus est in carne,* nempe in filio, imagine sua,
20 alioqui invisibilis. non venit Christus ut se, sed ut patrem conspicuum faceret, Ioan. xiv. 8, 9. *Iustificatus est in spiritu,* quis enim iustificetur potius quam pater: *conspectus est ab angelis;* in hoc scilicet mysterium introspicere cupientibus.

honor, not only as God, but even as man. Rev. v. 12. "worthy
is the Lamb that was slain to receive power and riches and
wisdom and strength and honor and glory and blessing";
and hence, v. 13. "blessing, and honor, and glory, and power,
5 be unto him that sitteth upon the throne, and unto the Lamb
for ever and ever."

There is a still greater doubt respecting the reading in 1
Tim. iii. 16. "God was manifest in the flesh." Here again
Erasmus asserts that neither Ambrose nor the *Vetus Interpres*
10 reads the word God in this verse, and that it does not appear in
a considerable number of the early copies. However this may
be, it will be clear, when the context is duly examined, that
the whole passage must be understood of God the Father in
conjunction with the Son. For it is not Christ who is "the
15 great mystery of godliness," but God the Father in Christ, as
appears from Col. ii. 2. "the mystery of God and of the Father,
and of Christ." 2 Cor. v. 18, 19. "all things are of God, who
hath reconciled us to himself by Jesus Christ . . . to wit,
that God was in Christ, reconciling the world unto himself,
20 not imputing their trespasses unto them." Why therefore
should God the Father not be in Christ through the medium
of all those offices of reconciliation which the apostle enu-
merates in this passage of Timothy? "God was manifest in
the flesh"; namely, in the Son, his own image; in any other
25 way he is invisible: nor did Christ come to manifest himself,
but his Father, John xiv. 8, 9. "Justified in the Spirit"—and
who should be thereby justified, if not the Father? "Seen of
angels"—inasmuch as they desired to look into this mystery,

1 Pet. i. 12. *prædicatus est gentibus;* Pater nimirum in Christo. *fides illi habita est in mundo;* cui potissimum, nisi patri per Christum. *sursum receptus est in gloriam;* nempe in filio qui fuit, facta reconciliatione, reversus cum filio est in gloriam,

5 vel recepit se in gloriam, quam in filio summam reportaverat. quid plura? qui receptam tueri sententiam omnino malunt, hæc non de Patre, sed tantum de filio dici, cum de utroque dispari licet ratione dici possunt; filium quidem esse Deum facile obtinuerint, non enim ibimus inficias; Deum esse sum-

10 mum cum Patre unum, nequaquam ex hoc loco probaverint.

Proximus est locus Tit. ii. 13. *apparentiam gloriæ magni Dei ac servatoris nostri Iesu Christi.* Nam et intelligi hic potest gloria Dei patris cum qua Christus sit adventurus Matt. xvi. 27. ut ex analogia scripturæ intellexit Ambrosius: vis

15 enim tota arguendi, ab articulo pendet, qui sine momento fere græcis nominibus vel adesse potest vel abesse, vel utrique nomini communis esse: et sane aliis in linguis ubi usus articuli nullus est, vel de uno vel de duobus æque possunt verba ista intelligi: et sine articulo eadem pene verba de duobus pro-

1 Pet. i. 12. "Preached unto the Gentiles"—that is, the Father in Christ. "Believed on in the world"—and to whom is faith so applicable, as to the Father through Christ? "Received up into glory"—namely, he who was in the Son from
5 the beginning, after reconciliation had been made, returned with the Son into glory, or was received into that supreme glory which he had obtained in the Son. But there is no need of discussing this text at greater length: those who are determined to defend at all events the received opinion, according
10 to which these several propositions are predicated not of the Father but of the Son alone, when they are in fact applicable both to the one and the other, though on different grounds, may easily establish that the Son is God, a truth which I am far from denying; but they will in vain attempt to prove from
15 this passage that he is the supreme God, and one with the Father.

The next passage is Tit. ii. 13. "the glorious appearing of the great God and our Savior Jesus Christ." Here also the glory of God the Father may be intended, with which Christ
20 is to be invested on his second advent, Matt. xvi. 27. as Ambrose understands the passage from the analogy of Scripture. For the whole force of the proof depends upon the definitive article, which may be inserted or omitted before the two nouns in the Greek without affecting the sense; or the article pre-
25 fixed to one may be common to both. Besides, in other languages, where the article is not used, the words may be understood to apply indifferently either to one or two persons; and nearly the same words are employed without the article in

feruntur Philipp. i. 2. et Philem. 3; nisi quod pro μεγάλου illic
πατρὸς adiicitur: et 2 Pet. i. 1. *per iustitiam Dei nostri et ser-*
vatoris nostri Iesu Christi. hic sine articulo repetitum pro-
nomen ἡμῶν de duobus divisim hæc dici demonstrat, ut in
5 græcis codicibus legitur. Et fides certe ea est, in re præsertim
cum primis credenda, quæ non ex locis aliud agentibus, lectione etiam nonnunquam varia atque sensu dubiis, unde ex-
primi et quasi extorqueri, non ex articulis aut particulis au-
cupio quodam captari, non ex ambiguis aut obscuris quasi
10 pythia responsa erui, sed ex clarissimis fontibus pleno ore
hauriri debeat. Hæc enim est evangelii præ lege præstantia,
hæc aperta simplicitas, hæc vera lux et promissa doctrinæ perspicuitas, postremo qui *magnum Deum* dicit, neque summum continuo neque cum patre dicit essentia unum; nec
15 tamen ea ratione Christum esse *Deum magnum* negat, qua
supra demonstratum est.

Affertur etiam locus ex 1 Ioan. iii. 16. *charitatem Dei, quod*
ille animam suam pro nobis posuit. Sed hic Syrus interpres
pro *Dei* legit *illius,* et annon alii codices videndum: prono-
20 men ille ἐκεῖνος, videtur non ad Deum, sed ad filium Dei refe-

reference to two persons, Philipp. i. 2. and Philem. 3. except
that in the latter passages the word "Father" is substituted
for "great." So also 2 Pet. i. 1. "through the righteousness of
[our] God and our Savior Jesus Christ." Here the repetition
5 of the pronoun ἡμῶν without the article, as it is read by some
of the Greek manuscripts, shows that two distinct persons are
spoken of. And surely what is proposed to us as an object of
belief, especially in a matter involving a primary article of
faith, ought not to be an inference forced and extorted from
10 passages relating to an entirely different subject, in which the
readings are sometimes various, and the sense doubtful, nor
hunted out by careful research from among articles and par-
ticles, nor elicited by dint of ingenuity, like the answers of an
oracle, from sentences of dark or equivocal meaning; but
15 should be susceptible of abundant proof from the clearest
sources. For it is in this that the superiority of the gospel to
the law consists; this, and this alone, is consistent with its open
simplicity; this is that true light and perspicuity which we
had been taught to expect would be its characteristic. Lastly,
20 he who calls God, *great,* does not necessarily call him supreme,
or essentially one with the Father; nor on the other hand does
he thereby deny that Christ is *the great God,* in the sense in
which he has been above proved to be such.

Another passage which is also produced is 1 John iii. 16.
25 "hereby perceive we the love of God, because he laid down
his life for us." Here however the Syriac version reads *illius*
instead of *Dei,* and it remains to be seen whether other manuscripts do the same. The pronoun *he,* ἐκεῖνος, seems not to be

rendum; ut ex collatis superioribus huius epistolæ capitibus, et huius capitis versibus 1, 2, 5, 8. colligitur; et ex Rom. v. 8. *commendat suam erga nos charitatem Deus, eo quod cum* &c. *Christus pro nobis mortuus sit. Charitas* igitur *Dei* charitas
5 patris est, qua is mundum ita dilexit, ut *per proprium san-guinem acquisiverit* Act. xx. 28. et hic *animam suam,* id est, unigeniti filii, posuerit ac dederit, ut ex Ioan. iii. 16. et plu-rimorum locorum analogia interpretandum est. Quid si etiam *animam suam* pro dilectissimi vita filii Apostolus intellectam
10 voluit, cum nos quotidiano usu loquendi, amicum quemque dilectissimum, animam sæpe et partem animæ dicere soleamus.

Palmarius locus, ut putatur, est 1 Ioan. v. et decerpta pars versus vigesimi: nam si integer legatur, non id efficit cuius causa adducitur: *sed scimus filium Dei venisse, et dedisse*
15 *nobis mentem, ut cognoscamus verum illum, et sumus in vero illo, in eius filio Iesu Christo; hic est verus ille Deus et vita æterna:* Sumus enim in vero illo in eius filio, id est, qua-tenus in illius veri filio sumus, hic est *verus ille Deus.* Nimi-rum is qui modo *verus ille* dicebatur, omisso illic Deo hic
20 addito: etenim is est ille verus, quem ut cognosceremus, ve-nisse scimus filium Dei, et mentem nobis dedisse, non is qui

referred to God, but to the Son of God, as may be concluded
from a comparison of the former chapters of this epistle, and
the first, second, fifth, and eighth verses of the chapter before
us, as well as from Rom. v. 8. "God commendeth his love
5 toward us, in that, while we were yet sinners, Christ died for
us." "The love of God," therefore, is the love of the Father,
whereby he so loved the world, that "he purchased it with his
own blood," Acts xx. 28. and for it "laid down his life," that
is, the life of his only begotten Son, as it may be explained
10 from John iii. 16. and by analogy from many other passages.
Nor is it extraordinary that by the phrase, "his life," should
be understood the life of his beloved Son, since we are ourselves in the habit of calling any much-loved friend by the
title of life, or part of our life, as a term of endearment in
15 familiar discourse.

But the passage which is considered most important of all,
is 1 John v. part of the twentieth verse; for if the whole be
taken, it will not prove what it is adduced to support. "We
know that the Son of God is come, and hath given us an
20 understanding, that we may know him that is true, and we
are in him that is true, (even) in his Son Jesus Christ: this is
the true God, and eternal life." For "we are in him that is
true in his Son"; that is, so far as we are in the Son of him
that is true: "this is the true God"; namely, he who was just
25 before called "him that was true," the word "God" being
omitted in the one clause, and subjoined in the other. For he
it is that is "he that is true" (whom that we might know, "we
know that the Son of God is come, and hath given us an

illius veri filius dicitur, quamvis proxime nominatus: ipse enim sensus communis flagitat ut articulus hic ad illum verum de quo potissimum agitur, non ad illius veri filium referatur. Similia exempla non desunt: Act. iv. 10, 11. et x. 16. 2 Thess. ii. 8, 9. 2 Ioan. 7. conferatur denique Ioan. xvii. 3. cum quo loco locus iste, transpositis duntaxat verbis, sensu consentire prorsus videtur. At inquies, ex aliquot superioribus locis Christus est Deus: si autem solus verus Deus est pater, Christus non est verus Deus; si non verus, ergo falsus. Respondeo, id propere nimis arripi: potest enim esse non *verus ille,* vel quia imago duntaxat est illius veri, vel quia illo vero minorem se passim declarat. Nobis hoc semper licebit non dicere de Christo quod scriptura non dicit. Deum dicit scriptura; Deum illum verum non dicit: in hoc nos cur non acquiescimus? falsus sane Deus dicendus is non est, cum quo Deus ille verus utpote dilecto filio divinam suam potentiam ac gloriam communicavit. Affertur et Philipp. ii. 6. *qui in forma Dei existens.* Hoc autem non magis Deum esse demonstrat, quam quod sequitur, *formam servi accipiens,* demonstrat re vera fuisse servum: etenim forma pro ipso esse apud sacros scriptores nusquam legitur. quod si *forma Dei* pro forma

understanding"), not he who is called "the Son of him that
is true," though that be the nearest antecedent; for common
sense itself requires that the article "this" should be referred
to "him that is true" (to whom the subject of the context
5 principally relates), not to "the Son of him that is true." Ex-
amples of a similar construction are not wanting. See Acts
iv. 10, 11. and x. 16. 2 Thess. ii. 8, 9. 2 John 7. Compare
also John xvii. 3. with which passage the verse in question
seems to correspond exactly in sense, the position of the words
10 alone being changed. But it will be objected, that according
to some of the texts quoted before, Christ is God; now if the
Father be the only true God, Christ is not the true God; but
if he be not the true God, he must be a false God. I answer,
that the conclusion is too hastily drawn; for it may be that he
15 is not "he that is true," either because he is only the image of
him that is true, or because he uniformly declares himself to
be inferior to him that is true. We are not obliged to say of
Christ what the Scriptures do not say. The Scriptures call him
"God," but not "him that is the true God"; why are we not
20 at liberty to acquiesce in the same distinction? At all events
he is not to be called a false God, to whom, as to his beloved
Son, he that is the true God has communicated his divine
power and glory.

They also adduce Philipp. ii. 6. "who being in the form of
25 God"—but this no more proves him to be God than the
phrase which follows—"took upon him the form of a servant"—proves that he was really a servant, as the sacred
writers nowhere use the word "form" for actual being. But

essentiali contenderint hic sumi, non effugerint iidem, quin
posita forma ponatur et materia, ponatur et efficiens Dei,
quod merito negabant. Idem igitur videtur esse *in forma* ac
si in imagine Dei dictum esset; quod sæpe de Christo dicitur,
5 sicut et de homine, ratione licet longe inferiore, et imaginem
eum esse Dei, et in imagine Dei esse videlicet creatum. plura
de hoc loco infra adiiciemus. Postremus affertur locus ex
ep. Iudæ v. 4. *et solum dominatorem Deum ac dominum
nostrum Iesum Christum negant.* Quis hic despotam sive
10 *dominatorem* et *Dominum* non verbose nimis in unum quem-
libet simul conferri dixerit? quis non potius de duobus hæc
dici, de patre nimirum solo Deo, ac Domino nostro Iesu
Christo, ex collatis aliunde innumeris locis id clare confir-
mantibus, iudicaverit? sed qui ex articulis nescio quam vim
15 elicere solent, propterea quod hic duorum nominum priori
duntaxat articulus futilitatis vitandæ causa Græce præponitur,
de eodem dici posterius etiam nomen contendunt. Quod si
ea vis articulorum esset, quo pacto carere iis cæteræ linguæ
possent, non video. Multo minus valuerint citata ex vetere in
20 novo testamento loca, si ad aliud vel plus probandum adhi-
bentur quam ille scriptor evangelicus probandum sibi proposuit. Eo in genere sunt Psal. lxviii. 18, 19, 20. *curruum*

if it be contended that "the form of God" is here taken in a philosophical sense for the essential form, this consequence cannot be avoided, that when Christ laid aside the form, he laid aside also the substance and the efficiency of God; a
5 doctrine against which they protest, and with justice. "To be in the form of God," therefore, seems to be synonymous with being in the image of God; which is often predicated of Christ, even as man is also said, though in a much lower sense, to be the image of God, and to be in the image of God, that
10 is, by creation. More will be added respecting this passage hereafter.

The last passage that is quoted is from the epistle of Jude, v. 4. "denying the only Lord God, and our Lord Jesus Christ." Who will not agree that this is too verbose a mode of descrip-
15 tion, if all these words are intended to apply to one person? or who would not rather conclude, on a comparison of many other passages which tend to confirm the same opinion, that they were spoken of two persons, namely, the Father the only God, and our Lord Jesus Christ? Those, however, who are
20 accustomed to discover some extraordinary force in the use of the article, contend that both names must refer to the same person, because the article is prefixed in the Greek to the first of them only, which is done to avoid weakening the structure of the sentence. If the force of the articles is so great, I do not
25 see how other languages can dispense with them.

The passages quoted in the New Testament from the Old will have still less weight than the above, if produced to prove anything more than what the writer who quoted them in-

Dei duæ myriades &c. *Dominus cum illis. Ascendens in sublime* &c. *accepisti dona hominibus.* Hic præter quasdam elleipses, quas pro suo arbitrio interpretes varie supplere audent, duorum fit mentio, *Dei* et *Domini:* quod contra ipsos
5 facit qui, collato hoc loco cum Eph. iv. 5. 8. Christi summam deitatem hinc asserere conantur: quod apostolo in mentem non venerat; ut qui longe secus disputet v. 9. *illud ascendit quid est, nisi quod etiam descenderet prius in infimas partes terræ?* unde hoc tantum voluit ostendere, Christum Domi-
10 num modo mortuum, nunc cœlo receptum, hominibus dedisse dona quæ a patre acceperat.

Verum ab evangelio ad legis tempora, quod mirum est, recurrunt, qui patrem et filium essentia esse unum volunt; et lucem tenebris illustrare conantur. Nempe filius non tan-
15 tum Deus, sed Iehova quoque nominatur; ut ex collatis aliquot locis utriusque fœderis ostenditur. Iehova autem unus est, isque summus Deus; ergo filius et pater essentia unum sunt. At vero argumentum illud quam infirmum sit, facile apparebit; attributum nempe esse filio nomen Iehovæ, cum
20 nomen Iehovæ etiam angelis concessum sit, haud secus ac nomen Dei concessum esse supra docuimus, nimirum divi-

tended. Of this class are, Psal. lxviii. 17–19. "the chariots of God are twenty thousand," &c. "the Lord is among them," &c. "thou hast ascended on high . . . thou hast received gifts for men." Here (to say nothing of several ellipses, which the interpreters are bold enough to fill up in various ways, as they think proper) mention is made of two persons, "God" and "the Lord," which is in contradiction to the opinions of those who attempt to elicit a testimony to the supreme divinity of Christ, by comparing this passage with Eph. iv. 5–8. Such a doctrine was never intended by the apostle, who argues very differently in the ninth verse—"now that he ascended, what is it but that he also descended first into the lower parts of the earth?"—from which he only meant to show that the Lord Christ, who had lately died, and was now received into heaven, "gave gifts unto men" which he had received from the Father.

It is singular, however, that those who maintain the Father and the Son to be one in essence, should revert from the gospel to the times of the law, as if they would make a fruitless attempt to illustrate light by darkness. They say that the Son is called not only God, but also Jehovah, as appears from a comparison of several passages in both testaments. Now Jehovah is the one supreme God; therefore the Son and the Father are one in essence. It will be easy, however, to expose the weakness of an argument derived from the ascription of the name of Jehovah to the Son. For the name of Jehovah is conceded even to the angels, in the same sense as it has been already shown that the name of God is applied to them;

nam præsentiam atque personam verbaque ipsa Iehovæ refe-
rentibus. Gen. xvi. 7. *inveniens eam angelus Iehovæ.* cum
v. 10. *iterum dixit angelus Iehovæ, valde multiplicabo semen
tuum.* et 13. *tunc vocavit Hagar nomen Iehovæ alloquen-*
5 *tis ipsam.* et cap. xviii. 10. *et dixit Iehova* &c. apparet tamen
tres illos hospites fuisse angelos. Sic Gen. xix. v. 1. *duobus angelis.* et 13. *misit nos Iehova.* cum 18. 21, 24. *ne quæso*
אֲדֹנָי. *cui dixit ille, en acceptum habeo te. Iehova demisit pluviam ab Iehova e cœlis.* et cap. xxi. 17. *inclamans angelus Dei*
10 *Hagaram e cœlo* &c. *attendit Deus,* cum v. 18. *patrem gentis
magnæ efficiam ipsum.* Sic Exod. iii. 2, 4. *angelus Iehovæ.
videns Iehova. inclamavit Deus.* cum Act. vii. 30. *visus est
ei angelus Domini.* Si is Christus aut summus Deus fuisset,
videtur id Stephanus tum maxime fuisse palam dicturus vel
15 ad fidem aliis vel ad terrorem illis iudicibus incutiendum. Et
Exod. xx. ubi lex data est, nulla cuiusquam mentio fit qui
legem dederit Mosi præterquam Iehovæ; et tamen Act. vii.
38. idem Stephanus qui supra, *fuit* inquit, *cum angelo ipsum
alloquente in monte Sina.* Et v. 53. docet idem, acceptam esse
20 legem *per dispositionem angelorum.* Sic Gal. iii. 19. *ordinata
per angelos.* Heb. ii. 2. *si per angelos dictus sermo fuit firmus*

namely, when they represent the divine presence and person, and utter the very words of Jehovah. Gen. xvi. 7. "the angel of Jehovah found her," compared with v. 10. "the angel of Jehovah said unto her, I will multiply thy seed exceedingly,"

5 and v. 13. "she called the name of Jehovah who spake unto her—." xviii. 13. "and Jehovah said," &c. whereas it appears that the three men whom Abraham entertained were angels. Gen. xix. 1. "there came two angels." v. 13. "and Jehovah hath sent us"—compared with v. 18, 21, 24. "Oh,

10 not so, אֲדֹנָי: and he said unto him, See, I have accepted thee . . . then Jehovah rained . . . from Jehovah out of heaven." Gen. xxi. 17. "the angel of God called to Hagar out of heaven," &c. "God hath heard"—compared with v. 18. "I will make him a great nation." So Exod. iii. 2, 4. "the angel

15 of Jehovah . . . when Jehovah saw that he turned aside to see, God called unto him"—compared with Acts vii. 30. "there appeared to him an angel of the Lord in a flame of fire in a bush." If that angel had been Christ or the supreme God, it is natural to suppose that Stephen would have de-

20 clared it openly, especially on such an occasion, where it might have tended to strengthen the faith of the other believers, and strike his judges with alarm. In Exod. xx. on the delivery of the law to Moses, no mention is made of any one except Jehovah, and yet Acts vii. 38. the same Stephen says,

25 "this is he that was in the church in the wilderness with the angel which spake to him in the mount Sinai"; and verse 53. he declares that "the law was received by the disposition of angels." Gal. iii. 19. "it was ordained by angels." Heb. ii. 2.

&c. Ergo quæ illic Iehova locutus esse dicitur, non ipse, sed angeli locuti sunt nomine Iehovæ. Nec mirum; non enim convenisse videtur, ut Christus evangelii minister, idem fuerit minister legis, *quanto præstantioris pacti est mediator,* 5 Heb. viii. 6. Illud vero mirum, si legis mediator fuit Christus, id tot apostolos nunquam indicasse, immo contrarium videtur monuisse. Heb. i. 1. *multis vicibus, multisque modis olim Deus loquutus Patribus in Prophetis, ultimis diebus hisce loquutus est nobis in filio.* porro Num. xxii. 22. *accensa est* 10 *ira Dei, et opposuit se angelus Iehovæ.* Et. v. 31. *tum detexit Iehova oculos Baleami, qui vidit angelum Iehovæ.* Mox ille angelus v. 32. tanquam Iehova ipse; *ecce ego egressus sum, ut sim tibi adversarius, quia declinat hæc via in conspectu meo.* Et Baleamus v. 34. *si malum videtur in oculis tuis.* Et rursum 15 angelus, *tantum quod edixero tibi* v. 35. cum 20. et cum cap. xxiii. 8, 20. Ios. v. 14. *sum princeps militiæ Iehovæ,* cum cap. vi. 2. *dixit Iehova.* Iudic. vi. 11, 12. *angelus Iehovæ. Iehova tecum.* cum v. 14. *Iehova dixit.* Et rursus 20, 21. *angelus Dei. Angelus Iehovæ.* et 22. *animadvertit angelum Iehovæ* 20 *eum esse* &c. cum 23. *dixit ei Iehova:* quamquam angelus, ut fere alias, pro Iehova se gessit: v. 14. *nonne mitto te.* et 16. *facies; nam ero tecum.* et ipse Gideon tanquam Iehovam

"if the word spoken by angels was steadfast," &c. Therefore what is said in Exodus to have been spoken by Jehovah, was not spoken by himself personally, but by angels in the name of Jehovah. Nor is this extraordinary, for it would seem un-
5 suitable that Christ the minister of the gospel should also have been the minister of the law: "by how much more also he is the mediator of a better covenant," Heb. viii. 6. On the other hand it would indeed have been wonderful if Christ had actually appeared as the mediator of the law, and none of the
10 apostles had ever intimated it. Nay, the contrary seems to be asserted Heb. i. 1. "God who at sundry times and in divers manners spake in times past unto the fathers by the prophets, hath in these last days spoken unto us by his Son." Again it is said, Num. xxii. 22. "God's anger was kindled . . . and
15 the angel of Jehovah stood in the way for an adversary unto him." v. 31. "then Jehovah opened the eyes of Balaam, and he saw the angel of Jehovah." Afterwards the same angel speaks as if he were Jehovah himself, v. 32. "behold I went out to withstand thee, because thy way is perverse before me":
20 and Balaam says, v. 34. "if it displease thee—"; to which the angel answers, "only the word that I shall speak unto thee, that thou shalt speak." v. 35. compared with v. 20. and with chap. xxiii. 8, 20. Josh. v. 14. "as captain of the host of Jehovah am I come," compared with vi. 2. "Jehovah said
25 unto Joshua." Judg. vi. 11, 12. "an angel of Jehovah . . . the angel of Jehovah"—compared with v. 14. "Jehovah looked upon him, and said—." Again, v. 20, 21. "the angel of God . . . the angel of Jehovah": and v. 22. "Gideon

ipsum alloquitur. v. 17. *te illum esse qui loqueris mecum.* Sic
1 Chron. xxi. 15. *miserat Deus angelum.* et v. 16, 17. *tum
David vidit angelum, ideoque procidit, et dixit Deo.* et v. 18,
19. *tum angelus Iehovæ edixit Gadi. Ascendit itaque David*
5 *secundum verbum Gadis, quod edixerat nomine Iehovæ.*

At duæ nonnunquam personæ in eadem sententia Iehova
nominantur. ut Gen. xix. 24. *Iehova demisit pluviam ab
Iehova e cœlis.* 1 Sam. iii. 21. *postquam revelasset se Iehova
Schemueli shilunti in sermone Iehovæ.* Ier. xxxiv. 12. *fuit*
10 *verbum Iehovæ ad Ieremiam a Iehova, dicendo.* Hos. i. 7.
servabo eos per Iehovam Deum ipsorum. Zech. iii. 1, 2, 3.
coram angelo. dicebat autem Iehova, increpat Iehova te, et
rursus, *coram ipso angelo.* Respondeo, his in locis, aut alterum horum esse angelum, ut supra, aut emphatico loquendi
15 more atque usu, bis nomen Iehovæ, de eadem tamen persona
reciproce dici; nam *Iehova Deus Israel, Iehova unus.* At si hic
uterque sua natura ac proprie Iehova est, non iam unus, sed

perceived that he was an angel of Jehovah—" compared with v. 23. "Jehovah said unto him—" although the angel here, as in other instances, personated the character of Jehovah:—v. 14. "have not I sent thee?" v. 16. "surely I will be with thee, and thou shalt smite the Midianites": and Gideon himself addresses him as Jehovah, v. 17. "show me a sign that thou talkest with me." 1 Chron. xxi. 15. "God sent an angel—." v. 16, 17. "and David saw the angel of Jehovah . . . and fell upon his face, and said unto God—." v. 18, 19. "then the angel of Jehovah commanded Gad to say unto David . . . and David went up at the saying of Gad, which he spake in the name of Jehovah."

But it may be urged, that the name of Jehovah is sometimes assigned to two persons in the same sentence. Gen. xix. 24. "Jehovah rained . . . from Jehovah out of heaven." 1 Sam. iii. 21. "Jehovah revealed himself to Samuel in Shiloh by the word of Jehovah." Jer. xxxiv. 12. "the word of Jehovah came to Jeremiah from Jehovah, saying—." Hos. i. 7. "I will save them by Jehovah their God." Zech. iii. 1–3. "standing before the angel . . . and Jehovah said unto Satan, Jehovah rebuke thee"—and again "before the angel." I answer, that in these passages either one of the two persons is an angel, according to that usage of the word which has been already explained; or it is to be considered as a peculiar form of speaking, in which, for the sake of emphasis, the name of Jehovah is repeated, though with reference to the same person; "for Jehovah the God of Israel is one Jehovah." If in such texts as these both persons are to be understood prop-

duo plane Iehovæ sunt; itaque emphaseos duntaxat causa nomen illud interatur. Similis locutio extat Gen. ix. 16. *aspiciam, ad recordandum fœderis inter Deum et omnem animantem.* et 1 Cor. i. 7, 8. *expectantibus revelationem Domini nostri Iesu Christi.* et 1 Thess. iii. 12, 13. *faxit Dominus, ut* &c. *ut corda vestra stabiliat coram Deo et patre nostro in adventum Domini nostri Iesu Christi.* hic sive Deus et pater, sive Dominus Iesus is est qui superiore versu Dominus appellatur, utrobique similis redundantia est. certe si in locis supra citatis aliisque eiusmodi duos esse intellexissent Hebræi, quorum uterque Iehova pari iure diceretur et esset, credidissent sine dubio sicuti nunc fere creditur, inculcantibus toties prophetis, aut saltem scrupulo gravi laborassent: at ita unquam intellexisse ea loca ecclesiam illam, aut credidisse duos esse, quorum uterque pari ratione et nominaretur Iehova et esset, intelligentem credo neminem affirmaturum: non alio igitur modo intellexisse ea loca videntur atque nos hic intelligimus. Sic de hominibus 1 Reg. viii. 1. *congregari iussit Solomon seniores Israelis* &c. *ad regem Solomonem Hierosolymas.*

erly and in their own nature as Jehovah, there is no longer one
Jehovah, but two; whence it follows that the repetition of the
name can only have been employed for the purpose of giving
additional force to the sentence. A similar form of speech
5 occurs Gen. ix. 16. "I will look upon it, that I may remember
the everlasting covenant between God and every living creature": and 1 Cor. i. 7, 8. "waiting for the coming of our Lord
Jesus Christ." 1 Thess. iii. 12, 13. "the Lord make you to
increase," &c. "to the end he may stablish your hearts . . .
10 before God, even our Father, at the coming of our Lord Jesus
Christ." Here whether it be "God, even our Father," or "our
Lord Jesus," who is in the former verse called "Lord," in
either case there is the same redundance. If the Jews had
understood the passages quoted above, and others of the same
15 kind, as implying that there were two persons, both of whom
were Jehovah, and both of whom had an equal right to the
appellation, there can be no doubt that, seeing the doctrine
so frequently enforced by the prophets, they would have
adopted the same belief which now prevails among us, or
20 would at least have labored under considerable scruples on
the subject: whereas I suppose no one in his senses will venture to affirm that the Jewish Church ever so understood the
passages in question, or believed that there were two persons,
each of whom was Jehovah, and had an equal right to assume
25 the title. It would seem, therefore, that they interpreted them
in the manner above mentioned. Thus in allusion to a human
being, 1 Kings viii. 1. "then Solomon assembled the elders of
Israel . . . unto king Solomon in Jerusalem." No one is

Quis tam est fatuus ut putet, duas hic personas in eadem sententia Solomonem nominari? Constat ergo, et ipso auctore
sacro id affirmante, et iis ipsis ita credentibus quibus angeli
apparuerunt, impositum angelo nomen Iehovæ; nec angelo
5 solum verum etiam universæ ecclesiæ Ier. xxxiii. 16. ut infra.
Sed quoniam hoc mirum videtur Placæo Salmuriensi, angelum præ se ferre nomen Iehovæ, et personatum quendam Iehovam sic esse, et quasi in scena histricum, ostendam ubi Deus
ipse declarat suum nomen esse in angelo. Exod. xxiii. 20, 21.
10 *ecce ego mitto angelum ante te, ad servandum te in hac via*
&c. *cave tibi ob præsentiam eius, et ausculta voci eius ne exa-*
cerbes eum: quia non feret defectionem vestram, quia nomen
meum est in eo. Ille angelus qui ex eo tempore Israelitas allo-
quebatur, et cuius voci auscultare iubentur, Iehova semper
15 dictus est, et tamen Iehova ipse non fuit. Immo inquiunt fuit;
nam Christus fuit 1 Cor. x. 9. *neque tentemus Christum* &c.
Respondeo, nihil nunc interesse fueritne Christus necne: illud
nunc quæro, an filii Israelis eum angelum revera Iehovam
esse intellexerint? si ita intellexerunt, necesse est vel duos esse
20 Iehovas intellexerint, vel Iehovam et illum angelum essentia
unum: quod nemo sanus de illo populo dixerit: dicentem

so absurd as to suppose that the name of Solomon is here applied to two persons in the same sentence. It is evident, therefore, both from the declaration of the sacred writer himself, and from the belief of those very persons to whom the angels appeared, that the name of Jehovah was attributed to an angel; and not to an angel only, but also to the whole Church, Jer. xxxiii. 16.

But as Placæus of Saumur thinks it incredible that an angel should bear the name of Jehovah, and that the dignity of the supreme Deity should be degraded by being personated, as it were, on a stage, I will produce a passage in which God himself declares that his name is in an angel. Exod. xxiii. 20, 21. "behold, I send an angel before thee, to keep thee in the way," &c. "beware of him, and obey his voice; provoke him not, for he will not pardon your transgressions; for my name is in him." The angel who from that time forward addressed the Israelites, and whose voice they were commanded to hear, was always called Jehovah, though the appellation did not properly belong to him. To this they reply, that he was really Jehovah, for that angel was Christ; 1 Cor. x. 9. "neither let us tempt Christ," &c. I answer, that it is of no importance to the present question, whether it were Christ or not; the subject of inquiry now is, whether the children of Israel understood that angel to be really Jehovah? If they did so understand, it follows that they must have conceived either that there were two Jehovahs, or that Jehovah and the angel were one in essence; which no rational person will affirm to have been their belief. But even if such an assertion were advanced,

refutabit cap. xxxiii. 2, 3, 5. *mittam angelum: non ascen-*
dam, ne consumam te. et audiens populus verbum malum
istud, luctui se dederunt. Si credidit populus Iehovam et
illum angelum essentia esse unos, divinitate ac gloria pares,
5 cur lugebat, et Iehovam iratiorem ante se ascendere malebat,
quam illum angelum, mediatorem certe, si Christus fuisset
et pacificum? si non intellexerunt illum angelum esse Iehovam, necesse est intellexisse, quo modo nos intelligimus,
nomen Iehovæ præ se tulisse: idque nec absurdum esse nec
10 histrionicum. exoratus tandem ut ipse ascenderet, hoc tantum annuit, v. 14. *facies meæ præcedent:* quod aliud quid
est, nisi eius nominis et gloriæ in angelo aliquo repræsentatio?
Quisquis autem is fuit, sive Christus sive angelorum quisquam alius, non unum fuisse cum Iehova neque parem, verba
15 etiam Iehovæ demonstrant: auscultare voci eius iussi sunt, non
propter ipsius nomen, sed quod nomen Iehovæ in eo esset.
Si porro affirmant, illum angelum fuisse Christum, quid aliud
evincunt, nisi Christum fuisse angelum, sicut et dici volunt
Gen. xlviii. 16. *angelus ille qui vindicat me.* Isa. lxiii. 9. *ange-*
20 *lus faciei eius,* id est, qui faciem eius sive gloriam refert et personam sustinet. officio, inquiunt angelus, natura Iehova. sed

it would be refuted by chap. xxxiii. 2, 3, 5. "I will send an angel before thee . . . for I will not go up in the midst of thee . . . lest I consume thee in the way. And when the people heard these evil tidings, they mourned." If the people had believed that Jehovah and that angel were one in essence, equal in divinity and glory, why did they mourn, and desire that Jehovah should go up before them, notwithstanding his anger, rather than the angel? who, if he had indeed been Christ, would have acted as a mediator and peace-maker. If, on the contrary, they did not consider the angel as Jehovah, they must necessarily have understood that he bore the name of Jehovah in the sense in which I suppose him to have borne it, wherein there is nothing either absurd or histrionic. Being at length prevailed upon to go up with them in person, he grants thus much only, v. 14—"my presence shall go with thee"—which can imply nothing else than a representation of his name and glory in the person of some angel. But whoever this was, whether Christ, or some angel different from the preceding, the very words of Jehovah himself show that he was neither one with Jehovah, nor co-equal, for the Israelites are commanded to hear his voice, not on the authority of his own name, but because the name of Jehovah was in him. If on the other hand it is contended that the angel was Christ, this proves no more than that Christ was an angel, according to their interpretation of Gen. xlviii. 16. "the angel which redeemed me from all evil"; and Isa. lxiii. 9. "the angel of his presence saved them"; that is, he who represented his presence or glory, and bore his character; an angel, or messen-

hæc cui probaverint? dicitur is quidem Mal. iii. 1. *angelus fœderis;* et ex loco supra citato Exod. xxiii. 20, 21. cum 1 Cor. x. 9. At non idcirco ubicunque angelus de cœlo mittitur, is continuo Christus existimandus est; nec ubi Christus, is con-
5 tinuo Deus cum patre unus. Enimvero legis et prophetarum obscuritas ad refutandam evangelii lucem adhiberi non debet, sed contra lux evangelica ad illustrandam prophetarum obscuritatem et tropos. Utcunque Moses certe de Christo vaticinans Deut. xviii. 15. *Prophetam,* inquit, *e medio tui, e fratribus*
10 *tuis sicut ego sum suscitabit tibi Iehova Deus tuus; ei auscultate.* Humanam hic inquies Christi naturam prædicit. at versu inquam sequente, divinam etiam naturam, eam dico quam Iehovæ vis esse coessentialem, plane a Christo removet, cum ait, *secundum omnia quæ petiisti a Iehova Deo Tuo in Horebo,*
15 *dicendo, ne pergam audire vocem Iehovæ Dei* &c. Christum igitur audituri, prædicente atque testante ipso Mose, non erant Iehovam Deum audituri, neque Iehovam Christum habituri.

Eadem ratione expendendus est prophetici quoque libri
20 stylus Apocalypseos: cap. i. 1. cum v. 8, 11. *significavit mittens per angelum suum;* mox ille angelus (qui verbis iisdem pene describitur quibus ille angelus Dan. x. 5. &c.) *ego sum*

ger, as they say, by office, but Jehovah by nature. But to whose satisfaction will they be able to prove this? He is called indeed, Mal. iii. 1. "the messenger of the covenant": see also Exod. xxiii. 20, 21. compared with 1 Cor. x. 9. as before. But it does
5 not therefore follow, that whenever an angel is sent from heaven, that angel is to be considered as Christ; nor where Christ is sent, that he is to be considered as one God with the Father. Nor ought the obscurity of the law and the prophets to be brought forward to refute the light of the gospel, but on
10 the contrary the light of the gospel ought to be employed to illustrate the obscurity necessarily arising from the figurative language of the prophets. However this may be, Moses says, prophesying of Christ, Deut. xviii. 15. "Jehovah thy God will raise up unto thee a prophet from the midst of thee, of thy
15 brethren, like unto me; unto him ye shall hearken." It will be answered, that he here predicts the human nature of Christ. I reply that in the following verse he plainly takes away from Christ that divine nature which it is wished to make co-essential with the Father—"according to all that thou de-
20 siredst of Jehovah thy God in Horeb . . . saying, Let me not hear again the voice of Jehovah my God," &c. In hearing Christ therefore, as Moses himself predicts and testifies, they were not to hear the God Jehovah, nor were they to consider Christ as Jehovah.
25   The style of the prophetical book of Revelation, as respects this subject, must be regarded in the same light. Chap. i. 1, 8, 11. "he sent and signified it by his angel." Afterwards this angel, who is described nearly in the same words as the angel,

Alpha et Omega dicit Dominus, qui est, et qui erat, et qui venturus est; et 13. *similem filio hominis;* et 17. *ego sum primus ille* &c. et cap. ii. 7. et sæpius, *quid spiritus dicat ecclesiis:* et xxii. 6. *misit angelum suum;* v. 8. *ante pedes angeli*

5 *qui mihi hæc ostendebat.* et 9. *vide ne feceris; conservus tuus sum* &c. Mox idem angelus v. 12. *et ecce venio cito; et merces mea* &c. et 13. idem ait, *sum Alpha et Omega* &c. idem 14. *beati qui præstant eius mandata;* et 16. *ego Iesus misi angelum meum* &c. Hæc Bezam eo redegerunt, ut librum hunc

10 tarde ab ecclesia pro Apostolico agnitum, adeoque negligentius habitum, versusque quosdam postremi capitis ab Arriano quopiam confusos atque transpositos arbitratus, eos in suum, quem ipsi videbatur, locum restituendos esse censuerit. Id quod nihil necesse erat, si animadvertisset, quod toto vetere

15 Testamento animadvertere cuivis licet, angelos et nomen Dei atque Iehovæ et personam et verba ipsa quasi sua suscipere solere. nonnunquam enim et personam et verba ipsa Dei præ se fert angelus, etiam sine nomine vel Iehovæ vel Dei. sed duntaxat angeli, immo hominis, ut sentit ipse Iunius in Iudic.

20 ii. 1. &c. Sed nomen Iehovæ duas res aiunt significare Theo-

Dan. x. 5, &c. "I am Alpha and Omega, the beginning and the ending, saith the Lord, which is, and which was, and which is to come." v. 13. "like unto the Son of man." v. 17. "I am the first and the last." ii. 7, &c. "what the Spirit saith unto the churches." xxii. 6. "the Lord God sent his angel." v. 8. "before the feet of the angel which showed me these things." v. 9. "see thou do it not; for I am thy fellow-servant," &c. Again, the same angel says, v. 12. "behold I come quickly, and my reward is with me," &c. and again, v. 13. "I am Alpha and Omega," &c. and v. 14. "blessed are they that do his commandments"; and v. 16. "I Jesus have sent my angel," &c. These passages so perplexed Beza, that he was compelled to reconcile the imaginary difficulty by supposing that the order of a few verses in the last chapter had been confused and transposed by some Arian, which he attributed to the circumstance of the book having been acknowledged as canonical by the Church at a comparatively late period, and therefore less carefully preserved, whence he thought it necessary to restore them to what he considered their proper order. This supposition would have been unnecessary, had he remarked, what may be uniformly observed throughout the Old Testament, that angels are accustomed to assume the name and person, and the very words of God and Jehovah, as their own; and that occasionally an angel represents the person and the very words of God, without taking the name either of Jehovah or God, but only in the character of an angel, or even of a man, as Junius himself acknowledges, Judges ii. 1, &c. But according to divines the name of Jehovah signifies

logi; vel Dei naturam, vel verborum ac promissionum eius impletionem: Si naturam adeoque personam Dei significat, cur cui personam atque præsentiam suam imponit, ei nomen eam significans non imponat? Si verborum ac promissionum
5 eius impletionem, cur cui verba uni Deo convenientia toties attribuit, ei nomen quoque Iehovæ, quo nomine verborum illorum et promissionum impletio significatur, non attribuat? aut si nomen illud usque eo gratum Deo fuit, ut hoc sibi uni sacrosanctum et proprium semper esse voluerit, cur in novo
10 fœdere, ubi promissiones maxime implentur, illud nomen prorsus deposuit, illud Domini solum retinuit, quod angelis atque hominibus commune semper fuit? Si nomen denique quodcunque sic Deo cordi esset, cur se nobis sub evangelio sine ullo prorsus nomine proprio exhibuit?
15 At instant, esse ubi Christus ipse suo nomine ac persona Iehova dicatur: ut Isa. viii. 13, 14. *Iehovam exercituum ipsum sanctificate, et ipse sit timori vobis,* &c. *et erit sanctificationi vobis: in lapidem autem allisionis et in rupem offensionis ambabus domubus Israelis.* &c. Cum 1 Pet. ii. 7. *hic*
20 *factus est caput anguli, et lapis ad quem impingitur* &c. Respondeo, collato versu 13. cum 11. *nam ita edixit Iehova mihi* &c. hæc verba non Christi hortantis Israelitas ut ipsum se sanctificarent et timerent, quem nondum norant; sed verba,

two things, either the nature of God, or the completion of his word and promises. If it signify the nature, and therefore the person of God, why should not he who is invested with his person and presence, be also invested with the name which
5 represents them? If it signify the completion of his word and promises, why should not he, to whom words suitable to God alone are so frequently attributed, be permitted also to assume the name of Jehovah, whereby the completion of these words and promises is represented? Or if that name be so acceptable
10 to God, that he has always chosen to consider it as sacred and peculiar to himself alone, why has he uniformly disused it in the New Testament, which contains the most important fulfilment of his prophecies; retaining only the name of the Lord, which had always been common to him with angels and men?
15 If, lastly, any name whatever can be so pleasing to God, why has he exhibited himself to us in the gospel without any proper name at all?

They urge, however, that Christ himself is sometimes called Jehovah in his own name and person; as in Isa. viii. 13,
20 14. "sanctify Jehovah of hosts himself, and let him be your fear, and let him be your dread: and he shall be for a sanctuary; but for a stone of stumbling and for a rock of offence to both the houses of Israel," &c. compared with 1 Pet. ii. 7. "the same is made the head of the corner, and a stone of
25 stumbling," &c. I answer, that it appears on a comparison of the thirteenth with the eleventh verse—"for Jehovah spake thus to me," &c.—that these are not the words of Christ exhorting the Israelites to sanctify and fear himself, whom they

sicubi alias, Patris esse interminantis fore se *in lapidem* &c. *ambabus domubus Israelis,* id est, Israelitis eius præcipue ætatis omnibus. quod si Christum hæc respiciunt, inusitatum non est apud Prophetas, ut Deus Pater se id facturum pro-

5 nuntiet, quod postea sub evangelio per filium fecit. hinc Petrus ait *factus est caput anguli, et lapis ad quem impingitur.* a quo autem factus, nisi a Patre? et cap. iii. citato hoc ipso Isaiæ loco v. 12, 13. haud obscure Patrem indicat hæc de se locutum. v. 15. *Sed Dominum Deum sanctificate,* quo no-

10 mine Christum hic intelligere nemo confirmaverit. et Zech. xi. 13. *edixit Iehova mihi, proiice eos conferendos in figulum, magnificum pretium quo pretiose æstimatus sum ab illis.* Respondeo, id non negari; modo hoc simul memoria tenea-tur, Exod. xxiii. 21. non suum hoc nomen, sed Iehovæ in eo

15 esse: Quod infra planius fiet. Quamquam nihil obstat quo-minus ipsius Patris nomine hæc etiam dici intelligantur; qui ita accipiat quæ in filium commissuri erant Iudæi, ac si in ipsum commissa essent; quemadmodum et filius quæ suis fidelibus facta sunt, sibimet ipsi facta esse pronuntiat: Matt.

20 xxv. 35, 40. *esurivi et dedistis mihi* &c. *quatenus id fecistis uni ex istis fratribus meis minimis, mihi fecistis.* cuiusmodi et illud Act. ix. 4, 5. *Saul, Saul, quid me persequeris?* Idem

had not yet known, but of the Father threatening, as in other places, that he would be "for a stone of stumbling," &c. "to both the houses of Israel," that is, to the Israelites, and especially to the Israelites of that age. But supposing the words to refer to Christ, it is not unusual among the prophets for God the Father to declare that he would work himself, what afterwards under the gospel he wrought by means of his Son. Hence Peter says, "the same is made the head of the corner, and a stone of stumbling." By whom made, except by the Father? And in the third chapter, a quotation of part of the same passage of Isaiah clearly proves that the Father was speaking of himself; v. 15. "but sanctify the Lord God"— under which name no one will assert that Christ is intended. Again, they quote Zech. xi. 13. "Jehovah said unto me, Cast it unto the potter; a goodly price that I was prized at of them." That this relates to Christ I do not deny; only it must be remembered, that this is not his own name, but that the name of Jehovah is in him, Exod. xxiii. 21. as will presently appear more plainly. At the same time there is no reason why the words should not be understood of the Father speaking in his own name, who would consider the offences which the Jews should commit against his Son, as offences against himself; in the same sense as the Son declares that whatever is done to those who believed in him, is done to himself. Matt. xxv. 35, 40. "I was an hungred, and ye gave me meat," &c. "inasmuch as ye have done it unto one of the least of these my brethren, ye have done it unto me." An instance of the same kind occurs Acts ix. 4, 5. "Saul, Saul, why persecutest thou

respondendum de Zech. xii. 10. præsertim si conferatur cum Apoc. i. 7. *videbit eum omnis oculus, etiam quem transfixerunt:* etenim Iehovam nemo unquam vidit, nedum Iehovam hominem vidit nedum transfixit: deinde eum transfixerunt 5 qui *effudit spiritum gratiæ* v. 10. Pater autem is erat qui per filium effudit spiritum gratiæ, Act. ii. 33. *adeptus a patre effudit:* ergo Pater is est quem in filio transfixerunt. hinc Ioannes non dicit *intuebuntur me,* sed *intuebuntur quem transfixerunt* cap. xix. 37. et eodem Zechariæ versu mutata persona 10 dicitur, *et plangent super eum, quasi planctu super unicum et primogenitum,* plane quasi de alio, id est, de filio potissimum, non de se proprie loquatur Iehova. Eiusdem explicationis est illud Mal. iii. 1. *ecce ego missurus sum angelum meum, qui expediat viam meam ante me: et repente veniet* 15 *in templum suum Dominus quem vos quæritis, et angelus fœderis quo vos delectamini ecce venturus est, ait Iehova exercituum.* Unde sic argumentatur Placæus. Ille ante cuius faciem mittendus est angelus Baptista, est Deus Israelis; Christus ille est; non enim missus est Baptista ante faciem 20 patris. At vero si Ioannes Baptista dictus est Elias, Matt. xi. 14. *qui præcessit cum spiritu et virtute Eliæ,* Luc. i. 17. cur

me ?" The same answer must be given respecting Zech. xii. 10. especially on a comparison with Rev. i. 7. "every eye shall see him, and they also that pierced him": for none have seen Jehovah at any time, much less have they seen him as a man;
5 least of all have they pierced him. Secondly, they pierced him who "poured upon them the spirit of grace," v. 10. Now it was the Father who poured the spirit of grace through the Son; Acts ii. 33. "having received of the Father the promise of the Holy Ghost, he hath shed forth this." Therefore it was
10 the Father whom they pierced in the Son. Accordingly, John does not say, "they shall look upon me," but "they shall look upon him whom they pierced," chap. xix. 37. So also in the verse of Zechariah alluded to a change of persons takes place —"they shall look upon me whom they have pierced, and
15 they shall mourn for him as one mourneth for his only son"; as if Jehovah were not properly alluding to himself, but spoke of another, that is, of the Son. The passage in Malachi iii. 1. admits of a similar interpretation: "behold I will send my messenger, and he shall prepare the way before me, and
20 Jehovah, whom ye seek, shall suddenly come to his temple, even the messenger of the covenant, whom ye delight in: behold he shall come, saith Jehovah of hosts." From which passage Placæus argues thus: He before whose face the Baptist is to be sent as a messenger, is the God of Israel; but the
25 Baptist was not sent before the face of the Father; therefore Christ is that God of Israel. But if the name of Elias could be ascribed to John the Baptist, Matt. xi. 14. inasmuch as he "went before him in the spirit and power of Elias," Luke i.

non mittere dicatur Pater ante faciem suam, cum mittit ante faciem eius qui in nomine patris venturus erat? nam Patrem esse qui misit hunc angelum, verba ipsa sequentia declarant: *me* enim *qui mittam,* et *angelum fœderis qui venturus est,* et *Iehovam exercituum qui hæc ait,* in prima ac tertia eandem esse personam, intelligi vix potest: immo hæc verba esse Patris angelum illum mittentis, interpretatur ipse Christus Matt. xi. 10. *ecce ego mitto nuntium meum ante faciem tuam.* Quis iam nunc misit? Filius, ut placet Placæo. cuius ante faciem? filii. ergo hic filius sese alloquitur, se mittit ante faciem suam: novum plane et inauditum; præsertim cum Baptista ipse testetur se a Patre missum Ioan. i. 33. *ego non noveram eum; sed qui misit me—, ille mihi dixerat* &c. Misit ergo Deus Pater angelum illum ante faciem filii sui, quia filium venturum ille angelus præcessit: misit ante faciem suam, quia ipse erat *in Christo,* vel quod idem est, in filio, *mundum reconcilians sibi* 2 Cor. v. 19. Sic usurpari nomen et præsentiam Dei pro virtute ac Potestate Dei quasi præsentis in filio, demonstrat alter locus de Ioanne Baptista: Isa. xl. 3. *vox clamantis in deserto parate viam Iehovæ, adæquate in solitudine aggerem Deo nostro.* Baptista enim nusquam clamavit, Christum esse Iehovam aut Deum nostrum.

17. why may not the Father be said to send him before his own face, inasmuch as he sends him before the face of him who was to come in the name of the Father? for that it was the Father who sent the messenger, is proved by the subse-
5 quent words of the same verse, since the phrases "I who sent," and "the messenger of the covenant who shall come," and "Jehovah of hosts who saith these things," can scarcely be understood to apply all to the same person. Nay, even according to Christ's own interpretation, the verse implies that
10 it was the Father who sent the messenger; Matt. xi. 10. "behold, I send my messenger before thy face." Who was it that sent?—the Son, according to Placæus. Before the face of whom?—of the Son:—therefore the Son addresses himself in this passage, and sends himself before his own face,
15 which is a new and unheard of figure of speech; not to mention that the Baptist himself testifies that he was sent by the Father, John i. 33. "I knew him not, but he that sent me . . . the same said unto me," &c. God the Father therefore sent the messenger before the face of his Son, inasmuch as that
20 messenger preceded the advent of the Son; he sent him before his own face, inasmuch as he was himself in Christ, or, which is the same thing, in the Son, "reconciling the world unto himself," 2 Cor. v. 19. That the name and presence of God is used to imply his vicarious power and might resident in the
25 Son, is proved by another prophecy concerning John the Baptist, Isa. xl. 3. "the voice of him that crieth in the wilderness, Prepare ye the way of Jehovah; make straight in the desert a highway for our God." For the Baptist was never heard to cry that Christ was "Jehovah," or "our God."

Ex ipso autem Evangelio, quo nos præcipue fundamento niti debemus, et præsertim ex eo evangelii scriptore Ioanne, qui id maxime operam dabat, ut deitatem filii, cuiusmodi esset, palam assereret, pergo illud alterum præstare quod in partitione supra sum pollicitus, Ipsum filium, non nomen Dei et Iehovæ solum, verum etiam quicquid præterea habet, patri acceptum referre; quod idem etiam post eum testantur Apostoli, ipsum videlicet esse id quod est, vitam ipsam, attributa, opera, honorem denique divinum: Ioan. iii. 35. *pater diligit filium, et omnia dedit ei in manum.* et xiii. 3. *sciens Iesus patrem omnia dedisse sibi in manum, et se a deo prodiisse.* Matt. xi. 27. *omnia mihi tradita sunt a patre meo.* Verum hic etiam, quod supra fecerunt, fortasse rursus interpellabunt qui adversantur: habent enim duas naturas Christi earumque simul officium mediatorium quasi parata quædam diverticula responsionum suarum, ut vertumnum facilius comprehendas. Quod scriptura dicit de filio, id illi divisim, quoties libet, de filio nunc Dei nunc hominis dictum volunt; nunc de mediatore vel Deo, vel homine, vel utroque simul. Atqui ipse filius diserte, *pater,* inquit, *diligit filium et omnia dedit ei in ma-*

Recurring, however, to the Gospel itself, on which, as on a foundation, our dependence should chiefly be placed, and adducing my proofs more especially from the evangelist John, the leading purpose of whose work was to declare explicitly the nature of the Son's divinity, I proceed to demonstrate the other proposition announced in my original division of the subject; namely, that the Son himself professes to have received from the Father, not only the name of God and of Jehovah, but all that pertains to his own being, that is to say, his individuality, his existence itself, his attributes, his works, his divine honors; to which doctrine the apostles also, subsequent to Christ, bear their testimony. John iii. 35. "the Father loveth the Son, and hath given all things unto him." xiii. 3. "Jesus knowing that the Father had given all things unto him, and that he was come from God." Matt. xi. 27. "all things are delivered unto me of my Father."

But here perhaps the advocates of the contrary opinion will interpose with the same argument which was advanced before; for they are constantly shifting the form of their reasoning, Vertumnus-like, and using the twofold nature of Christ developed in his office of mediator, as a ready subterfuge by which to evade any arguments that may be brought against them. What Scripture says of the Son generally, they apply, as suits their purpose, in a partial and restricted sense; at one time to the Son of God, at another to the Son of Man, now to the Mediator in his divine, now in his human capacity, and now again in his union of both natures. But the Son himself says expressly, "the Father loveth the Son, and hath given all

num, Ioan. iii. 35. Nempe quia diligit, non quia genuit;
nempe etiam filio, non mediatori duntaxat. Quanto satius,
quanto ad intellectum nostrum accommodatius dixisset, si
id intelligi voluisset, quod illi volunt, *Pater diligit Christum,*
5 vel *mediatorem,* vel *filium hominis?* non dixit, sed absolute,
filium; id est, quicquid filii nomen sua significatione com-
plectitur. Quæro etiam ut supra ex quo mediator est factus,
maneatne idem Deus qui ex eorum sententia fuit, annon? Si
idem, cur a patre potius quam a seipso petit accipitque omnia?
10 Si a patre omnia, quid opus est ad officium mediatoris, quod
docent, ut sit verus et summus Deus, cum a patre omnia accipiat, non mediatoris tantum quæ sunt, sed quæ etiam filii?
Si idem Deus non manet, summus nunquam fuit. hinc plane
intelligitur illud Ioan. xvi. 15. *omnia quæ habet Pater mea*
15 *sunt.* dono scilicet Patris. et xvii. 9, 10.—*quos dedisti mihi*
quia tui sunt, et mea omnia tua sunt, et tua mea sunt.

Primum itaque apertissime nomen accipit a Patre: Isa. ix.
6. *cuius nomen vocat Iehova, admirabilem,* &c. *patrem æter-*
nitatis. Si huius loci elleipses recte intelligantur: nam profecto

things into his hand," John iii. 35.—namely, because "he loveth him," not because he hath begotten him—and he hath given all things to him as "the Son," not as Mediator only. If the words had been meant to convey the sense attributed to
5 them by my opponents, it would have been more satisfactory and intelligible to have said, "the Father loveth Christ," or "the Mediator," or "the Son of Man." None of these modes of expression are adopted, but it is simply said, "the Father loveth the Son"; that is, whatever is comprehended under
10 the name of the Son. The same question may also be repeated which was asked before, whether from the time that he became the Mediator, his Deity, in their opinion, remained what it had previously been, or not? If it remained the same, why does he ask and receive every thing from the Father, and
15 not from himself? If all things come from the Father, why is it necessary, as they maintain it to be, for the mediatorial office, that he should be the true and supreme God; since he has received from the Father whatever belongs to him, not only in his mediatorial, but in his filial character? If his Deity
20 be not the same as before, he was never the Supreme God. From hence may be understood John xvi. 15. "all things that the Father hath are mine"—that is, by the Father's gift. And xvii. 9, 10. " them which thou hast given me, for they are thine; and all mine are thine, and thine are mine."
25   In the first place, then, it is most evident that he receives his name from the Father. Isa. ix. 6. "his name shall be called Wonderful," &c. "the everlasting Father"; if indeed this elliptical passage be rightly understood; for, strictly speaking, the

proprie loquendo, filius non est pater, nec dici potest, neque alias usquam est dictus; ut dictum vel hic esse quoquomodo concedamus: etenim plerique patrem futuri sæculi vertunt, non æternitatis; id est, doctorem sæculi qui et pater sæpe dici-
5 tur. Philipp. ii. 7, 9. *quapropter etiam ipsum Deus extulit;* καὶ ἐχαρίσατο; *ex gratia largitus est ei nomen, quod est supra omne nomen.* Heb. i. 4. *quanto excellentius præ illis hæreditate* vel *sorte accepit nomen.* Eph. i. 20, 21. *quem collocavit —longe supra omne imperium—, et omne nomen quod no-*
10 *minatur non solum in hoc sæculo, verum etiam in futuro.* Quidni autem illud nomen Iehova sit, aut si quod excellentius Dei nomen est: nominis autem impositio ad maiorem semper; puta patrem vel dominum pertinere conceditur.

Sed quid de nomine dubitemus, cum filius ipsum esse itidem
15 a Patre accipiat? Ioan. vii. 29. *ab ipso sum.* Idem innuitur Ioan. i. 1. *in principio.* Æternitati enim hic repugnat et decretum, ut supra dictum est, et nomen filii, et illa vox *ego hodie genui te,* et *ero illi in patrem;* et *principium* fuisse tantummodo ante mundum conditum, ut est Ioan. xvii. 5. demon-
20 strant Col. i. 15, 16, 17. *Primogenitus omnis rei conditæ:*

Son is not the Father, and cannot properly bear the name, nor is it elsewhere ascribed to him, even if we should allow that in some sense or other it is applied to him in the passage before us. The last clause, however, is generally translated
5 not "the everlasting Father," but "the Father of the age to come"; that is, its teacher, the name of father being often attributed to a teacher. Philipp. ii. 9. "wherefore God also hath highly exalted him, and hath given him (καὶ ἐχαρίσατο) a name which is above every name." Heb. i. 4. "being made so much
10 better than the angels, as he hath by inheritance obtained a more excellent name than they." Eph. i. 20, 21. "when he set him at his own right hand . . . far above all principality," &c. "and every name that is named, not only in this world, but also in that which is to come." There is no reason
15 why that name should not be Jehovah, or any other name pertaining to the Deity, if there be any still higher: but the imposition of a name is allowed to be uniformly the privilege of the greater personage, whether father or lord.

We need be under no concern, however, respecting the
20 name, seeing that the Son receives his very being in like manner from the Father. John vii. 29. "I am from him." The same thing is implied John i. 1. "in the beginning." For the notion of his eternity is here excluded not only by the decree, as has been stated before, but by the name of Son, and by the
25 phrases—"this day have I begotten thee," and, "I will be to him a father." Besides, the word "beginning" can only here mean "before the foundation of the world," according to John xvii. 5. as is evident from Col. i. 15–17. "the first born

nam per eum condita sunt omnia quæ in cælis sunt, et quæ in terra &c. *Estque ipse ante omnia, et omnia per eum constant.* Hic non homo, non mediator, sed creator filius primogenitus ipse omnis rei creatæ dicitur. Sic Heb. ii. 11. *et qui*
5 *sanctificat et qui sanctificatur, ex uno sunt omnes* &c. et iii. 2. *fidum ei qui fecit eum.* Nam qui ab æterno genitus est, eum certe pater genuit nunquam: Quod enim ab æterno est factum, id nunquam fiebat; quem pater ab æterno genuit, eum profecto adhuc gignit; quem adhuc gignit, is nondum est
10 genitus, nondum ergo filius: quæ enim actio initium non habet, ea neque habet finem. Nec profecto posse fieri ullo modo videtur, ut filius ab æterno vel gigneretur vel genitus sit. Si filius est, aliquando certe aut in Patre fuit, et ab eo prodiit, aut separatim ut nunc a patre in se perque se, semper extitit:
15 Si aliquando in patre fuit, nunc vero separatim existit, mutatus olim est, adeoque mutabilis: Si separatim a Patre semper in se extitit, quomodo est a Patre, quomodo genitus, quomodo filius, quomodo denique subsistentia separatim, quin essentia quoque; cum essentia substantialis et subsistentia, si
20 metaphysicas ineptias mittere velimus, idem sint? utcunque hæc se habeant, differre nunc numero filium a patre nemo

of every creature: for by him were all things created that are in heaven, and that are in earth," &c. "and he is before all things, and by him all things consist." Here the Son, not in his human or mediatorial character, but in his capacity of
5 creator, is himself called the first born of every creature. So too Heb. ii. 11. "for both he that sanctifieth, and they that are sanctified, are all of one"; and iii. 2. "faithful to him that appointed him." Him who was begotten from all eternity the Father cannot have begotten, for what was made from all
10 eternity was never in the act of being made; him whom the Father begat from all eternity he still begets; he whom he still begets is not yet begotten, and therefore is not yet a son; for an action which has no beginning can have no completion. Besides, it seems to be altogether impossible that the Son
15 should be either begotten or born from all eternity. If he is the Son, either he must have been originally in the Father, and have proceeded from him, or he must always have been as he is now, separate from the Father, self-existent and independent. If he was originally in the Father, but now exists
20 separately, he has undergone a certain change at some time or other, and is therefore mutable. If he always existed separately from, and independently of, the Father, how is he from the Father, how begotten, how the Son, how separate in subsistence, unless he be also separate in essence? since, laying
25 aside metaphysical trifling, a substantial essence and a subsistence are the same thing. However this may be, it will be universally acknowledged that the Son now at least differs numerically from the Father; but that those who differ nu-

non fatebitur: qui differunt numero, eos propriis essentiis, ut loquuntur dialectici, inter se differre, clarius est quam ut quisquam ratione præditus possit inficiari. Pater itaque et Filius essentia inter se differunt. Hæc ita se habere, omni ratione
5 constat; non itidem scriptura constare, quod adhuc reponunt adversarii, id ipsi ostendant. Neque enim obstat illud quo tantopere confiditur, adumbratum in Melchesedecho, Heb. vii. 3. *sine patre, sine matre, sine genere; nec initium dierum, neque vitæ finem habens, sed assimilatus filio Dei.* Sic enim
10 initium dierum non habuit filius, ut fuit sine patre terreno: non habuisse ab æterno initium dierum, non magis ostenditur, quam non habuisse patrem, non fuisse filium. Quod si essentiam habuit a Patre, ea quo pacto summe divina, id est, una eademque cum patris essentia esse potuerit, ostendatur; cum
15 divina essentia quæ una semper est, generare eandem et ab eadem generari nullo modo possit: nec possit huiusmodi quicquam subsistentia sive persona agere aut pati, quin essentia quoque tota idem agat et patiatur. generatio autem cum producat aliquid quod extra generantem sit atque existat, Deus
20 certe Deum sibi æqualem gignere non potest, cum quia ipse unus semper est, tum quia infinitus. Cum itaque filius a patre essentiam habeat, filius certe non ordine solum (quæ dis-

merically must differ also in their proper essences, as the logicians express it, is too clear to be denied by any one possessed of common reason. Hence it follows that the Father and the Son differ in essence.

5   That this is the true doctrine, reason shows on every view of the subject; that it is contrary to Scripture, which my opponents persist in maintaining, remains to be proved by those who make the assertion. Nor does the type of Melchisedec, on which so much reliance is placed, involve any difficulty.
10   Heb. vii. 3. "without father, without mother, without descent; having neither beginning of days, nor end of life; but made like unto the Son of God." For inasmuch as the Son was without any earthly father, he is in one sense said to have had no beginning of days; but it no more appears that he had
15   no beginning of days from all eternity, than that he had no Father, or was not a Son. If however he derived his essence from the Father, let it be shown how that essence can have been supremely divine, that is, identically the same with the essence of the Father; since the divine essence, whose property it is to be always one, cannot possibly generate the same
20   essence by which it is generated, nor can a subsistence or person become an agent or patient under either of the circumstances supposed, unless the entire essence be simultaneously agent or patient in the same manner also. Now as the effect
25   of generation is to produce something which shall exist independently of the generator, it follows that God cannot beget a co-equal Deity, because unity and infinity are two of his essential attributes. Since therefore the Son derives his essence

tinctio sine scriptura multis imponit) verum etiam essentia
patre posterior est: nomenque filii, quo potissimum nomine
summam ei divinitatem astruere solent, sententiam ipsorum
maxime refellit. Summus enim Deus a seipso est; Qui autem
5 a seipso non est, qui non genuit, sed genitus est, is non causa
prima sed effectum est; non igitur summus Deus. Et sane qui
ab æterno genitus est, ab æterno fuit; si genitus est qui ab
æterno fuit, reddi nulla ratio potest, cur non et pater sit genitus, et habuerit Patrem; Quid? quod pater et filius, relata
10 cum sint, quæ et ratione et re differunt, et iuxta leges opposi-
torum pater non sit filius, nec filius pater, si essentiæ unius
essent quod relatis impossibile est, sequeretur patrem esse filii
filium, filium esse patris patrem: quod cuiusmodi sit quili-
bet mentis compos iudicato. Nam ne ad unius essentiæ plures
15 hypostases confugere possint, satis iam supra disseruimus.
Postremo si filius est eiusdem essentiæ cum Patre, idemque
filius post unionem hypostaticam in unam personam cum
homine coalescit, non video evadi qui possit, quin homo
eadem cum patre quoque persona sit. ex quo affirmato para-
20 doxa non pauca nascerentur: Sed de his fortasse, cum de in-
carnatione Christi agendum erit.

from the Father, he is posterior to the Father not merely in rank, a distinction unauthorized by Scripture, and by which many are deceived, but also in essence; and the filial character itself, on the strength of which they are chiefly wont to build his claim to supreme divinity, affords the best refutation of their opinion. For the supreme God is self-existent; but he who is not self-existent, who did not beget, but was begotten, is not the first cause, but the effect, and therefore is not the supreme God. He who was begotten from all eternity, must have been from all eternity; but if he can have been begotten who was from all eternity, there is no reason why the Father himself should not have been begotten, and have derived his origin also from some paternal essence. Besides, since father and son are relative terms, distinguished from each other both in theory and in fact, and since according to the laws of contraries the father cannot be the son, nor the son the father, if, which is impossible from the nature of relation, they were of one essence, it would follow that the father stood in a filial relation to the son, and the son in a paternal relation to the father, a position, of the extravagance of which any rational being may judge. For the doctrine which holds that a plurality of hypostasis is consistent with a unity of essence, has already been sufficiently confuted. Lastly, if the Son be of the same essence with the Father, and the same Son after his hypostatical union coalesce in one person with man, I do not see how to evade the inference, that man also is the same person with the Father, an hypothesis which would give birth to not a few paradoxes. But more may perhaps be said on this point,

Vitam. Ioan. v. 26. *sicut pater habet vitam in seipso, sic dedit et filio habere vitam in seipso:* et vi. 57. *sicut misit me vivens ille pater, et ego vivo vel propter patrem, ita* &c. idque in æternum: Heb. ii. 8. *ad filium autem, thronus tuus Deus in sæculum sæculi:* hinc v. 11, 12. *ipsi peribunt, tu autem permanes: tu autem idem es, et anni tui non deficient.*

Attributa et primum. Omnipræsentiam: nam si pater dedit filio omnia, si ipsum esse et vivere, dedit etiam esse ubicunque est: hinc ista intelligenda: Ioan. i. 49. *priusquam te Philippus vocaret, videbam te.* Nam ex hoc Nathanael nihil aliud credidit quam quod professus est v. 50. *tu es filius Dei;* et cap. iii. 13. *filius hominis qui est in cœlo.* Hæc filium, sive hominis sive Dei, nunquam demonstraverint eiusdem esse essentiæ cum patre; sed filium quidem hominis tum cœlo descendisse cum in utero virginis conceptus est, esse in cœlo, toto nempe animo ac spiritu ut propheta summus, tamen corpore in terris tum versabatur: vel eum, qui virtute altissima nunc factus est homo, eadem virtute vel potiore natura in principio accepta esse etiam nunc in cœlo, vel potius qui erat, ut ὤν utrumvis significat. et Matt. xviii. 20. *illic sum in medio eorum:*

when the incarnation of Christ comes under consideration.

With regard to his existence. John v. 26. "as the Father hath life in himself, so hath he given to the Son to have life in himself." vi. 57. "as the living Father hath sent me, and I live by the Father, so he that eateth me," &c. This gift of life is for ever. Heb. ii. 8. "unto the Son he saith, Thy throne, O God, is for ever and ever"—hence xi. 12. "they shall perish, but thou remainest . . . but thou art the same, and thy years shall not fail."

With regard to the divine attributes. And first, that of Omnipresence; for if the Father has given all things to the Son, even his very being and life, he has also given him to be wherever he is. In this sense is to be understood John i. 48. "before that Philip called thee . . . I saw thee." For Nathanael inferred nothing more from this than what he professes in the next verse—"thou art the Son of God," and iii. 13. "the Son of man which is in heaven." These words can never prove that the Son, whether of man or of God, is of the same essence with the Father; but only that the Son of man came down from heaven at the period of his conception in the womb of the Virgin, that though he was ministering on earth in the body, his whole spirit and mind, as befitted a great prophet, were in the Father, or that he, who when made man was endowed with the highest degree of virtue, by reason of that virtue, or of a superior nature given to him in the beginning, is even now in heaven; or rather "which was in heaven," the Greek ὤν having both significations. Again, Matt. xviii. 20. "there am I in the midst of them." xxviii. 20.

et xxviii. 20. *ero vobiscum usque* &c. Verum neque hæc infinitatem omnipræsentiæ assequuntur: ut sequente capite dicetur.

Omniscientiam: Matt. xi. 27. *omnia mihi tradita sunt a*
5 *Patre meo: et nemo novit filium nisi pater, neque patrem quisquam novit nisi filius* &c. Ioan. v. 20. *pater amat filium, et omnia monstrat ei:* et viii. 26. *quæ audivi ab eo hæc loquor;* et v. 28. *tunc agnoscetis me* &c.; *sed prout docuit me pater ita loqui;* et 38. *loquor quod vidi apud patrem meum:* et
10 cap. xv. 15. *omnia quæ audivi a patre meo nota feci vobis:* hinc cap. ii. 24, 25. *eo quod nosset omnes* &c.; et xxi. 17. *tu nosti omnia.* et xvi. 30. *nunc scimus te scire omnia; per hoc credimus te a Deo prodiisse.* Et iii. 31, 32, 33, 34. *qui e cœlo venit—: quod vidit et audivit—. is quem misit Deus verba*
15 *Dei loquitur; non enim ad mensuram dat Deus spiritum:* Apoc. i. 1. *revelatio Iesu Christi quam dedit ipsi Deus:* hinc cap. ii. 23. *me esse scrutatorem renum—.* nam et fideles quoque dicuntur nosse omnia: 1 Ioan. ii. 20. *vos unctionem habetis a sancto illo profectam, et nostis omnia.* absolute au-
20 tem omnia ne filius quidem novit; sunt enim quæ pater sibi soli arcana reservavit. Marc. xiii. 32. *sed de die illo ac hora*

"I am with you alway, even unto the end of the world." Even these texts, however, do not amount to an assertion of absolute omnipresence, as will be demonstrated in the following chapter.

5 Omniscience. Matt. xi. 27. "all things are delivered unto me of my Father, and no man knoweth the Son, but the Father, neither knoweth any man the Father, save the Son, and he to whomsoever the Son will reveal him." John v. 20. "the Father loveth the Son, and showeth him all things." viii. 10 26. "I speak those things that I have heard of him." v. 28. "then shall ye know that . . . as my Father hath taught me, I speak these things." v. 38. "I speak that which I have seen with my Father." xv. 15. "all things that I have heard of my Father, I have made known unto you." ii. 24, 25. "he knew 15 all men . . . for he knew what was in man." xxi. 17. "thou knowest all things." xvi. 30. "now are we sure that thou knowest all things . . . by this we believe that thou camest forth from God." iii. 31–34. "he that cometh from heaven . . . what he hath seen and heard . . . he whom God hath 20 sent speaketh the words of God; for God giveth not the Spirit by measure unto him." Rev. i. 1. "the revelation of Jesus Christ, which God gave unto him"— whence it is written of him, ii. 23. "I am he which searcheth the reins and hearts" —even as it is said of the faithful, that they know all things; 25 1 John ii. 20. "ye have an unction from the Holy One, and ye know all things." Even the Son, however, knows not all things absolutely; there being some secret purposes, the knowledge of which the Father has reserved to himself alone.

nemo scit: ne angeli quidem qui in cœlo sunt, neque ipse filius, sed pater. Matt. xxiv. 36. *sed pater meus solus.* Act. i. 7. *tempora et opportunitates quas pater in sua ipsius auctoritate posuit.*

5   Auctoritatem: Matt. xxviii. 18. *data est mihi omnis auctoritas in cœlo et in terra:* Luc. xxii. 29. *ego vero dispono vobis, sicut disposuit mihi pater meus, regnum:* Ioan. v. 22. *omne iudicium dedit filio;* et v. 43. *ego veni nomine patris mei:* et cap. vii. 16. *mea doctrina non est mea, sed eius qui misit*
10   *me:* et viii. 42. *ego a deo egressus sum et venio; nec a meipso veni, sed ille me misit:* et xii. 49, 50. *ego ex meipso non locutus sum, sed qui misit me pater, ipse mihi præcepit quid dicam et quid loquar* &c. et xiv. 24; *sermo quem auditis non est meus, sed eius qui misit me, nempe patris:* et xvii. 2. *sicut*
15   *dedisti ei auctoritatem in omnem carnem—:* Apoc. ii. 26, 27. *dabo ei auctoritatem—sicut et ego accepi a patre meo.*

Omnipotentiam: Ioan. v. 19. *non potest filius a semetipso operari, nisi viderit patrem operantem: quæcunque enim ille facit, hæc etiam filius similiter facit;* et v. 30. *non possum a*
20   *meipso facere quicquam—:* et cap. x. 18. *potestatem habeo deponendi eam, et rursus assumendi: hoc mandatum accepi a patre meo:* hinc Philipp. iii. 21. *potest subiicere sibi omnia;* Apoc. i. 8. *ego ille omnipotens:* quamquam hoc annon de Deo Patre dicatur ab asseverante auctoritatem suam filio vel
25   angelo, ut supra, videndum: quemadmodum Psal. ii. 7.

Mark xiii. 32. "of that day and that hour knoweth no man, no not the angels which are in heaven, neither the Son, but the Father"; or as it is in Matt. xxiv. 36. "my Father only." Acts. i. 7. "the times and the seasons, which the Father hath
5 put in his own power."

Authority. Matt. xxviii. 18. "all power is given unto me in heaven and in earth." Luke xxii. 29. "I appoint unto you a kingdom, as my Father hath appointed unto me." John v. 22. "the Father hath committed all judgment unto the Son."
10 v. 43. "I am come in my Father's name." vii. 16. "my doctrine is not mine, but his that sent me." viii. 42. "I proceeded forth and came from God; neither came I of myself, but he sent me." xii. 49, 50. "I have not spoken of myself, but the Father which sent me, he gave me a commandment what I
15 should say, and what I should speak." xiv. 24. "the word which ye hear is not mine, but the Father's which sent me." xvii. 2. "as thou hast given him power over all flesh." Rev. ii. 26, 27. "to him will I give power . . . even as I received of my Father."
20 Omnipotence. John v. 19. "the Son can do nothing of himself, but what he seeth the Father do; for what things soever he doeth, these also doeth the Son likewise." v. 30. "I can of my own self do nothing." x. 18. "I have power to lay it down, and I have power to take it again: this commandment have I
25 received of my Father." Hence Philipp. iii. 21. "he is able even to subdue all things unto himself." Rev. i. 8. "I am . . . the Almighty": though it may be questioned whether this is not said of God the Father by the Son or the angel repre-

Opera: Ioan. v. 20, 21. *pater enim—, et opera illis maiora monstrabit ei: sicut enim pater—, ita et filius quos vult vivificat;* et v. 36. *opera quæ dedit mihi pater ut ea consummem; ipsa opera quæ ego facio, testantur de me quod pater*

5 *miserit me:* non igitur deitatem testantur, sed missionem a deo; ut passim. et cap. viii. 28; *tunc agnoscetis me eum esse et a meipso nihil facere:* et x. 32. *multa bona opera ostendi vobis a patre meo.* et xi. 22. *scio fore ut quæcunque petieris a Deo, det tibi:* et v. 41. *pater gratias ago tibi quod me au-*

10 *dieris:* Sic passim in miraculis edendis: etiam ubi divinam opem non implorat fatetur tamen; Matt. xii. 28. cum Luc. xi. 20. *per spiritum, per digitum Dei, eiicio dæmonia:* Ioan. xiv. 10. *pater qui in me manet, ipse facit opera.* Quamquam hæc non sic divina plane fuerunt, ut non ab angelis eadem quoque

15 fierent eodem tempore, eodem in loco ubi Christus ipse quotidie versabatur: Ioan. v. 4. *angelus enim descendebat—.* et a discipulis; cap. xiv. 12. *Qui credit in me, opera quæ ego facio et ipse faciet et maiora istis.* Et quæ sequuntur quidem maxima, a patre tamen accepta; primum, conversionem. Ioan.

senting his authority, as has been explained before: so also Psal. ii. 7.

Works. John v. 20, 21. "for the Father . . . will show him greater works than these . . . for as the Father raiseth up the dead, and quickeneth them; even so the Son quickeneth whom he will." v. 36. "the works that my Father hath given me to finish, the same works that I do, bear witness of me that the Father hath sent me":—it is not therefore his divinity of which they bear witness, but his mission from God; and so in other places. viii. 28. "then shall ye know that I am he, and that I do nothing of myself." x. 32. "many good works have I showed you from my Father." xi. 22. "I know that even now, whatsoever thou wilt ask of God, God will give it thee." v. 41. "Father, I thank thee that thou hast heard me." So likewise in working miracles, even where he does not expressly implore the divine assistance, he nevertheless acknowledges it. Matt. xii. 28. compared with Luke xi. 20. "I cast out devils by the spirit," or "finger, of God." John xiv. 10. "the Father that dwelleth in me, he doeth the works." Yet the nature of these works, although divine, was such, that angels were not precluded from performing similar miracles at the same time and in the same place where Christ himself abode daily: John v. 4. "an angel went down at a certain season into the pool." The disciples also performed the same works. John xiv. 12. "he that believeth on me, the works that I do, shall he do also; and greater works than these shall he do."

The following gifts also, great as they are, were received by

vi. 44; *nemo potest venire ad me nisi pater traxerit eum:* et
xvii. 2. *ut quotquot dedisti ei, det iis vitam æternam;* et passim: unde Matt. xxiv. 31. *electos eius.* quoties igitur Christus elegisse dicitur ut Ioan. xiii. 18. et xv. 16, 19. ad aposto-
5 licum munus duntaxat electio ea intelligenda est.

Creationem. sed ita tamen ut per eum semper, non ab eo,
sed a patre: Isa. li. 16. *posui verba mea in ore tuo, et umbra
manus meæ texi te ad plantandum cœlos, et ad fundandum
terram, et ad dicendum Tzioni, populus meus es:* hoc sive de
10 vetere sive de nova creatione intelligatur, perinde valet. Rom.
xi. 36. *ex eo* (nimirum Patre) *et per eum, et in ipsum sunt
omnia ipsi gloria in sæcula:* 1 Cor. viii. 6. *unus Deus pater
ille a quo omnia, et unus Dominus Iesus Christus per quem
omnia.* cætera loca vide infra cap. vii. de Creatione. *Per* autem
15 præpositio minus principalem causam efficientem significet
necesse est, ubi efficiens a quo, id est, principalis, aut nominatur aut intelligitur: intelligitur autem ex iis omnibus et
quæ iam dicta sunt. et quæ post dicentur, patrem omnibus

him from the Father. First, the power of conversion. John vi. 44. "no man can come to me, except the Father which hath sent me draw him." xvii. 2. "that he should give eternal life to as many as thou hast given him": and so uniformly;

5 whence arises the expression, Matt. xxiv. 31.—"his elect." Wherever therefore Christ is said to have chosen any one, as John xiii. 18. and xv. 16, 19. he must be understood to speak only of the election to the apostolical office.

Secondly, creation—but with this peculiarity, that it is
10 always said to have taken place *per eum,* through him, not by him, but by the Father. Isa. li. 16. "I have put my words in thy mouth, and I have covered thee in the shadow of mine hand, that I may plant the heavens, and lay the foundations of the earth, and say unto Zion, Thou art my people."
15 Whether this be understood of the old or the new creation, the inference is the same. Rom. xi. 36. "for of him" (*ex eo*) —that is, of the Father—"and through him (*per eum*), and to him are all things; to whom be glory for ever." 1 Cor. viii. 6. "to us there is but one God, the Father, of whom (*a quo*)
20 are all things, and we in him; and one Lord Jesus Christ, by whom (*per quem*) are all things." The remaining passages on the same subject will be cited in the seventh chapter, on the Creation. But the preposition *per* must signify the secondary efficient cause, whenever the *efficiens a quo,* that is, the
25 principal efficient cause, is either expressed or understood. Now it appears from all the texts which have been already quoted, as well as from those which will be produced hereafter, that the Father is the first or chief cause of all things.

in rebus priorem ac potiorem causam esse: id quod vel Heb. iii. a v. 1. ad 6. satis liquet. *considerate apostolum—. fidum ei qui ipsum fecit. conditorem domus suæ,* id est, ecclesiæ. Sed qui et *ipsum* v. 2. et *hæc omnia construxit, est Deus,* pater nempe, v. 4.

Remissionem peccatorum: etiam homo; Ioan. v. 22. *omne iudicium dedit filio.* Matt. ix. 6. *ut sciatis auctoritatem habere filium hominis in terra remittendi peccata, tunc dicit* &c. Act. v. 31. *hunc Deus dextera sua evectum constituit principem ac servatorem, ut det resipiscentiam Israeli et remissionem peccatorum:* hinc cap. vii. 60. *Domine, ne statuas iis hoc peccatum.* Ex his omnibus illud Isaiæ clarius intelligitur de Deo Patre primario dici, cap. xxxv. 4, 5, 6. *ecce Deus vester, ultio advenit, retributio Dei, ipse advenit servaturus nos. Tunc aperient se oculi cæcorum* &c. Nam pater et *servatorem* Christum constituit Act. v. ut supra, et *venire* dicitur, Ioan. xiv. 23. et ipsi edere opera, ut supra.

Conservationem: Ioan. xvii. 11, 12. *pater sancte, conserva eos per nomen tuum quos dedisti mihi. ego custodivi eos per nomen tuum.* et v. 15. *rogo—; ut eos a maligno illo conserves.* hinc Col. i. 17. *omnia in eo consistunt.* Heb. i. 3. *sustinens omnia verbo potentiæ suæ.* Sed Græce legitur non *suæ* sed *illius,* nempe patris. plura vide infra, cap. viii. de

This is evident even from the single passage, Heb. iii. 1–6. "consider the Apostle . . . who was faithful to him that appointed him . . . who hath builded the house," that is, the Church. But he "that appointed him," v. 2. and "builded all things, is God," that is, the Father, v. 4.

Thirdly, the remission of sins, even in his human nature. John v. 22. "the Father hath committed all judgment unto the Son." Matt. ix. 6. "that ye may know that the Son of man hath power on earth to forgive sins, then saith he," &c. Acts v. 31. "him hath God exalted with his right hand to be a Prince and a Savior, for to give repentance to Israel, and forgiveness of sins." Hence Stephen says, vii. 60. "Lord, lay not this sin to their charge." It clearly appears from these passages that the following expression in Isaiah refers primarily to God the Father, xxxv. 4–6. "behold, your God will come with vengeance, even God with a recompense, he will come and save you: then the eyes of the blind shall be opened," &c. For it was the Father who appointed Christ "to be a Savior," Acts v. 31. and the Father is said "to come unto him," John xiv. 23. and "do the works," as has been proved before.

Fourthly, preservation. John xvii. 11, 12. "holy Father, keep through thine own name those whom thou hast given me . . . I kept them in thy name." v. 15. "I pray . . . that thou shouldest keep them from the evil." Col. i. 17. "by him all things consist." Heb. i. 3. "upholding all things by the word of his power," where it is read in the Greek, not "of his own power," but "of his," namely, of the Father's power. But this subject will come under consideration again

Providentia, ubi summa rerum gubernatio solius patris primario esse ostenditur. unde non conservator solum, sed servator etiam Pater Iehova sæpe a prophetis dicitur; quod qui de filio propter nomen servatoris interpretantur, haud leve argumentum deitatis eius nactos se esse putant: quasi vero in evangelio pater etiam servator non sæpenumero dicatur, ut infra cap. xiii. patebit.

Renovationem: Act. v. 31. *hunc Deus dextera sua evectum constituit principem ac servatorem, ut det resipiscentiam Israeli.* 1 Cor. i. 30. *ex ipso vos estis in Christo Iesu qui factus est nobis sapientia a deo, iustitiaque, et sanctificatio, et redemptio:* et 2 Ep. iv. 6. *quoniam Deus qui dixit, ut e tenebris lux splendesceret, is est qui splenduit in cordibus nostris ad præbendum lumen cognitionis in facie Iesu Christi.* et v. 17, &c. *ecce nova facta sunt omnia: hæc enim omnia sunt ex Deo, qui reconciliavit nos sibi per Iesum Christum. nempe quia Deus erat in Christo mundum reconcilians sibi. rogamus Christi nomine, reconciliamini Deo; fecit enim ut qui non noverat peccatum, pro nobis peccatum esset, ut nos efficeremur iustitia Dei in eo.* hinc facile explicantur loca illa Ier. xxiii. 6. *et hoc est nomen quo vocabit eum Iehova iustitia nostra* cum cap. xxxiii. 16. *et hoc est quod vocabit eam* (nempe ecclesiam, non idcirco essentia cum Deo unam) *Iehova iustitia nostra;* vel clariore syntaxi, *Iehovam iustitiam nostram;* vel si quis mavult, *hic qui vocabit eam* eodem pertinet.

Potestatem conferendi dona: quippe quam a patre accepit:

in the eighth chapter, on Providence, where the chief government of all things will be shown to belong primarily to the Father alone; whence the Father, Jehovah, is often called by the prophets not only the Preserver, but also the Savior.
5 Those who refer these passages to the Son, on account of the appellation of Savior, seem to conceive that they hereby gain an important argument for his divinity; as if the same title were not frequently applied to the Father in the New Testament, as will be shown in the thirteenth chapter.

10 Fifthly, renovation. Acts v. 31. "him hath God exalted with his right hand, to be a Prince and a Savior, for to give repentance to Israel." 1 Cor. i. 30. "of him are ye in Christ Jesus, who of God is made unto us wisdom, and righteousness, and sanctification, and redemption." 2 Cor. iv. 6. "for God,
15 who commanded the light to shine out of darkness, hath shined in our hearts to give the light of the knowledge of the glory of God in the face of Jesus Christ." v. 17–21. "behold, all things are become new, and all things are of God, who hath reconciled himself to us by Jesus Christ . . . we pray
20 you in Christ's stead, be ye reconciled unto God: for he hath made him to be sin for us, who knew no sin, that we might be made the righteousness of God in him." Hence Jer. xxiii. 6. may be explained without difficulty: "this is his name whereby he shall be called, Jehovah our righteousness, and
25 xxxiii. 16. "this is the name wherewith she shall be called" (that is, the Church, which does not thereby become essentially one with God) "Jehovah our righteousness."

Sixthly, the power of conferring gifts; namely, that vica-

Ioan. xvii. 18. *sicut me misisti in mundum, ita et ego misi eos in mundum:* et xx. 21. idem: hinc Matt. x. 1. *dedit iis auctoritatem adversus spiritus impuros:* Act. iii. 6. *in nomine Iesu ambula:* et ix. 34. *sanat te Iesus.* Repetantur quæ supra
5 dicta sunt de operibus ipsius: Ioan. xiv. 16. *rogabo patrem et alium advocatum dabit vobis:* et xvi. 13, &c. *ille spiritus de meo accipiet—. omnia quæ habet pater mea sunt; propterea dixi illum de meo accepturum.* sic cap. xx. 21, 22. *sicut misit me pater, ita* &c. *accipite spiritum sanctum:* hinc Eph. iv. 8.
10 *dedit dona hominibus* cum Psal. lxviii. 19. (unde hoc petitum est) *accipiens dedisti dona hominibus.*

Ipsum opus mediatorium vel potius passionis. Matt. xxvi. 39. *Pater mi si possibile est, abeat a me poculum istud.* Luc. xxii. 43. *conspectus est angelus e cœlo corroborans eum.* Heb.
15 v. 7, 8. *Qui in diebus carnis suæ deprecationibus et supplicationibus oblatis, cum clamore valido et lachrymis apud eum qui poterat ipsum servare a morte; et ex auditis precibus liberatus ex metu quamvis filius esset, tamen ex iis quæ passus est didicit obedientiam.* Si etiam filius tota persona passionis opus
20 superare per se potuit, cur se deseruit? cur Patris opem imploravit? cur angelus ad corroborandum missus? Qua igitur ratione filius cum patre essentia unus aut æqualis credendus? Sic in crucc, Matt. xxvii. 40. *Deus mi, Deus mi, cur deseruisti*

rious power which he has received from the Father. John xvii. 18. "as thou hast sent me into the world, even so have I also sent them into the world." See also xx. 21. Hence Matt. x. 1. "he gave them power against unclean spirits." Acts iii. 6. "in 5 the name of Jesus Christ of Nazareth, rise up and walk." ix. 34. "Jesus Christ maketh thee whole." What was said before of his works, may be repeated here. John xiv. 16. "I will pray the Father, and he shall give you another Comforter." xvi. 13, &c. "the Spirit shall receive of mine . . . all things 10 that the Father hath are mine, therefore said I that he shall take of mine." xx. 21, 22. "as my Father hath sent me, even so send I you . . . receive the Holy Ghost." Hence Eph. iv. 8. "he gave gifts to men"; compared with Psal. lxviii. 18. whence it is taken, "thou hast received gifts for men."

15   Seventhly, his mediatorial work itself, or rather his passion. Matt. xxvi. 39. "O my Father, if it be possible, let this cup pass from me." Luke xxii. 43. "there appeared an angel unto him from heaven, strengthening him." Heb. v. 7, 8. "who in the days of his flesh, when he had offered up prayers and 20 supplications with strong crying and tears unto him that was able to save him from death, and was heard in that he feared: though he were a Son, yet learned he obedience by the things which he suffered." For if the Son was able to accomplish by his own independent power the work of his passion, why did 25 he forsake himself; why did he implore the assistance of his Father; why was an angel sent to strengthen him? How then can the Son be considered co-essential and co-equal with the Father? So too he exclaimed upon the cross, "My God, my

me? Deus filii etiam Dei est pater. cur Patrem inclamavit? sensit nimirum se ad perferendos mortis dolores ne divina quidem natura sua sibi sufficere. et moriens, Luc. xxiii. 46. *Pater in manus tuas depono spiritum meum.* at cuinam potius quam sibi Deo se hominem commendasset, si divina etiam natura sua se satis potenter liberare a morte valuisset. pater itaque solus resuscitavit. quod nunc proximum est ut videamus.

Resuscitationem ad vitam: 2 Cor. iv. 14. *scientes fore, ut qui suscitavit Dominum Iesum, nos quoque per Iesum suscitet, et sistat vobiscum.* 1 Thess. iv. 14. *Deus eos qui obdormiverint per Iesum ducet cum eo.* Sed de hoc supra hoc ipso capite locis pluribus citatis uberius iam diximus.

Adventum in iudicium. Rom. ii. 16. *quo die iudicabit Deus occulta hominum secundum evangelium meum, per Iesum Christum.* 1 Tim. vi. 14. *usque ad illustrem adventum Domini nostri Iesu Christi.*

Honorem divinum: Ioan. v. 22, 23. *omne iudicium dedit filio, ut omnes honorent filium prout honorant patrem—, ut qui miserit eum:* Philipp. ii. 9, 10, 11. *extulit; largitus est, ut ad nomen Iesu—: omnisque lingua profiteatur Iesum Christum esse Dominum ad gloriam Dei patris:* Heb. i. 6.

God, why hast thou forsaken me?" He whom the Son, himself God, addresses as God, must be the Father; why then did the Son call upon the Father? Because he felt even his divine nature insufficient to support him under the pains of death.

5 Thus also he said, when at the point of death, Luke xxiii. 46. "Father, into thy hands I commend my spirit." To whom rather than to himself as God would he have commended himself in his human nature, if by his own divine nature alone he had possessed sufficient power to deliver himself from

10 death? It was therefore the Father only who raised him again to life; which is the next particular to be noticed.

Eighthly, his resuscitation from death. 2 Cor. iv. 14. "knowing that he which raised up the Lord Jesus, shall raise up us also by Jesus, and shall present us with you." 1 Thess.

15 iv. 14. "them also which sleep in Jesus shall God bring with him." But this point has been sufficiently illustrated by ample quotations in a former part of the chapter.

Ninthly, his future judicial advent. Rom. ii. 16. "in the day when God shall judge the secrets of men by Jesus Christ

20 according to my gospel." 1 Tim. vi. 14. "until the appearing of our Lord Jesus Christ."

Tenthly, divine honors. John v. 22, 23. "the Father hath committed all judgment unto the Son; that all men should honor the Son, even as they honor the Father . . . which

25 hath sent him." Philipp. ii. 9–11. "God hath highly exalted him, and hath given him a name . . . that at the name of Jesus every knee should bow . . . and that every tongue should confess that Jesus Christ is Lord, to the glory of God

quum inducit primogenitum in orbem terrarum, dicit, et adorent eum omnes angeli Dei: Apoc. v. 12. *dignus est agnus ille mactatus qui accipiat—.* unde Act. vii. 59. *invocantem et dicentem, Domine Iesu;* et ix. 14. *qui invocant nomen tuum;* 1 Cor. i. 2. *cum omnibus qui invocant nomen Domini nostri Iesu Christi;* 2 Tim. ii. 22. *cum iis qui invocant Christum ex puro corde.* id est quemadmodum explicatur Col. iii. 17. *quicquid feceritis—, in nomine Domini Iesu Christi istud agite, gratias agentes Deo et patri per eum.* 2 Tim. ii. 19. *quisquis nominat nomen Christi.* Non alia igitur ratione filium Dei videmur invocare quam veluti advocatum nostrum ad patrem. Sic Apoc. xxii. 20. *Veni igitur Domine Iesu;* ad iudicium nempe exercendum, *quod pater ei dedit, ut omnes honorent filium* &c. Ioan. v. 22, 23. ut supra.

Baptizari in nomen eius. Matt. xxviii. 18, 19. *data est mihi omnis auctoritas in cœlo et in terra; profecti igitur docete—, baptizantes eos in nomen patris et filii et spiritus sancti:* sed de hoc amplius cap. sequente. Tum credere in eum, siquidem is honor duntaxat divinus est: creditur enim in Deum et in Mosen Exod. xiv. 31. et in Prophetas 2 Chron. xx. 20. et in omnes sanctos Philem. 5. speratur etiam in Mosen Ioan. v. 45. et credere in aliquem nihil aliud videtur He-

the Father." Heb. i. 6. "when he bringeth in the first-begotten into the world, he saith, And let all the angels of God worship him." Rev. v. 12. "worthy is the Lamb that was slain to receive power," &c. Hence Acts. vii. 59. "calling upon God, and saying, Lord Jesus, receive my spirit." ix. 14. "all that call upon thy name." 1 Cor. i. 2. "with all that in every place call upon the name of Jesus Christ our Lord." 2 Tim. ii. 22. "with them that call upon the Lord out of a pure heart," that is, as it is explained Col. iii. 17. "whatsoever ye do . . . do it in the name of the Lord Jesus, giving thanks to God and the Father by him." 2 Tim. ii. 19. "every one that nameth the name of Christ." It appears therefore that when we call upon the Son of God, it is only in his capacity of advocate with the Father. So Rev. xxii. 20. "even so, come, Lord Jesus"; namely, to execute judgment, "which the Father hath committed unto him, that all men might honor the Son," &c. John v. 22, 23.

Eleventhly, baptism in his name. Matt. xxviii. 18, 19. "all power is given unto me in heaven and in earth; go ye therefore and teach all nations, baptizing them in the name of the Father, and of the Son, and of the Holy Ghost." More will be said on this subject in the next chapter.

Twelfthly, belief in him; if indeed this ought to be considered as an honor peculiar to divinity; for the Israelites are said, Exod. xiv. 31. "to believe Jehovah and his servant Moses." Again, "to believe the prophets" occurs 2 Chron. xx. 20. and "faith toward all saints," Philem. 5. and "Moses in whom ye trust," John v. 45. Whence it would seem, that "to

braico sermone esse quam sermone Græco aut Latino credere alicui. quicquid est distinctiunculæ, ex scholis non ex
scriptura ortum habet: nam credere in aliquem, est ubi
fiduciam nullam notat; Ioan. ii. 23, 24. *multi crediderunt*
5 *in nomen eius—; ipse autem Iesus non credebat iis seme-*
tipsum—; et xii. 42. *multi crediderunt in eum, sed propter*
Pharisæos hoc non profitebantur: et credere alicui summam
sæpius fidem significat; Ioan. v. 24. *Qui credit ei qui misit*
me, habet vitam æternam; Rom. iv. 3. *credidit Abrahamus*
10 *Deo et imputatum est ei ad iustitiam.* 1 Ioan. v. 10. *qui*
non credit Deo. Tit. iii. 8. idem. Sed et hoc etiam a patre
habet: Ioan. iii. 35, 36. *pater omnia dedit ei in manum;*
qui credit in filium, habet—: et vi. 40. *hæc est voluntas eius*
qui misit me, ut quisquis credit in filium, habeat: et xii. 44.
15 *Iesus clamavit et dixit—, non in me, sed in eum qui—:* hinc
xiv. 1. *creditis in Deum? etiam in me credite.* 1 Ioan. iii. 23.
hoc est mandatum eius, ut credamus nomini filii eius Iesu
Christi. Hinc statuamus, *credere in Christum,* nihil esse aliud
nisi credere Christum esse filium Dei a patre missum ad salu-
20 tem nostrum: Ioan. xi. 25, 26, 27. *dixit ei Iesus, ego sum*
resurrectio et vita; qui credit in me, etiamsi mortuus fuerit,

believe in any one" is nothing more than an Hebraism, which the Greeks or Latins express by the phrase "to believe any one"; so that whatever trifling distinction may be made between the two, originates in the schools, and not in Scripture.

5 For in some cases "to believe in any one" implies no faith at all. John ii. 23, 24. "many believed in his name . . . but Jesus did not commit himself unto them." xii. 42. "many believed on him, but because of the Pharisees they did not confess him." On the other hand, "to believe any one" often

10 signifies the highest degree of faith. John v. 24. "he that believeth on him (*qui credit ei*) that sent me, hath everlasting life." Rom. iv. 3. "Abraham believed God, and it was counted unto him for righteousness." 1 John v. 10. "he that believeth not God." See also Tit. iii. 8. This honor, however,

15 like the others, is derived from the Father. John iii. 35, 36. "the Father hath given all things into his hand: he that believeth on the Son hath everlasting life." vi. 40. "this is the will of him that sent me, that every one which seeth the Son, and believeth on him, may have everlasting life." xii. 44.

20 "Jesus cried and said, He that believeth on me, believeth not on me, but on him that sent me." Hence xiv. 1. "ye believe in God, believe also in me." 1 John iii. 23. "this is his commandment, that we should believe on the name of his Son Jesus Christ." It may therefore be laid down as certain,

25 that "believing in Christ" implies nothing more than that we believe Christ to be the Son of God, sent from the Father for our salvation. John xi. 25–27. "Jesus said unto her, I am the resurrection and the life; he that believeth in me, though he

vivet: et quisquis vivit et credit in me non morietur in æternum. credis hoc? ait illi, etiam Domine; ego credo te esse Christum filium Dei qui in mundum venturus erat.

Gloriam denique divinam: Ioan. i. 1. *sermo erat apud*
5 *Deum, eratque sermo Deus.* et v. 14. *spectavimus gloriam ut unigeniti egressi a patre,* παρὰ πατρός; et 18. *Deum nemo vidit unquam, unigenitus filius qui est in,* vel *ad sinum patris sui, ille enarravit:* et vi. 46. *non quod patrem viderit quisquam, nisi is qui est a deo,* ὁ ὢν παρὰ τοῦ Θεοῦ *cum capite* xvii.
10 5. *glorifica me tu pater apud temetipsum ea gloria quam habui apud te priusquam mundus esset.* Nemo hic dubitat quin Pater ascendentem ad se filium, in eum quem petebat pristinum gloriæ locum restituerit: is autem locus, quod nemo non fatebitur, est dextera Dei; erat igitur idem a principio
15 gloriæ locus unde descenderat: dextera autem Dei gloriam quidem significat, non primario summe divinam, sed Deo duntaxat proximam. itaque v. 24. *ut spectent gloriam illam meam quam dedisti mihi; quia dilexisti me ante iactum mundi fundamentum:* his in locis, sicubi alias, de natura filii
20 divina docemur, ut distincta tamen a natura Patris ac plane minore: esse enim apud Deum πρὸς Θεὸν, et παρὰ Θεῷ; esse Deum, et esse in sinu Dei patris; esse Deum, et esse a Deo; esse unum Deum invisibilem, et esse unigenitum aspecta-

were dead, yet shall he live: and whosoever liveth and believeth in me shall never die. Believest thou this? She saith
unto him, Yea, Lord; I believe that thou art the Christ, the
Son of God, which should come into the world."

5   Thirteenthly, divine glory. John i. 1. "the Word was with
God, and the Word was God." v. 14. "we beheld his glory,
the glory as of the only-begotten of the Father," παρὰ Πατρός.
v. 18. "no man hath seen God at any time; the only-begotten
Son, which is in the bosom of the Father, he hath declared
10   him." vi. 46. "not that any man hath seen the Father, save
he which is of God," ὁ ὢν παρὰ τοῦ Θεοῦ. xvii. 5. "glorify
thou me with thine own self with the glory which I had with
thee before the world was." No one doubts that the Father
restored the Son, on his ascent into heaven, to that original
15   place of glory of which he here speaks. That place will be
universally acknowledged to be the right hand of God; the
same therefore was his place of glory in the beginning, and
from which he had descended. But the right hand of God
primarily signifies a glory, not in the highest sense divine, but
20   only next in dignity to God. So v. 24. "that they may behold
my glory which thou hast given me; for thou lovedst me
before the foundation of the world." In these, as in other
passages, we are taught that the nature of the Son is indeed
divine, but distinct from and clearly inferior to the nature of
25   the Father—for to be with God, πρὸς Θεὸν, and to be from
God, παρὰ Θεῷ—to be God, and to be in the bosom of God
the Father—to be God, and to be from God—to be the one
invisible God, and to be the only-begotten and visible, are

bilem disparata sunt; quæ de una eademque essentia dici non possunt: gloriam autem habere datam non ab se sibi sed a patre quia sit dilectus, etiam in divina natura ante iacta mundi fundamenta, minorem plane declarat. Sic Matt. xvi. 27. *cum* 5 *gloria patris sui:* Act. iii. 13. *Deus ille Abrahami, et Isaaci, et Iacobi, Deus ille patrum nostrorum glorificavit filium suum Iesum.* Col. i. 19. *quoniam libuit patri ut omnis plenitudo in eo inhabitaret* cum cap. ii. 9. *in eo inhabitat omnis plenitudo Deitatis corporaliter.* et Eph. iii. 19. *ut impleamini ad* 10 *omnem usque plenitudinem illam Dei:* hæc apertissime demonstrant, ita Christum suam plenitudinem accepisse a Deo, ut nos a Christo accepturi sumus: illud enim *corporaliter* quod adiicitur, vel idem est quod *solide,* ut opponatur *inani deceptioni,* cuius fit mentio versu præcedente, vel ad eandem 15 cum Deo essentiam arguendam nihil penitus facit. 1 Pet. i. 21. *gloriam ei dedit, ut fides ac spes vestra sit in Deo.* et ii. 4. *apud Deum electus, honoratus.* et 2 Ep. i. 16, 17. *qui oculis nostris aspeximus illius maiestatem: acceperat enim a Deo patre honorem et gloriam voce ad eum delata huiusmodi*—. 20 et 1 Ep. iv. 11. cum 2 Ep. iii. 18. *ut in omnibus glorificetur Deus per Iesum Christum: cui est gloria et robur in sæcula sæculorum. crescite in gratia et notitia Domini nostri et servatoris Iesu Christi: cui gloria et nunc, et in diem sæculi.* Hic ex priore loco videtur Domini nomen, ut sæpe alias, de patre

things so different that they cannot be predicated of one and the same essence. Besides, considering that his glory, even in his divine nature before the foundation of the world, was not self-derived, but given by the love of the Father, it is plainly demonstrated to be inferior to the Father. So Matt. xvi. 27. "in the glory of his Father." Acts iii. 13. "the God of Abraham, and of Isaac, and of Jacob, the God of our fathers, hath glorified his Son Jesus." Col. i. 19. "it pleased the Father that in him should all fulness dwell." ii. 9. "in him dwelleth all the fulness of the Godhead bodily." Eph. iii. 19. "that ye might be filled with all the fulness of God." These passages most clearly evince that Christ has received his fulness from God, in the sense in which we shall receive our fulness from Christ. For the term "bodily," which is subjoined, either means "substantially," in opposition to the "vain deceit" mentioned in the preceding verse, or is of no weight in proving that Christ is of the same essence with God. 1 Pet. i. 21. "who gave him glory, that your faith and hope might be in God." ii. 4. "chosen of God and precious." 2 Pet. i. 16, 17. "we were eye-witnesses of his majesty; for he received from God the Father honor and glory, when there came such a voice to him——." 1 Pet. iv. 11. compared with 2 Pet. iii. 18. "that God in all things may be glorified, through Jesus Christ, to whom be praise and dominion for ever and ever: but grow in grace, and in the knowledge of our Lord and Savior Jesus Christ; to whom be glory both now and for ever." On a collation of the two passages, it would seem that the phrase "our Lord," in the latter, must be understood of the Father,

esse intelligendum. Si de filio, eodem tamen recidit; doctrina enim superioris loci non variat. hinc Ioan. xii. 41. ex Isa. lxiii. 5. *hæc dixit Isaias, quando vidit gloriam eius:* id est, gloriam unigeniti, quam pater filio dedit. Neque obstat quod legitur Isa. xlii. 8. *ego sum Iehova, illud est nomen meum; et gloriam meam alteri non dabo, et laudem meam sculptilibus:* tametsi enim filius alter est a patre, hic tamen gloriam sculptilibus et alienis diis negat se daturum: non filio qui effulgentia gloriæ illius et character substantiæ est, et super quem positurum se spiritum suum promiserat, v. 1. Quam enim gloriam filio dat pater, ab se non alienat; filius enim patrem ubique glorificat: Ioan. xiii. 31. *nunc glorificatus est filius hominis, et Deus glorificatus est in eo.* et cap. viii. 50. *ego vero non quæro gloriam meam; est qui quærat et iudicet.*

Hinc patris quæ sunt, qua ratione dicantur esse filii, perspicuum est. Ioan. xvi. 15. *omnia quæ habet pater, mea sunt.* et xvii. 6, 7. *tui erant, et mihi eos dedisti. nunc noverunt omnia quæ dedisti, a te esse.* hinc v. 10. *mea omnia tua sunt, et tua mea sunt.* Nimirum quo pacto regnum suum esse dixit, Luc. xxii. 30; quia priore versu dixerat, *ego paciscor vobis, prout pactus est mihi pater meus, regnum.* Adventum deni-

as is frequently the case. If however it be applied to the Son, the inference is the same, for it does not alter the doctrine of the former passage. John xii. 41. citing Isa. lxiii. 5. "these things said Esaias, when he saw his glory, and spake of him,"

5 that is, the glory of the only-begotten, given to the Son by the Father. Nor is any difficulty created by Isa. xlii. 8. "I am Jehovah, that is my name; and my glory will I not give to another, neither my praise to graven images." For though the Son be "another" than the Father, God only means that

10 he will not give his glory to graven images and strange gods, not that he will not give it to the Son, who is the brightness of his glory, and the express image of his person, and upon whom he had promised that he would put his Spirit, v. 1. For the Father does not alienate his glory from himself in

15 imparting it to the Son, inasmuch as the Son uniformly glorifies the Father. John xiii. 31. "now is the Son of man glorified, and God is glorified in him." viii. 50. "I seek not mine own glory; there is one that seeketh and judgeth."

Hence it becomes evident on what principle the attributes

20 of the Father are said to pertain to the Son. John xvi. 15. "all things that the Father hath are mine." xvii. 6, 7. "thine they were, and thou gavest them me; . . . now they have known that all things whatsoever thou hast given me are of thee." It is therefore said, v. 10. "all mine are thine, and thine are

25 mine"; namely, in the same sense in which he had called the kingdom his. Luke xxii. 30. for he had said in the preceding verse, "I appoint unto you a kingdom, as my Father hath appointed unto me."

que in iudicium: 1 Tim. vi. 14. *usque ad illustrem illum adventum Domini nostri Iesu Christi, quem præstitutis* vel *suis temporibus ostendet ille beatus, Rex ille regum et Dominus dominorum; qui solus habet immortalitatem, lucem habitans* 5 *inaccessam, quem vidit nemo hominum neque videre potest.*

Cum hæc omnia a patre acceperit, et in forma Dei esset, *rapinam non duxit hoc æqualia esse cum Deo,* Philipp. ii. 6. Nempe quia id dono acceperat, non rapto. esse autem æqualem, si is sensus loci illius est, unitatem essentiæ refellit potius 10 quam probat. æqualitas enim non nisi duarum saltem potest essentiarum esse. Sicuti et istæ voces *non duxit,* vel *non arbitratus est,* et *sese exinanivit,* &c. convenire summo Deo non videntur: Arbitrari enim quid est aliud, nisi opinari? Opinio autem in Deum non cadit: nec magis exinanire se Deus infi-15 nitus potest, quam sibi contradicere; infinitum enim et inane sibi invicem repugnant. At vero cum in qua forma Dei extitit, eam exinaniverit, si forma Dei pro ipsa essentia Dei sumenda, ipsam Dei essentiam exinaniisse arguetur; quod fieri non potest.

20 Patrem itaque maiorem esse filio (quod postremo loco demonstrandum suscepi) filius ipse profitetur palam, atque declarat: Ioan. x. 29. *pater maior omnibus est.* et xiv. 28. *pater maior me est.* homine inquis. Itane vero crediderunt disci-

Lastly, his coming to judgment. 1 Tim. vi. 14. "until the appearing of our Lord Jesus Christ, which in his time he shall show, who is the blessed and only Potentate, the King of kings and Lord of lords; who only hath immortality, dwell-
5 ing in the light which no man can approach unto; whom no man hath seen, nor can see."

Christ therefore, having received all these things from the Father, and "being in the form of God, thought it not robbery to be equal with God," Philipp. ii. 5. namely, because
10 he had obtained them by gift, not by robbery. For if this passage imply his co-equality with the Father, it rather refutes than proves his unity of essence; since equality cannot exist but between two or more essences. Further, the phrases "he did not think it," "he made himself of no reputation"
15 (literally, "he emptied himself"), appear inapplicable to the supreme God. For "to think" is nothing else than to entertain an opinion, which cannot be properly said of God. Nor can the infinite God be said to empty himself, any more than to contradict himself; for infinity and emptiness are opposite
20 terms. But since he emptied himself of that form of God in which he had previously existed, if the form of God is to be taken for the essence of the Deity itself, it would prove him to have emptied himself of that essence, which is impossible.

Again, the Son himself acknowledges and declares openly,
25 that the Father is greater than the Son; which was the last proposition I undertook to prove. John x. 29. "my Father is greater than all." xiv. 28. "my Father is greater than I." It will be answered, that Christ is speaking of his human nature.

puli hominem duntaxat hæc loqui? siccine in se credi voluit
Christus? non dices opinor. Si igitur non homo tantum hæc
dixit, (nam se homine maiorem esse patrem nemini erat dubium) sed, qualis ipse credi voluit, et homo et Deus, intelligi
5 procul dubio sic debet, ac si palam dixisset, pater maior me
est, quantuscunque sum, et homine et Deo: aut certe is non
dixit in quem isti crediderunt, non is docuit, sed in ambiguo
lusit. Naturam igitur cum persona, non naturam Dei patris
cum natura filii hominis comparavit. Et v. 31. *prout man-*
10 *datum dedit mihi pater, ita facio.* Et cap. v. 18, 19. insimu-
latus ab Iudæis quasi parem fecisset se Deo, id diserte negat:
non potest, inquit, filius a semetipso operari—. et v. 30.
prout audio, iudico; et iudicium meum iustum est, quia non
quæro voluntatem meam, sed voluntatem eius qui misit me;
15 id est *patris.* et cap. vi. 38. *descendi e cœlo ut exequar non*
voluntatem meam, sed voluntatem eius qui misit me. Misit
autem filium unigenitum: voluntas ergo patris et alia est et
maior voluntate unigeniti. Et vii. 28. *clamabat in templo,*
dicens—a meipso non veni. et viii. 29. *nam qui misit me*
20 *mecum est: pater me solum non reliquit; quia ego quæ pla-*
cent ipsi facio semper. hæc si loquitur ut Deus, qui potuit eum

But did his disciples understand him as speaking merely of his human nature? Was this the belief in himself which Christ required? Such an opinion will scarcely be maintained. If therefore he said this, not of his human nature only 5 (for that the Father was greater than he in his human nature could not admit of a doubt), but in the sense in which he himself wished his followers to conceive of him both as God and man, it ought undoubtedly to be understood as if he had said, My Father is greater than I, whatsoever I am, both in 10 my human and divine nature; otherwise the speaker would not have been he in whom they believed, and instead of teaching them, he would only have been imposing upon them with an equivocation. He must therefore have intended to compare the nature with the person, not the nature of God the 15 Father with the nature of the Son in his human form. So v. 31. "as the Father gave me commandment, even so I do." John v. 18, 19. Being accused by the Jews of having made himself equal with God, he expressly denies it: "the Son can do nothing of himself," v. 30. "as I hear I judge, and my 20 judgment is just; because I seek not mine own will, but the will of my Father which sent me." vi. 38. "I came down from heaven, not to do mine own will, but the will of him that sent me." Now he that was sent was the only begotten Son; therefore the will of the Father is other and greater than the will 25 of the only begotten Son. vii. 28. "Jesus cried in the temple, saying . . . I am not come of myself." viii. 29. "he that sent me is with me: the Father hath not left me alone; for I do always those things that please him." If he says this as

pater relinquere essentia unus? si ut homo, quid sit solum æquali deitatis potentia fultum? cur denique non reliquit solum? non quia essentia unus, sed quia *quæ placent ipsi facio semper.* minor scilicet quæ placent maiori. Et v. 42.

5 *nec enim a meipso veni,* (ergo ne a deitate quidem sua) *sed ille misit me.* Alter ergo a meipso et major. v. 49. *honoro patrem meum.* 50. *non quæro gloriam meam.* et 54. *si ego glorifico meipsum, gloria mea nihil est.* minor ergo quam patris gloria. Et cap. x. 24, 25. *si tu es Christus—. opera quæ*

10 *ego facio in nomine patris mei, hæc testantur de me.* et xv. 10. *sicut ego patris mei mandata observavi, et maneo in eius charitate—.* et xvi. 25. *veniet tempus cum non amplius per similitudines loquar vobis, sed aperte de patre meo nuntium afferam vobis.* et xx. 17. *ascendo ad patrem meum et patrem*

15 *vestrum, et ad Deum meum et Deum vestrum.* conferatur Apoc. i. 11. *dicentis ego sum Alpha et Omega—.* et v. 17. *ego sum primus ille et ultimus.* et cap. ii. 8. idem cum cap. iii. 12. *faciam ut is sit columna in templo Dei mei.* et ter deinceps idem. hic qui *primum et ultimum* se modo dixerat, mox pa-

20 trem fatetur Deum suum: Matt. xi. 25, 26. *confiteor,* vel *gratias ago tibi pater Domine cœli ac terræ, quod hoc—: etiam pater propterea quod ita erat bene placitum coram te.*

Hactenus filii testimonia de patre habuimus, nunc patris

God, how could he be left by the Father, with whom he was
essentially one? if as man, what is meant by his being "left
alone," who was sustained by a Godhead of equal power?
And why "did not the Father leave him alone?"—not be-
5 cause he was essentially one with him, but because he "did
always those things that pleased him," that is, as the less con-
forms himself to the will of the greater. v. 42. "neither came
I of myself"—not therefore of his own Godhead—"but he
sent me": he that sent him was therefore another and greater
10 than himself. v. 49. "I honor my Father." v. 50. "I seek not
mine own glory." v. 54. "if I honor myself, my glory is
nothing"; it is therefore less than the Father's glory. x. 24,
25. "if thou be the Christ, tell us plainly . . . the works that
I do in my Father's name, they bear witness of me." xv. 10.
15 "as I have kept my Father's commandments, and abide in
his love." xvi. 25. "the time cometh when I shall no more
speak to you in proverbs, but I shall show you plainly of the
Father." xx. 17. "I ascend unto my Father and your Father;
and to my God, and your God." Compare also Rev. i. 11. "I
20 am Alpha and Omega," and v. 17. "I am the first and the
last." See also ii. 8. iii. 12. "him that overcometh will I
make a pillar in the temple of my God," which is repeated
three times successively. Here he, who had just before styled
himself "the first and the last," acknowledges that the Father
25 was his God. Matt. xi. 25, 26. "I thank thee, O Father, Lord
of heaven and earth; because thou hast hid these things," &c.
"even so, Father, for so it seemed good in thy sight."

Thus far we have considered the testimony of the Son re-

de filio audiamus: scribitur enim Matt. xi. 27. *nemo novit filium, nisi pater; neque patrem quisquam novit, nisi filius, et cuicunque voluerit filius eum retegere:* 1 Ioan, v. 9. *hoc est testimonium Dei quod testificatus est de filio suo*—: hic

5 pater de filio testaturus absolute *Deus* dicitur; testimonium autem illud clarissimum est: Matt. iii. 17. *hic est filius meus dilectus in quo acquievi:* Isa. xlii. 1. cum Matt. xii. 18. *en servus meus quem sustento, electus meus quem benigne accipit anima mea: indam spiritum meum ipsi;* et rursus Matt.

10 xvii. 5. idem. 2 Pet. i. 17. *acceperat enim a Deo patre honorem et gloriam, voce ad eum delata huiusmodi a magnifica illa gloria, hic est filius ille meus dilectus in quo acquievi:* Mal. iii. 1. *et angelus fœderis ecce venturus est ait Iehova exercituum.* et apertissime Psal. ii. ubi introductus Deus Pater

15 et naturam et officia filii sui ipse palam declarat. v. 7, 8, 11, 12. *decretum; Iehova dixit mihi, filius meus es. pete a me, et dabo. colite Iehovam: osculamini filium.* his adde Heb. i. 8, 9. *ad filium autem, thronus tuus, Deus, in sæculum sæculi*—. *dilexisti iustitiam, et odisti legis transgressionem;*

20 *propterea unxit te Deus Deus tuus, oleo exultationis ultra consortes tuos.* His denique adiiciatur testimonium Gabrielis angeli. Luc. i. 32. *hic erit magnus, et filius altissimi vocabitur: dabitque ei Dominus Deus sedem Davidis patris ipsius.* filius

specting the Father; let us now enquire what is the testimony of the Father respecting the Son: for it is written, Matt. xi. 27. "no man knoweth the Son, but the Father; neither knoweth any man the Father, save the Son, and he to whomsoever the Son will reveal him." 1 John v. 9. "this is the witness of God which he hath testified of his Son." Here the Father, when about to testify of the Son, is called God absolutely; and his witness is most explicit. Matt. iii. 17. "this is my beloved Son, in whom I am well pleased." Isa. xlii. 1. compared with Matt. xii. 18. "behold my servant, whom I uphold; mine elect in whom my soul delighteth; I have put my spirit upon him":—see also Matt. xvii. 5. 2 Pet. i. 17. "for he received from God the Father honor and glory, when there came such a voice to him from the excellent glory, This is my beloved Son, in whom I am well pleased." Mal. iii. 1. "even the messenger of the covenant, behold he shall come, saith Jehovah of hosts": and still more clearly Psal. ii. where God the Father is introduced in his own person as explicitly declaring the nature and offices of his Son. Psal. vii. 8, 11, 12. "I will declare the decree; Jehovah hath said unto me, Thou art my Son . . . ask of me and I shall give . . . serve Jehovah . . . kiss the Son." Heb. i. 8, 9. "unto the Son he saith, Thy throne, O God, is for ever and ever . . . thou hast loved righteousness, and hated iniquity; therefore God, even thy God, hath anointed thee with the oil of gladness above thy fellows." To the above may also be added the testimony of the angel Gabriel, Luke i. 32. "he shall be great, and shall be called the Son of the Highest, and the Lord God shall give

Altissimi: non ergo ipse altissimus. Idem undique confirmant apostoli: et primus omnium Baptista; Ioan. i. 29. *ecce agnus Dei;* et v. 33, 34. *ego non noveram eum; sed qui misit me ut baptizarem aqua, ille mihi dixerat—. ego igitur vidi,* 5 *et testor hunc esse filium Dei.* et cap. iii. 32. &c. *quod vidit et audivit, hoc testatur—.* Non terrenus solum; hic non terrena solum loquitur: sed qui supra omnes est, qui e cœlo est v. 31. ne quis hæc atque huismodi de Christo homine dicta esse semper obtundat. 2 Cor. iv. 46. *ne irradiet eos illustratio* 10 *evangelii gloriæ Christi, qui est imago Dei.* Col. i. 15. *qui est imago Dei invisibilis, et primogenitus omnis rei creatæ:* Philipp. ii. 6. *in forma Dei:* Heb. i. 2. *quem constituit hæredem—;* v. 3. *effulgentia gloriæ et character substantiæ eius.* hæc omnia relata cum sint, idque in personis numero duabus, 15 essentiam declarant et non unam, et alteram altera minorem. Sic. v. 4. *tanto præstantior factus angelis, quanto excellentius præ illis hæreditate accepit nomen.* 1 Cor. iii. 23. *vos autem Christi; Christus vero Dei est.* ubinam potius conveniebat Christum nominasse Deum? non nominavit sed, Dei; id 20 etiam clarius in iis quæ sequuntur: cap. xi. 3. *velim vos scire —caput Christi Deum:* Eph. i. 17. *Deus Domini nostri Iesu*

unto him the throne of his father David." If then he be the Son of the Most High, he is not himself the Most High.

The apostles every where teach the same doctrine; as the Baptist had done before them. John i. 29. "behold the Lamb of God." v. 33, 34. "I knew him not, but he that sent me to baptize with water, the same said unto me," &c. "and I saw, and bare record that this is the Son of God." iii. 32. "what he hath seen and heard, that he testifieth," &c.—not he alone that was "earthly," nor did he speak only of "earthly things," but he that is "above all," and that "cometh from heaven," v. 31. lest it should be still contended that this and similar texts refer to the human nature of Christ. 2 Cor. iv. 4. 6. "lest the light of the glorious Gospel of Christ, who is the image of God, should shine unto them." Col. i. 15. "who is the image of the invisible God, the first-born of every creature." Philipp. ii. 6, "in the form of God." Heb. i. 2. "whom he hath appointed heir." v. 3. "the brightness of his glory, and the express image of his person." The terms here used, being all relative, and applied numerically to two persons, prove, first, that there is no unity of essence, and secondly, that the one is inferior to the other. So v. 4. "being made so much better than the angels, as he hath by inheritance obtained a more excellent name than they." 1 Cor. iii. 23. "ye are Christ's, and Christ is God's." Here, if any where, it might have been expected that Christ would have been designated by the title of God; yet it is only said that he is "of God." The same appears even more clearly in what follows: xi. 3. "I would have you know that . . . the head of Christ is God." Eph. i. 17.

Christi: 1 Cor. xv. 27. *cum dicit omnia esse ei subiecta, palam est hoc dici, excepto eo qui subiecit ei omnia: postquam vero subiecta fuerint ei omnia, tunc et ipse filius subiicietur ei qui subiecerit ipsi omnia; ut Deus sit omnia in omnibus.* Non est

5 ut hic adversarii quod solent, ad mediatorium munus ullo subterfugio possint recurrere: hic enim filius cum mediatorium munus impleverit, et nihil restabit, quo minus ad pristinam unigeniti filii gloriam restituendus sit, Patri tamen subiicietur.

10 Hæc fuit sanctorum de Dei filio fides, hæc eadem illius fidei celebrata confessio, hæc sola docetur, Deo accepta est, æternæ salutis promissionem habet: Matt. xvi. 15, 16, 17, 18, 19. *vos quem me dicitis esse? respondit Petrus, tu es Christus filius Dei viventis: tum Iesus, beatus es Simon, quia caro et*

15 *sanguis non revelavit tibi, sed pater meus qui est in cælis. super hanc petram ædificabo ecclesiam meam*—: Luc. ix. 20. *Christum illum Dei.* Ioan. i. 50, 51. *respondit Nathanael, tu es filius Dei, tu es Rex Israel:* et vi. 69. *nos credidimus et novimus te esse Christum illum filium Dei viventis:* et ix. 35,

20 36, 37, 38. *tune credis in filium Dei? respondit, quis est, Domine, ut credam in eum? dixit Iesus, vidisti eum, et is est*

"the God of our Lord Jesus Christ." 1 Cor. xv. 27. "when he saith, all things are put under him, it is manifest that he is excepted, which did put all things under him: and when all things shall be subdued unto him, then shall the Son also him-self be subject unto him that put all things under him, that God may be all in all." Here the usual subterfuge of the op-ponents of this doctrine, that of alleging the mediatorial office of Christ can be of no avail; since it is expressly declared, that when the Son shall have completed his functions as mediator, and nothing shall remain to prevent him from resuming his original glory as only begotten Son, he shall nevertheless be subject unto the Father.

Such was the faith of the saints respecting the Son of God; such is the tenor of the celebrated confession of that faith; such is the doctrine which alone is taught in Scripture, which is acceptable to God, and has the promise of eternal salvation. Matt. xvi. 15–19. "whom say ye that I am? and Simon Peter answered and said, Thou art the Christ, the Son of the living God: and Jesus answered and said unto him, Blessed art thou, Simon Bar-jona: for flesh and blood hath not revealed it unto thee, but my Father which is in heaven . . . upon this rock I will build my Church." Luke ix. 20. "the Christ of God." John i. 49, 50. "Nathanael answered and saith unto him, Rabbi, thou art the Son of God; thou art the King of Israel." vi. 69. "we believe and are sure that thou art that Christ, the Son of the living God." ix. 35–38. "dost thou believe on the Son of God? he answered and said, Who is he, Lord, that I might believe on him? and Jesus saith unto him, Thou hast

qui loquitur tecum: ille ait, credo, Domine et adoravit eum:
et xi. 22, 26, 27. scio fore, ut quæcunque petieris a Deo, det
tibi. Quisquis vivit, et credit in eum, non morietur in æter-
num; credis hoc? ait illi, etiam Domine; ego credo te esse
5 *Christum filium Dei qui in mundum venturus erat: et xvi.*
27, 30, 31. pater amat vos, quia vos me amastis, et credidistis
me a Deo prodiisse. nunc scimus te scire omnia; per hoc cre-
dimus te a Deo prodiisse: et xvii. 3, 7, 8, 21. hæc est vita
æterna, ut cognoscant te esse illum solum verum Deum, et
10 *quem misisti Iesum Christum. nunc noverunt, omnia quæ*
dedisti mihi, a te esse: verba quæ tradidisti mihi tradidi iis:
et vere norunt me a te prodiisse. ut credat mundus, me a te
missum esse: et xx. 31. hæc scripta sunt ut credatis Iesum
esse Christum filium Dei, et ut credentes, vitam habeatis in
15 *nomine ipsius:* Act. viii. 37. *si credis—. credo Iesum Chris-*
tum esse filium Dei. Rom. x. 9. *si credideris in corde tuo quod*
Deus eum suscitavit ex mortuis, servaberis. Col. ii. 2. *ut con-*
solationem habeant corda eorum, ipsis charitate compactis
ad omnem opulentiam plenæ ac certissimæ intelligentiæ ad
20 *agnitionem mysterii Dei ac patris, et Christi:* Philipp. iv. 6, 7.
petitiones vestræ innotescant apud Deum; et pax Dei quæ
exsuperat omnem mentem custodiet corda vestra et cogita-

both seen him, and it is he that talketh with thee: and he said, Lord, I believe; and he worshipped him." xi. 22, 26, 27. "I know that even now, whatsoever thou wilt ask of God, God will give it thee: whosoever liveth and believeth in me, shall
5 never die: believest thou this? she saith unto him, Yea, Lord, I believe that thou art the Christ, the Son of God, which should come into the world." xvi. 27, 30, 31. "the Father himself loveth you, because ye have loved me, and have believed that I came out from God: now are we sure that thou
10 knowest all things; by this we believe that thou camest forth from God." xvii. 3, 7, 8, 21. "this is life eternal, that they might know thee the only true God, and Jesus Christ whom thou hast sent: now they have known that all things, whatsoever thou hast given me, are of thee; for I have given unto
15 them the words which thou gavest me; and they have received them, and have known surely that I came out from thee: that the world may believe that thou hast sent me." xx. 31. "these are written, that ye might believe that Jesus is the Christ, the Son of God, and that believing, ye might have life through
20 his name." Acts viii. 37. "if thou believest, thou mayest . . . I believe that Jesus Christ is the Son of God." Rom. x. 9. "if thou shalt believe in thine heart that God hath raised him from the dead, thou shalt be saved." Col. ii. 2. "that their hearts might be comforted, being knit together in love, and
25 unto all riches of the full assurance of understanding, to the acknowledgment of the mystery of God, and of the Father, and of Christ." Philipp. iv. 6, 7. "let your requests be made known unto God: and the peace of God, which passeth all

tiones vestras in Christo Iesu: 1 Pet. i. 21. *per eum credentes in Deum qui suscitavit eum ex mortuis, et gloriam ei dedit ut fides ac spes vestra sit in Deo:* 1 Ioan. iv. 15. *quisquis profes-sus fuerit Iesum esse filium Dei, Deus in eo habitat, et ipse in* 5 *Deo:* et v. 1. *quisquis credit Iesum esse Christum illum, ex Deo genitus est;* et v. 5. *quis est qui vincit mundum, nisi qui credit Iesum esse filium Dei?* Postremo, symbolum etiam apostolicum in ecclesia antiquissimum et receptissimum non aliam nobis fidem proponit.

CAPUT VI.

DE SPIRITU SANCTO.

A PATRE et Filio proximum est ut de Sancto Spiritu dicamus; quando et patris et filii spiritus appella-tur. Quod autem ad naturam eius attinet, quomodo existat, quove extiterit, scriptura tacet: unde nos temerarii ne simus, admonemur. Nam etsi spiritus est, sicuti et pater et 15 filius recte dicitur, etsi Christus Ioan. xx. 22. flando dedisse spiritum sanctum vel eius quoddam symbolum potius aut pignus discipulis suis memoratur, spirari idcirco a patre et

understanding, shall keep your hearts and minds through Christ Jesus." 1 Pet. i. 21. "who by him do believe in God, that raised him up from the dead, and gave him glory; that your faith and hope might be in God." 1 John iv. 15. "who-
5 soever shall confess that Jesus is the Son of God, God dwelleth in him, and he in God." v. 1. "whosoever believeth that Jesus is the Christ, is born of God." v. 5. "who is he that over-cometh the world, but he that believeth that Jesus is the Son of God?" Finally, this is the faith proposed to us in the
10 Apostles' Creed, the most ancient and universally received compendium of belief in the possession of the Church.

CHAPTER VI.

OF THE HOLY SPIRIT.

HAVING concluded what relates to the Father and the Son, the next subject to be discussed is that of the Holy Spirit, inasmuch as this latter is called the
15 Spirit of the Father and the Son. With regard to the nature of the Spirit, in what manner it exists, or whence it arose, Scripture is silent; which is a caution to us not to be too hasty in our conclusions on the subject. For though it be a Spirit, in the same sense in which the Father and Son are properly
20 called Spirits; though we read that Christ by breathing on his disciples gave to them the Holy Ghost, or rather perhaps some symbol or pledge of the Holy Ghost, John xx. 22. yet in treating of the nature of the Holy Spirit, we are not au-thorized to infer from such expressions, that the Spirit was

filio spiritum, si de natura spiritus sancti loquamur, quis hinc
ausit statuere? Neque vero id naturam sancti spiritus attingit,
quod emanare aut procedere Theologi vocant ex Ioan. xv.
26. ubi dicitur, *spiritus veritatis,* ὁ παρὰ τοῦ πατρὸς ἐκπορεύεται,
5 *qui a patre procedit,* seu egreditur. quod solum verbum ad
plenam tanti mysterii fidem, exile admodum argumentum
est; et missionem spiritus, non naturam significat: quo sensu
etiam filius ἐξελθεῖν sive *egredi* sive *procedere* a patre id malit
quisquam interpretari, quod, quantum nobis liquet, idem
10 valet, sæpius dicitur: immo *omni verbo* ἐκπορευομένῳ, id est,
procedente vel exeunte *per os Dei* dicimur *vivere,* Matt. iv. 4.
Cum itaque spiritus nec generari dicatur, neque creari, neque
quo alio existat modo ex scriptura constet, in tanto sacrorum
auctorum silentio dehiscat methodus necesse est.

15   Nomen spiritus et Deo et angelis et hominum quoque men-
tibus tribui solet. Spiritus autem Dei vel spiritus sanctus quoties dicitur, sciendum est in veteri testamento nunc ipsum
Deum patrem, ut Gen. vi. 3. *non disceptabit spiritus meus.*

  Nunc patris potentiam atque virtutem, illum imprimis
20 afflatum divinum omnia creantem ac foventem significari:
quomodo locum illum Gen. i. 2. *spiritus Dei incubabat,*

breathed from the Father and the Son. The terms "emanation" and "procession," employed by theologians on the authority of John xv. 26. do not relate to the nature of the Holy Spirit; "the Spirit of truth," ὁ παρὰ τοῦ Πατρὸς ἐκπο-
5 ρεύεται, "who proceedeth" or "goeth forth from the Father"; which single expression is too slender a foundation for the full establishment of so great a mystery, especially as these words relate rather to the mission than to the nature of the Spirit; in which sense the Son also is often said ἐξελθεῖν, which
10 in my opinion may be translated either "to go forth" or "to proceed" from the Father, without making any difference in the meaning. Nay, we are even said "to live by every word (ἐκπορευομένῳ) that proceedeth," or "goeth forth from the mouth of God," Matt. iv. 4. Since therefore the Spirit is
15 neither said to be generated nor created, nor is any other mode of existence specifically attributed to it in Scripture, we must be content to leave undetermined a point on which the sacred writers have preserved so uniform a silence.

The name of Spirit is also frequently applied to God and
20 angels, and to the human mind. When the phrase, the Spirit of God, or the Holy Spirit, occurs in the Old Testament, it is to be variously interpreted; sometimes it signifies God the Father himself, as Gen. vi. 3. "my Spirit shall not alway strive with man"; sometimes the power and virtue of the
25 Father, and particularly that divine breath or influence by which every thing is created and nourished. In this sense many both of the ancient and modern interpreters understand the passage in Gen. i. 2. "the Spirit of God moved upon the

multi intelligunt et antiqui et recentiores. Quamquam illic filius intelligendus videtur potius, per quem pater omnia creasse toties dicitur. Iob. xxvi. 13. *spiritu suo cœlos ornavit.* et xxvii. 3. *spiritus Dei in naribus meis.* et xxxiii. 4. *spiritus* 5 *Dei fortis, et efflatus omnipotentis.* Psal. civ. 30. *emittente Spiritum tuum, recreantur.* et cxxxix. 7. *quo irem a spiritu tuo?* Ezech. xxxvii. 14. *indam spiritum meum vobis, ut reviviscatis.* et multis aliis in locis.

Vel angelum aliquem. Isa. xlviii. 16. *Dominus Iehova* 10 *mittit me, et spiritus eius.* Ezech. iii. 12. *tum sustulit me spiritus—;* Sic v. 14. et 24. et passim.

Vel Christum, quem misit pater, ut plerique volunt, qui Israelitas duceret in terram Cananæam. Isa. lxiii. 10, 11. *dolore afficientibus spiritum sanctitatis eius. Qui posuit in* 15 *medio istius spiritum sanctitatis suæ.* Nempe angelum illum, in quo nomen suum posuit, id est, Christum quem tentaverunt, Num. xxi. 5, &c. cum 1 Cor. x. 9.

Nunc illam sive vim sive vocem Dei, quæ quoquomodo prophetis inspiratur, Neh. ix. 30. *cum contestatus esses eos* 20 *spiritu tuo per prophetas tuos.*

Nunc lucem veritatis, sive ordinariam sive extraordinariam, qua suos illuminat Deus atque deducit, Num. xiv. 24. *at servum meum Calebum, quia fuit spiritus alius cum eo—.* Neh. ix. 20. *spiritum etiam tuum optimum dedisti ad in-* 25 *telligentiam—.* Psal. li. 13, 14. *spiritum sanctitatis tuæ*

face of the waters." Here, however, it appears to be used with reference to the Son, through whom the Father is so often said to have created all things. Job xxvi. 13. "by his Spirit he hath garnished the heavens." xxvii. 3. "the Spirit of God is in my
5 nostrils." xxxiii. 4. "the Spirit of God hath made me, and the breath of the Almighty hath given me life." Psal. civ. 30. "thou sendest forth thy Spirit, they are created." cxxxix. 7. "whither shall I go then from thy Spirit?" Ezek. xxxvii. 14. "I shall put my Spirit in you, and ye shall live." See also
10 many other similar passages.

Sometimes it means an angel. Isa. xlviii. 16. "the Lord Jehovah and his Spirit hath sent me." Ezck. iii. 12. "then the Spirit took me up." See also v. 14, 24, &c.

Sometimes it means Christ, who according to the common
15 opinion was sent by the Father to lead the Israelites into the land of Canaan. Isa. lxiii. 10, 11. "they rebelled, and vexed his Holy Spirit . . . where is he that put his Holy Spirit within them?" that is, the angel to whom he transferred his own name, namely, Christ "whom they tempted," Num.
20 xxi. 5, &c. compared with 1 Cor. x. 9.

Sometimes it means that impulse or voice of God by which the prophets were inspired. Neh. ix. 30. "thou testifiedst against them by thy Spirit in thy prophets."

Sometimes it means that light of truth, whether ordinary
25 or extraordinary, wherewith God enlightens and leads his people. Num. xiv. 24. "my servant Caleb, because he had another Spirit within him—." Neh. ix. 20. "thou gavest also thy good Spirit to instruct them." Psal. li. 11, 12. "take

ne recipias a me; spiritu ingenuitatis tuæ sustenta me. et cxliii. 10. *tuo spiritu bono deduc me.* Certe nec David nec quisquam alius sub vetusto fœdere Hebræus, spiritum illum sanctum et bonum, personam aliquam, nisi forte angelum,
5 crediderunt.

Etiam qua ipsum Christum. Isa. xi. 2. *super quo quiescet spiritus Iehovæ, spiritus sapientiæ et intelligentiæ, spiritus consilii et potentiæ, spiritus scientiæ et reverentiæ Iehovæ.* et xlii. 1. *indam spiritum meum ipsi,* cum Act. x. 38. *ut Iesum*
10 *illum unxerit Deus spiritu sancto et potentia.*

In alios etiam dona Dei spiritualia, ipsamque donationem. Gen. xli. 38. *virum in quo spiritus Dei sit.* Num. xi. 17, 25, 26, 29. *seponam de spiritu qui est super te, ponamque in iis—.* 2 Reg. ii. 9. *sit ergo, quæso portio dupla de tuo spiritu*
15 *penes me.* et v. 15. *quievit spiritus Eliæ super Elisæum.*

Hæc omnia et huiusmodi multa alia de virtute et potentia Dei patris fuisse in vetere testamento intellecta, certissimum est; cum spiritus sanctus neque datus adhuc esset, neque creditus, ne ab iis quidem qui ultimis temporibus effusum iri
20 cecinerunt.

Sub Evangelio itidem nomen spiritus Dei vel sancti significat nunc ipsum Patrem. Matt. i. 18, 20. *quod in ea geni-*

not thy Holy Spirit from me . . . renew a right Spirit within me." cxliii. 10. "thy Spirit is good; lead me into the land of uprightness." Undoubtedly neither David, nor any other Hebrew, under the old covenant, believed in the per-sonality of that "good" and "Holy Spirit," unless perhaps as an angel.

More particularly, it implies that light which was shed on Christ himself. Isa. xi. 2. "the Spirit of Jehovah shall rest upon him, the Spirit of wisdom and understanding, the Spirit of counsel and might, the Spirit of knowledge and of the fear of Jehovah." xlii. 1. "I have put my Spirit upon him," com-pared with Acts x. 38. "how God anointed Jesus of Nazareth with the Holy Ghost and with power."

It is also used to signify the spiritual gifts conferred by God on individuals, and the act of gift itself. Gen. xli. 38. "a man in whom the Spirit of God is." Num. xi. 17, 25, 26, 29. "I will take of the Spirit which is upon thee, and will put it upon them." 2 Kings ii. 9. "I pray thee, let a double portion of thy Spirit be upon me." v. 15. "the Spirit of Elijah doth rest upon Elisha."

Nothing can be more certain, than that all these passages, and many others of a similar kind in the Old Testament, were understood of the virtue and power of God the Father, inas-much as the Holy Spirit was not yet given, nor believed in, even by those who prophesied that it should be poured forth in the latter times.

So likewise under the Gospel, what is called the Holy Spirit, or the Spirit of God, sometimes means the Father himself.

tum est, ex spiritu sancto est. Luc. i. 35. *spiritus sanctus su-*
perveniet in te, et virtus Altissimi inumbrabit te. propterea id
etiam quod gignetur ex te sanctum, vocabitur filius Dei.

Nunc Patris virtutem, et potentiam. Matt. xii. 28. cum
5 Luc. xi. 20. *per spiritum Dei. per dignitum Dei.* Rom. i. 4.
definito filio Dei potenter, secundum spiritum sanctificationis
ex resurrectione mortuorum. Sic enim scriptura passim docet
patris virtute suscitatum, indeque filium Dei definitum, et
præsertim, Act. xiii. 32, 33. ut capitis initio superioris. *secun-*
10 *dum* autem *spiritum* videtur idem valere quod Eph. iv. 24.
secundum Deum conditus; et 1 Pet. iv. 6. *ut viverent secun-*
dum Deum, spiritu. Isa. xlii. 1. cum Heb. ix. 14. *indam*
spiritum meum ipsi. qui per spiritum æternum seipsum ob-
tulit inculpatum Deo. Luc. iv. 1. *Iesus plenus spiritu sancto.*
15 et v. 18. cum Isa. lxi. 1. *spiritus Domini Iehovæ super me,*
eo quod unxit me, admisit me ad—, cum Act. x. 38. *ut Iesum*
illum a Nazaretha unxerit Deus spiritu sancto et potentia.
cap. i. 2. *cum præcepta dedisset apostolis, quos per spiritum*
sanctum elegerat. hæc probabilius est de patris virtute, quam

Matt. i. 18, 20. "that which is conceived in her is of the Holy Ghost." Luke i. 35. "the Holy Ghost shall come upon thee, and the power of the Highest shall overshadow thee; therefore also that holy thing which shall be born of thee, shall be called
5 the Son of God."

Again, it sometimes means the virtue and power of the Father. Matt. xii. 28. compared with Luke xi. 20. "I cast out devils by the Spirit" or "finger of God." Rom. i. 4. "declared to be the Son of God with power, according to the Spirit
10 of holiness, by the resurrection from the dead." For thus the Scripture teaches throughout, that Christ was raised by the power of the Father, and thereby declared to be the Son of God. See particularly Acts xiii. 32, 33. quoted in the beginning of the last chapter. But the phrase, "according to the
15 Spirit" (*secundum Spiritum*) seems to have the same signification as Eph. iv. 24. "which after God (*secundum Deum*) is created in righteousness and true holiness"; and 1 Pet. iv. 6. "that they might live according to God (*secundum Deum*) in the Spirit." Isa. xlii. 1. compared with Heb. ix. 14. "I
20 have put my Spirit upon him . . . who through the eternal Spirit offered himself without spot to God." Luke iv. 1. "Jesus, being full of the Holy Ghost," and v. 18. compared with Isa. lxi. 1. "the Spirit of the Lord Jehovah is upon me, because he hath anointed me to preach the gospel to the poor;
25 he hath sent me," &c. Acts x. 38. "God anointed Jesus of Nazareth with the Holy Ghost and with power." i. 2. "after that he through the Holy Ghost had given commandments unto the apostles whom he had chosen." It is more probable

de ipso spiritu sancto intelligi oportere: quid enim opus erat ipso spiritu sancto Christum impleri, de quo ipse Christus, *de meo,* inquit, *accipiet,* Ioan. xvi. 15. Hinc etiam in Christi baptismo Matt. iii. descendisse in Christum crediderim spiri-
5 tum, non tam suo nomine, quam a patre missum, virtutis divinæ symbolum ac ministrum. Quid enim ipse conferre potuit Christo, a quo et mittendus erat, et omnia accepturus? an testimonium perhibere? at nondum ipse notus. an ecclesiæ tum primum erat patefaciendus? at neque de eo neque
10 de eius munere tum cum appareret, quicquam est dictum: Et vox illa de cœlo nihil de spiritu, sed tantum de filio testificata est; Descensio igitur, et columbina species illa spiritus sancti, aliud nihil videtur fuisse, quam repræsentatio quædam summi amoris ac dilectionis paternæ erga filium a spiritu sancto sub
15 columbæ mansuetissima specie administrata, voce illa interprete cœlitus testata.

Significat tertio spiritus instinctum, et lucem, et vocem, aut verbum divinum, sive per Christum qui Dei sermo est, sive modo quovis alio divinitus missum. Marc. xii. 36. *David*
20 *dixit per spiritum sanctum.* Act. i. 16. *prædixit spiritus sanctus per os Davidis.* et xxviii. 25. *recte spiritus sanctus locutus est per Isaiam prophetam.* Heb. iii. 7. *dixit spiritus sanctus,*

that these phrases are to be understood of the power of the
Father, than of the Holy Spirit himself; for how could it
be necessary that Christ should be filled with the Holy Spirit,
of whom he had himself said, John xvi. 15. "he shall take of
5 mine?" For the same reason I am inclined to believe that the
Spirit descended upon Christ at his baptism, not so much in
his own name, as in virtue of a mission from the Father, and
as a symbol and minister of the divine power. For what could
the Spirit confer on Christ, from whom he was himself to be
10 sent, and to receive all things? Was his purpose to bear witness
to Christ? But as yet he was himself not so much as known.
Was it meant that the Spirit should be then manifested for the
first time to the church? But at the time of his appearance
nothing was said of him or of his office; nor did that voice
15 from heaven bear any testimony to the Spirit, but only to the
Son. The descent therefore and appearance of the Holy Spirit
in the likeness of a dove, seems to have been nothing more
than a representation of the ineffable affection of the Father
for the Son, communicated by the Holy Spirit under the ap-
20 propriate image of a dove, and accompanied by a voice from
heaven declaratory of that affection.

Thirdly, the Spirit signifies a divine impulse, or light, or
voice, or word, transmitted from above either through Christ,
who is the Word of God, or by some other channel. Mark
25 xii. 36. "David himself said by the Holy Ghost." Acts i. 16.
"the Holy Ghost by the mouth of David spake before concerning Judas." xxviii. 25. "well spake the Holy Ghost by Esaias
the prophet." Heb. iii. 7. "wherefore, as the Holy Ghost

hodie—. et ix. 8. *hoc declarante spiritu sancto, nondum fac-*
tam fuisse manifestam ad sacrarium viam—. et x. 15. *testi-*
ficatur nobis spiritus sanctus. 2 Pet. i. 21. *acti a spiritu sancto,*
locuti sunt sancti Dei homines. Luc. ii. 25, 26. *et spiritus*
5 *sanctus erat super eum: fueratque ipsi divinitus nuntiatum a*
spiritu sancto. Hæc et similia loca præcise de sancti spiritus
persona intelligi, puto non posse, cum quia is nondum erat
datus, tum quia solus Christus, ut modo dixi, sermo Dei est,
et propheta ecclesiæ, primario videlicet ac proprie; tametsi
10 *multifariam multisque modis olim Deus locutus est patribus*
in prophetis. Heb. i. 1. non ergo solum per spiritum sanctum,
nisi latiore omnino, quam postea, atque ea maxime quam
attulimus, spiritus sancti significatione. Hinc 1 Pet. i. 11.
qui in iis (nempe prophetis) *erat spiritus Christi,* aut intelli-
15 gendus est ipse Christus, ut infra cap. iii. 18, 19. *vivificatus*
spiritu, in quo, vel *per quem, spiritibus in carcere profectus*—,
aut intelligendus est spiritus Christi sermonis et summi prophetæ vicarius.

Significat tandem spiritus ipsam spiritus sancti personam,
20 aut symbolum eius. Matt. iii. 16. *vidit spiritum Dei descen-*
dentem quasi columbam, et manentem super eum. Marc. i.
10. idem. Luc. iii. 22. *corporea specie, tanquam columba.*

saith, To-day if ye will hear his voice," &c. ix. 8. "the Holy
Ghost this signifying, that the way into the holiest of all was
not yet made manifest." x. 15. "whereof the Holy Ghost also
is a witness to us." 2 Pet. i. 21. "holy men of God spake as
5 they were moved by the Holy Ghost." Luke ii. 25, 26. "the
Holy Ghost was upon him: and it was revealed unto him by
the Holy Ghost——." It appears to me, that these and similar
passages cannot be considered as referring to the express person of the Spirit, both because the Spirit was not yet given,
10 and because Christ alone, as has been said before, is, properly
speaking, and in a primary sense, the Word of God, and the
Prophet of the Church; though "God at sundry times and in
divers manners spake in time past unto the fathers by the
prophets," Heb. i. 1. whence it appears that he did not speak
15 by the Holy Spirit alone, unless the term be understood in the
signification which I have proposed, and in a much wider
sense than was subsequently attributed to it. Hence, 1 Pet.
i. 11. "searching what or what manner of time the Spirit of
Christ which was in them"—that is, in the prophets—"did
20 signify," must either be understood of Christ himself, as iii.
18, 19. "quickened by the Spirit, by which also he went and
preached unto the spirits in prison," or it must be understood
of the Spirit which supplied the place of Christ the Word and
the Chief Prophet.

25   Further, the Spirit signifies the person itself of the Holy
Spirit, or its symbol. Matt. iii. 16. Mark i. 10. "he saw the
Spirit of God descending like a dove, and lighting upon him."
Luke iii. 22. "in a bodily shape like a dove." John i. 32, 33.

Ioan. i. 32, 33. *quasi columbam.* Nec dixerit mihi hic quispiam, columbam non esse personam; substantia enim intelligens, quavis sub specie, persona est; quemadmodum visa illa ab Ezechiele quatuor animalia. Ezech. i. Ioan. xiv. 16, 17.
5 *alium advocatum.* et v. 26. idem. et cap. xv. 26. et xvi. 7, 13. idem. et xx. 22. *inhalavit iis, ac dixit, accipite spiritum sanctum.* Nempe hoc symbolum erat et quasi certissimum pignus illius promissi, quod impletum est Act. ii. 2, 3, 4, 33. *et promissione spiritus sancti accepta a patre, effudit hoc—.* Matt.
10 xxviii. 19. *in nomine—, et spiritus sancti.* Act. xv. 28. *visum est spiritui sancto.* Rom. viii. 16. *testatur.* v. 26. *sublevat, intercedit.* Eph. i. 13, 14. τῷ πνεύματι τῷ ἁγίῳ· ὅς ἐστιν ἀῤῥαβών. Et iv. 30. *ne tristitia afficite spiritum illum.* Donationem denique et dona eius. Ioan. vii. 39. *hoc autem*
15 *dixit de spiritu illo quem accepturi erant—. nondum enim erat spiritus sanctus—.* Matt. iii. 11. *ipse vos baptizabit spiritu sancto et igne.* Act. i. 5. et xi. 16. idem. 1 Thess. v. 19. *spiritum ne extinguite.*

Quis autem sit sanctus ille spiritus, unde sit, quæque eius
20 officia, expressius nemo docet quam ipse Dei filius: Matt. x. 20. *spiritus patris vestri is est qui loquitur in vobis.* Luc. xi. 13. *quanto magis pater cœlestis dabit spiritum sanctum pe-*

"like a dove." Nor let it be objected, that a dove is not a person; for an intelligent substance, under any form whatever, is a person; as for instance, the four living creatures seen in Ezekiel's vision, ch. i. John xiv. 16, 17. "another Comforter." See also v. 26. xv. 26. xvi. 7, 13. xx. 22. "he breathed on them, and saith unto them, Receive ye the Holy Ghost"— which was a kind of symbol, and sure pledge of that promise, the fulfilment of which is recorded Acts ii. 2–4, 33. "having received of the Father the promise of the Holy Ghost, he hath shed forth this." Matt. xxviii. 19. "in the name of the Father, and of the Son, and of the Holy Ghost." Acts xv. 28. "it seemed good to the Holy Ghost." Rom. viii. 16. "the Spirit itself beareth witness with our spirit." v. 26. "it helpeth our infirmities . . . it maketh intercession for us." Eph. i. 13, 14. τῷ πνεύματι τῷ ἁγίῳ· ὅς ἐστιν ἀῤῥαβών. "ye were sealed with that Holy Spirit of promise which is the earnest of our inheritance." iv. 30. "grieve not the Holy Spirit of God."

Lastly, it signifies the donation of the Spirit itself, and of its attendant gifts. John vii. 39. "but this spake he of the Spirit, which they that believe on him should receive; for the Holy Ghost was not yet given." Matt. iii. 11. "he shall baptize you with the Holy Ghost and with fire." See also Acts i. 5. and xi. 16. 1 Thess. v. 19. "quench not the Spirit."

Who this Holy Spirit is, and whence he comes, and what are his offices, no one has taught us more explicitly than the Son of God himself. Matt. x. 20. "it is not ye that speak, but the Spirit of your Father that speaketh in you." Luke xi. 13. "how much more shall your heavenly Father give the Holy

tentibus ab ipso. et xxiv. 49. *ecce, ego mittam promissum patris mei in vos: vos autem residete Hierosolymis usque quo induamini virtute ex alto.* Ioan. xiv. 16, 17. *rogabo patrem, et alium advocatum dabit vobis, spiritum veritatis.* et v. 26.

5 *advocatus ille spiritus sanctus quem mittet pater in nomine meo.* et cap. xv. 26. *advocatus ille quem ego vobis mittam a patre—; qui a patre egreditur, ille testabitur de me.* et xvi. 7. *mittam eum ad vos.* v. 8. *cum venerit, arguet mundum—.* et 13. *non loquitur a semetipso; sed quæcunque audierit, lo-*

10 *quitur.* et 14. *ille me glorificabit quia de meo accipiet.* 15. *omnia quæ habet pater, mea sunt: propterea dixi illum de meo accepturum.* cap. xx. 22. *cum hoc dixisset, inhalavit iis, ac dixit. accipite spiritum sanctum.* Act. ii. 2, 3, 4, 33. *et promissione spiritus sancti accepta a patre, effudit hoc—.*

15 et v. 32. *nos sumus ei testes horum quæ dicimus; atque etiam spiritus sanctus, quem dedit Deus iis qui dicto sunt audientes ipsi.* Rom. xv. 13. *utinam vero Deus spei impleat vos omni gaudio et pace credendo, ut spe abundetis per virtutem spiritus sancti.* 1 Cor. xii. 3. *et neminem posse dicere Iesum Domi-*

20 *num, nisi per spiritum sanctum.* Heb. ii. 4. *testimonium illis præbente Deo et signis et prodigiis variisque virtutibus. et spiritus sancti distributionibus, pro sua voluntate.* Hinc spiritus patris, spiritus Dei, etiam Spiritus Christi vocatur. Matt.

Spirit to them that ask him." xxiv. 49. "behold, I send the promise of my Father upon you; but tarry ye in the city of Jerusalem, until ye be endued with power from on high." John xiv. 16, 17. "I will pray the Father, and he shall give you another Comforter, that he may abide with you for ever, even the Spirit of truth." v. 26. "the Comforter, which is the Holy Ghost, whom the Father will send in my name." xv. 26. "the Comforter, whom I will send unto you from the Father . . . which proceedeth from the Father, he shall testify of me." xvi. 7. "I will send him unto you." v. 8. "when he is come, he will reprove the world—." v. 13. "he shall not speak of himself; but whatsoever he shall hear, that shall he speak." v. 14. "he shall glorify me, for he shall receive of mine." v. 15. "all things that the Father hath are mine; therefore said I that he shall take of mine." xx. 22. "when he had said this, he breathed on them, and saith unto them, Receive ye the Holy Ghost." Acts. ii. 2–4, 33. "having received of the Father the promise of the Holy Ghost, he hath shed forth this—." v. 32. "we are his witnesses of these things, and so is also the Holy Ghost whom God hath given to them that obey him." Rom. xv. 13. "now the God of hope fill you with all joy and peace in believing, that ye may abound in hope through the power of the Holy Ghost." 1 Cor. xii. 3. "no man can say that Jesus is the Lord, but by the Holy Ghost." Heb. ii. 4. "God also bearing them witness both with signs and wonders, and with divers miracles, and gifts of the Holy Ghost, according to his own will." Hence he is called the Spirit of the Father, the Spirit of God, and even the

x. 20. *spiritus patris vestri is est.* Rom. viii. 9. *vos autem non estis in carne, sed in spiritu; siquidem spiritus Dei habitat in vobis: quod si quis spiritum Christi non habet, is non est eius.* et v. 15, 16. *spiritum adoptionis, per quem clamamus, Abba,*
5 *Pater: et ipse spiritus testatur una cum spiritu nostro, nos esse filios Dei.* 1 Cor. vi. 11. *per spiritum Dei nostri.* 2 Ep. i. 21, 22. *qui nos confirmat vobiscum in Christum, et qui unxit nos, Deus est, qui etiam obsignavit nos, et dedit arrhabonem spiritus.* Gal. iv. 6. *misit Deus spiritum filii sui in corda vestra,*
10 *clamantem Abba, pater.* Eph. i. 13, 14. *spiritu promissionis illo sancto, qui est arrhabo hæreditatis nostræ.* et iv. 30. *ne tristitia afficite spiritum sanctum Dei, per quem obsignati estis.* et ii. 18. *quoniam utrique per ipsum habemus aditum in uno spiritu ad patrem.* 1 Pet. i. 12. *per emissum e cœlo*
15 *spiritum sanctum.* Ex his omnibus existit illud, Matt. xxviii. 19. *baptizantes eos in nomen patris, filii et spiritus sancti.* 1 Ioan. v. 7. *tres sunt qui testificantur in cœlo, pater, sermo, et spiritus sanctus, et hi tres unum sunt.* Sed de hoc loco egimus capite superiore; de illo altero, deque hoc rursus infra
20 hoc capite agemus.

Et sane si Deus quam doctrinam cum primis intelligi a nobis atque inde credi vult, eam non obscure aut perplexe, sed explicate atque perspicue totidem disertis verbis, ut par est,

Spirit of Christ. Matt. x. 20. "it is the Spirit of your Father
that speaketh in you." Rom. viii. 9. "but ye are not in the
flesh, but in the Spirit, if so be that the Spirit of God dwell in
you: now if any man have not the Spirit of Christ, he is none
5 of his." v. 15, 16. "ye have received the spirit of adoption,
whereby we cry, Abba, Father; the Spirit itself beareth witness with our spirit, that we are the sons of God." 1 Cor. vi.
11. "by the Spirit of our God." 2 Cor. i. 21, 22. "he which
stablisheth us with you in Christ, and hath anointed us, is
10 God; who hath also sealed us, and given the earnest of the
Spirit in our hearts." Gal. iv. 6. "God hath sent forth the Spirit
of his Son into your hearts, crying, Abba, Father." Eph. i.
13, 14. "that holy Spirit of promise, which is the earnest of
our inheritance." iv. 30. "grieve not the holy Spirit of God,
15 whereby ye are sealed." ii. 18. "through him we both have
access by one Spirit unto the Father." 1 Pet. i. 12. "the Holy
Ghost sent down from heaven." From all which results the
command in Matthew xxviii. 19. "baptizing them in the
name of the Father, and of the Son, and of the Holy Ghost."
20 1 John v. 7. "there are three that bear witness in heaven, the
Father, the Word, and the Holy Ghost; and these three are
one." The latter passage has been considered in the preceding
chapter; but both will undergo a further examination in a
subsequent part of the present.

25   If it be the divine will that a doctrine which is to be understood and believed as one of the primary articles of our faith,
should be delivered without obscurity or confusion, and explained, as is fitting, in clear and precise terms; if it be certain

docet, si hoc potissimum in religione cavendum est, ne quis nobis merito obiiciat quod Samaritanis Christus, Ioan. iv. 22. *vos adoratis quod nescitis,* ratumque in fide hoc dictum Christi esse debet, *nos adoramus quod scimus,* quæ de sancto spiritu expressissima traduntur, quæque adeo de ipso scire possumus ac debemus, hæc fere sunt: sunt autem eiusmodi, ut, etiamsi spiritus sanctus nusquam subiecisse se, quod de Christo dicitur, ad mediatorium aliquod munus, dicatur, nec filii nomine ad obedientiam Patri obstringeretur, tamen et patre et filio plane minorem, utpote per omnia obsequentem, et obtemperantem, promissum, missum, datum, nihil a seipso loquentem, arrhabonem etiam datum, describant atque constituant. Nullum hic ad humanam naturam subterfugium; hæc omnia de sancto spiritu dicuntur eorum quidem sententia, Summo Deo. ex quo plane evincitur, quoties horum consimilia passim de filio Dei leguntur, quibus is patre minor manifesto declaratur, ea non ad humanam solum eius naturam, sed ad divinam etiam referri oportere. Quod enim spiritu sancto, Patris, ut volunt, æquali indignum non est, id filio quantumvis Deo indignum censeri non debet. Quibus etiam in locis

that particular care ought to be taken in every thing connected
with religion, lest the objection urged by Christ against the
Samaritans should be applicable to us—"ye worship ye know
not what," John iv. 22.; if our Lord's saying should be held
5 sacred wherever points of faith are in question—"we know
what we worship"; the particulars which have been stated
seem to contain all that we are capable of knowing, or are required to know respecting the Holy Spirit, inasmuch as revelation has declared nothing else expressly on the subject. The
10 nature of these particulars is such, that although the Holy
Spirit be nowhere said to have taken upon himself any mediatorial functions, as is said of Christ, nor to be engaged by the
obligations of a filial relation to pay obedience to the Father,
yet he must evidently be considered as inferior to both Father
15 and Son, inasmuch as he is represented and declared to be
subservient and obedient in all things; to have been promised,
and sent, and given; to speak nothing of himself; and even to
have been given as an earnest. There is no room here for any
sophistical distinction founded on a twofold nature; all these
20 expressions refer to the Holy Spirit, who is maintained to be
the supreme God; whence it follows, that wherever similar
phrases are applied to the Son of God, in which he is distinctly
declared to be inferior to the Father, they ought to be understood in reference to his divine as well as to his human char-
25 acter. For what those, who believe in the Holy Spirit's co-
equality with the Father, deem to be not unworthy of him,
cannot be considered unworthy of the Son, however exalted
may be the dignity of his Godhead. Wherefore it remains now

cum officium quidem eius totum explicetur, divinitas nusquam in sacris literis nominatim doceatur, neque ubi de uno
Deo disertissime, ut Ioan. xvii. 3. 1 Cor. viii. 4. &c. docetur,
neque ubi Deus vel describitur, vel solio sedens inducitur,
5 immo cum spiritus Dei passim, et spiritus sanctus Dei nominetur, Eph. iv. 30. spiritus autem Dei a Deo distinctus re et
numero, esse Deus essentia unus cum eo cuius est spiritus non
possit, nisi miris quibusdam et absurdis hypothesibus, non ex
scriptura sacra, sed ex humano cerebro ad hanc solam doc-
10 trinam fulciendam conquisitis duci velimus; si ubicunque
patris et spiritus sancti simul fit mentio, solus pater Deus
nominatur, solus pater etiam praeterito spiritu unus verus
Deus ab ipso Christo agnoscitur, ut superiore capite quam-
plurimis testimoniis ostendimus; si is qui confirmat nos in
15 Christum, qui unxit, qui obsignavit nos, deditque arrhabonem spiritus, ut supra, 2 Cor. i. 22. Deus est, isque unus,
isque pater; Si Deus misit spiritum filii sui in corda nostra
clamantem Abba, Pater. Gal. iv. 6. unde is qui et spiritum
filii misit et ipsum filium, is quem et nos invocare docemur,
20 et ipse spiritus invocat, et Deus unus est et solus pater; Qua
tandem ratione, quibus argumentis credendum sit, spiritum

to be seen on what grounds, and by what arguments, we are constrained to believe that the Holy Spirit is God, if Scripture nowhere expressly teach the doctrine of his divinity, not even in the passages where his office is explained at large, nor in 5 those where the unity of God is explicitly asserted, as in John xvii. 3. 1 Cor. viii. 4, &c. nor where God is either described, or introduced as sitting upon his throne; if, further, the Spirit be frequently named the Spirit of God, and the Holy Spirit of God, Eph. iv. 30. so that the Spirit of God being actually and 10 numerically distinct from God himself, cannot possibly be essentially one God with him whose Spirit he is (except on certain strange and absurd hypotheses, which have no foundation in Holy Scripture, but were devised by human ingenuity for the sole purpose of supporting this particular doc- 15 trine); if, wherever the Father and the Holy Spirit are mentioned together, the Father alone be called God, and the Father alone, omitting all notice of the Spirit, be acknowledged by Christ himself to be the one true God, as has been proved in the former chapter by abundant testimony; if he be 20 God who "stablisheth us in Christ," who "hath anointed us," who "hath sealed us," and "given us the earnest of the Spirit," 2 Cor. i. 22. if that God be one God, and that one God the Father; if, finally, "God hath sent forth the Spirit of his Son into our hearts, crying, Abba, Father," Gal. iv. 6. whence it 25 follows that he who sent both the Spirit of his Son and the Son himself, he on whom we are taught to call, and on whom the Spirit himself calls, is the one God and the only Father. It seems exceedingly unreasonable, not to say dangerous, that

sanctum esse Deum, reliquum est ut videamus. Quamquam in re tam ardua imponi id oneris credentibus, ut quod in fide primum atque firmissimum censetur, id non claris divini verbi testimoniis discendum, sed humanæ rationi cum sit contra-
5 rium, humana tamen ratione, vel incerta potius disputatione investigandum cuique sit, durum admodum atque lubricum est.

Itaque spiritum sanctum esse Deum defendi solet, primo, quod Dei nomen spiritui sancto attribui videtur. Act. v. 3.
10 cum 4. *ut mentireris spiritui sancto, non mentitus es homi-nibus, sed Deo.* At vero si superius quæ de spiritu sancto ex ore filii accepimus, attendantur satis, infirmus admodum hic locus est ad asserendam tanti mysterii doctrinam. Cum enim spiritus a patre mitti, nomine etiam filii disertissime dicatur,
15 sane qui mentitur spiritui, mentitur Deo; ut qui recipit apos-tolum, recipit Deum qui misit, Matt. x. 40. Ioan. xiii. 20. Atque ab hoc loco removet omnem controversiam ipse Paulus, eumque appositissime interpretatur, dum eundem plane sen-sum uberius expromit; 1 Thess. iv. 8. *qui hæc spernit, non*
20 *hominem spernit, sed Deum, qui etiam dedit spiritum suum sanctum in nobis.* Quicquid incertum est annon hoc loco spiritus sanctus Deum patrem significat: idem enim Petrus v. 9. *cur—, ut tentaretis spiritum Domini;* id est, ipsum Deum patrem divinamque eius mentem, quam latere aut fal-

in a matter of so much difficulty, believers should be required to receive a doctrine, represented by its advocates as of primary importance and of undoubted certainty, on anything less than the clearest testimony of Scripture; and that a point which is confessedly contrary to human reason, should nevertheless be considered as susceptible of proof from human reason only, or rather from doubtful and obscure disputations.

First, then, it is usual to defend the divinity of the Holy Spirit on the ground, that the name of God seems to be attributed to the Spirit: Acts v. 3, 4. "why hath Satan filled thine heart to lie to the Holy Ghost? . . . thou hast not lied unto men, but unto God." But if attention be paid to what has been stated before respecting the Holy Ghost on the authority of the Son, this passage will appear too weak for the support of so great a doctrinal mystery. For since the Spirit is expressly said to be sent by the Father, and in the name of the Son, he who lies to the Spirit must lie to God, in the same sense as he who receives an apostle, receives God who sent him, Matt. x. 40. John xiii. 20. St. Paul himself removes all ground of controversy from this passage, and explains it most appositely by implication, 1 Thess. iv. 8. where his intention is evidently to express the same truth more at large: "he therefore that despiseth, despiseth not man, but God, who hath also given unto us his Holy Spirit." Besides, it may be doubted whether the Holy Spirit in this passage does not signify God the Father; for Peter afterwards says, v. 9. "how is it that ye have agreed together to tempt the Spirit of the Lord?" that is, God the Father himself, and his divine intelligence, which

lere nemo mortalium potest. Et sane v. 32. spiritus sanctus
non Deus dicitur, sed testis Christi cum Apostolis, *quem dedit
Deus obedientibus ipsi.* et Act. ii. 38. *accipietis donum spiritus sancti.* a Deo nempe datum: donum autem Dei quemad-
5 modum Deus, præsertim summus.

Secundus locus est Act. xxviii. 25. cum Isa. vi. 8, 9. *Dominus dixit. spiritus sanctus locutus est,* et Ier. xxxi. 31. cum
Heb. x. 15. idem. Atqui hoc supra compertum est, nomen
Domini et Iehovæ etiam angelis quibusque divinitus missis in
10 veteri testamento passim tribui: in novo autem ipse filius de
spiritu sancto palam testatur, Ioan. xvi. 13. *non loqui eum
a semetipso, sed quæ audierit loqui.* Deum igitur esse neque
ex hoc loco demonstrari potest.

Tertius locus est 1 Cor. iii. 16. cum cap. vi. 19. et 2 Ep.
15 vi. 16. *templum Dei. templum spiritus.* Sed neque hic dicitur neque ullo modo hinc sequitur spiritum sanctum esse
Deum: non enim est quod solus spiritus, sed quod pater etiam
et filius, Ioan. xiv. 23. *habitat in nobis,* cur *templum Dei*
dicamur. Itaque 1 Cor. vi. 19. ubi *templum spiritus* dicimur,
20 quasi sedulo cavisset Paulus ne quid de sancto spiritu ob illud
dictum erraremus, addidit, *quem habetis a Deo.* hinc deduci

no one can elude or deceive. And in v. 32. the Holy Spirit is not called God, but a witness of Christ with the apostles, "whom God hath given to them that obey him." So also Acts ii. 38. "ye shall receive the gift of the Holy Ghost," the gift, that is, of God. But how can the gift of God be himself God, much more the supreme God?

The second passage is Acts xxviii. 25. compared with Isa. vi. 8, 9. "I heard the voice of the Lord, saying—" &c. . . . "well spake the Holy Ghost by Esaias the prophet," &c. See also Jer. xxxi. 31. compared with Heb. x. 15. But it has been shown above, that the names Lord and Jehovah are throughout the Old Testament attributed to whatever angel God may entrust with the execution of his commands; and in the New Testament the Son himself openly testifies of the Holy Spirit, John xvi. 13. that "he shall not speak of himself, but whatsoever he shall hear, that shall he speak." It cannot therefore be inferred from this passage, any more than from the preceding, that the Holy Ghost is God.

The third place is 1 Cor. iii. 16. compared with vi. 19. and 2 Cor. vi. 16. "the temple of God . . . the temple of the Holy Ghost." But neither is it here said, nor does it in any way follow from hence, that the Holy Spirit is God; for it is not because the Spirit alone, but because the Father also and the Son "make their abode with us," that we are called "the temple of God." Therefore in 1 Cor. vi. 19. where we are called "the temple of the Holy Ghost," St. Paul has added, "which ye have of God," as if with the purpose of guarding against any error which might arise respecting the Holy Spirit

quo pacto potest, quem habemus a Deo, eum esse Deum. Quo autem sensu *templum spiritus* dicamur, explanatius docet Eph. ii. 22. *in quo et vos una ædificamini, ut sitis domicilium Dei per spiritum.*

5   Tum proprietates divinæ attributæ spiritui afferuntur. Primo Omniscientia; quasi ex eadem penitus essentia. 1 Cor. ii. 10, 11. *spiritus omnia scrutatur, etiam profunditates Dei. Quis enim hominum novit ea quæ sunt hominis, nisi spiritus hominis qui est in eo? ita etiam ea quæ sunt Dei nemo novit,*
10 *nisi spiritus Dei.* Respondeo ad v. 10. ex sententia Theologorum, non hic agi de omniscientia divina, sed de illa duntaxat profunda *quam nobis Deus revelavit per spiritum suum;* quæ ipsa verba proxime præcedunt. Deinde illud *omnia* restringendum esse ad ea quæ nobis expedit scire. Quid! quod Deum
15 scrutari Deum cum quo unus essentia sit, absurde diceretur. Tum ad v. 11. non hic agi de essentia spiritus: nam si ut spiritus hominis est ad hominem, ita intelligetur spiritus Dei esse ad Deum, quid non absurdi sequatur? alluditur itaque solum ad intimam propinquitatem et communionem spiritus cum
20 Deo, a quo est egressus. Quod quin ita sit, tollere omnem

in consequence of his expression. How then can it be deduced from this passage, that he whom we have of God, is God himself? In what sense we are called "the temple of the Holy Ghost," the same apostle has explained more fully Eph. ii. 22.
5 "in whom ye also are builded together for an habitation of God through the Spirit."

The next evidence which is produced for this purpose, is the ascription of the divine attributes to the Spirit. And first, Omniscience; as if the Spirit were altogether of the same es-
10 sence with God. 1 Cor. ii. 10, 11. "the Spirit searcheth all things, yea the deep things of God: for what man knoweth the things of a man, save the spirit of man which is in him? even so the things of God knoweth no man, but the Spirit of God." With regard to the tenth verse, I reply, that in the
15 opinion of divines, the question is not respecting the divine omniscience, but only respecting those deep things "which God hath revealed unto us by his Spirit" the words imme-diately preceding. Besides, the phrase "all things" must be restricted to mean whatever it is expedient for us to know:
20 not to mention that it would be absurd to speak of God search-ing God, with whom he was one in essence. Next, as to the eleventh verse, the essence of the Spirit is not the subject in question; for the consequences would be full of absurd-ity, if it were to be understood that the Spirit of God was
25 with regard to God, as the spirit of a man is with regard to man. Allusion therefore is made only to the intimate rela-tionship and communion of the Spirit with God, from whom he originally proceeded. That no doubt may remain as to the

dubitationem, versus sequens non differt: *accepimus spiritum,
qui ex Deo est.* Esse autem ex Deo, non est esse Deum, qui
unus est. Quanto planius ipse filius omniscientiam spiritui
non concedit? Matt. xi. 27. *nemo novit filium, nisi pater:*
5 *neque patrem quisquam novit, nisi filius, et cuicunque voluerit filius eûm retegere.* Quid ergo spiritus sanctus? nam tertius hic nemo qui vel patrem vel filium noverit, nisi per patrem
vel filium. Marc. xiii. 32. *de die illo ac hora nemo scit; ne
angeli quidem qui in cœlo sunt, nec ipse filius, sed pater.* Si
10 nec ipse filius, qui itidem in cœlo est, certe nec ipse filii spiritus, qui a filio accipit omnia, Ioan. xvi. 14.

Secundo, omnipræsentiam; Quod *spiritus Dei habitat in
nobis.* Verum ne universum quidem terrarum orbem cum
toto cœlo, id est, totam hanc mundi machinam si impleret,
15 omnipræsens continuo esse probaretur: quod enim sol suo
lumine, quidni spiritus sua virtute facile compleat, nec idcirco
infinitus necessario credendus sit. Certe si spiritus ille mendax
quadringentos simul prophetas potuit implere, 1 Reg. xxii.
22. quot millia spiritus sanctus merito credatur posse; nec
20 tamen infinitus aut immensus esse?

Tertio opera divina. Act. ii. 4. *donum linguarum.* et cap.
xiii. 2. *dixit spiritus sanctus separate mihi——.* et xx. 28. *spi-*

truth of this interpretation, the following verse is of the same import: "we have received . . . the Spirit which is of God." That which is "of" God, cannot be actually God, who is unity. The Son himself disallows the omniscience of the Spirit

5 still more plainly. Matt. xi. 27. "no man knoweth the Son, but the Father, neither knoweth any man the Father, save the Son, and he to whomsoever the Son will reveal him." What then becomes of the Holy Spirit? for according to this passage, no third person whatever knoweth either the Father or the

10 Son, except through their medium. Mark xiii. 32. "of that day and that hour knoweth no man, no, not the angels which are in heaven, neither the Son, but the Father." If not even the Son himself, who is also in heaven, then certainly not the Spirit of the Son, who receiveth all things from the Son him-

15 self; John xvi. 14.

Secondly, Omnipresence, on the ground that "the Spirit of God dwelleth in us." But even if it filled with its presence the whole circle of the earth, with all the heavens, that is, the entire fabric of this world, it would not follow that the Spirit

20 is omnipresent. For why should not the Spirit easily fill with the influence of its power, what the Sun fills with its light; though it does not necessarily follow that we are to believe it infinite? If that lying spirit, 1 Kings xxii. 22. were able to fill four hundred prophets at once, how many thousands

25 ought we not to think the Holy Spirit capable of pervading, even without the attributes of infinity or immensity?

Thirdly, divine works. Acts ii. 4. "the Spirit gave them utterance." xiii. 2. "the Holy Ghost said, Separate me Barna-

ritus sanctus constituit vos episcopos. 2 Pet. i. 21. *acti a spiritu sancto locuti sunt.* hæc uno responso facillime solvuntur, si meminerimus modo quæ Christus de sancto illo spiritu paracleto ipse nos docuit, missum a patre per filium; non suo nomine, a semetipso non loqui, ergo neque agere, ergo neque aliis dare ut loquantur, quæ dedit accepisse. At 1 Cor. xii. 11. dicitur *distribuere singulis sicut vult:* et ipse, inquam distribui singulis pro voluntate Dei patris, Heb. ii. 4. et *ventus* quoque Ioan. iii. 8. *ubi vult spirat.* Quod autem Mariæ et Iosepho annuntiatum est conceptionis illius sanctæ auctorem esse spiritum sanctum Matt. i. 18, 20. Luc. i. 35. id de sola illius persona intelligendum non est. Nam in vetere testamento spiritus Dei et spiritus sancti nomine, vel ipsum Deum patrem, vel divinam vim eius intelligi satis constat; De alio spiritu sancto et Maria et Iosephus nihil dum audierant: cum Iudæis in hodiernum usque diem sancti spiritus persona et divinitas ignota sit: itaque et in locis citatis, πνεῦμα ἅγιον utrobique sine solito articulo est; vel si hoc est parum, explanate apud Lucam

bas and Saul for the work." Acts xx. 28. "the Holy Ghost
hath made you overseers to feed the Church of God." 2 Pet.
i. 21. "holy men of God spake as they were moved by the
Holy Ghost." A single remark will suffice for the solution of
5 all these passages, if it be only remembered what was the
language of Christ respecting the Holy Spirit, the Comforter; namely, that he was sent by the Son from the Father,
that he spake not of himself, nor in his own name, and consequently that he did not act in his own name; therefore that
10 he did not even move others to speak of his own power, but
that what he gave he had himself received. Again, 1 Cor. xii.
11. the Spirit is said "to divide to every man severally as he
will." In answer to this it may be observed, that the Spirit
himself is also said to be divided to each according to the will
15 of God the Father, Heb. ii. 4. and that even "the wind blow-
eth where it listeth," John iii. 8. With regard to the annun-
ciation made to Joseph and Mary, that the Holy Spirit was the
author of the miraculous conception, Matt. i. 18, 20. Luke
i. 35. it is not to be understood with reference to his own per-
20 son alone. For it is certain that, in the Old Testament, under
the name of the Spirit of God, or of the Holy Spirit, either
God the Father himself, or his divine power was signified;
nor had Joseph and Mary at that time heard anything of any
other Holy Spirit, inasmuch as the personality and divinity
25 of the Holy Spirit are not acknowledged by the Jews even to
the present day. Accordingly, in both the passages quoted,
πνεῦμα ἅγιον is without the customary article; or if this be not
considered as sufficiently decisive, the angel speaks in a more

angelus loquitur. *spiritus sanctus superveniet in te, et virtus altissimi inumbrabit te: propterea— vocabitur filius Dei;* patris nempe, nisi duos patres, unum filii Dei, alterum filii hominis existimari velimus.

5   Quarto honores Divini. Matt. xxviii. 19. *baptizantes eos in nomen patris, filii, et spiritus sancti.* hic numerantur quidem tres; trium autem horum vel divinitatem vel unitatem vel æqualitatem denique quod statuat, verbum hic nullum. Nam et prophetam in nomen prophetæ, et iustum in nomen

10 iusti recipere, et potum cuiquam in nomen discipuli dare Matt. x. 41. Ioan. xiii. 20. legitur: id aliud nihil esse, nisi eo quod sit propheta, quod sit iustus, quod sit discipulus, luce clarius est. Deinde *baptizabatur in Mosen* 1 Cor. x. 2. id est, in legem vel doctrinam Mosis: et *in baptizmum Ioannis*

15 Act. xix. 3, eodem sensu; et *in nomen Iesu Christi in remissionem peccatorum* Act. ii. 38. et *in Christum Iesum et in mortem eius* Rom. vi. 3. et *in unum corpus* 1 Cor. xii. 13. baptizamur igitur *in nomen,* id est, in ea beneficia ac dona quæ per filium et spiritum accepimus. Hinc lætatus est Pau-

20 lus, neminem potuisse dicere se in nomen Pauli esse baptizatum 1 Cor. i. 13, 14, 15. non quo pertimesceret ne quis eum divinitatis, sed maioris auctoritatis affectatæ argueret, quam Paulo conveniret. Ex his omnibus palam est, baptizari

circumstantial manner in St. Luke: "the Holy Ghost shall come upon thee, and the power of the Highest shall overshadow thee; therefore that holy thing which shall be born of thee shall be called the Son of God"—that is, of the Father: unless we suppose that there are two Fathers—one Father of the Son of God, another Father of the Son of man.

Fourthly, divine honors. Matt. xxviii. 19. "baptizing them in the name of the Father, and of the Son, and of the Holy Ghost." Here mention is undoubtedly made of three persons; but there is not a word that determines the divinity, or unity, or equality of these three. For we read, Matt. x. 41. John xiii. 20. of receiving a prophet in the name of a prophet, and a righteous man in the name of a righteous man, and of giving a cup of cold water in the name of a disciple; which evidently means nothing more, than because he is a prophet, or a righteous man, or a disciple. Thus too the Israelites "were baptized unto Moses," 1 Cor. x. 2. that is, unto the law or doctrine of Moses; and "unto the baptism of John" occurs in the same sense, Acts xix 3. and "in the name of Jesus Christ for the remission of sins," Acts ii. 38. and "into Jesus Christ" and "into his death," Rom. vi. 3. and "into one body," 1 Cor. xii. 13. To be baptized therefore "in their name," is to be admitted to those benefits and gifts which we have received through the Son and the Holy Spirit. Hence St. Paul rejoiced that no one could say he had been baptized in his name, 1 Cor. i. 13–15. It was not the imputation of making himself God that he feared, but that of affecting greater authority than was suitable to his character. From all which it is clear that when

nos *in nomen patris, filii, et spiritus sancti,* non ut hinc trium illorum in se aut inter se natura quæ sit, sed quid in baptizmo in iis qui credunt efficiant admoneamur: Pater nempe salutem æternam, filius redemptionem, spiritus sanctificationem.
5 Pater quidem a seipso, filius et spiritus a patre potestate accepta: Patris enim nomine filium, patris et filii Spiritum omnia agere, iam sæpe ex ore filii demonstratum est; etiam ex verbis proxime præcedentibus v. 18. *data est mihi omnis auctoritas—; profecti ergo—, baptizantes in nomen—.* id quod ex
10 1 Cor. vi. 11. planissimum sit; *sed abluti estis, sed sanctificati estis, sed iustificati estis, in nomine Domini Iesu et per spiritum Dei nostri.* hic trium itidem fit mentio in baptizmo, filii, spiritus, et Dei nostri: reliquum est igitur, ut Deus ille noster solus pater sit, cuius et filius et spiritus est.
15   Sed invocatur spiritus: 2 Cor. xiii. 13. *gratia Domini Iesu, charitas Dei, et communicatio spiritus sancti sit cum omnibus vobis.* At vero hæc non est invocatio, sed benedictio; ubi spiritus non ut persona invocatur, sed ut donum petitur ab eo qui solus illic Deus nominatur: Nempe pater a quo et spiritum
20 communicandum Christus ipse iubet nos petere Luc. xi. 13. Si unquam spiritus esset invocandus, tunc certe potissimum,

we are baptized in the name of the Father, Son, and Holy Ghost, this is not done to impress upon our minds the inherent or relative natures of these three persons, but the benefits conferred by them in baptism on those who believe; namely,

5 that our eternal salvation is owing to the Father, our redemption to the Son, and our sanctification to the Spirit. The power of the Father is inherent in himself, that of the Son and the Spirit is received from the Father; for it has been already proved on the authority of the Son, that the Son does every

10 thing in the name of the Father, and the Spirit every thing in the name of the Father and the Son; and a confirmation of the same truth may be derived from the words immediately preceding the verse under discussion: v. 18. "all power is given unto me . . . go ye therefore . . . baptizing in the

15 name," &c. and still more plainly by 1 Cor. vi. 11. "but ye are washed, but ye are sanctified, but ye are justified in the name of the Lord Jesus, and by the Spirit of our God." Here the same three are mentioned as in baptism, "the Son, the Spirit," and "our God"; it follows therefore that the Father

20 alone is our God, of whom are both the Son and the Spirit.

But invocation is made to the Spirit. 2 Cor. xiii. 14. "the grace of the Lord Jesus Christ, and the love of God, and the communion of the Holy Ghost, be with you all." This, however, is not so much an invocation as a benediction, in which

25 the Spirit is not addressed as a person, but sought as a gift from him who alone is there called God; namely, the Father, from whom Christ himself directs us to seek the communication of the Spirit, Luke xi. 13. If the Spirit were ever to be

cum a nobis petitur; iubemur tamen non se a seipso sed a patre tantum petere. cur ipsum spiritum, si Deus est, non invocamus ut se nobis daret? qui a patre, non a seipso, et petitur et datur, nec Deus esse potest, nec invocandus. Eadem
5 forma benedictionis extat Gen. xlviii. 15, 16. *Deus ille ante cuius conspectum—, angelus ille—, benedicat—;* ut supra: et Apoc. i. 4. *gratia vobis et pax ab eo qui est—, et a septem spiritibus.* hic septem illi spiritus certe non invocantur; de quibus etiam statim amplius dicemus. Atque in hac bene-
10 dictione, rerum potius quam personarum ordo vel dignitas spectanda est: per filium enim accedimus ad patrem, a quo demum spiritus sanctus mittitur. Sic 1 Cor. xii. 4, 5, 6. *distinctiones donorum sunt, sed idem spiritus; et distinctiones mysteriorum sunt, sed idem Dominus; et distinctiones actio-*
15 *num sunt, sed idem Deus, qui intus agit omnia in omnibus.* hic tres ordine inverso nominantur; unus autem Deus qui agit omnia in omnibus, etiam in filio et spiritu, ut passim docemur.

Ex quo perspicitur Matt. xii. 31, 32. de persona spiritus
20 sancti nihil dici: Si enim in spiritum sanctum gravius quam in patrem et filium, si in spiritum solum sine venia peccaretur, maior profecto spiritus patre et filio esset: de illa itaque

invoked personally, it would be then especially, when we pray
for him; yet we are commanded not to ask him of himself, but
only of the Father. Why do we not call upon the Spirit himself, if he be God, to give himself to us? He who is sought
5 from the Father, and given by him, not by himself, can neither
be God, nor an object of invocation. The same form of benediction occurs Gen. xlviii. 15, 16. "the God before whom my
fathers did walk . . . the angel which redeemed me from
all evil, bless the lads": and Rev. i. 4. "grace be unto you and
10 peace from him which is . . . and from the seven spirits."
It is clear that in this passage the seven spirits, of whom more
will be said hereafter, are not meant to be invoked. Besides
that in this benediction the order or dignity of the things signified should be considered, rather than that of the persons;
15 for it is by the Son that we come to the Father, from whom
finally the Holy Spirit is sent. So 1 Cor. xii. 4–6. "there are
diversities of gifts, but the same Spirit: and there are differ-
ences of administrations, but the same Lord: and there are
diversities of operations, but it is the same God which work-
20 eth all in all." Here the three are again mentioned in an
inverse order; but it is one God which worketh all in all, even
in the Son and the Spirit, as we are taught throughout the
whole of Scripture.

Hence it appears that what is said Matt. xii. 31, 32. has
25 no reference to the personality of the Holy Spirit. For if to
sin against the Holy Spirit were worse than to sin against the
Father and Son, and if that alone were an unpardonable sin,
the Spirit truly would be greater than the Father and the Son.

summa et ordine quidem postrema illuminatione qua pater
per spiritum nos illuminat, et cui si quis repugnat, nihil ei
restat unde salvus esse possit, verba illa fieri. Sed crediderim
potius spiritum sanctum hic dici ipsum patrem, cuius *per*
5 *spiritum* v. 28. vel *digitum* Luc. xi. 20. Christus eiicere se
dæmonia profitebatur; quem Pharisæi cum Beelzebulem esse
calumniarentur, sine spe veniæ peccasse dicuntur, cum dice-
rent *spiritum impurum habet,* Marc. iii. 30. qui patris spiritum habebat. Quid, quod ad Pharisæos hæc est locutus qui
10 alium spiritum quam ipsum patrem nullum agnoverunt. Hoc
si verum est, quod sane locum integrum a v. 24. ad 32. per-
pendenti obscurum esse nequit, formidolosum illud peccatum
in spiritum sanctum erit re vera peccatum in patrem qui spiritus sanctitatis est; Si quis nempe dixerit, spiritum illum
15 patris qui agebat in Christo, esse principem dæmoniorum seu
spiritum impurum; ut dilucide ostendit Marcus loco supra
citato.

　　At Spiritus cum patre et filio gratiam et benedictionem in
ecclesias confert. Apoc. i. 4, 5. *gratia sit vobis et pax ab illo*
20 *qui est—. et a septem spiritibus, qui in conspectu throni eius*
sunt, et a Iesu Christo. Verum et hic quoque ne sancti spiritus
mentio fiat, repugnat et numerus et stantium locus quasi an-

The words must therefore apply to that illumination, which, as it is highest in degree, so it is last in order of time, whereby the Father enlightens us through the Spirit, and which if any one resist, no method of salvation remains open to him. I am inclined to believe, however, that it is the Father himself who is here called the Holy Spirit, by whose "Spirit," v. 28. or "finger," Luke xi. 20. Christ professed to cast out devils; when therefore the Pharisees accused him falsely of acting in concert with Beelzebub, they are declared to sin unpardonably, because they said of him who had the Spirit of his Father, "he hath an unclean spirit," Mark iii. 30. Besides, it was to the Pharisees that he spoke thus, who acknowledged no other Spirit than the Father himself. If this be the true interpretation of the passage, which will not be doubted by any one who examines the whole context from v. 24 to v. 32. that dreaded sin against the Holy Spirit will be in reality a sin against the Father, who is the Spirit of holiness; of which he would be guilty, who should affirm that the Spirit of the Father which was working in Christ was the prince of the devils, or an unclean spirit; as Mark clearly shows in the passage quoted above.

But the Spirit bestows grace and blessing upon the churches in conjunction with the Father and the Son; Rev. i. 4, 5. "grace be unto you and peace from him which is . . . and from the seven spirits which are before his throne, and from Jesus Christ." It is clear, however, that the Holy Spirit is not here meant to be implied; the number of the spirits is inconsistent with such a supposition, as well as the place which they

gelorum in conspectu throni, et cap. iv. 5. et v. 6. ubi septem
illi spiritus *septem lampades igneæ ardentes ante thronum,* et
agni cornua et *oculi* dicuntur. Hos spiritus qui ad unum redi-
gunt spiritum sanctum eiusque gratiam septiformem, quos
5 Beza merito refellit, viderint ne personarum proprietates virtutibus attribuendo, eorum rem agant, qui spiritum sanctum
nihil aliud nisi virtutem ac potentiam patris interpretantur.
Hæc sane abunde erudire nos possint, ne in huiusmodi ternæ
enumeratione trium personarum doctrinam subesse, vel æqua-
10 litatem vel ordinem spectari arbitremur: ne in illo quidem
loco de quo supradictum est, et quo plerique tantopere nituntur, 1 Ioan. v. 7. *tres sunt qui testificantur in cœlo; pater,*
sermo, et spiritus sanctus; et hi tres unum sunt. ubi quod vel
Deitatem, vel essentiæ saltem unitatem affirmet, nihil prorsus
15 est: nam neque solus Deus testificari dicitur in cœlo; 1 Tim.
v. 21. *obtestor etiam atque etiam in conspectu Dei, et Domini*
Iesu Christi, et electorum angelorum. ubi spiritum sanctum
expectasset quis tertio loco nominandum, si in huiusmodi ter-
nariis id ageretur; et unitas cuiusmodi intelligenda sit, tria illa
20 sequente versiculo nominata, *spiritus, aqua et sanguis,* quæ
ad unum, sive ad id unum nempe testificandum sunt, satis
propemodum declarant. Ipse Beza Trinitatis alioqui acerri-

are said to occupy, standing like angels before the throne. See also iv. 5. and v. 6. where the same spirits are called "seven lamps of fire burning before the throne," and the "seven horns" and "seven eyes" of the Lamb. Those who reduce
5 these spirits to one Holy Spirit, and consider them as synonymous with his sevenfold grace (an opinion which is deservedly refuted by Beza) ought to beware, lest, by attributing to mere virtues the properties of persons, they furnish arguments to those commentators who interpret the Holy
10 Spirit as nothing more than the virtue and power of the Father. This may suffice to convince us, that in this kind of threefold enumerations the sacred writers have no view whatever to the doctrine of three divine persons, or to the equality or order of those persons; not even in that verse which has been
15 mentioned above, and on which commentators in general lay so much stress, 1 John v. 7. "there are three that bear record in heaven, the Father, the Word, and the Holy Ghost, and these three are one," where there is in reality nothing which implies either divinity or unity of essence. As to divinity, God
20 is not the only one who is said to bear record in heaven; 1 Tim. v. 21. "I charge thee before God, and the Lord Jesus Christ, and the elect angels," where it might have been expected that the Holy Spirit would have been named in the third place, if such ternary forms of expression really con-
25 tained the meaning which is commonly ascribed to them. What kind of unity is intended, is sufficiently plain from the next verse, in which "the spirit, the water, and the blood" are mentioned, which "are to bear record to one," or "to that one

mus assertor per *unum sunt* intelligit in unum consentiunt.
Quid autem testificentur, versus 5. et 6. ostendunt; id nimirum, quod qui credit *mundum vincit, Iesum* scilicet *esse filium
Dei;* Iesum etiam *Christum,* id est, unctum; non ergo unum
5 neque parem ei qui unxit: testimonium hoc ipsum avertit
plane essentialem, quam hinc statuunt, testium unitatem.
Nam sermo et filius est et Christus, id est, inquam unctus.
utque ut imago est qua Deus fit conspicuus, ita sermo est, quo
Deus est audibilis; talis cum sit, non potest cum invisibili et
10 inaudibili Deo unus essentia esse. idem de spiritu aliis ratio-
nibus supra demonstratum est: hi tres ergo non sunt essentia
unum, ut nihil amplius de suspicione huius loci commemore-
mus, in quo non fides, sed opinio duntaxat legentium versetur,
necesse est. De Spiritu insuper quæro sitne alius qui in cœlo,
15 alius qui in terra testificatur, an idem? Si idem, quid is in
cœlo testificetur, nusquam alias legimus; cum in terra, id
est, in cordibus nostris testificatio eius clarissima semper fuit:
certe Christus Ioan. viii. 16, 18. se et Patrem solos testes de
se adhibet: deinde præter alteros duos testes sane locupletis-
20 simos cur idem Spiritus bis testificatur? Si alius, novum hoc
et inauditum. Sunt et alia quæ multorum suspicionem de hoc

thing." Beza himself, who is generally a staunch defender of the Trinity, understands the phrase *unum sunt* to mean, "agree in one." What it is that they testify, appears in the fifth and sixth verses; namely, that "he that overcometh the world 5 is he that believeth that Jesus is the Son of God, even Jesus Christ," that is, "the anointed"; therefore he is not one with, nor equal to, him that anointed him. Thus the very record that they bear is inconsistent with the essential unity of the witnesses, which is attempted to be deduced from the passage. 10 For the Word is both Son and Christ, that is, as I say, "the anointed"; and as he is the image, as it were, by which we see God, so is he the word by which we hear him. But if such be his nature, he cannot be essentially one with God, whom no one can see or hear. The same has been already proved, by 15 other arguments, with regard to the Spirit; it follows, therefore, that these three are not one in essence. I say nothing of the suspicion of spuriousness attached to the passage, which is a matter of criticism rather than of doctrine. Further, I would ask whether there is one Spirit that bears record in 20 heaven, and another which bears record in earth, or whether both are the same Spirit. If the same, it is extraordinary that we nowhere else read of his bearing witness in heaven, although his witness has always been most conspicuously manifested in earth, that is, in our hearts. Christ certainly brings 25 forward himself and his Father as the only witnesses of himself, John viii. 16, 19. Why then, in addition to two other perfectly competent witnesses, should the Spirit twice bear witness to the same thing? On the other hand, if it be another

loco adaugeant; et tamen hoc loco pene solo fundata TRIADIS doctrina tota, atque arrepta hinc esse potissimum videtur.

Quis autem vel quid sit Spiritus sanctus ne prorsus nesciamus, etsi scripturæ verbis disertis non docent, ex scripturis tamen supra citatis intelligere est, spiritum sanctum, cum sit Deo minister, ac proinde non increatus, ex substantia Dei, non necessitate naturæ, sed libera voluntate agentis creatum, id est, productum fuisse ante iacta, ut credibile est, mundi fundamenta, post Filium, filioque longe inferiorem. Dices hæc spiritum sanctum a Filio non distinguere. Dico itidem illud *egredi* et *prodire a patre* et *procedere,* quod græce idem est, Filium non distinguere a Spiritu sancto; cum hæc et de utroque dicantur et missionem non naturam utriusque significent. Satis est in divinis ad nomen, atque etiam naturam Filii præ Spiritu Sancto accipiendam, quod effulgentia gloriæ et character subsistentiæ divinæ Filio, non Spiritui Sancto impressus dicatur.

Spirit, we have here a new and unheard-of doctrine. There are besides other circumstances, which in the opinion of many render the passage suspicious; and yet it is on the authority of this text, almost exclusively, that the whole doctrine of the 5 Trinity has been hastily adopted.

Lest however we should be altogether ignorant who or what the Holy Spirit is, although Scripture nowhere teaches us in express terms, it may be collected from the passages quoted above, that the Holy Spirit, inasmuch as he is a min-
10 ister of God, and therefore a creature, was created or produced of the substance of God, not by a natural necessity, but by the free will of the agent, probably before the foundations of the world were laid, but later than the Son, and far inferior to him. It will be objected, that thus the Holy Spirit is not sufficiently
15 distinguished from the Son. I reply, that the Scriptural expressions themselves, "to come forth, to go out from the Father, to proceed from the Father," which mean the same in the Greek, do not distinguish the Son from the Holy Spirit, inasmuch as these terms are used indiscriminately with ref-
20 erence to both persons, and signify their mission, not their nature. There is however sufficient reason for placing the name as well as the nature of the Son above that of the Holy Spirit in the discussion of topics relative to the Deity; inasmuch as the brightness of the glory of God, and the express
25 image of his person, are said to have been impressed on the one, and not on the other.

COLUMBIA UNIVERSITY PRESS
Columbia University
New York

————

FOREIGN AGENT
OXFORD UNIVERSITY PRESS
Humphrey Milford
Amen House, London, E.C.